Music at Midnight

The Effigies of M.r George Herbert
Author of those Sacred Poems called
The Temple.

A Christian's state and case
Is not a corpulent, but a thin and spare
Yet active strength: whose long and bony face
Content and care
Do seem to equally divide ...
'The Size'

JOHN DRURY

Music at Midnight

The Life and Poetry of George Herbert

ALLEN LANE
an imprint of
PENGUIN BOOKS

ALLEN LANE

Published by the Penguin Group
Penguin Books Ltd, 80 Strand, London WC2R ORL, England
Penguin Group (USA) Inc., 375 Hudson Street, New York, New York 10014, USA
Penguin Group (Canada), 90 Eglinton Avenue East, Suite 700, Toronto, Ontario, Canada M4P 2Y3
(a division of Pearson Penguin Canada Inc.)
Penguin Ireland, 25 St Stephen's Green, Dublin 2, Ireland (a division of Penguin Books Ltd)
Penguin Group (Australia), 707 Collins Street, Melbourne, Victoria 3008, Australia
(a division of Pearson Australia Group Pty Ltd)
Penguin Books India Pvt Ltd, 11 Community Centre, Panchsheel Park, New Delhi – 110 017, India
Penguin Group (NZ), 67 Apollo Drive, Rosedale, Auckland 0632, New Zealand
(a division of Pearson New Zealand Ltd)
Penguin Books (South Africa) (Pty) Ltd, Block D, Rosebank Office Park,
181 Jan Smuts Avenue, Parktown North, Gauteng 2193, South Africa

Penguin Books Ltd, Registered Offices: 80 Strand, London WC2R ORL, England

www.penguin.com

First published 2013
001

Copyright © John Drury, 2013

The moral right of the author has been asserted

All rights reserved
Without limiting the rights under copyright
reserved above, no part of this publication may be
reproduced, stored in or introduced into a retrieval system,
or transmitted, in any form or by any means (electronic, mechanical,
photocopying, recording or otherwise) without the prior
written permission of both the copyright owner and
the above publisher of this book

Set in 10.5/14 pt Sabon LT Std
Typeset by Jouve (UK), Milton Keynes
Printed in Great Britain by Clays Ltd, St Ives plc

ISBN: 978-1-846-14248-2

To Caroline

In another walk to Salisbury he saw a poor man with a poorer horse that was fallen under his load; they were both in distress, and needed present help, which Mr. Herbert perceiving, put off his canonical coat, and helped the poor man to unload, and after to load his horse. The poor man blessed him for it, and he blessed the poor man; and so was like the good Samaritan, that he gave him money to refresh both himself and his horse, and told him, that if he loved himself, he would be merciful to his beast. Thus he left the poor man, and at his coming to his musical friends at Salisbury, they began to wonder that Mr. George Herbert, who used to be so trim and clean, came into that company so soiled and discomposed; but he told them the occasion; and when one of the company told him he had disparaged himself by so dirty an employment, his answer was, that the thought of what he had done would prove music to him at midnight, and that the omission of it would have upbraided and made discourse in his conscience, whensoever he would pass by that place. 'For if I be bound to pray for all that be in distress, I am sure that I am bound, so far as it is in my power, to practise what I pray for. And though I do not wish for the like occasion every day, yet let me tell you, I would not willingly pass one day of my life without comforting a sad soul, or showing mercy; and I praise God for the occasion. And now let's tune our instruments.'

Izaak Walton,
The Life of Mr. George Herbert, 1670

Contents

List of Illustrations

ENDPAPERS

Front endpapers: Map of Middlesex, from John Speed, *The Theatre of the Empire of Great Britain,* 1616. (© The British Library Board (Maps. C.7.c.20))

Rear endpapers: Map of Wiltshire, from John Speed, *The Theatre of the Empire of Great Britain,* 1616. (© The British Library Board (Maps. C.7.c.20))

COLOUR PLATES

1. The Herbert tomb in St Nicholas Parish Church, Montgomery. (Photo: Adam Cusack / g17 photography)

2. Magdalen Herbert, portrait by Federico Zuccaro. (© The Trustees of the Weston Park Foundation. Photo: Bridgeman Art Library)

3. The Summerhouse at Eyton–upon–Severn, Shropshire. (Photo: The Vivat Trust)

4. Edward Herbert, 1st Baron Herbert of Cherbury, *c.*1610–14, portrait by Isaac Oliver. (Private Collection. Photo: The Bridgeman Art Library)

5. Lancelot Andrewes, portrait by an anonymous artist. (Bodleian Library, University of Oxford (Cat. LP84))

INTEGRATED ILLUSTRATIONS

Preface and Acknowledgements

From the start, Herbert's life story has served as an introduction to his poetry. When his friend Nicholas Ferrar of Little Gidding first published his collected verse in 1633, the year of Herbert's death, under the title of *The Temple* (Ferrar's choice rather than Herbert's), he prefaced it with three pages under the heading of 'The Printers to the Reader'. In ten lines he traced the outline of Herbert's forty-year life: his academic success, culminating in the Oratorship of the University of Cambridge; his abandonment of the hopes of a career at court which that office promised; and his final three years as a country parson. That was it in a nutshell: a quiet life with a crisis in the middle of it. Nineteen years later in 1652, a Fellow of Clare Hall in Cambridge called Barnabas Oley published Herbert's prose work, *The Country Parson*,[1] under the title of *A Priest to the Temple* – a deliberate capitalizing on the success of *The Temple*. As a Cambridge don, Oley was particularly interested in Herbert's midlife crisis and career change, still a matter of speculation and gossip in the colleges.

By his early death Herbert escaped the distress of civil war, the execution of Charles I and the suppression of his kind of moderate Anglicanism during the Commonwealth. In 1670, ten years after monarchy and the Church of England were restored, Izaak Walton published *The Life of Mr. George Herbert*,[2] a biography of some fifty pages which set Herbert up as a shining example of conservative Anglican sanctity, exemplary for Walton's own times. Walton's text is therefore tricky. He had been interested in Herbert for twenty years and consulted people who had known him. This gives his *Life* abiding authority. But he is not dependable. Admiration led him into hagiography and the invention of affecting scenes, particularly those surrounding Herbert's institution as rector of Bemerton, which are variously impossible, improbable, plausible and convincing. Walton has been subjected to rigorous critique by David Novarr.[3] The polymath John Aubrey made some notes about Herbert which have been collected in the selection from his voluminous papers called *Brief Lives*, edited by Oliver Lawson Dick. Like Walton, he was writing a generation after Herbert and is not entirely dependable. His appetite for information, particularly about his native Wiltshire, was voracious and often undiscriminating. Unlike Walton he had not the slightest inclination to hagiography. Walton and Aubrey have been superseded as biographers by Amy Charles,[4] to whose painstaking researches the present book owes a great deal.

But Amy Charles, though she established the facts of Herbert's life with scrupulous care, only occasionally and incidentally referred them to his poetry. That is the main concern of Joseph Summers's *George Herbert: His Religion and Art*.[5] Summers's excellent literary criticism of Herbert is separated from, and preceded by, chapters on his life and his religion – things which in reality were woven together. Helen Vendler's *The Poetry of George Herbert*[6] is something else again: a brilliant reading of the poetry, alert to form and feeling, but much less interested in matters of history. Chana Bloch's *Spelling the Word: George Herbert and the Bible*[7] is a wonderful study of that major topic. Most recently Helen Wilcox has made a lifetime of Herbert scholarship available to the public in her *The English Poems of George Herbert*.[8] Poem by poem, she collects just about everything which previous critics have written, which she presents along with her own notes and interpretations. Apart from being a bit skimpy about forms, it is a gold mine. I have used it constantly, along with *A Concordance to the Complete Writings of George Herbert* edited by Mario di Cesare and Rigo Mignani,[9] and F. E. Hutchinson's unsurpassed *The Works of George Herbert*.[10]

In this book I have tried to bring together life and poetry, history and literary criticism as closely as possible. The reason for doing this is commanding enough. The circumstances of a poet's life and times are the soil in which the work is rooted – not just the outward and material circumstances but also, and still more, the inward patterns of thought and feeling prevailing in the poet's world. Understanding these enriches and clarifies the reading of the poems, particularly since Herbert's are frequently autobiographical: 'a picture of the many spiritual conflicts that passed betwixt God and my soul' in his own words.[11] Stimulated by this confession, the Bostonian philosopher George Herbert Palmer honoured his own baptismal names by producing an edition of Herbert's English works with the poems from *The Temple* rearranged in his own chronological order, based on Herbert's biography.[12] Unfortunately, this was a tour de force of gullible speculation. Apart from the survival of a manuscript of about a third of Herbert's poetry with corrections and Latin poems in his own hand, which can reasonably be dated to around 1623 and which allows us to distinguish in general terms between poems written before and after it,[13] such precision is impossible (see the Interlude at p. 139). Palmer's work has withered on the vine. But it leaves behind it an all-important warning: namely that while Herbert's poems obviously and confessedly arise from his life-experiences, only in a very few instances can we even guess responsibly exactly *when* they were written. A poem can recollect. It can take its cue from other literature or from pondering on things in the world which are by no means special or unique to the poet and, far from occurring just at one particular moment, are around all the time. In Herbert's case, things he learned and felt as a child were often a source of his adult meditations, and influences from the public church liturgy which ordered his years and accompanied him throughout his life could come to the point of his pen at any moment in any year. Above all, occasions of sorrow and happiness, regret, sensual pleasure, hope and resignation arise in the ordinary course of day-to-day life, often and over and over again. Most of us let them pass, but the poet seizes upon them and with truthfulness and imaginative craft – an interesting and demanding combination – makes them into works of art. These are the points, common to humanity at large, at which Herbert's readers feel closest to him: points at which his accuracy and sympathy make him, they may feel, a friend.

The point of knowing about Herbert's life and embedding his poems in it, as I have done, is not to imitate Palmer's flawed method. Rather, the biographical structure of this book maps out the ground which produced the poetry. Poetry comes from life: from the contemplative life of the imagination as well as from the active life, both of them historical or 'in time'. From there it addresses other lives in their own particular times: from life to life. T. S. Eliot wrote that 'in his poems we can find ample evidence of his spiritual struggles, of self-examination and self-criticism, and of the cost at which he acquired godliness . . . What we can confidently believe is that every poem in the book [*The Temple*, Herbert's collection of his English poetry] is true to the poet's experience.'[14]

But times differ: occasions of shame, fear or pleasure can vary from one generation to another. So my introduction, 'Herbert's World', describes important features of his historical context: the Church, the Bible, God, spirituality and poetry. After that, the course of his life takes over until the final chapters about his afterlife.

The spelling is modernized in this book, but not the punctuation. Herbert's differs only slightly from our own, so the question of whether to keep it or not is nicely balanced. Since the whole purpose of this book is to make Herbert familiar to the modern reader, I believe that modernized spelling enhances accessibility and fluent reading, while removing slight difficulties and – the last thing one wants – the possibility of an inappropriate air of quaintness.

It is much more important than this for readers to realize at the out-set that when Herbert uses a past participle such as 'lodged' he expects each of the two syllables to be heard: 'lodg-ed'. When he wants to reduce it to one syllable he substitutes an apostrophe for the 'e': 'lodg'd'. The technical terms for various metres in poetry look for-midable but denote simple things. Verse moves along on metaphorical 'feet': units with differences of emphasis or stress. 'Iambics march from short to long,' wrote Coleridge. In other words they go 'ti-tum', short–long. Trochees do the opposite: 'tum-ti' or long–short. The spondee is a solemn 'tum-tum'.

Finally, my own context. The writing of this book has been greatly helped by a number of institutions and individuals. All Souls College has provided every kind of support: in particular from Jim Adams, Keith Thomas, Noel Malcolm and Ian Maclean. Colin Burrow read a draft and commented on it with acute sympathy. I am also grateful to helpful staff at the Codrington Library in All Souls, the British Library, the Bodleian Library, Dr Williams's Library and Christ Church Library.

Laurence Dreyfus taught me about Jacobean music, Mark Girouard kindly advised me about Jacobean mansions, and Victoria Moul improved my Latin. Stuart Proffitt of Penguin trustingly commissioned the book and, like Colin Burrow, read and annotated a draft. I am also grateful to Francis Warner, Robert Cummings, Helen Wilcox and Jasper Griffin. Peter James's copy-editing wonderfully combined sensitivity with thoroughness. Cecilia Mackay was a resourceful researcher of images. I wish that Frank Kermode, who favoured my project and from whom I learned so much in the arts of literary criticism when we were both at King's College, Cambridge, had lived to see it. Alas, my first wife Clare died just when it was in its early stages. Our family, Jessica, Susannah and Matt, have kept a kindly eye on it. Perhaps one day my grandchildren, Zoe and Alex, will have a look at it. Above all, my wife Caroline Elam's contribution to it all has been deep, detailed and immeasurably sympathetic. She has read what I have written, piece by piece, and commented on it with the expert eye of an historian and an editor. Dedicating this book to her is a slight acknowledgement of all that she has given to it and to me.

In ye name of God. Amen.

1° Higher opportunities of doeing good are to be prefferd
before lower, even where to continue in ye lower is no
sinn. by ye Apostles rule. 1 Cor. 7, 21. & in ye whole chapter
therfore your choice at first was good.

2° yet are you now ingaged. It is a different thing
to advise you now, & before you took to Sr Johns
affaires. you have bin at charges: you have stockd
the grounds: you have layed out thoughts & prayers

3° you have sowed: therfore Expect a harvest.
To Change shewes not well. & you are by ye A-
-postles rule (Philip. 4, 8.) not only to pursue pure
things, but things y^t are lovely, & of good report
if there be any vertue or any praise: now Con-
-stancy is such & of great esteem wth all. As in
things inwardly good to have an Eye to ye world
may be phariaicall: So in things naturally visible
& apparent, as ye course of our life & ye chan-
-ges therof, wi are to regard others, & neither
to scandalize them, nor wound our owne reputation.

4° when two things dislike you: the one for the
nature therof (as your trade) the other only for
the success (as assistance of Sr John) doe

Herbert's handwriting, in a letter to Arthur Woodnoth (see page 226)

Introduction: Herbert's World

PAST AND PRESENT IN 'LOVE (III)'

Herbert's masterpiece 'Love (III)' is saturated in the conditions of life in seventeenth-century England. It is set in the hall of some substantial household, given to hospitality, such as Herbert lived in for most of his life. It draws on the manners and etiquette expected of guests and hosts which were the subject of numerous books.[1] At the same time its truth and beauty speak directly to readers anywhere and at any time at the deepest psychological level: its setting is the inmost heart or soul. How does it do it?

Love (III)

Love bade me welcome: yet my soul drew back,
    Guilty of dust and sin.
But quick-ey'd Love, observing me grow slack
    From my first entrance in,
Drew nearer to me, sweetly questioning,
    If I lack'd any thing.

A guest, I answer'd, worthy to be here:
    Love said, You shall be he.
I the unkind, ungrateful? Ah my dear,
    I cannot look on thee.
Love took my hand, and smiling did reply,
    Who made the eyes but I?

> Truth Lord, but I have marr'd them: let my shame
> > Go where it doth deserve.
> And know you not, says Love, who bore the blame?
> > My dear, then I will serve.
> You must sit down, says Love, and taste my meat:
> > So I did sit and eat.

A moving poem. Among other things, it moves us because of how it moves. Simply put, a poem, like ordinary language, is a pattern of short syllables and long ones. They are the pulse of its music. Herbert's sensitivity to metre was honed by his schoolday studies of Latin poetry, which depends on it entirely and does not rhyme. His skill as a lutanist and viol player in a great age of English music, particularly accompanied song, further tuned his ear for metre. Here these high-level arts, classical poetry and contemporary music, sustain the rhythms of simple, everyday speech. In the first scene-setting line of 'Love (III)' the short syllables in 'Love bade me welcome', springing from a stress on the first syllable, give it a sprightly alacrity. Then the three stressed syllables at the end of the line, 'soul drew back', make a heavy drag. This sets the tune for the dialogue in the rest of the poem between Love, coaxing the soul in light-footed metres, and the soul responding with ponderous reluctance. They are resolved in the wonderful last line of all, where rhyme, the great feature of English verse (as opposed to Latin), is decisive. Its light monosyllables are pinned down by the settling stress on the verbs 'sit' and 'eat' – 'eat' rhyming so satisfyingly with 'meat' (meaning food) at the end of the line before. This metrical movement towards the rhyming resolution reflects the resolution of the great and crucial problem in Herbert's life and verse: who, or what, is he up against all the time? The obvious answer is 'God'. But that simply restates the problem, for who or what is 'God'? Herbert's Bible, *the* book for readers in his day, gave him the ultimate answer: 'God is love.'[2] This cuts through the knot of theology tangled with its opposite, atheism. Belief and disbelief apart, love is everyone's ultimate and constant concern. It makes life and makes it worth living. It is altruistically redemptive ('bore the blame') as well as creatively nourishing. When it occurs in anyone's life in anything like a strong and pure form it amazes by its simple just-happenedness. This makes it difficult to understand in terms of normal patterns of cause and effect, particularly moral ones. It transcends them, having no other ends in view than the beloved. The achievement of Herbert's poem is that it, likewise, steps gracefully over the regular encumbrances of religion, with all its assertions and qualifications, to attain the radiant modesty of its last line. We need only think of how it would all suffer if its first word were 'God' rather than 'Love' to get the point.

It is astonishing to notice that within the short and lucid compass of 'Love (III)' Christianity's whole grand biblical narrative of humanity is contained as its subtext. The guest is 'guilty of dust and sin'. He is descended from Adam, the primal man who sinned against his Creator's command not to eat the fruit of the 'tree of the knowledge of good and evil' in the middle of paradise and was punished for it by mortality: 'dust thou art and unto dust thou shalt return.'[3] The divine creation of man is held in the host's punning riposte 'Who made the eyes but I?' Love likes jokes. Then the redemption in Christ, his divine taking upon himself of man's sin and punishment, is as deftly and lightly put in the host's next parry: 'And know you not, says Love, who bore the blame?' Finally, the prophetic promise that at the end of history redemption would be sealed and celebrated with a banquet, 'a feast of fat things, a feast of wines on the lees, of fat things full of marrow, of wine on the lees well refined'[4] is settled into that last, monosyllabic line 'So I did sit and eat.' The whole thing is replete with biblical references, among them Psalm 23:5 'Thou hast prepared a table before me'; Song of Songs 2:4 'He brought me to the banqueting house, and his banner over me was love'; Luke 12:37 the lord 'shall make them sit down to meat, and will come forth and serve them'. And more than that: the Church's great sacrament of eating and drinking, the Holy Communion, is powerfully present. In Herbert's day some communicants took the sacred bread and wine kneeling, some sitting. He himself was in two minds about it. 'The feast indeed requires sitting', he wrote, 'because it is a feast; but man's unpreparedness requires kneeling.'[5] In 'Love (III)' the domestic setting requires sitting. Seventeenth-century readers, church-going and full of their Bibles, were more likely to notice this wonderful feat of condensation, without the slightest heaviness, than we are. They would have admired it all the more for that.

Readers may well get the sense that this poem takes them as far as poetry can ever go: 'the most beautiful poem in the world' in Simone Weil's judgement when she came upon it at a time of crisis in 1938, tormented by migraines and the gathering storm in Europe.[6] At the same time they feel themselves presented with a little scene of everyday life in the seventeenth century, like a Dutch interior by Vermeer or Terborch in its quietly well-mannered realism, even its touch of comedy. That is its beauty. It is the work of a man who valued common experience, common sense and courtesy so highly as to collect 1,184 proverbs[7] – at the same time a mystic for whom the actuality of immediate religious experience mattered intensely, and more than orthodox doctrine.

Herbert's poems, like their pictorial counterparts, give their readers the sense of a particular moment in time. Yet none of them can be precisely dated. Apart from those that he wrote in Latin, none was published in his lifetime. They were kept in manuscript, corrected and rearranged, until he handed the whole lot over at the end to a man called Edmund Duncon, asking him to take the little book which contained them to 'Little Gidding', where Nicholas Ferrar, the leader of the devoutly Christian community there, was to decide whether to get them published. Thanks to him, they were printed within the year.

The circumstances of Herbert's life which bore on his poetry included pre-eminently the Church of England as a socio-political as well as religious institution, the Bible, beliefs about God derived from both these, the spirituality of individuals, and the state and status of English poetry in his time.

THE CHURCH

The Church of England was Herbert's mother and his home. It was the product of the protestant reformations of the previous century which had replaced the authority of the Pope with that of the vernacular Bible and swept away a panoply of complex Latin ritual as well as (to our regret nowadays) much of its attendant visual imagery. The Church of England was somewhat milder in this respect than the

Calvinist churches elsewhere in Europe. Herbert was glad of this. Stained-glass windows, deplored by puritans, figure positively in his verse. He loved old customs, such as processions through the fields to bless the crops, for their social value.[8] But radical Calvinists within his Church felt that reformation had not gone far enough and disputed, for example, the wearing of surplices by the clergy, signing baptized children on their foreheads with the cross and the use of the ring in marriage. During Herbert's lifetime these and more substantial quarrels about doctrine were just about contained, but after his death they erupted into war.

The Church pervaded the life of the nation from the King as its supreme governor to the country parson and his flock. Ecclesiastically, James I felt much more at home in England than he had been as James VI among the Presbyterians in Scotland, presbyters being laymen with power of governance in local churches. In England there were bishops, appointed by the crown as supreme governor of the Church, an office which James enjoyed and took seriously. In Scotland he had come under the lash of the Calvinist Andrew Melville who had told him that he was in charge of the Commonwealth but not of the Church where 'there is Christ Jesus, the king of the Church, whose subject James the Sixth is, and of whose kingdom, he is not a king, nor a lord, nor a head, but a member'.[9] On his way from Scotland to England in 1603 clergy sympathetic to Melville presented James with the Millenary Petition, asking to be relieved from 'the burden of human rites and ceremonies' of the English Church. The universities of Oxford and Cambridge were hostile to it, bringing Melville's wrath upon themselves in a satire with the laborious title *Anti-Tami-Cami-Categoria*: *Tami* signifying Oxford and *Cami* Cambridge. Herbert wrote a response to Melville in a series of Latin poems entitled *Musae Responsoriae* ('Poems in Answer' – most of them in a relaxed and witty style), with a dedication to the King. No doubt it pleased him. And Herbert may well have hoped, at the time, that it would lead to preferment, possibly secular.

If so, it was a reasonable hope, for Herbert was the sort of man James liked, as he showed when he visited Cambridge in 1620 and asked for a copy of Herbert's epigram thanking the King for his gift to the University of his Latin works. Their admiration was mutual.

Herbert set one of the King's orations as a text for his rhetoric class 'which he analysed, showed the concinnity of the parts, the propriety of the phrase, the height and power of it to move affections'.[10] James was perhaps the only intellectual to have occupied the throne of England. A contemporary said that his court was 'as Constantine's court, *ecclesiae instar* [an image of the Church], a little university, compassed with learned men in all professions; and his Majesty in the midst of them ... a living library, furnished at all hands, to reply, answer, object, resolve, discourse, explain'.[11] James enjoyed debate among the learned but discouraged public controversy, particularly about the doctrine of predestination. Derived from the Bible, and therefore fundamental to Calvinists, this doctrine held that the ultimate fate of every human being – salvation or damnation – was decided by God in advance and was unalterable. It was deeply troubling – not least to Herbert ('I cannot skill of these thy ways')[12] – and James regarded it as a disturbance of the tranquillity and consensus of the Church, which he successfully fostered.

The Jacobean clergy were better educated than ever before, thanks to growth in the numbers at the universities and the foundation of new colleges there. They were 'the most learned of the world', according to one witness,[13] and in Patrick Collinson's judgement 'ranked as honorary or pseudo-gentry, far above any status which would have been theirs by right of wealth'.[14] The King and the Lord Keeper of the Great Seal, who ranked with the Lord Chancellor, took care to appoint men with university degrees to the parishes in their gift. There was no lack of ordained graduates.

The civilized and inclusive character of Jacobean Anglicanism was exemplified by St Martin-in-the-Fields, the parish church of Herbert's youth in London. As well as the Herbert family, the congregation included Sir Walter Raleigh, Sir George More (John Donne's father-in-law and guardian to George Herbert's elder brother Edward), Inigo Jones and the painter Nicholas Hilliard. The Rector was Thomas Mountford, Doctor of Divinity and a man of parts eulogized by the preacher at his funeral in 1632 as a model of Anglican balance,[15] 'a true son of the Church of England, I mean a true Protestant; he was as far from popish superstition, as factious singularity, nor more addicted to the conclave of Rome than addicted to the parlour of

[Calvinist] Amsterdam.' He was a learned preacher, 'a devourer of books' and 'in his ordinary discourse abounded in witty, pleasant and facetious passages'. He had 'a true and hearty love unto music, and his skill in it showed he was as well able to set in tune his affections, as his voice or instrument'. He was assiduous in his 'daily private devotions and soliloquies with God'. Puritan and mainstream Anglican preferences were happily combined at St Martin's. There was a 'lecturer', the kind of additional preacher favoured by puritans, who held forth once a week. The church had been refurbished in the 1590s so that the people might better hear the preacher. Communion, in line with puritan practice, was served to the people in the pews. On the other hand, the music was fine and at Christmas the church was decorated with rosemary, bay, holly and ivy: things suspect to puritans but valued by Herbert as man and country parson.[16]

Both town and country parsons were deeply embedded in their parishes. Patrick Collinson gives an excellent example.

> John Favour, the Jacobean vicar of Halifax, described his life as consisting of 'preaching every Sabbath day, lecturing every day in the week, exercising justice in the commonwealth, practising of physic and chirurgery in the great penury and necessity thereof in the country where I live'. He was also the author of a book of poetry.[17]

Herbert too was an amateur medic – and the prince of clerical poets. Favour, like many clergymen, was a justice of the peace. There is no record of Herbert having held that office during his last years as rector of Bemerton, but he was enthusiastic in his encouragement of others to take on its duties: 'no Commonwealth in the world hath a braver institution than that of Justices of the Peace.'[18] In Northampton there was 'a weekly assembly of the magistrates and preachers for the correction of notorious blasphemy, whoredom, drunkenness, railing against religion or preachers, scolds and ribalds'.[19] 'The clergy', according to Collinson, 'had an acknowledged out-of-court role as peacemakers, arbitrating and composing quarrels.' The subject of Herbert's *Country Parson* spent his Sundays after church 'in reconciling neighbours that are at variance'.[20] As well as being a fellow-poet, he shared Favour's 'practising of physic', gathering herbs from the rectory garden to make medicines for his parishioners.[21] Being a parson was often uphill work, a good number of people being religiously indifferent, ignorant or hostile, or believing that 'a man might be saved by his own well-doing' without ecclesiastical interference.[22] For all that, the parson was the focus of unity, welfare and order in his parish, constantly visiting his people, whether they came to church or not, 'and every one is more awaked, when he come, and say, *Thou art the man.*'[23]

THE BIBLE

Herbert yielded to no Calvinist in his enthusiasm for the Bible, widely available in English translations which culminated in the Authorized or King James Bible of 1611 when he was eighteen. The vernacular scriptures dominated his Church's liturgy. The Bible is not so much a book, in the ordinary sense of the word, as a library: a collection of books held together within a span from the beginning of its history to its end. Within that span there are narratives, including myths, legends, chronicles and novels, books of proverbs and pragmatic philosophy, prophecies and poems (secular as well as sacred), legal codes and letters. There are also various and contradictory views of events and their meanings. There is much dispute. The Psalms argue with God, his providence and his absence. The books of Job and Ecclesiastes subject such consensus as there is to radically sceptical critique – and these were particular favourites of Herbert's in his darker moods. For the Christian reader like Herbert it all held together in Jesus. But even there, in the New Testament, versions of him abounded in four different Gospels and in the imagery of the Epistles. For Herbert this variety was not a problem to be solved by theological or historical-critical exertions, but a store of wonders and delights for everyday use. At all events, he was more devoted to the Bible as a resource, a guide to life and a mirror of his human self than as an authority – which, being a churchman, he took for granted.

He wrote two sonnets on 'The Holy Scriptures'. The first is deliciously medicinal, launching off from the dangerously artless double stress of 'Oh Book!' then hopping along on light feet through plentiful broken lines and enjambments which continue the sense over the line-breaks.

(A 'lidger' is an ambassador, a 'handsell' a new year's present to wish good luck – also a foretaste.)

> Oh Book! infinite sweetness! Let my heart
> > Suck ev'ry letter, and a honey gain
> > Precious for any grief in any part;
> To clear the breast, to mollify all pain.
>
> Thou art all health, health thriving till it make
> > A full eternity: thou art a mass
> > Of strange delights, where we may wish and take.
> Ladies, look here; this is the thankful glass
>
> That mends the looker's eyes: this is the well
> > That washes what it shows. Who can endear
> > Thy praise too much? thou art heav'ns lidger here,
> Working against the states of death and hell.
>
> > Thou art joy's handsell: heav'n lies flat in thee,
> > Subject to ev'ry mounter's bended knee.

The pervasive sprightliness (the huckster's cry of 'Ladies, look here' for example) comes to a head in the multiple paradox of the last lines: the Bible is a flat map of encircling heaven; it becomes a rider's mounting block; the rider bends his knee to mount his horse; the devout reader bends his knee in prayer.

The second sonnet turns from the praise of scripture to its use. Its diffuse variety is a spur to the creative fun of making one's own links and connections. It is a 'book of stars' which the reader can enjoy mapping into constellations, a garden of medicinal herbs which he can gather together to make a potion:

> Seeing not only how each verse doth shine,
> But all the constellations of the story.
> This verse marks that, and both do make a motion
> > Unto a third, that ten leaves off doth lie:
> > Then as dispersed herbs do watch [wait to contrive]
> > > a potion,
> These three make up some Christian's destiny.

9

So it was a guidebook to life. As the reader comments on it with connective skill, it comments shrewdly on the reader,

> for in ev'ry thing
> Thy words do find me out, and parallels bring,
> And in another make me understood.

Reading about 'another', any of the host of biblical pilgrims through life's twists and turns, contributes to self-understanding – something the modern secular reader gets from novels.

Thanks to translators and printing presses, the English Bible was more available in Herbert's time than ever before. Big English Bibles for church lecterns had appeared under Henry VIII and Elizabeth I. But it was the translation of 1560, made by English protestant exiles in Geneva, which held the field. It had gone through more than fifty editions when Herbert was born. It was cheap and available in handy quarto and octavo formats. It kept selling after the King James translation appeared in 1611 when he was an undergraduate at Trinity College, Cambridge. The King James Bible first appeared in large folio format to sit on church lecterns, printed in gothic black-letter type. But it was soon available in the smaller formats and the clearer roman typeface, slowly overtaking the Geneva translation in popularity. [24] As well as being the central ingredient of church services, it was affordable and could be studied at home. It was exhilarating to have the authoritative text, God's word, in your own hands, as Herbert testifies. There were commentaries to assist study. Calvin's were popular: 'worthy to be compared to the ancients', according to John Donne.[25] Herbert possessed 'the comment of Lucas Brugensis [a catholic writer] upon the Scripture' and valued it enough to leave it to his curate John Hayes in his will. His country parson 'hath one Comment at least upon every book of the Scripture, and ploughing with this, and his own meditations, he enters into the secrets of God treasured in the holy Scripture' which was 'the book of books, the storehouse and magazine of life and comfort'.[26]

GOD

'In him we live, and move, and have our being.' Those words of St Paul to the philosophers of Athens (according to Chapter 17 of the Acts of the Apostles) need to be taken at full strength for the understanding of Herbert and his God. Divinity saturated and enclosed his world: the whole of it, from the slightest movements of his own inmost being to his external circumstances in time and the natural world – the last of these topped by the divinely populated heaven beyond its sky. It followed that proofs or disproofs of God's existence just didn't arise: there was no place outside God where they could be contrived, nor any to which they could reasonably be addressed. Divinity was the cause and the sum of how things are, without remainder. Herbert's profound sense of this can be called mystical. For him believing in God, in the sense in which we raise that question nowadays, was not an issue. The issue, confronting him in his experience over and over again, was how you could trust – 'believe in' in a more existential and urgent way than mere assent to a doctrine or notion – the Father God whose absences were as unpredictable as his irresistible actions too often belied his reputation for justice. Herbert, in his continual searching for a clear and stable reciprocity, found plenty to complain about there, as we shall see. Fortunately there was more to divinity than that. There was the divine Christ, Son of the Father, whose essence was love, and whose love was invincible even by the direst affliction.

Herbert took the images of God in his Bible as ineluctable facts. They marked out the pitch on which human lives were lived. Before the protestant reformations a host of saints, commemorated on practically every day of the year and presiding over the lives of individuals and all sorts of groups and institutions, were available for the prayers and benefits of the devout: the Blessed Virgin Mary above all. With them cleared away, the world of a Christian's imagination was suddenly concentrated. The Bible, for all its variety and dissensions, is held together by the belief that the world, everything in it and everything that happened in it, was the work of the one God, absolute and exclusive. It was a unity sowing seeds of anxiety.

The world was complete and finished in six days, with God pronouncing it good at the end of each day: and good the natural world remained for Herbert and his contemporaries. Long before the discoveries of Darwin and modern astrophysics, some explanation of how everything had come into existence and how it worked was required. Divine creation provided that, had no challengers and held the field. The natural world presented no moral problems. Rather, it provided ample scope for the investigation of the heavens and the earth which was beginning to gather pace among intellectuals, led by Herbert's older friend Sir Francis Bacon. In his early poem 'Vanity (1)' Herbert was chary about such 'philosophy' as it was called, dismissing astronomy and chemistry as too speculative to occupy the valuable time of the practical Christian. For him, like most people with time to reflect, it was more a matter of wonder and admiration, such as sustains his own nature-poem 'Providence'. That wonder in the face of nature remains in common between him and us nowadays. It is not a negligible remainder in itself, and it enables us to engage with his praise of nature. But the biblical account of creation on which he stood is no longer so much as an approximation to science. It is appreciated as an impressive work of the imagination, doing what it could to answer the question of origins by projecting human creativity and craft on to the unseen deity. Once generally accepted as straightforwardly true, it is now old poetry.

The world as divine creation had another aspect which was a lot more problematic. God was not only the maker and lord of space and all its contents. He was also the lord of time, setting it on its course, ordaining and governing everything that happened. The resulting riddle was formidable and all too familiar. God is just and good. Why, then, is so much that happens bad and unjust? The question resonates through the Jewish scriptures of the Old Testament: psalms complaining of the unmerited sufferings of good individuals, prophets doing their best to interpret national disasters as just punishments for infidelity, chroniclers interpreting history in the same way, the Book of Job confronting what Muriel Spark has called 'the only problem' with unsparing insistence but ending up (again) with wonder in the face of the incomprehensible as the only answer. Once again, we can sympathize. 'Why is this happening to me?' is a question implying that an affliction is personally meant when it is so personally experienced. It is hard not to ask it, but it hangs in the air. It hangs there long enough for us to sense that the question is misconceived. Our sufferings are not punishments. They are misfortunes. Bad things just happen and do not discriminate between good and bad people. That is reality and it does not sit comfortably with the notion of a personal deity as its benevolent and omnipotent author, even micro-manager and director. Herbert felt the discomfort keenly. He did not hesitate to accuse this God, his God, of enticing him into grief under false pretences, of being a torturer, of being absent or silent when most needed. The reader of his poem 'Discipline' naturally expects that title to introduce a poem about discipline in the life of the Christian. It turns out differently. It is God who needs to behave himself, stop lashing about and learn to love. Interestingly, love is figured in the pagan form of Cupid, the little archer: a signal that there is nothing abject here, but a lively answering back in springing long–short trochaic feet.

Discipline

Throw away thy rod,
Throw away thy wrath:
> O my God,
Take the gentle path.

For my heart's desire
Unto thee is bent:
> I aspire
To a full consent.

Not a word or look
I affect to own,
> But by book,
And thy book alone.

Though I fall, I weep:
Though I halt in pace,
> Yet I creep
To the throne of grace.

Then thy wrath remove;
Love will do the deed:
> For with love
Stony hearts will bleed.

Love is swift of foot;
Love's a man of war,
                And can shoot,
And hit from far.

Who can scape his bow?
That which wrought on thee,
                Brought thee low,
Needs must work on me.

Throw away thy rod:
Though man frailties hath,
                Thou art God:
Throw away thy wrath.

The crucial reference there – to love which so 'wrought on' the deity that it brought him low – brings in Christianity's belief in the compassionate descent of deity to earth in Christ and asserts the primacy of love over godhead. Christianity, in its New Testament scriptures, could not abandon the image of deity deeply rooted in its Old Testament origins. But it gave religious people another focus of attention and wonder: the human sufferer as epiphany of the divine. In this way the problem became, paradoxically, the answer. Tragic misfortune and death were taken into the absolute. Jesus – to Herbert simply 'My Master' – was divinity incarnate, born into the world and history and suffering the worst that it could do. It was not just that this happened to him. As with all things seen from a moral aspect, it was a matter of how: how he had taken it all and why. The reason given by the more profound New Testament writers, Paul and John, mattered supremely to Herbert. It was love: a love of mankind ardent and reckless to the point of self-sacrifice. Love was the revelation: the motive, manner and meaning of Jesus' life and, most of all, his death. It was the ultimate divine quality or virtue: sublime in its depth and, at the same time, practical and practicable in everyday existence. When the country parson dealt with someone in despair, 'not so much doubting a God, as that he is theirs; then he dives unto the boundless ocean of God's love and the unspeakable riches of his loving-kindness'.[27] It was the 'exceeding great victory, which in the creation needed not', whereby God gave humanity 'love for love'. It was the gift of reciprocity, the heart's basic desire, the parson's 'business'[28] and the poet's dominant theme. At this crucial point the modern reader, of whatever persuasion concerning religion, can be free from intellectual reserve and enjoy Herbert's poetry (to use his own word) 'heart-deep', finding in it 'the grace of finding a way to live that keeps faith with the importance of goodness and love even in the face of everything that can happen to you'.[29]

Love, the divine motive for the great reversal of the terms and conditions of human life, stood revealed as the ultimate virtue: virtue understood as both quality and power. It was, we might say, the God within God and beyond God (as usually understood): the be-all and end-all of Herbert's life. When in 'Love (III)' he hesitates to accept Love's invitation to 'sit down and taste my meat [food]' because he does not deserve it, he is met by the response:

'And know you not', says Love, 'who bore the blame?'

T. S. Eliot reached the same destination in 'Little Gidding' IV.

Who then devised the torment? Love.
Love is the unfamiliar Name
Behind the hands that wove
The intolerable shirt of flame
Which human power cannot remove.

The primacy of love over theology and everything else is a major reason for the hold Herbert's Christian poetry has on modern readers – secular and even atheist as they may be.

SPIRITUALITY

If love is the heart and soul of the good life, then the inner or 'spiritual' life is all important. Nourished by the regular services of the Church and by the Bible, it expressed itself in private devotions. Herbert's teacher and friend Lancelot Andrewes, the learned Bishop of Winchester, used to pray in solitude all morning. His *Preces Privatae*[30] take the whole world, as well as his own occasions of penitence and thanks, into the consciousness of a man on his own. When Herbert on his deathbed entrusted his poems to Nicholas Ferrar for publication he described them as 'a picture of the many spiritual conflicts that have passed betwixt God and my soul' which might 'turn to the advantage of any dejected poor soul'.[31] He was not alone in making such a record and intending it to help others. In Colchester at that time two women, Cicely Johnson and Rose Thurgood, like Herbert subject to religious anxiety and apparently God-sent illness, read spiritual autobiographies by others and wrote their own.[32] Their representations of physical and mental agony were to be standard in this popular genre. A passage of Rose Thurgood's about illness in her family is typical in its realism and theism. Being sick in the seventeenth century was dire, as Herbert himself knew all too well.

> And thus we lay very sick a month, and my children were sometimes so hot in their fits, that none could quench their drought, and fainted away, that were driven to watch with them, for fear they would have died, and my husband had so hot fits, that I could not keep in bed, and I was so weak withal, that I could not sit up of three weeks together, not while my bed was made, but swooned away. Then it pleased God we were somewhat better one week, and then we all fell sick again but one and that was Mary. And I now seeing myself in this extreme poverty and want and all my household was sick again, and withal the Lord gave me over to hardness of heart again, then I began to rage and swell at God himself, saying to myself, what a God is this, what doth he mind to do with my children, surely they will die. And thus I began to quarrel with God.[33]

And so it went on from bad to worse until on 'the day before the Gunpowder treason day [1605]' the scriptures which had aggravated her sufferings suddenly relieved them: 'I felt a sweet flash coming over my heart and suddenly withal these words were pronounced in my heart: Thy name is written in the book of life: Thou hast that white stone and a new name.' The words were from Revelation 21:27 referring to 'they which are written in the Lamb's book of life' and 2:17: 'To him that overcometh will I give . . . a white stone, and in the stone a new name written . . .' The Bible was the one and only resource for protestants in their solitary agonies, sometimes appalling and sometimes comforting them.

Towards the end of her account Rose Thurgood reflects on its status. It is not the product of 'brain knowledge' or 'divinity and scholarship', but 'that which I have written is out of mine own experience, which the

Lord hath wrought in me by his holy spirit, and not by the traditions of men.' Thurgood was emphatic in telling the fellow-sufferers whom she expected to read her manuscript that she wrote 'out of my experimental knowledge'.[34] The adjective is striking and shows that the methods of the spiritual life were parallel to those of intellectual life at large. What the individual knew for herself was what counted. It was the same with philosophy. Montaigne's essays in solitary reflection under the motto 'what do I know?' were widely read in John Florio's translation of 1603. 'Retire into yourself,' wrote Herbert's brother Edward in his philosophical treatise *de Veritate*, 'and enter into your own faculties; you will find there God, virtue, and the other universal truths.' For him that was a more comfortable exercise than for his brother or Rose Thurgood, but for each of them it entailed autobiographical writing – in Edward's case one of the first autobiographies since St Augustine, the founder of autobiography as a search for truth in his *Confessions*, a book which worked powerfully on George Herbert.

POETRY

Even when timeless in quality, poetry owes a good deal of that quality to its particular time and place. In the second half of the sixteenth century poetry in English had asserted its rights over and against Latin poetry, which needed no defence, being part of the school syllabus. In 1557 Richard Tottel, a publisher of legal texts, published his *Miscellany: Songs and Sonnets of Henry Howard, Earl of Surrey, Sir Thomas Wyatt and Others*. It stayed in print until 1585. In a short preface 'To the reader' he staked his claim and that of English poetry.

> That to have well written in verse, yea and in small parcels, deserveth great praise, the works of divers Latins, Italians and other, do prove sufficiently. That our tongue is able in that kind to do as praiseworthily as the rest, the honourable style of the noble Earl of Surrey, and the weightiness of the deep-witted Sir Thomas Wyatt the elder's verse, with several graces in sundry good English writers, do show abundantly. It resteth now (gentle reader) that thou think it not evil done, to publish, to the honour of the English tongue, and for profit of the studious of

English eloquence, those works which the ungentle hoarders up of such treasure have heretofore envied thee.[35]

In that last sentence 'envied' bears the old sense of 'begrudged'. Tottel was bringing off a publishing coup: turning the sort of commonplace note-books, in which individuals ('hoarders') copied by hand poems which took their fancy, into a printed book for the general market.

In 1589, the year of Shakespeare's first play *Henry VI Part 1*, George Puttenham, a disreputable lawyer, echoed Tottel in the second chapter of his *The Art of English Poesy*, 'That there may be an art of our English poesy, as well as there is of the Latin and Greek'.[36] 'Why', he asked, 'may not the same be with us as well as with them, our language being no less copious, pithy and significative than theirs, our conceits [ideas] the same, and our wits no less apt to devise and imitate than theirs were?' The beauty of their poetry was its composition by metrical feet, but we can do as well or better with 'rhyme and tunable concords'. Puttenham's much used and discussed book provided English poets and readers with an encyclopaedic guide to poetic forms and fashionings.

A much better book than Puttenham's appeared six years later and a couple of years before Herbert was born: Philip Sidney's *An Apology for Poetry*. Sidney championed English verse in an age of Latinity: 'our tongue is most fit to honour Poesy, and to be honoured by Poesy.'[37] Herbert agreed:

> Let foreign nations of their language boast,
> What fine variety each tongue affords:
> I like our language, as our men and coast:
> Who cannot dress it well, want wit, not words.[38]

Herbert had family, as well as literary, reasons for being interested in Sidney. As a boy at Shrewsbury School, Sidney had stayed with the Newports, Herbert's maternal grandparents, at nearby Eyton. Sidney's sister Mary had married Henry Herbert, Earl of Pembroke, the pre-eminent grandee of the extensive Herbert family. The aristocratic couple lived in their great house at Wilton near Salisbury (and nearer still to Bemerton where Herbert was to end his days). Mary's enthusiasm and talent for literature made Wilton into a sort of school or college for writers. She and her brother Philip were close. At Wilton he began writing his romance with poems, *The Countess of Pembroke's Arcadia* – 'in loose sheets of paper', he recalled to her, 'most of it in your presence'. When Philip died, Mary completed their version of the biblical psalms, the origin and foundation of all Christian poetry. The Sidney *Psalms* influenced Herbert in two ways: positively, by their variety of forms, and negatively because it was not for him to repeat an exercise well done by illustrious forebears and praised by his friend John Donne as equal in inspiration to King David's originals.[39] There is only one psalm version in *The Temple*, 'The 23d Psalm', though it is at least the equal of Sidney's. Compare the fluency of Herbert's:

> He leads me to the tender grass,
> > Where I both feed and rest;
> Then to the sreams that gently pass:
> > In both I have the best

with Sidney's less vivid and somewhat jerky:

> He rests me in green pasture his;
> > By waters still and sweet
> > He guides my feet.

There was room for improvement.

Above all, Sidney's *Apology for Poetry* gave Herbert reasons and incentive for his own writing. Sidney believed that poetry could 'be used with the fruit of comfort by some, when, in sorrowful pangs of their death-dealing sins, they find the consolation of the never-leaving goodness'.[40] Poetry as consolation 'of any dejected poor soul'[41] was Herbert's motive for allowing what he had written for so long in the privacy of manuscript to be published after his death.

Thinking of the 'songs and sonnets' of the time, Sidney hoped that they could be turned to religious use:

> which, Lord, if he gave us so good minds, how well it might be employed, and with how heavenly fruit, both private and public, in singing the praises of the immortal beauty, the immortal goodness of the God who giveth us hands to write, and wits to conceive; of which we might well want words, but never matter; of which we could turn our eyes to nothing, but we should ever have new-budding occasions.[42]

That would have reinforced Herbert's resolution to devote his talents exclusively to religious poetry as he promised his mother in 1609, when he was sixteen.

The poetic self-consciousness which marked Sidney's *Apology* is reflected in two poems by Herbert, 'The Quiddity' and 'Jordan (II)'. He posed the question of the value of poetry, and answered it, in 'The Quiddity': the word means the essence of something, its particular nature.

The Quiddity

My God, a verse is not a crown,
No point of honour, or gay suit,
No hawk, or banquet, or renown,
Nor a good sword, nor yet a lute:

It cannot vault, or dance, or play;
It never was in *France* or *Spain*;
Nor can it entertain the day
With my great stable or demain:

It is no office, art, or news,
Nor the Exchange, or busy Hall;
But it is that which while I use
I am with thee, and *most take all*.

This is a lively poem, moving along quickly with four beats to the line in a simple rhyme scheme of *a b a b*. It is enjoyable too for the vivid, tightly packed richness of its contents, gathered from a world of gaiety, travel, sport and business. 'Suit' in the second line is a word Herbert used for courtship, usually of putting his case to God – not for posh clothes. The glamour of Jacobean life among the aristocracy is obviously something the poet knows and has a liking for, but views from a quizzical distance. He could do that because he occupied a standpoint apart from it: a rendezvous with God. While he was writing he was 'with' the God whom he addressed at the beginning, before the glamorous social excursion which comes to rest in the last two lines. '*Most take all*' was the triumphant call of the winner in a game of cards. It is a poetic triumph too. It steals a phrase from the public and secular world which the poet has toured only to deny with all his 'noes', 'nors' and 'never', and uses it to assert its opposite: the transcendent value of the simple privacy (what could be simpler than 'I am with thee'?) of being an individual in the company of the Other who is everything to him.

Simplicity, therefore, was what Herbert sought in his life and in the writing which accompanied it. 'Give me simplicity, that I may live.'[43] In 'Jordan (II)' the reader is admitted to the process of Herbert's writing: creativity and inspiration fighting it out with dissatisfaction and correction until the end when the bustling poet is told by 'a friend' to stop striving for effect and just 'copy out' love, the *sweetness ready penn'd* in his Bible.

Jordan (II)

When first my lines of heav'nly joys made mention,
Such was their lustre, they did so excel,
That I sought out quaint words, and trim invention;
My thoughts began to burnish, sprout, and swell,
Curling with metaphors a plain intention,
Decking the sense, as if it were to sell.

Thousands of notions in my brain did run,
Off'ring their service, if I were not sped:
I often blotted what I had begun;
This was not quick enough, and that was dead.
Nothing could seem too rich to clothe the sun,
Much less those joys which trample on his head.

As flames do work and wind, when they ascend,
So did I weave myself into the sense.
But while I bustled, I might hear a friend
Whisper, *How wide is all this long pretence!*
There is in love a sweetness ready penn'd:
Copy out only that, and save expense.

The title 'Jordan' is worth clarifying as an enigmatic key to the poem. It refers to the story of Naaman, in the Bible at II Kings 5. Naaman was a Syrian general but a leper. Desperately seeking a cure, he resorted to the Israelite prophet Elisha. Rudely refusing to come out and talk to him, Elisha sent an underling to tell him to wash seven times in the River

Jordan. Naaman, offended, proudly protested that he had greater rivers at home than Israel's little stream. But his servants reasoned with him. He did what he was told and 'his flesh came again like unto the flesh of a little child, and he was clean.' Herbert, ever keen on cleanliness and childhood, turned the story into a narrative of the poet's pride and glory in his work contradicted by his being set to copying out 'love' like a schoolboy with his elementary copy-book.

The experience of writing has rarely been so exactly or succinctly presented as in 'Jordan (II)'. In the first verse the poet is brimming over with ideas and enjoying the expression of them in 'quaint words and trim invention'. A slight shadow falls in the last line, where he finds himself in the writer's trap of seeking his reader's approval, 'Decking [adorning] the sense as if it were to sell' with the ornaments to which Puttenham devoted a long section of his book. But the exhilaration of fertility carries over into the second verse, then turns into the business of correction and revision – even this in the same high spirits. One way and another he is carried away: and that is the trouble. The third verse surprises the reader. 'So did I weave myself into the sense': surely this is positive, to wind self and sense, poet and his matter, into fusion? Yet it is the height of what he calls mere 'bustling'. Literary self-indulgence and self-proccupation, however enjoyable, is precisely not, for him, the point of writing poetry. It should be objective, transitive, and deal with something other. That is what the 'friend' indicates in a tactful whisper. And it was there all the time, *'ready penn'd'* in Holy Writ and particularly in the record there of Christ: yet again, love.

'Jordan (II)' is so candid as to convince its readers that they are in open contact with the poet at work and that he is giving them a direct account of his doings. It is something of a let-down to learn that the poem is so similar to poems by Shakespeare and Sidney, to which Herbert had access, that these look very like models, even sources, for it. Considered less emotionally, this is a reminder that Herbert was a poet among poets, that he drew on the abundant products of the great age of English poetry which preceded him. He was, to make the obvious point again, a poet in his own time.

'Jordan (II)' is strongly reminiscent of lines 1296–1302 of Shakespeare's *Lucrece*, published in 1594 and reissued three times after that, in which the heroine sits down to write a letter to her husband after her rape by Tarquin.

> Her maid is gone, and she prepares to write,
> First hovering o'er the paper with her quill:
> Conceit [thought] and grief an eager combat fight;
> What wit sets down is blotted straight with will;
> This is too curious good, this blunt and ill:
> > Much like a press of people at the door,
> > Throng her inventions, which shall go before.

Poetic self-consciousness made the process of writing and its 'inventions' an interesting and appealing subject to a fellow-poet. The vivid actuality of Herbert's poem is not damaged by noticing the ghost of Shakespeare's hand in it. Rather, it sets it in its context as a reminder of the historical commerce and succession of poetry.

Knowledgeable readers have more often been struck by the similarity of Herbert's Jordan poem, particularly at the end, to the first sonnet in Philip Sidney's popular *Astrophil and Stella*, published twice in 1591 and again in 1598.

> Loving in truth, and fain in verse my love to show,
> That she (dear she) might take some pleasure in my pain;
> Pleasure might cause her read, reading might make her know;
> Knowledge might pity win, and pity grace obtain;
> > I sought fit words to paint the blackest face of woe,
> Studying inventions fine, her wits to entertain;
> Oft turning others' leaves, to see if thence would flow
> Some fresh and fruitful showers upon my sunburnt brain.
> > But words came halting forth, wanting invention's stay;
> Invention, nature's child, fled step-dame study's blows;
> And others' feet still seemed but strangers in my way.
> Thus great with child to speak, and helpless in my throes,
> > Biting my truant pen, beating myself for spite,
> > 'Fool,' said my muse to me; 'look in thy heart and write.'

Sidney's poem and Herbert's are alike in their subject matter, grace and narrative structure, with their definitive and mind-changing endings. But Sidney wrote about not being able to write to his own satisfaction or at all. And Herbert wrote about having all too many notions and all too much 'invention' of clever ways to put it. Sidney had writer's block. Herbert had writer's incontinence. Sidney's ending has his muse telling him to stop casting about outside himself and among previous love poems and look inward: 'look in thy heart and write.' Herbert's 'friend' points him in the other direction: to look beyond himself and pay attention to what was already written, the love recorded in the Gospels. He does not need invention, but the elementary ability to copy what is there. And what is there yet again, the given and one-thing-necessary, is love.

Herbert was seven when John Donne first met his beloved mother Magdalen in Oxford. Donne was her friend for the rest of her life and preached her memorial sermon. In 1610 he sent her the manuscript of his series of religious poems entitled *La Corona*: a sign of his turning from the erotic to the sacred. It looks like more than a coincidence that, at the same time, Herbert sent her from Cambridge the two sonnets in which he declared his exclusive devotion to writing religious verse. From July to December in 1625, when plague was raging in London, Donne (now dean of St Paul's) and Herbert (withdrawing himself from Cambridge) were together at Magdalen's house in Chelsea. The other poet in the Herbert family, Edward, summarily recalled to London from his embassy in Paris, was around too. He turned Donne's great love poem 'The Ecstasy' into his own elaborately platonic 'Ode Upon a Question Moved, Whether Love Should Continue for Ever'. Such moving of questions in conversations, along with the reading and exchange of manuscript poems, must have been frequent at Chelsea then. What did Herbert owe to Donne? The two of them are usually contrasted: simplicity against complexity, modesty against hyperbole, quiet against loud. But Donne was a master of those poetic turns and techniques which served Herbert so well: the bold attack at the start and the transformative last line; the variety of forms to suit varieties of mood and matter; the ear for the rhythms and images of plain idiomatic speech; the ability to find different voices for the self in its changing states from anger to serenity. Herbert brought all these into making the chamber music of his individual voice, expressing itself in an even greater variety of moods and forms.

PART ONE

I

Childhood

The first three years of George Herbert's life were spent at Montgomery on the border between England and Wales. He was born into a family of six children: four brothers and two sisters. After him came two more brothers and another sister – ten of them all together and all surviving into adulthood. The little town with its market place is on an eastern slope: the mountains of Wales behind and an expansive view of the fields and wooded hills of the Severn valley below. Above it, on a rocky eminence, are the ruins of the great castle built by Henry III as a frontier post to keep out the wild and poorer Welsh in the mountainous country to the west, the source of frequent raids. The Herberts had been lords of the castle on the hill since the time of Henry VIII, but, according to George Herbert's elder brother Edward, their grandfather had built himself a more comfortable 'low building but of great capacity' called Blackhall down in the town.[1] 'He delighted also much in hospitality, as having a very long table twice covered every meal with best meats that could be gotten, and a very great family. It was an ordinary saying in the country at that time, when they saw any fowl rise, "Fly where thou wilt, thou wilt light at Blackhall".[2] There, very probably, George Herbert was born in 1593, the seventh child of old Edward Herbert's son Richard and his wife Magdalen Newport.

Blackhall has since disappeared, leaving its name to a street in the town. So has the renaissance mansion, including his library, which George's brother Edward Herbert built for himself within the castle's ruins in the 1630s. He had been made Baron Herbert of Cherbury, a little nearby town, as a reward for being ambassador to France. He would have liked Montgomery to be his title, but the senior Herberts

Montgomery, from John Speed, The Theatre of the Empire of Great Britain, *1611, Montgomeryshire.*

MONTGOMERY

A. The Castle
B. Backe Lane
C. Chery Stret
D. Orchard stret
E. Old gates
F. High stret
G. The Ruines of the old wall.

| 40 | 80 | 120 | 160 |

A. SCALE. OF. PASES.

in Wiltshire had already snapped it up. Edward Herbert was a renaissance man if ever there was one. As well as being a diplomat and a soldier, he wrote good poetry derived from his association with John Donne, which survives in modern anthologies (it is usually erotic or platonic, often both, and noticeably more metaphysical than his brother's), a hard-hitting and reductionist book of philosophy called *de Veritate* which he dedicated to George (see Chapter 4), a history of *The Life and Reign of King Henry the Eighth* and a famous and boastful *Autobiography*, recording with pride the exploits of his ancestors against the Welsh and, at greater length, his own achievements at home and abroad. Isaac Oliver's portrait of him,[3] a delicate and unusually large miniature, shows him relaxing in a woodland glade with a view of the Severn valley beyond. Among the trees, his squire holds his armour and three richly caparisoned horses, as if he were a knight of romance out of Spenser's *Faire Queene*. But he is in rich civilian dress, his thoughtful head supported by one hand and a shield over his side bearing the emblem of a heart above flames and the motto *magica sympathiae*, 'the magic of sympathy': soldier, lover and philosopher in his local landscape.

His forebears were less refined, going about their business of keeping order in Britain's wild west with all necessary violence. Edward Herbert tells a ferocious story of his grandfather and namesake.

> Some outlaws being lodged in an alehouse upon the hills of Llandinam, my grandfather and a few servants coming to apprehend them, the principal outlaw shot an arrow which stuck in the pummel of his saddle, whereupon my grandfather coming up to him with his sword in his hand, and taking him prisoner, he showed him the said arrow, bidding him look what he had done, whereof the outlaw was no further sensible than to say he was sorry that he left his better bow at home, which he conceived would have carried his shot to his body, and the outlaw being brought to justice, suffered for it.[4]

As a justice of the peace, old Edward Herbert on one occasion abused his powers appallingly.

> [He] intervened in a dispute about land and mendaciously informed one of the disputants, John Richard, that he had received an order for

his eviction from the Council of the Welsh Marches. When Richard asked to see the order, Herbert arrested him. During his imprisonment and despite a writ of Habeas Corpus from the Court of Requests to take the prisoner to London, Herbert deliberately ordered his men to destroy Richard's crops, incarcerate his wife and leave his children to starve. One of them, in fact, died from lack of food and care and was left unburied for a fortnight.[5]

Edward Herbert remembered his father Richard, son of this terrifying patriarch, as 'black haired and bearded, as all my ancestors on his side are said to have been, of a manly or somewhat stern look, but withal very handsome and well compact in his limbs.' He was:

> of a great courage, whereof he gave proof, when he was so barbarously assaulted by many men in the churchyard at Llanerfyl, at what time he would have apprehended a man who denied to appear to justice; for, defending himself against them all . . . he chased his adversaries until a villain, coming behind him, did over the shoulders of others wound him in the head with a forest bill until he fell down, though recovering himself again, notwithstanding his skull was cut through to the *pia mater* of the brain, he saw his adversaries fly away, and after walked to his house.[6]

Richard Herbert died in 1596 when Edward was fourteen and George only three. At this point their mother Magdalen came into her own, moving her family some 20 miles west from the edge of the wild, to live with her widowed mother, Margaret Bromley Newport, at Eyton upon Severn, a few miles south-east of Shrewsbury. The Newports were a lot richer than the Herberts, owned much of Shropshire and were more civilized. The five-bay house at Eyton, familiar to Sir Philip Sidney from his days at Shrewsbury School, has disappeared, but its site is idyllic: on a plateau just south of the church and Roman ruins of Wroxeter, overlooking the river with views of the pastures and the wooded hills beyond: which could all be enjoyed (and no doubt was by small George) from a surviving summerhouse or banqueting house, originally one of a pair, three storeys high with a stair-turret, a fenestrated room and a flat, balustrade roof. Old Lady Newport was very proud and fond of her family, not least of her grandchildren. Edward

Shrewsbury with Eyton upon Severn downriver to the south-east, from John Speed, The Theatre of the Empire of Great Britain, *1611, Shropshire.*

Alscot
Rocadyne
Wellyn
Walcot
Orleton
Carleton cast.
Aston
Uppinton
Ucketon
Norton
Rushton
Wrekin hill
Bestaw
Roxalter
Great Bildas
Leghton
Eaton upō Seueren
Little Bildas
Belserdyne
Draton
Shenton
Greßedge
Cunde
Harnydge Grange
Wike
Attonburnell cast
Horley
Wenlok

admired her 'incomparable piety and love to her children' and her hospitality, which 'Exceeded all either of her country or time; for, besides abundance of provision and good cheer for guests . . . she used ever after dinner to distribute with her own hands to the poor, who resorted to her in great numbers, alms in money, to every one of them more or less, as she thought they needed it'.[7] Little George must have been happy at Eyton, and Edward, at the early age of sixteen, was married to Mary Herbert while they were there. Mary came from another branch of the Herbert family and her father had stipulated that, unless she married a man with the name of Herbert, she would forfeit her inheritance of lands in Monmouthshire and Ireland. So as far as Magdalen Herbert and Margaret Newport were concerned, this was a way of securing Edward's future.

Margaret Newport's family piety is witnessed by the fine tomb in Wroxeter Church which she erected to her husband and (in advance) herself: there are alabaster effigies of both. In the same church the tomb of her father and mother, Sir Thomas and Lady Bromley, both in coloured alabaster effigies, is even grander. Margaret's daughter followed suit. While she was at Eyton, Magdalen Herbert set about erecting a tomb for her late husband Richard and herself (both husband and wife again) in Montgomery Church.

Nothing else in that church is so grandiose. Indeed even by the high Elizabethan standards of display the tomb is magnificent. A large semi-circular arch, its main feature, has two painted figures in its spandrels: Old Father Time with his hourglass and sickle and a naked woman who might be Truth. Above this, heraldry abounds to display the family's connections. A row of shields above the arch supports a gigantic strapwork pediment with Richard Herbert's arms in the middle. Above them, to subdue the pomp a little, are two skulls with bones and the inscription 'olim fui: sic eritis': 'I was once, you will be so.' The great arch forms the front of a vaulted canopy over the recumbent effigies of Richard and his wife Magdalen. But only he is buried there, with a sculpted representation of his corpse below the table on which the two effigies lie. Magdalen died thirty-one years later, having married again, and was buried at Chelsea.

Sir Richard, 'black-haired and bearded' as Edward remembered him, is in full armour.[8] The armour is conventional, but apt enough.

As an enforcer of law and order in the disorderly Welsh Marches, deputy lieutenant and principal justice of the peace, he needed to be prepared to fight. But in his monument it is his wife Magdalen, George's mother, who predominates. Her effigy is at the front, richly gowned. Her face above her ruff is youthful and alert, surmounted by the coiffure which also appears in her portrait:[9] her hair pulled up from her forehead in two high rolls. Her maternity is displayed by a row of little kneeling figures of their children (not likenesses, more like dolls) behind the two effigies: six boys and two girls, for some reason a boy and a girl short of her total of ten. George was her fourth son. It is in the inscription, in gilded gothic lettering above the arch, that Magdalen's control is most blatantly asserted. Although it is her husband's tomb, most of the text is about her and her family, to which she referred in capital letters.

> Heare Lyeth the Body of Richard Herbert Esquire whose Monument was Made at the Coste of Magdalene his wife Daughter of Sir Richard NEWPORT of High Arcoall in the County of Salop, Knighte (deceased) & of Dame Margaret his wife Daughter & Sole heyr to Sir Thomas BROMLEY Knighte Late Lord Chiefe Justice of England & one of the Executors of the Late Kinge of Most Famous Memorye Kinge Henry the Eighte Ano Dom 1600.

Verses in Latin, advertising learning, are in a cartouche over the effigies. They celebrate Magdalen's virtue, piety and love in erecting the monument and the couple's fidelity.

Richard Herbert's tomb is, then, more a monument to his formidable widow and her family than to him and his. For its design and making Magdalen employed the builder Walter Hancock. Her brother, Sir Francis Newport, Member of Parliament for Shropshire, was an enthusiastic patron of Hancock. In 1595 he recommended him strongly to the Bailiffs of Shrewsbury for the building of their new Market House as 'a Mason of approved skill and honesty . . . you cannot match the man in these parts with any of his occupation, neither in science and judgement of workmanship, nor in plainness and honesty to deal withal'.[10] Hancock got the job and built the Market House on broad semi-circular arches like the one on the monument in Montgomery Church. In his will of 1599 he referred to '£4.19s. owed to Wm. Reed wh. he is to receive of Mrs. Magd. Herbert out of that work which he and others have done by my appointment at Montgomery'.[11]

In the same year, 1599, old Margaret Newport died and Magdalen Herbert with her brood moved to Oxford to keep an eye on Edward Herbert who was an undergraduate at University College. When the monument was completed, according to the date of 1600 inscribed on it, George Herbert was seven years old. It is not known whether he ever saw it, but he had certainly heard plenty about it. In his later life he took a more sceptical view than his mother or his grandmother of monumental magnificence, as his poem 'Church Monuments' testifies.

The lines of 'Church Monuments' are solemn pentameters, varied and fluent. There is much enjambment, the continuing of sense and sentences over the line-breaks. Most strikingly, this happens over the gaps between the verses, giving the whole thing the continuous and inevitable flow of time's 'ever rolling stream'.[12] The sentences are long: only four of them over the four verses. The rhyme scheme is drawn out too, the first three lines of each verse having to wait for the next three to get their rhymes (*a b c a b c*). Herbert had learned from his friend Lancelot Andrewes, the great preacher and linguist who was dean of Westminster when he was a scholar there, to make the most of a word by situating it in one context after another (see Chapter 2). Here the word is 'dust'. It occurs six times, as well as the adjective 'dusty'. The dust of death, the ordinary dust on the monuments, the sand-dust in the hourglass, all echo God's sonorous verdict on fallen Man: 'dust thou art, and unto dust thou shalt return.'[13] The 'lines' and the 'stem' referred to are genealogical.

Church Monuments

> While that my soul repairs to her devotion,
> Here I entomb my flesh, that it betimes
> May take acquaintance of this heap of dust;
> To which the blast of death's incessant motion,
> Fed with the exhalation of our crimes,
> Drives all at last. Therefore I gladly trust

My body to this school, that it may learn,
To spell his elements, and find his birth
Written in dusty heraldry and lines:
Which dissolution sure doth best discern,
Comparing dust with dust, and earth with earth.
These laugh at Jet and Marble put for signs,

To sever the good fellowship of dust,
And spoil the meeting. What shall point out them,
When they shall bow, and kneel, and fall down flat
To kiss those heaps, which now they have in trust?
Dear flesh, while I do pray, learn here thy stem
And true descent; that when thou shalt grow fat,

And wanton in thy cravings, thou mayst know,
That flesh is but the glass, which holds the dust
That measures all our time; which also shall
Be crumbled into dust. Mark here below
How tame these ashes are, how free from lust,
That thou mayst fit thyself against thy fall.

'Dusty heraldry and lines' – all those shields of the family line of
descent and all those inscriptions on the tomb at Montgomery
Church – testify to death's 'dust to dust and earth to earth' rather than
to dynastic splendour. 'Jet and Marble put for signs' only:

> sever the good fellowship of dust
> And spoil the meeting

of mortal with mortality. The monuments themselves will eventually
crumble and 'fall down flat' (excellently apt and deliberate bathos) to
be one with the dust they had 'in trust'. The penultimate line brings a
shudder:

> How tame these ashes are, how free from lust.

They are a lesson in humility in its strictest Latin-derived sense of
being of the earth. Family pride was beside the point.

But, for all that, family mattered. In particular, the traditions of
hospitality maintained by both the Herberts and the Newports were

engrained in George Herbert. Hospitality is the master-metaphor of 'Love (III)', with its dialogue between welcoming host and diffident guest resolved by sitting down at table. He was to end his days as the hospitable rector of a country parish, seeing to it that on festival days none of his parishioners should 'want a good meal suiting to the joy of the occasion'.

While Magdalen Herbert was in Oxford with her family, including the seven-year-old George, she got to know John Donne. He was secretary to Sir Thomas Egerton, Lord Keeper of the Great Seal. But he was on thin ice because he was in love with Egerton's niece Ann More, whose father disapproved of the affair (he married her secretly in December 1601). Twenty-six years later, in 1627, he had risen to be dean of St Paul's and preached in commemoration of Magdalen Herbert, who had meanwhile remarried, to Sir John Danvers.[14] Donne was wittily laudatory of the benefit of the move to Oxford in 1599 to Magdalen's children. It 'recompensed to them, the loss of a *Father*, in giving them *two mothers*; her own personal care and the advantage of that place; where she contracted a friendship, with divers reverend persons, of eminency, and estimation there; which continued to their ends'.[15] Donne may well have considered himself one of these persons. More modestly, he may just have been an observer of Magdalen Herbert's ability to gather interesting people into her circle when he met her in Oxford and first admired her 'conversation, naturally cheerful, and merry, and loving facetiousness, and sharpness of wit'.[16] His friendship with her was to grow and include her son George. They both dedicated poems to her.

The Herberts were not long in Oxford. In April 1601, they moved to London and settled there at last. They had a house at Charing Cross, the district named after the elaborate cross, still there in the Herberts' time, erected by Edward I to mark a staging post in his wife Eleanor's funeral procession. George Herbert was eight when they got there.

London, one needs to remember, was and is a double-yolked riverside city: the mercantile City of London with its port and, a little further upstream on the Thames, Westminster, the seat of government with its royal palace, Abbey church and School. Charing Cross came between the two. It was rural, a character which survives in place names in and around it: Covent Garden, St Martin-in-the-Fields,

St Giles in the Fields, Long Acre, Haymarket. It also had a barbarous aspect: its use as a place for public executions and punishments. If you were lucky enough to escape such horrors, stood at the Cross and the water conduit beside it and looked north, the river was behind you, just beyond a row of houses (one of them probably the Herberts') with gardens and yards, Scotland Yard among them, going down to the water. In front of you to your right was the Herberts' parish church, St Martin-in-the-Fields. To the right of that was the Strand, a waterside appellation, along which the mansions of the great in Church and state led east to the lawyers' Inns of Court and the densely populated City of London beyond. In front of you, and to the left of St Martin's Church, were the Royal Mews or stables, the richly smelling accommodation for all the horses and hawks of the royal household. Beyond the Mews was open country, threaded by lanes leading eventually to the main road to Oxford and the west. Some sense of what Charing Cross was like in Herbert's time can be got from the landscape around Hampton Court nowadays: the royal palace by the river, the Mews at a short distance from it, and the surrounding parkland as far as the eye can see. To live at Charing Cross was to be surrounded by the royal court.

The Mews at Charing Cross served the royal palaces: St James's, then the other side of a deerpark, and Whitehall. Whitehall announced itself with two magnificent buildings to your left. There was the Banqueting House, a Tudor predecessor of Inigo Jones's present masterpiece, where great state occasions, receptions and masques were held. The trappings of the beau monde which Herbert fended off in 'The Quiddity'[17] were all around him to dazzle his eyes in his childhood: the hawks and banquets, the 'gay suits' and good swords, the dances and plays, the Exchange up the Strand in the City, the 'great stable' and 'busy hall'. The Banqueting House was next to the Holbein Gate, a magnificent turreted Tudor affair like the great gates of Cambridge colleges, but grander. It was encrusted in royal heraldry, with the King's Chamber set over its central arch. Through it you could walk or ride down King Street through the palace buildings: lodgings on the right, chapel and the Privy Garden on the left, until the King Street gate let you out on to Palace Yard and confronted you with the superb spectacle of Westminster Abbey, Westminster Hall

Westminster and Charing Cross, from John Speed, The Theatre of the Empire of Great Britain, *1611, Middlesex. Charing Cross itself is in the middle of the image. The Royal Mews are to its right, with the church of St Martin-in-the-Fields just to their right. The Strand, with the riverside mansions of the great, leads away east to the City of*

London. To the left of the Cross, the Palace of Whitehall is entered through the Holbein Gate and stretches westwards to Westminster Abbey, with St Margaret's Church beside it to its right and the School to its left.

(both still surviving) and the tall Parliament House. On the other side of the Abbey, nestling in its shadow, was the royal foundation of Westminster School.

Charing Cross was altogether well placed for Magdalen Herbert's careful upbringing of her brood. There were masques and plays at the Banqueting House. Shakespeare was at the Globe Theatre over the river. Great sermons were preached at the royal chapel of Whitehall. At Westminster Abbey the music was famous and fine. There was plenty of space for play and exercise, and one of the best schools in the land a short walk away.

It also suited her social talents. She could draw on court and city, aristocrats, gentry in town, clergy, musicians and writers for company at her parties. Her hospitality was famous. John Donne made a point of it in his sermon of commemoration on her in 1627. She was a Newport, he reflected, and 'from that worthy family, whence she had her original extraction, and birth, she sucked that love of hospitality, (hospitality, which hath celebrated that family, in many generations, successively) which dwelt in her, to her end'.[18] It had been a hospitality which created a salon of witty conversation and extended beyond family and friends to the poor and the sick: 'And as her house was a Court, in the conversation of the best, and an Almshouse, in feeding the poor, so was it also an Hospital in ministering relief to the sick.'

Her 'Kitchin Book' for the first year at Charing Cross has survived.[19] The 'number of my household' was twenty-eight people: six 'gentlewomen' and six 'gentlemen' (her family), four female and ten male domestic staff. They were kept busy. Magdalen started off with a house-warming or 'drinking' for twenty-six guests. The next day, Easter Sunday, twenty-nine people, not all the same as the day before, sat down to dinner. In the following three months ninety-six different visitors were entertained, some of them so frequently as to be semi-resident. There was music, once from 'a Blind harper and his boys'. The composers John Bull and William Byrd were each at her table more than once. Morris dancers came to the house. There were card games. There were prayers. And so it went merrily on. Her eldest son Edward thought that all this went too far, that she 'kept a greater family than became either her widow's estate, or such young beginners as we were'.[20] There was reason for complaint. The house was a

London base for Magdalen's Newport family. Her nephew Richard Newport was a regular member of the household. She frequently boarded another nephew and his servant, her brothers-in-law Robert Harley and John Barker and his servant, and a cousin on her mother's side, Lady Bromley and her servant.[21] Altogether, the place was something like a fair-sized college of the time.

With so many people milling around, good manners were important. The etiquette books of the day give us a good idea of what they entailed.[22] Their emphasis on diffidence is relevant to the behaviour of the guest in 'Love (III)'. *The Civil Conversation* (1581) advises that 'It is the part of him which receiveth these outward honours, first, modestly to refuse them, showing thereby that he looketh not for them, otherwise he shall show to be somewhat proud.' Castiglione's *Courtier*, translated into English in 1561, laid down that a guest should 'not receive favour and promotions so easily as they be offered him, but refuse them modestly, showing he much esteemeth them ... that he may give him an occasion that offereth them, to offer them with a great deal more instance.' As has been observed, 'Submission and obsequiousness were signals of the social order at work.'[23] But they could also make it all absurdly sticky, and then a simple directness was needed to cut the cackle. Guazzo's *Civil Conversation*, a courtesy book published in English in 1581, set out the:

> example of the discreet gentleman, who, after long strife between him and certain of his friends, who would first enter into the house, saith, You may now know well how much I am at your command, seeing I am ready to obey you in things which turn to my dishonour: which said, he entered in without straining courtesy any longer.

It was good manners to honour your host with protestations of modest unworthiness. It was also good manners, when your host insisted, to refrain from more polite altercation and 'sit and eat'. Religious and psychological depth apart, 'Love (III)' is a picture of the sort of polite behaviour which, with all its elaboration, ensured some order in the crowded house at Charing Cross.

But it was precarious, as Herbert recalled when he wrote his poem 'The Family', making it a metaphor for his own internal turmoil and its control. His mother's lively and argumentative family is detectable here, as is her reduction of it to peace and order with the help of her servants and the tutors who came to teach her children.

> What doth this noise of thoughts within my heart,
>> As if they had a part?
> What do these loud complaints and puling fears,
>> As if there were no rule or ears?
>
> But, Lord, the house and family are thine,
>> Though some of them repine.
> Turn out these wranglers, which defile thy seat:
>> For where thou dwellest all is neat.
>
> First Peace and Silence all disputes control,
>> Then Order plays the soul;
> And giving all things their set forms and hours,
>> Makes of wild woods sweet walks and bow'rs.
>
> Humble Obedience near the door doth stand,
>> Expecting a command:
> Than whom in waiting nothing seems more slow,
>> Nothing more quick when she doth go.
>
> Joys oft are there, and griefs as well as joys;
>> But griefs without a noise:
> Yet speak they louder then distemper'd fears.
>> What is so shrill as silent tears?
>
> This is thy house, with these it doth abound;
>> And where these are not found,
> Perhaps thou com'st sometimes, and for a day;
>> But not to make a constant stay.

The start of the poem is a good example of poetic attack. The poet's voice bursts out in sudden exasperation against the hubbub in his heart. Isn't it supposed to be God's 'house and family'? Why doesn't he turn out 'these wranglers'? But violent expulsion is not the way. With a characteristically light, domestic use of allegory, Herbert has Peace, Silence and Order take over. 'Humble Obedience' in the fourth verse is a model of the porter-cum-messenger of households of the time. She is a woman, we may be surprised to learn from 'Nothing more quick when *she* doth go', but in allegory the virtues are traditionally feminine. The fifth verse is full of tender realism. Even a well-ordered household has griefs as often as joys. But they do not disrupt it. The line 'What is so shrill as silent tears?' is a heart-stopper: emotional tension held tight between opposites. The poem ends with sober and rational reflection. God will only, and at best, make occasional visits to distracted households. The domestic scene is his when it is orderly. When he had a household of his own at Bemerton Rectory, Herbert insisted that 'the Parson is very exact in the governing of his house' and recommended having Psalm 101 inscribed on one of the walls with its banning of frowardness (cheek), slander and pride: 'whoso leadeth a godly life, he shall be my servant. There shall no deceitful person dwell in my house.'

One of Herbert's most extraordinary and arresting poems is about a row breaking out at table. When his elder brother Edward wrote about George in his *Autobiography* he acknowledged that 'about Salisbury, where he lived beneficed for many years [only three actually], he was little less than sainted', but went on to recall that 'he was not exempt from passion and choler, being infirmities to which all our race is subject.' [24] The Herberts were an inflammable lot. 'Choler' sounds just like 'Collar': the title of the poem in question. It may indeed be a triple pun, such as occurs in the first scene of *Romeo and Juliet* (1599), 'caller' sounding much the same as 'choler' and 'collar' in seventeenth-century pronunciation. The caller to order at the end of the chaotic poem is God calling '*Child*', as he did for the infant Samuel in the Bible.[25] But it is not out of the way to suspect that the voice of Magdalen or one of her servants is behind it.

The Collar

I struck the board, and cried, No more.
                    I will abroad.
          What? Shall I ever sigh and pine?
My life and lines are free; free as the road,
          Loose as the wind, as large as store.
                    Shall I be still in suit?

Have I no harvest but a thorn
To let me blood, and not restore
What I have lost with cordial fruit?
                        Sure there was wine
Before my sighs did dry it: there was corn
                  Before my tears did drown it.
Is the year only lost to me?
                  Have I no bays to crown it?
No flowers, no garlands gay? all blasted?
                  All wasted?
Not so, my heart: but there is fruit,
                  And thou hast hands.
Recover all thy sigh-blown age
On double pleasures: leave thy cold dispute
Of what is fit, and not. Forsake thy cage,
                  Thy rope of sands,
Which petty thoughts have made, and made to thee
Good cable, to enforce and draw,
                  And be thy law,
While thou dost wink and would'st not see.
                  Away; take heed:
                  I will abroad.
Call in thy deaths head there; tie up thy fears.
                  He that forbears
            To suit and serve his need,
                  Deserves his load.
But as I rav'd and grew more fierce and wild
                  At every word,
Methoughts I heard one calling, *Child!*
                  And I replied, *My Lord.*

'At one time', confessed L. C. Knights, 'I felt that in this well-known ending ... Herbert was evading the issue by simply throwing up the conflict and relapsing into the naïve simplicity of childhood.' But for Herbert 'childhood is health' and simplicity the 'much-desired end' for the man as for the poet, to be gained through difficulty. Knights had second thoughts.

But of course I was wrong. The really childish behaviour is the storm of rage in which the tempestuous desires – superbly evoked in the free movement of the verse – are directed towards an undefined 'freedom'. What the poet enforces is that to be 'loose as the wind' is to be as incoherent and purposeless; that freedom is to be found not in some undefined 'abroad', but, in Ben Jonson's phrase, 'here in my bosom, and at home'.[26]

The phrase from Morning Prayer in the Book of Common Prayer, 'whose service is perfect freedom', so familiar to Herbert, suggests itself too.

Presumably, what threw Knights off course in his earlier reading was Herbert's persuasively accurate and sincere description of the storm of rage. He resurrects the past experience complete and whole. The reader is there and with it – up to a point: for the fury goes on so recklessly that 'tantrum' becomes a better word for it. Around halfway we begin to feel that the speaker has got beyond himself, is starting to make a fool of himself. We get embarrassed, might soon feel bored. This near over-running is a tribute to the accuracy of Herbert's self-satire.

The poem is also a masterpiece in Herbert's marrying of form and content. One only has to look at it: no stanzas; long, short and middling-length lines all higgledy-piggledy; rhyme-endings all over the place. It is an eruption. If we use the letters of the alphabet to denote these rhyme endings we have to go at least as far as 's', the nineteenth letter. The last line before the final and resolving four lines ('Deserves his load') comes down with an onomatopoeic thump. Only in the last four lines do we get a stable rhyme-scheme of *a b a b* and a settled coming-together of the line-lengths, which have previously been scattered, in a diminuendo which applies the brakes to the careering vehicle: ten syllables, followed by four, eight and six. Joseph Summers has called it, aptly and succinctly, 'a formalised picture of chaos' and ranked it among 'Herbert's most deliberate ventures in "hieroglyphic form"' – that is, poems like 'The Altar' and 'Easter-wings' which are shaped and physically formed like their subjects.[27] Those poems, however, make shapes to fit order. The marvel of 'The Collar' is that it makes a shape to fit disorder. There was, perhaps, nothing like that again until T. S. Eliot wrote *The Waste Land*.

Herbert's childhood years gave him rich knowledge and insight into the social world beyond the family. Charing Cross was a great place for observing life: high, low and middling. Herbert's wide-awake watch on human behaviour in public informs 'The Quip'. A quip, according to *The Oxford English Dictionary*, is 'a sharp or sarcastic remark directed against a person; a clever hit'. Here the quip, '*But thou shalt answer, Lord, for me*' at the ends of the middle verses, is more of a deflection: no sarcasm but an evasion of the world's teasing solicitations which allows the poet to stand aside from them with a serenity which softens the satire.

> The merry world did on a day
> With his train-bands and mates agree
> To meet together, where I lay,
> And all in sport to jeer at me.
>
> First, Beauty crept into a rose,
> Which when I pluck'd not, Sir, said she,
> Tell me, I pray, Whose hands are those?
> *But thou shalt answer, Lord, for me.*
>
> Then Money came, and chinking still,
> What tune is this, poor man? said he:
> I heard in Music you had skill.
> *But thou shalt answer, Lord, for me.*
>
> Then came brave Glory puffing by
> In silks that whistled, who but he?
> He scarce allow'd me half an eye.
> *But thou shalt answer, Lord, for me.*
>
> Then came quick Wit and Conversation,
> And he would needs a comfort be,
> And, to be short, make an Oration.
> *But thou shalt answer, Lord, for me.*
>
> Yet when the hour of thy design
> To answer these fine things shall come;
> Speak not at large; say, I am thine:
> And then they have their answer home.

The poem is full of London imagery: the train-bands or City militia; the pretty woman figured as a rose from the town garden, perhaps the Privy Garden at Whitehall; the City financier; the magnificently dressed courtier of the sort Herbert saw flocking around the Banqueting House on great days; the witty party talk, tending to the monologues which made Herbert famous as University Orator in Cambridge – but which he advised against in ordinary conversation in line 303 of 'The Church Porch': 'give men turns of speech.' Herbert's friend John Donne wrote satires on London life, full of little caricatures like Herbert's. The first of them has:

> a brisk perfumed courtier
> Deign with a nod, thy courtesy to honour.

Perhaps the element of satire in all this means that Donne is a source here, but his courtier, returning his bow with a curt nod, is not as vivid as Herbert's, with his onomatopoeic whistling silks and arrogantly perfunctory 'half an eye'. And Donne's satire goes on and on with sustained and bitter sarcasm, whereas Herbert's poem is beautifully formed, good natured and musical.

'Redemption' is a sonnet which starts in the country but ends in the city. The subtext at its root is biblical: Christ's ministry in rural Galilee, followed by his suffering and death in Jerusalem. The title combines secular and sacred: the legal action of clearing off or cancelling a liability, and the salvation of mankind by Christ's sacrificial death.

Redemption

> Having been tenant long to a rich Lord,
>> Not thriving, I resolved to be bold,
>> And make a suit unto him, to afford
> A new small-rented lease, and cancel th' old.
>
> In heaven at his manor I him sought:
>> They told me there, that he was lately gone
>> About some land, which he had dearly bought
> Long since on earth, to take possession.

I straight return'd, and knowing his great birth,
  Sought him accordingly in great resorts;
  In cities, theatres, gardens, parks and courts:
At length I heard a ragged noise and mirth

  Of thieves and murderers: there I him espied,
  Who straight, *Your suit is granted*, said, and died.

Bit by bit the momentous allegory, based on the two meanings of the title, emerges.

The first four lines appear to be a matter-of-fact agricultural anecdote. That the landlord's manor house should be in heaven alerts the reader to some religious meta-narrative, but the realism of the poet's dealings with the people at the manor house restores the sense of the everyday. It carries through to the end of the poem. The poet/farmer seeks his landlord in the city. He hears the noise of a mugging, down some alley one imagines: 'a ragged noise and mirth'. With a shock he recognizes his landlord as its victim, whose dying words change his leasehold just as he wanted. The doubling of a nasty, all too common incident in urban life with the solution of the human predicament in the final, terse climax is astonishing and leaves the reader open-mouthed. The age-old contrast of simple country life with the vanities and squalor of the town was a well-established pastoral convention. As with all conventions, it is how it is used that counts. Herbert does it with a freshness born of sharp observation of both its aspects and the skill to turn them to urgent and deeply felt meaning.

Herbert did not come to pitch the blessings of childhood as high as Thomas Traherne was to do a few decades later in his *Centuries of Meditations,* or his disciple Henry Vaughan looking back on his happy early days when he 'shined in my Angel-infancy'.[28] But he certainly thought that it was better being a child than an adult. This is the theme of his poem 'H. Baptism (II)'. In the sacrament of Holy Baptism children were, and are, named and admitted into the fellowship of the Christian Church. For Calvinist puritans of his time the Church was emphatically a fellowship of conscious and confessing believers. So they had a worry. Could an inarticulate infant be said to believe? Richard Hooker, whose much read definition of mainstream Anglicanism, *Of the Laws of Ecclesiastical Polity,* had been published at the time of

Herbert's birth, had an answer reinforced by the authority of Herbert's favourite theologian, St Augustine (particularly mentioned in his will, in which he leaves his curate Augustine's *Works*):

> Touching which difficulty, whether it may truly be said for infants at the time of their baptism that they do believe, the effect of St Augustine's answer is yea, but with this distinction, a present *actual habit of faith there is not* in them, there is delivered to them that sacrament, a part of the due celebration thereof consisteth in answering to the articles of faith [by the godparents] *because* the habit of faith which afterwards doth come with years, is but a *farther* building up of the same edifice, the *first foundation whereof was laid by the sacrament* of baptism.[29]

Herbert is more lucid and succinct.

Holy Baptism (II)

Since, Lord, to thee
A narrow way and little gate
Is all the passage, on my infancy
Thou didst lay hold, and antedate
My faith in me.

O let me still
Write thee great God, and me a child;
Let me be soft and supple to thy will,
Small to my self, to others mild,
Behither ill.

Although by stealth
My flesh get on, yet let her sister
My soul bid nothing, but preserve her wealth;
The growth of flesh is but a blister;
Childhood is health.

The poem is as clear as a bell. Hooker's logic is reduced to a simple antedating, or anticipation, of faith. Each stanza is a diamond-shaped sentence, its lines growing in length until the third at the middle, then diminishing again. In sound and shape, this is a 'back-where-we-started' tune or pattern. In terms of thought, it is a reduction of the central matter to the utmost simplicity. And thought is in each stanza. In the first, Herbert shows that Christ's teaching is entirely consistent with infant baptism. He paraphrases St Matthew's Gospel 7:13–14: 'Enter ye in at the strait [Herbert: "little"] gate: for wide is the gate, and broad is the way, that leadeth to destruction, and many there be which go in thereat: because strait is the gate, and narrow is the way, which leadeth to life, and few there be that find it.'

Characteristically, Herbert uses only the positive and leaves out the balefully negative matter in this pronouncement. A 'strait' or 'little' gate would be no problem for children, more of an invitation. In the second verse, childhood is to be written down as the paradigmatic relation of the human to the divine, of the little to the great. But childish ill-nature and misbehaviour have to be noticed and excluded in the last line: 'behither' means 'short of', 'barring' or 'save'. Herbert is a realist, even about childhood. His dislike of having to grow up shows in the last stanza. His body grows, painfully and irksomely like a blister. His soul (apparently feminine, from the Latin anima) had better not, but rather 'bid nothing' and 'preserve her wealth'. The concluding and conclusive last line speaks his mind in three words: 'Childhood is health.'

2

Westminster

SCHOOL

Magdalen Herbert believed in education. Her eldest son Edward was the object of her particular care. He tells us in his *Autobiography* how his schooling began.

> My schoolmaster in the house of my said lady grandmother [Margaret Newport at Eyton], then began to teach me the alphabet, and afterwards grammar, and other books commonly read in schools, in which I profited so much, that upon this theme *Audaces fortuna juvat* [fortune helps the brave], I made an oration of a sheet of paper, and fifty or sixty verses in the space of one day.[1]

Edward was a fast worker in this as in everything else. When he was nine and the family was still at Montgomery, he was sent to learn Welsh with a tutor in Denbighshire, in the expectation that he would become a local bigwig like his tough forebears. But he was also prepared for higher things. From the same tutor he acquired an 'exact knowledge of Greek, Latin, French, Italian and Spanish' and an exemplary and necessary training – not entirely successful – in how to keep his temper. A year later he was with another tutor in Shropshire who prepared him for University College, Oxford, where he perfected his linguistic talents, by sheer reading rather than tuition, and learned the lute. All this educational moving about was necessary for a boy brought up in rural Shropshire by a mother who took education seriously. Edward and the rest of the family were in Oxford for two years before moving to Charing Cross, by which time Edward's peripatetic education was complete and it was the turn of the younger children.

Magdalen impressed the importance of education on George, who came to see it as the foundation of society. In the long didactic poem 'The Church Porch', at the beginning of *The Temple*, he satirized the uneducated English gentry as, on the whole, a lot of foolish stray sheep.

> O England! full of sin, but most of sloth;
> Spit out thy phlegm, and fill thy breast with glory:
> Thy gentry bleats, as if thy native cloth
> Transfus'd a sheepishness into thy story:
> Not that they all are so, but that the most
> Are gone to grass, and in the pasture lost.
>
> This loss springs chiefly from our education.
> Some till their ground, but let weeds choke their son:
> Some mark a partridge, never their child's fashion:
> Some ship them over, and the thing is done.
> Study this art, make it thy great design;
> And if God's image move thee not, let thine.[2]

Magdalen herself taught George to write and to fit thoughts and words together.[3] There were plenty of tutors and schoolmasters to hand: Magdalen's 'Kitchin Book' records ten occasions on which such men came to the house at Charing Cross. A certain Mr. Phillips came there regularly, often bringing another schoolmaster with him – there were six boys and three girls in need of their services. The 'Kitchin Book' also records purchases of educational materials, including a grammar, 'a copy and phrase book', Latin books and pens for George. So for the first three years in London, aged between eight and eleven, George was taught at home by his mother and the various teachers she called in. After that he went to Westminster School.

This famous institution was a short walk southwards, through the Palace of Whitehall, from home. It occupied buildings on the south side of Westminster Abbey, whose Dean and Canons governed it. They took an active part in its educational life, which at Westminster amounted to a long saturation in classical literature and Anglican devotion.

It all looks strange and arcane to us now: not just the frequent prayers, but still more the overwhelming predominance of Latin language and literature, amalgamated with Greek, to the exclusion of mathematics and modern languages which were left to private study. But in the sixteenth century it was new and reflected the commanding ideals of the European classical renaissance. The revival of classical literature went under the title of 'humanities', to distinguish it from theology or divinity. The Dean of St Paul's Cathedral in the City of London, John Colet, had founded a school there in 1509 with William Lily, who was to be the author of the standard Latin grammar, as its head. Colet had the help and advice of his friend Erasmus, the pre-eminent humanist, who wrote books for it: *de Copia* to inculcate rhetorical fluency and dialectical invention in Latin, and *de Ratione Studii* as a blueprint for Christian humanist aims in education. Herbert's Westminster School took full advantage of the pioneering example of St Paul's in its curriculum.

Westminster was a relatively recent foundation, by Queen Elizabeth I in 1560. The Queen was an able Latinist, having been taught by Roger Ascham, the author of *The Schoolmaster* which set up exercises for double translation and the imitation of classical models. Ascham also taught her that beautifully clear italic handwriting which resembles Herbert's. A former colleague of Ascham's was succeeded as headmaster of Westminster by William Camden, the great antiquary who rewrote Britain's earliest history 'to restore Britain to Antiquity and Antiquity to Britain'. Camden had retired, but was still around when George Herbert was at the School, and frequently came in for meals. His work on ancient Britain was to supply Herbert with interesting material for an oration at Cambridge in 1623.[4] His pupil Ben Jonson wrote that he owed Camden 'All that I am in arts, all that I know'.[5] Undogmatic erudition and a love of English poetry were Camden's contribution to the formation of his many pupils. He was well read in Chaucer and other medieval English poets, had known Sidney at Oxford and no doubt encouraged Westminster's young poets: Jonson, Herbert and King.[6]

Prayer and the precise use of language were the School's fundamental disciplines. For his first year as a town boy Herbert would have lived at home. After that, as a scholar, he lived a quasi-monastic life in the old monastic buildings which had been taken over by the School. The scholars slept in the Scholars' Chamber, the old granary, furnished with forty beds with coverlets. They were woken at five o'clock with the command 'Surgite!' ('Rise!') to say their morning prayers. These were elaborate, consisting of scripture readings, psalms, a Latin hymn, the Lord's Prayer ('Our Father . . .') and seasonal prayers: much the same as the Morning Prayer of the Anglican Book of Common Prayer. After that they washed. The town boys came in at six to more prayers and the inspection of hands and faces for cleanliness. At seven the Headmaster appeared to hear repetition of Latin texts learned by heart overnight and to set texts for translation. Breakfast was at eight. Then the younger boys turned to Latin prose, their seniors to Latin verse. For the rest of the day the pupils divided into forms, the lower studying elementary exercises and Aesop's Fables in Latin, the middle forms reading increasingly difficult Latin authors including the legendary poetry of Ovid and Cicero's elegant prose. Greek was introduced at fourth-form level. Virgil's Latin epic, the *Aeneid*, and his pastoral poetry, along with the Greek orations of Demosthenes, occupied the sixth form. Dinner at noon was accompanied by reading from the Old Testament and concluded with a long grace. The same studies were resumed in the afternoon, boys at the top of the School being introduced to Hebrew, with an hour of recreation and, twice a week, music with the Abbey's choirmaster. After supper the senior boys helped the younger ones with their translation of English into Latin. The day ended at eight with prayer and bed. On Sundays the scholars attended services in the Abbey, the upper forms then turning the sermon they had heard there into Latin verse. Herbert was loyal all his life to his Westminster education of classics punctuated by prayer. He kept up his music too.

The exacting discipline of learning Latin, so lapidary and so precise, was a training in scrupulous accuracy with words. It demanded care and concentration. As such, it was congenial to Herbert's ascetic temperament, to his love of purity and (one of his favourite words) cleanness. Latin, like Greek and unlike English, is an inflected language. In English we leave a verb like 'love' much as it is and add other words to it to say 'I will be loved'. In Latin, on the other hand, one word does the trick. The root-word, 'amo' ('I love'), is inflected to become 'amabor' ('I will be loved'). Nouns are inflected too. To take the commonest example in Latin grammars even now, the three English words 'of a table' are just one word in Latin: 'mensae', the genitive or possessive case of the noun 'mensa'. Latin is a thrifty language and demands a keen eye and ear for the single word which contains so much: particularly when the words are embedded in the ostentatiously involved complexities of syntax which were the pride of the writers of renaissance Latin prose, including Herbert himself in his heyday. The ancient writers on rhetoric, such as Quintilian and Cicero, discussed at large the relative merits of plain and ornamental style – as Herbert himself was to do when he lectured on rhetoric at Cambridge. He became one of the best Latinists of his day, a time when the competition was strong. He was capable of writing Latin prose of such lavish complexity that it is very difficult to translate into English.

Poetry was a different matter. There the control exerted by form and metre drilled language by holding it in rhythmic patterns. Herbert wrote excellent Latin poetry. It was the only poetry of his to be published in his lifetime. His brother Edward, despite the success of George's English poetry in *The Temple*, considered that it was 'far short of expressing those perfections he had in the Greek and Latin tongue'.[7] Certainly the Latin poems (and five in Greek) he wrote in memory of his mother (discussed in Chapter 7) and of his friend Sir Francis Bacon (discussed in Chapter 6) are as moving as his English verse.

It is Herbert's English verse which lives on now that a Latin education is far to seek. But his thorough acquaintance with Latin poetry and his practice of it left their mark on his achievements in English. His native language was the one he loved best and wrote in most.

> I like our language, as our men and coast:
> Who cannot dress it well, want wit, not words.[8]

That dressing ('dress' in the general sense of preparing things properly and cleanly) owed a good deal to Latin poetry. The old Roman authors provided the English poets of the renaissance with a variety of forms, above all Horace whose Odes were deliberately various and experimental in their forms.

Latin and English poetry differed in construction. Latin poetry had nothing to do with the rhymes which hold English poems together, tying the end of one line to the end of another by assonance. Instead, Latin poetry depended for its rhythmical strength on metre. Made up of various arrangements of long and short syllables in units called 'feet' (see Preface), metre gave the lines sustained internal and external coherence. The English language is more liquid, more free and easy, than Latin. Often it can conform to the rules of metre, but a slavish obedience to them forces it into sounding unnaturally rigid and grinding. Stress suits the looseness of English better, being the emphasis on the words which matter, as distinct from the instances of 'the' and 'a' and personal pronouns – which Latin does not have because it includes them in the important words by inflexion.

A particularly well-'dressed' and beautiful poem by Herbert shows the influence of Latin poetry on him, along with its limits and the looser rhythms – stresses rather than metre – of English.

Virtue

Sweet day, so cool, so calm, so bright,
The bridal of the earth and sky:
The dew shall weep thy fall to night;
   For thou must die.

Sweet rose, whose hue, angry and brave
Bids the rash gazer wipe his eye:
Thy root is ever in its grave,
   And thou must die.

Sweet spring, full of sweet days and roses,
A box where sweets compacted lie;
My music shows ye have your closes,
   And all must die.

Only a sweet and virtuous soul,
Like season'd timber, never gives;
But though the whole world turn to coal,
   Then chiefly lives.

The first line is in strict metre: four iambic feet with their short then long syllables. The effect is of quiet rapture, assisted by the repetition of 'so'. But it is essential to the effect that this Latinate rhythm, so suitable to sudden, happy exclamation, should not be insisted on or emphasized in what follows. Rather, it becomes a soft and distant drumming which is sensed under the loose lyricism of English speech with its random stresses. Strict iambics are kept for the severe drumbeat of the refrain, 'For thou must die', subtly becoming more ominous as it changes into 'And thou must die', then 'And all must die' until it is replaced by the final line, 'Then chiefly lives', which breaks the iambic pattern by requiring a stress on the first syllable as well as the second and fourth for its full effect: '<u>Then</u> <u>chiefly</u> <u>lives</u>'. The poem's form was a favourite of Horace's who had himself got it from the Greeks: verses of four lines with the last line shorter than the previous three. Making that last line into a refrain, altered then finally contradicted, was Herbert's own idea.

'Virtue' is as economical as an exacting Latinist could wish. Words of one syllable are preferred, with occasional words of two to relax and vary the rhythm. The word 'sweet' works hard, appearing no fewer than six times and in each of the four verses. It was a stronger and busier word then, spanning a range of pleasure and purity beyond the palate and not tainted by its patronizing modern usage. All the same, using the one adjective – particularly that one – again and again without cloying is fine poetic thrift. Likewise the refrain, just slightly altered each time and finally to be dramatically transcended by the last line of all, is repetition without monotony.

Then there are the phrases which contain so much in so few words. The 'bridal' in 'The bridal of the earth and sky' lets the reader imagine earth and sky married to each other in harmonious, mutual, luminous response, each revealing the loveliness of the other – a perfect and complete landscape. 'Thy root is ever in its grave' puts the age-old theme of the interdependence of life and death, flourishing and decay, in a simple horticultural image. 'My music shows ye have your closes' binds the poem's artifice and its natural subject together with spare delicacy: poems, like songs and everything else, draw inevitably to their ends, their closes. It is part of their beauty. The 'season'd timber' of the last verse is also worth a thought. Timber is seasoned by being left to dehydrate out of doors under cover for several years, enduring, like the soul, the extremes of weather and the seasons. After that it is stable and strong. Very typical of Herbert is his reduction of the terrible, universal fires of doomsday to 'the whole world turn to coal' – that is, charcoal, made by the country charcoal burners in their slow woodland bonfires and used indoors for heating and cooking.

The poem's lyrical grace suggests that afternoon music lessons at Westminster have had their effect as well as all the Latin lessons. Indeed 'my music' in the third verse suggests that it is a song. One easy tune, with little changes here and there as it goes, would fit each verse. It is easy to imagine accompaniment by the lute. There are breaks in the verses at the end of their second lines, marked by colons and semi-colons: a breathing space for a singer at the point where the happy positive turns to the sad negative. The first line not only lilts with its iambic succession of four short–longs, one after the other. It also rises in the scale from the low double 'o' of 'cool' to the higher long 'a' in 'calm' and the pinging high 'i' in 'bright'. By contrast, the first line of the last verse is on the level, conversationally secure like the rest of the verse and, indeed, the eternal stability of the 'virtuous soul' which, in the end, it is all about. The previous verses have risen, then fallen. But this last verse keeps itself straight and steady to rise quietly to its triumphant end.

LANCELOT ANDREWES

The intensive study of languages at Westminster School was fostered by the most brilliant linguist of the day, Lancelot Andrewes. Andrewes was a canon of the Abbey from 1598; and in 1601, the year of the Herberts' arrival at Charing Cross, he became its dean with overall responsibility for the School. He knew fifteen languages, and it was said of him that, when God punished men for building the hubristic Tower of Babel by dividing their single language into many so that they could not understand one another,[9] Andrewes could have helped them out and 'served as an INTERPRETER GENERAL at the confusion of tongues'.[10] He was to have a lasting effect on the English language by becoming one of the chief translators of the King James Bible. He was a paradigm of Anglican learning, piety with a catholic touch and pastoral skill: all greatly admired by James I, as by poets as far apart in churchmanship as Milton and Crashaw, who both wrote poems about him.[11]

Lancelot Andrewes, Herbert's 'Father in God', by Simon de Passe, 1618.

Herbert's contemporary and fellow Westminster scholar John Hacket has left a vivid picture of Andrewes. He dined with the scholars every day and 'never walked to Chiswick for his recreation without a brace of the young fry, and in that wayfaring leisure, had a singular dexterity to fill those narrow vessels with a funnel'. Hacket was impressed by:

> how strict that excellent man was, to charge our masters that they should give us lessons out of none but the most classical authors; that he did often supply the place both of Head School-Master and Usher for the space of an whole week together and gave us not an hour of loitering time from morning to night. How he caused our exercises in prose and verse to be brought to him to examine our style and proficiency. And which was the greatest burden of his toil, sometimes thrice in a week, sometimes oftener, he sent for the uppermost Scholars to his lodgings at night, and kept them with him from eight unto eleven, unfolding to them the best rudiments of the Greek tongue, and the elements of the Hebrew grammar, and all this he did to boys without any compulsion of correction; nay I never heard him utter so much as a word of austerity among us.[12]

Andrewes left Westminster to be bishop of Chichester in November 1605, at the end of Herbert's first year at the School, but not before electing Herbert to a scholarship. Most of Herbert's time was under Andrewes's successor, Richard Neile. But Andrewes's influence on him was strong and the friendship they developed at Westminster lasted until the great man's death. The proximity of Charing Cross to Westminster made the people of the Abbey and the School, not least the Dean who presided over both, familiar figures to the Herbert family.

On Good Friday 1604 Andrewes preached a sermon before the King in the chapel at Whitehall Palace of extraordinary power and beauty. The King ordered it to be printed.[13] Several impressions were issued during the year. So if the eleven-year-old Herbert was not there in the chapel to hear it, he had abundant opportunity to read it. The sermon began, as sermons should, with a biblical text: the Lamentations of Jeremiah, 1:12. Andrewes quoted it, first in the old Vulgate's Latin, then in English. He wanted the august resonance of the Latin words to sound like a tolling bell through the whole sermon. The English is based on the Geneva Bible (the King James Version, in which he was to have a dominant hand, was yet to be), scrupulously emended in the light of the Hebrew original by himself.

> O vos omnes qui transitis per viam, attendite, et videte si est dolor sicut dolor meus! Quoniam vindemiavit me, ut locutus est Dominus, in die furoris suae.

> *Have ye no regard, o all ye that pass by the way? Consider, and behold, If ever there were sorrow like my Sorrow, which was done unto me, wherewith the Lord did afflict me in the day of the fierceness of his wrath.*

From this seed of biblical poetry Andrewes grew his sermon, frequently punctuating it with the Latin *non sicut* (nothing like), to drive home the extremity of Christ's passion and get his hearers to 'regard' and 'consider' it: two words from his English text which he also uses again and again. These are examples of the feature of Andrewes's prose which delighted T. S. Eliot: 'squeezing and squeezing the word until it yields a full juice of meaning which we should never have supposed any word to possess'.[14] Such prose is very close to poetry. The topic was urgent, because Christ's sufferings and death needed to be deeply appropriated in the hearts and minds of his listeners as their only salvation, brought about by the shifting of human guilt on to his divine innocence.

The course or plan of the sermon is best given in the résumé of it towards the end. A staccato conversational style, broken into short and pithy units like the lines of a poem, carries through the whole thing.

> Thus have we considered and seen, not so much as in this sight we might or should, but as much as the time will give us leave. And now, lay all these before you, (every one of them a *Non sicut* of itself) the pains of the body, esteemed by Pilate's *Ecce* ['Behold' – when he showed the tormented Christ to the crowd]; the sorrows of his soul, by his sweat in the garden; the comfortless estate of his sorrows, by his cry on the cross ['My God, my God, why hast thou forsaken me?']: And with these, his person, as being the Son of the great and eternal God. Then join to these, the cause: in God his fierce wrath: in us, our heinous sins deserving it: in him, his exceeding great love, both suffering that for us which we had deserved; and procuring for us, that we could never

deserve: making that to pertain to himself, which of right pertained to us; and making that pertain to us, which pertained to him only, and not to us at all, but by his means alone. And after their view in several, lay all them together, so many *Non sicuts* into one, and tell me, if his complaint be not just, and his request most reasonable.[15]

Printed as continuous prose, this paragraph is a hard read. Breaking it up and indenting it both makes for easier reading and reveals that its syntax is so deliberately constructed that it has the rhythms of poetry. In particular, Andrewes imitates the poetry of the biblical psalms, with a little break or caesura in the middle of each clause making a rhythmical balance. For example:

> And now, lay all these before you,
> (every one of them a *Non sicut* of itself)
>
> the pains of the body,
> esteemed by Pilate's *Ecce*;
> the sorrows of his soul,
> by his sweat in the garden;
> the comfortless estate of his sorrows,
> by his cry on the cross:
>
> And with these, his person,
> as being the Son of the great and eternal God.

T. S. Eliot noticed the poetic character of the great preacher's prose and notoriously took a couple of sentences from Andrewes's Christmas Sermon of 1622 describing the journey of the Magi –

A cold coming they had of it, at this time of the year; just the worst time of the year, to make a journey, and especially a long journey, in. The ways deep, the weather sharp, the days short, the sun farthest off . . . the very dead of winter[16]

– and turned them easily into the first lines of his poem 'The Journey of the Magi'.[17]

> 'A cold coming we had of it,
> Just the worst time of the year
> For a journey, and such a long journey:

The ways deep and the weather sharp,
The very dead of winter.'

The content of the Good Friday Sermon, compressed into the recap-
itulatory paragraph quoted above, is founded in irony. What happened
was paradoxical. Christ took upon himself what was really ours and
gave us what was his, 'procuring for us, that we could never deserve:
making that to appertain to himself, which of right pertained to us;
and making that pertain to us, which pertained to him only, and not
to us at all'. This collision of opposites, such as 'sins' and 'love', is
irony at its most extreme and the central nerve of sacrifice, which, in
its definitive Christian form, turns on the unique combination of
opposites, human suffering and divine power, focused in Christ crucified. Pain is at its core. Considering and regarding it, Andrewes
showed himself to be as great a poet of pain as Herbert was to become.

> His skin and flesh rent with the whips and scourges, his hands and feet
> wounded with the nails, his head with the thorns, his very heart with
> the spear point; all his senses, all his parts loaden with whatsoever wit
> or malice could invent. His blessed Body given as an Anvil to be beaten
> upon . . . till they brought him into this case, of *Si fuerit sicut* [if there
> were ever the like].

But psychological pain is even worse than physical.

> In this one, peradventure some *Sicut* may be found, in the pains of the
> body: but in the second, the sorrow of the soul, I am sure, none. And
> indeed, the pain of the body is but the body of pain: the very soul of
> sorrow and pain, is the soul's sorrow and pain . . . And of this, this of
> the soul, I dare make a case, *Si fuerit sicut*.

And so he does, comparing Christ in his God-forsaken isolation to a
bare tree: 'No comfort, no supply at all'. 'Never, never the like person:
and if as the person is, the passion be, never the like passion to his'. And
then comes the critical and terrible assertion, driven home by
Andrewes's short, monosyllabic sentence: 'It was God that did it.' He
visited his hostility to human sin on his innocent Son instead of us. We
should 'have been smitten with these sorrows by the fierce wrath of
God, had not he stepped between the blow and us, and latched it in his

own body and soul, even the dint of the fierceness of the wrath of God. O the *Non sicut* of our sins, that could not otherwise be answered!' To most people, including a good many sensitive Christians nowadays, this transaction feels grotesque, even repulsive. But within the framework of orthodox Christian theology it is the answer to 'the only question': the sufferings of the innocent at the hands of a God believed to be benevolent, just and omnipotent. It is an answer in terms of the myth-made-actual of sacrifice. Outside that theological framework, sacrifice still bears the sense of an offering made above and beyond what is fair and just, a deed of grace – not obligation, not law.

Andrewes appealed to his hearers' imagination, particularly their sympathetic imagination. He was operating in the realm of poetic myth, treated with unsparing realism, rather than reason playing with ideas. Rousing the imagination to regard and consider the painful image was the whole purpose of the sermon. The relentless tension begins to wind down as Andrewes considers Christ's 'incomparable Love' in enduring all this for us and instead of us. It is the greatest *non sicut* of all, the ultimate. 'We were more dear to thee than thine own self.' The barbarous horrors, divine and human, mythical and actual, give way to the celebration of love, the heart of the matter, whereby 'all is turned about clean contrary.' 'It was love that caused him to suffer these sorrows.' So beyond 'It was God that did it,' Andrewes more than implies that it was love that did it: or rather, that it was love that suffered it and, by steadfastly remaining itself, did it. This is the belief at the heart of Herbert's poetry. Andrewes's final appeal to his audience is to 'spend a few thoughts' on the love which makes this Friday good, paradoxically 'a day of joy and jubilee'.

The almost crushing weight of Andrewes's matter was supported by the strength of his language. It is terse and urgent. He believed that single words contained a vast amount of meaning. 'He had an almost obsessive fondness for curt, short syntactical units that were shorn of connectives.'[18] 'It fareth with *sentences* as with coins: In *coins*, they that in smallest compass contain greatest value, are best esteemed: and, in sentences, those that in fewest words comprise most matter, are most praised.'[19] This muscularity was graced with courtesy towards his hearers, delicate play on words, the rhythmical balance of antitheses, and subtle alliteration.

In all these things, and particularly in graceful strength, Andrewes was a model for the young George Herbert, who appropriated the virtues of his prose, so close to poetry, for himself. Hearing and reading Andrewes was an education for him. Westminster School taught him Latin and Greek to the highest standards. Andrewes taught him to 'love our language' and showed him what English could do. He went ahead and did it: throughout his writing, and particularly in 'The Sacrifice', which is the counterpart in verse of Andrewes's Good Friday Sermon in intention, matter and manner.

Andrewes had taken his biblical text from Lamentations: 'Have ye no regard, o all ye that pass by the way? Consider, and behold if ever there were sorrow like unto my Sorrow, which was done unto me, wherewith the Lord did afflict me in the day of the fierceness of his wrath. He built each and every word and phrase of it into the fabric of his discourse.' 'Like', *sicut*, and its negative counterpart, *non sicut*, sounded through it again and again as its solemn refrain. Biblical poetry was the source and origin. In 'The Sacrifice' Herbert followed him from start to finish, beginning with:

> *Oh all ye, who pass by*, whose eyes and mind
> To worldly things are sharp, but to me blind;
> To me, who took eyes that I might you find:
> Was ever grief like mine?

Each of the sixty-three verses ends with that last line, the English equivalent of Andrewes's repeated *sicuts* and *non sicuts*, right up to the last:

> But now I die; now all is finished.
> My woe, mans weal: and now I bow my head.
> Only let others say, when I am dead,
> Never was grief like mine.

The irony implicit in sacrifice generally, and in Christ's sacrifice most acutely and conclusively, runs though Herbert's poem as constantly as through Andrewes's sermon. It is evident in the two verses just quoted. In the first man's blindness is coupled with Christ's taking eyes, by his incarnation, to find him. In the second Christ's woe is man's weal or well-being.

But in one major respect Herbert was able, because he was writing a poem, to go further than his master and Dean. The whole poem is spoken by Christ. He is his own preacher, addressing the reader directly, and so with extraordinary force and pathos. He is himself the narrator of the tale of his own sufferings. In the Gospels they are told in the third person, 'he', but here in the first person singular, 'I'. He tells it all in iambic pentameters: that is, with five short–longs or light–heavies to every line. This Latin metre gives his monologue a sort of solemn and insistent monotony like a tolling bell, rounded off by the three iambics of the refrain. The form is undecorative and plain. Like Andrewes's prose, Herbert's poetry is curt and repetitive. His metre is able to sustain the complex and enigmatic irony, founded in Christ's double nature as man and God, in each verse. Let us pick out a few outstanding examples. When Judas and his posse from the High Priest come with lanterns and staves to arrest Christ, he rouses his sleeping disciples with:

> Arise, arise, they come. Look how they run!
> Alas, what haste they make to be undone!
> How with their lanterns do they seek the sun!
> > Was ever grief like mine? (lines 33–6)

Andrewes himself could not have done better in putting great irony into little, hasty sentences.

Herbert packs weighty typological allusion into few words. According to Genesis 2:7 when God made Adam, the first man, he 'breathed into his nostrils the breath of life, and man became a living soul'. Herbert reverses the process in Christ's words describing his condemnation to death ('rendereth' means 'gives back').

> Then they condemn me all with that same breath,
> Which I do give them daily, unto death.
> Thus *Adam* my first breathing rendereth:
> > Was ever grief like mine? (lines 69–72)

A still more extreme example of compact allusion occurs when the soldiers give Christ his crown of thorns. The thorns recall both Genesis 3:18 where the ground is cursed with thorns and thistles after Adam's fall, and Matthew 7:16 where Christ riddles 'Do men gather grapes of thorns, or figs of thistles?' The grapes in turn recall Isaiah 5 where Israel is the vineyard planted by God but neglected by the Israelites and then laid waste by God so that 'there shall come up briars and thorns.' All these biblical images are gathered up and, once more, put into reverse.

> Then on my head a crown of thorns I wear:
> For these are all the grapes *Sion* doth bear,
> Though I my vine planted and water'd there:
>> Was ever grief like mine?

> So sits the earth's great curse in *Adam's* fall
> Upon my head; so I remove it all
> From th' earth unto my brows, and bear the thrall:
>> Was ever grief like mine? (lines 161–8)

Finally, the typology of Adam and Christ, the primal man and the ultimate man, recurs in the extraordinarily homely imagery of tree-climbing and fruit-stealing (shadowed by climbing the scaffold to the tree of execution by hanging), as Christ hangs on the tree of the cross – a moment recalling and reversing the Tree of Life in Adam's Paradise. It is emphasized by the text from Lamentations appearing in italics. The second 'but' means 'except'.

> O *all ye who pass by, behold and see;*
> Man stole the fruit, but I must climb the tree;
> The tree of life to all, but only me.
>> Was ever grief like mine? (lines 201–5)

The most ferociously anti-Christian of literary critics, William Empson, admired 'The Sacrifice' enormously. In *Seven Types of Ambiguity*,[20] the knotty and wayward masterpiece which he wrote in his early twenties, he proclaimed that 'Herbert deals, in this poem, on the scale and by the methods necessary to it, with the most complicated and deeply-rooted notion of the human mind.'[21] Sacrifice is indeed a remarkably and interestingly persistent survivor from our primitive past. Herbert's poem appealed to Empson as an extreme example of ambiguity, the category which fascinated him and to which he was strongly attached. He believed maturity to consist in the ability to hold contradictory thoughts and feelings together simultaneously, not one after the other. Ambiguity was maturity. His teacher, I. A. Richards, had taught him to value the equilibrium and balance of opposites in poetry. Empson preferred to see this balance less serenely than Richards and more in terms of clash and conflict. 'Here, with a magnificence he [Herbert] never excelled, the various sets of conflicts in the Christian doctrine of sacrifice are stated with an assured and easy simplicity, a reliable and unassuming grandeur.'[22] Herbert's imagination got inside a thing and found the right words to describe it. 'It is only because this presentment of the sacrificial idea is so powerfully and beautifully imagined that all its impulses are involved.'[23]

Those 'various sets of conflicts' were already present in the New Testament Epistles. The first of them could be called 'moral displacement' and was fundamental to St Paul. 'Christ redeemed us from the curse of the law, having become a curse for us, for it is written "cursed is every one that hangeth upon a tree." '[24] It is more simply put in Herbert's 'Man stole the fruit, but I must climb the tree.' Another is the solidarity of the sacrificial victim with the people who offer it. 'Weep not, dear friends, since I for both have wept,' says Herbert's Christ. This solidarity is attributed to Christ's passion in the New Testament's most thorough discussion of sacrifice, the Epistle to the Hebrews: 'Forasmuch then as the children are partakers of flesh and blood, he also himself likewise took part of the same; that through death he might destroy him that hath the power of death, that is, the devil.'[25] The benefit of the sacrifice is nothing less than delivery from death. 'Alas! what have I stolen from you? Death' (line 231). So Herbert's Christ asks and answers as he hangs between the thieves. 'The Sacrifice' is not only a retelling of the passion narratives in the Gospels. It saturates the story with these sacrificial ideas from the more overtly doctrinal Epistles. Deep and thorough knowledge of the Bible, with the ability to handle and interpret it, was a major part of Herbert's education, read daily at school and often at home.

SIR JOHN DANVERS

In the winter of 1609, Herbert's last year at Westminster, his mother got married again to Sir John Danvers. He was half her age, the same age as her elder son Edward and only ten years older than George. Aubrey relates that Magdalen 'was old enough to have been Sir John's mother, but he married her for love of her wit. The Earl of Danby [Sir John's elder brother] was displeased with him for this disagreeable match.'[26] The displeasure did not last: in 1628, when George Herbert was motherless and at a loss over what to do with his life, Danby was prepared to put him up in his house at Dauntsey in Wiltshire. Besides, the marriage proved very happy; and Sir John was a solicitous step-father to Edward and George. As a young man he had:

> travelled France and Italy and made good observations. He had in a fair body an harmonical mind. In his youth his complexion was so exceeding beautiful and fine, that Thomas Bond . . . who was his companion in his travels, did say that the people would come after him in the street to admire him. He had a very fine fancy, which lay chiefly for gardens and architecture. The garden at Chelsea in Middlesex (as likewise the house there) do remain monuments of his ingenuity.[27]

All that remains of them now is the name of Danvers Street, London SW3. He built both house and garden at the time of his marriage to Magdalen, and John Aubrey has left us detailed descriptions of them.[28] The house had a central hall flanked by a chapel and a drawing room with a 'curious floor'[29] of yew and boxwood. Sitting in the hall you enjoyed a view of the Thames to the south and the garden to the north. In the centre of the garden was a bowling green – a very English feature such as George Herbert referred to in two of his poems, 'Constancy' and 'Affliction (I)'. It was surrounded by statues of Hercules and Antaeus, Cain and Abel, and a shepherd and shepherdess 'who have the honestest innocent countenances that can be imagined'. The banqueting house at the centre of the far end had a dark grotto underneath it which affected its visitors 'with a kind of religious horror'. All these were Italian features such as Danvers had seen on his travels. ''Twas Sir John Danvers of Chelsea', wrote Aubrey, 'who first taught us the way of Italian gardens.' Aubrey records endearingly that 'Sir John, being my relation and faithful friend, was wont in fair mornings in the summer to brush his beaver hat on the hyssop and thyme, which did perfume them with its natural spirit; and would last a morning or longer.'[30]

Herbert spent a good deal of time at Chelsea. We know that he and John Donne were there together for several months in 1625 when

London was in the grip of the plague. He was on easy terms with his stepfather, even preferring to write to him rather than to his mother when he was in need of funds or influence with the great at Cambridge. Danvers contributed much to his well-being.

JOHN DONNE

During George Herbert's time as a scholar at Westminster School his mother's friendship with Donne, begun in Oxford in 1599, grew. In 1607 Donne, having lost his job as secretary to Sir Thomas Egerton in 1602, was unemployed, living unhappily with his wife Ann and their seven children in a damp house at Mitcham in Surrey. He often visited London, where he had lodgings in Whitehall. The widow Magdalen Herbert was attractive to Donne for several reasons: for her beauty and her character certainly, but also as someone with excellent connections who might help him find a job.

In the summer of 1607, when George Herbert was fourteen, Magdalen and Donne were in frequent correspondence. Four of Donne's letters to Magdalen survive, thanks to Izaak Walton.[31] Walton prefaces the most interesting of these with a delicate discussion of their relationship. It was 'not an amity that polluted their souls, but an amity made up of a chain of suitable inclinations and virtues'. Money, as well as platonic love, was integral to it. It 'was begun in a happy time for him, he being then near to the fortieth year of his age, which was some years before he entered into sacred orders – a time when his necessities needed a daily supply for the support of his wife, seven children, and a family; and in time she proved one of his most bountiful benefactors, and he was as grateful an acknowledger of it'.

Donne's letter, written from Mitcham to Magdalen Herbert of 11 July 1607, tells of much coming and going between them, on this occasion resulting in some embarrassment. Donne found a messenger from Magdalen waiting for him when he got back to Mitcham from London early on Sunday morning. This prompted him to play, a little awkwardly, with her name – recalling Mary Magdalen in St John's Gospel coming early to Christ's tomb on the first Easter Sunday (like him to Mitcham). Along with the letter, he sent a sonnet with still

Viri seraphici Joannis Donne Qua=
dragenarij Effigies vera, Qui post
eam ætatem Sacris initiatus Ec=
clesiæ Sti Pauli Decanus obijt.
Anõ { Dõm 1631°
     { Ætatis suæ 59°

John Donne, friend of Herbert and admirer of Herbert's mother,
by Pierre Lombart, 1631.

more of this Magdalen name-play, and some other 'holy hymns and sonnets': altogether quite a package.

MADAM,

Your favours to me are everywhere; I use them, and have them. I enjoy them at London, and leave them there; and yet find them at Mitcham. Such riddles as these become things inexpressible, and such is your goodness. I was almost sorry to find your servant here this day, because I was loath to have any witness of my not coming home last night, and indeed of my coming this morning; but my not coming was excusable, because earnest business detained me; and my coming this day is by the example of your St Mary Magdalen, who rose early upon Sunday to seek that which she loved most; and so did I. And from her [his wife] and myself, I return such thanks as are due to one whom we owe all the good opinion that they whom we need most have of us. By this messenger, and on this good day, I commit the enclosed holy hymns and sonnets (which for the matter, not the workmanship, have yet escaped the fire) to your judgment, and to your protection too, if you think them worthy of it; and I have appointed this enclosed sonnet to usher them to your happy hand.

Your unworthiest servant,
Unless your accepting him to be so have mended him,
JO. DONNE.
Mitcham, July 11, 1607

'This enclosed sonnet' is entitled 'To The Lady Magdalen Herbert, Of St Mary Magdalen'.

Her name, once again, is its subject. It conflates, in line with the usual tradition, three women from the Gospels: the sinner who anointed Christ's feet; Mary of Bethany ('Bethina' in the poem), who 'did harbour Christ himself, a guest'; and Mary Magdalene ('Magdalo' in the poem), who stood at the foot of the cross and was the first to see the risen Christ. As Donne notes, with a wary and ostentatious eye on scholarship, 'some Fathers [that is, theologians] think these Magdalenes were two or three.' But he disagrees, and recommends the addition of Mrs. Herbert to the trio. As all this suggests, the poem is laboured, if a labour of love. The biblical Magdalen, who discovered Christ's resurrection before the apostles and the Church, is represented as a pious and hospitable woman of property like Mrs. Herbert.

> Her of your name, whose fair inheritance
>   Bethina was, and jointure Magdalo:
> An active faith so highly did advance,
>   That she once knew, more than the Church did know,
> The Resurrection; so much good there is
>   Delivered of her, that some Fathers be
> Loath to believe one woman could do this;
>   But think these Magdalenes were two or three.
> Increase their number, Lady, and their fame:
>   To their devotion, add your innocence;
> Take so much of th' example, as of the name;
>   The latter half; and in some recompense
> That they did harbour Christ himself, a guest,
>   Harbour these hymns, to his dear name addressed.
>
>   J.D.

As to Donne's 'enclosed holy hymns and sonnets', the third ingredient of his package, Walton says that 'these hymns are now lost to us'. Modern authorities on Donne do not agree with him. R. C. Bald believes that 'these hymns, to his dear name addressed' in the last line of this dedicatory sonnet are 'the group of sonnets entitled *La Corona*'.[32]

La Corona is dedicated to Christ, 'thou which of good, hast, yea art treasury'. As the last line of the dedicatory sonnet to Magdalen Herbert promised, the series is 'to his dear name addressed': seven sonnets on Christ's life from 'Annunciation' to 'Ascension'. They are linked together by the last line of one becoming the first line of the next, and the opening line of the series, '*Deign at my hands this crown of prayer and praise*' reappearing as its end. So it all begins with:

> *Deign at my hands this crown of prayer and praise,*
> Weaved in my low devout melancholy,
> Thou which of good, hast, yea art treasury,
> All changing unchanged Ancient of days,

> But do not, with a vile crown of frail bays,
> Reward my muse's white sincerity,
> But what thy thorny crown gained, that give me,
> A crown of glory, which doth flower always.

And the series ends with:

> Mild lamb, which with thy blood hast marked the path;
> Bright torch, which shin'st, that I my way may see,
> Oh, with thine own blood quench thine own just wrath,
> And if thy holy Spirit, my Muse did raise,
> *Deign at my hands this crown of prayer and praise.*

The title was a reminiscence of Donne's catholic upbringing in which 'the Corona of our Lady' was a way of saying the rosary. The sonnets announce Donne's turning from the 'frail bays' of erotic poetry to religious poetry's 'crown of glory, which doth flower always'. It achieves the change with quiet beauty. The sonnets are replete with the paradoxes inherent in the conjunction of the human and the divine in Christ's story. But the paradoxes are not strident. They move through the sequence with a devotion which combines attention to its subject with minimal self-concern. They are, for Donne, unusually tranquil, assured and modest. In other words, their whole temper is very close to that of George Herbert's poetry to come. As treasured items among Magdalen Herbert's papers, her son would have known them well.

In two poems of his maturity, George Herbert was to use a similar interlacing pattern to Donne's in 'La Corona'. In 'Sin's round' he copies Donne's form with the last line of one verse serving as the first line of the next and the last line of the whole poem repeating the first. Melancholy self-examination is its subject. A round was either a dance by a ring of people holding hands, as in 'Ring a ring of roses', or a song with the melody passed from singer to singer *ad infinitum*. Accordingly, it lends its sad subject a certain playfulness, comparable to Donne's tone in *La Corona*. The quizzical, conversational tone, however, is Herbert's own. Each verse contains an emblematic simile gathered from Herbert's store of learning, and therefore abstruse to the modern reader.

In the first verse it is the cockatrice. According to Pliny[33] and alchemical tradition, this was a mythical serpent, coiled and fiery, perversely hatched from a cock's egg. The biblical prophet Isaiah denounced the wicked with 'they conceive mischief and bring forth iniquity. They hatch cockatrice's eggs.'[34] According to *The Oxford English Dictionary* the word 'draught' has no fewer than fourteen meanings. Since Herbert is here dealing with 'my words', the 'perfected draughts' are most likely drafts of a piece of writing, emended to 'take fire from my inflamed thoughts'.

In the second verse 'the Sicilian Hill' is the volcano Etna. Its eruptions are like the poet's expression of his internal faults, heated by ventilation. As in the first verse, the last two lines are about the speaker or writer and his words. But now they are not enough: he wants to turn his sinful 'inventions' or imaginations into actions.

'Babel' in the third verse was the first large-scale human invention. In the Bible at Genesis 11:4 the reader overhears ambitious mankind as it invents its great project: 'Go to, let us build us a city and a tower, whose top may reach unto heaven.' First the idea, then the work. But God put a stop to it, scattering mankind into groups with different languages so that people could not understand one another and lived in 'dissensions' (the myth explained differences of human language). In the last three lines 'ill deeds' beget 'new thoughts of sinning' and we are back where we started, round and round in the vicious circle.

So the form suits the matter, holding dark reflections in a clever pattern and making a desperate situation into a pleasant and witty poem. This may strike the reader as discordant and embarrassing, or as a nice example of poetry's ability to make the intractable tractable.

Sin's round

Sorry I am, my God, sorry I am,
That my offences course it in a ring.
My thoughts are working like a busy flame,
Until their cockatrice they hatch and bring:
And when they once have perfected their draughts,
My words take fire from my inflamed thoughts.

My words take fire from my inflamed thoughts,
Which spit it forth like the Sicilian Hill.
They vent their wares, and pass them with their faults,
And by their breathing ventilate the ill.

But words suffice not, where are lewd intentions:
My hands do join to finish the inventions.

My hands do join to finish the inventions:
And so my sins ascend three storeys high,
As Babel grew, before there were dissensions.
Yet ill deeds loiter not: for they supply
New thoughts of sinning: wherefore, to my shame,
Sorry I am, my God, sorry I am.

Herbert's other interlacing poem is cheerful, not at all abstruse, and altogether better. 'A Wreath', his counterpart to Donne's wreathed 'crown of prayer and praise', perfects interlacing by weaving, not just verse to verse, but line to line with subtle repetitions until the last line ties up with the first. It is a little masterpiece, another figure-poem of apparently artless art. Its sincerity and longing for simplicity are set in the cunning complexity of its form. The result is a surprisingly easy poem which reads like ordinary speech with its hesitations and resumptions.

A Wreath

A wreathed garland of deserved praise,
Of praise deserved, unto thee I give,
I give to thee, who knowest all my ways,
My crooked winding ways, wherein I live,
Wherein I die, not live: for life is straight,
Straight as a line, and ever tends to thee,
To thee, who art more far above deceit,
Than deceit seems above simplicity.
Give me simplicity, that I may live,
So live and like, that I may know, thy ways,
Know them and practise them: then shall I give
For this poor wreath, give thee a crown of praise.

With this gem of happy, modest aspiration, this singing prayer, Herbert has outdone Donne in their mutual craft.

In 1608 Donne dedicated a poem 'To Mrs. M. H.'. It is not one of his great poems, but in some lines he captures the Magdalen Herbert whom we know from Walton and Herbert's commemoration of her in

Sir John Danvers

From a fine & curious Drawing in the Collection of Rob.t Stearne Tighe Esq.r

His Autograph from an Original in the Possession of

John Thane.

John Danvers, Herbert's good-natured stepfather: the only known likenesss, engraved from a contemporary drawing now lost. 'His complexion so beautiful and fine . . . that people would come after him in the street to admire him' (Aubrey).

Memoriae Matris Sacrum. Donne praises her love of truth compared with the mendacity of princes:

> for she,
> Truth, whom they dare not pardon, dares prefer.

Wondering whether she will accept his poem, he glimpses her:

> as a mother which delights to hear
> Her early child mis-speak half-uttered words

'Wit, and virtue, and honour her attend.' Her cabinet, in which he hopes his poem will be harboured, is a place:

> Whither all noble ambitious wits do run,
> A nest almost as full of good as she.

But in the latter verses a 'him' appears who is likely to reverse her oaths not to remarry. Donne, eager to keep in her good books all the same, includes him in his last two lines.

> But so much do I love her choice, that I,
> Would fain love him that shall be loved of her.

This is Sir John Danvers, the excellent and cultivated younger man whom Magdalen married in February 1609. John Donne stayed on good terms with the couple and he and George Herbert (who liked his stepfather too) were friends for life. Izaak Walton relates:

> that a little before his [Donne's] death he caused many seals to be made, and in them to be engraven the figure of Christ crucified on an anchor (the emblem of hope), and of which Dr Donne would often say, *crux mihi ancora* [the cross is an anchor for me]. These seals he gave or sent to most of those friends on which he put a value; and, at Mr. Herbert's death, these verses were found wrapped up with that seal which was by the doctor given to him:
>
> > When my dear friend could write no more,
> > He gave this seal, and so gave o'er.
> >
> > When winds and waves rise highest, I am sure,
> > The anchor keeps my faith, that me, secure.[37]

3

A Young Man at Cambridge

Apart from his mother's remarriage to Sir John Danvers, the major event in Herbert's life in 1609 was his election as a scholar of Trinity College, Cambridge. Trinity and Christ Church, Oxford are royal colleges, both foundations of Henry VIII, whose daughter Elizabeth I founded Westminster School. Every year the Dean of Christ Church and the Master of Trinity went down to Westminster to choose the brightest pupils. In 1609 one of those chosen for Trinity was the sixteen-year-old Herbert.

It was a good year. Alongside Herbert, John Hacket was also chosen for Trinity. He wrote the biography of John Williams, Archbishop of York, his patron – and Herbert's too in time: a lively book containing the vivid description of Lancelot Andrewes among the Westminster schoolboys quoted in the previous chapter. Christ Church chose Henry King, who was to be a great poet of bereavement – his 'The Exequy: To his Matchless never to be forgotten Friend', in memory of his wife, has been much anthologized. He and Hacket both became bishops. Of the two, the sensitive Henry King was closer to Herbert in temperament.

Thomas Nevile was the Master of Trinity concerned in Herbert's and Hacket's elections. According to Hacket, he 'never had his like for a splendid, courteous and bountiful gentleman'.[1] James I had particular reason to be fond of Nevile: he had been chosen to go to Scotland on James's accession with the greetings of the English clergy. When James visited Trinity in 1615, Herbert and Hacket then being fellows, Nevile was dying and too ill to preside over the lavish hospitality he had provided for him. So the King went to see him in his room, raised him from kneeling with his own hands, and said he was proud to have such a subject.

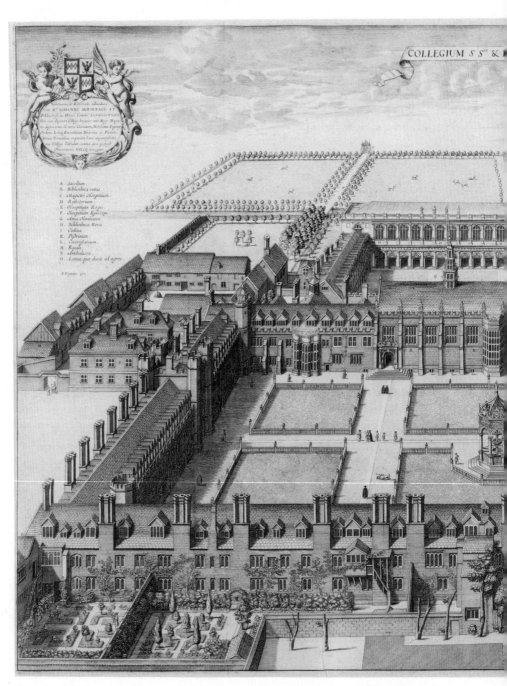

Trinity College, Cambridge by David Loggan, 1690. The great and royal college as Nevile rebuilt it and Herbert knew it, apart from the furthest building, Wren's Library of 1695.

VIDUÆ TRINITATIS

Nevile had been master of Trinity since 1593, the year of Herbert's birth, and had brought about a transformation of the college. The number of scholars and fellows rose to 300. The music in the chapel was greatly improved. Above all, Nevile demolished, rebuilt and built on the grand scale. He created the present Great Court out of a jumble of hostels and halls in an eight-year campaign which involved moving a whole towered gateway stone by stone. The splendid result was there for Herbert when he arrived in 1609. Pevsner praises its 'eminently English diversity':[2] a mixture of styles and materials, varied and asymmetrical but so large and open to the skies that it conveys a sense of dignified domestic peace. Nevile's new buildings, set around the vast space which he had cleared, included an extended Master's Lodge for himself, a new hall and library, and a whole new range of rooms along the southern and eastern sides. In the centre he placed a tall and elaborate fountain, domed and adorned with strapwork. It all remains to this day.

A little later in Herbert's time at Trinity, Nevile erected a new court between the Great Court and the river, now named after him. It is a cloister, then open to the river but now closed by Wren's Library, with rooms above. Tuscan columns support round-headed arches with, says Nikolaus Pevsner, 'an elegance which seems more Mediterranean than anything Cambridge knew shortly after 1600'[3] – classical architecture for classical scholars. Nevile's Trinity was spectacularly sure of itself as the University's greatest college. The biographer of John Hacket, Herbert's friend and contemporary, recalled that Hacket often gave:

> great thanks to God that he was not bred among rude and barbarous people, but among civil and learned Athenians; that he was not disposed to some monkish society, or ignorant cloister, but to the Greece of Greece itself, the most learned and royal society of Trinity College, which in that and all other ages since the foundation equalled any other college in Europe for plenty of incomparable divines, philosophers and orators.[4]

Trinity was to be Herbert's spacious home for the next fifteen years. As Izaak Walton relates:

> the generous Dr Nevile was a cherisher of his studies, and such a lover of his person, his behaviour, and the excellent endowments of his mind,

that he took him often into his own company, by which he confirmed his [Herbert's] native gentleness; and if during this time he expressed any error, it was that he kept himself too much retired, and at too great a distance with all his inferiors; and his clothes seemed to prove that he put too great a value on his parts and parentage.[5]

Adverse criticism of Herbert did not come readily to Walton, so these mild strictures are important. 'Gentleness' here denotes the social quality of belonging to the upper classes, so Nevile's favour can be understood as encouraging a certain innate snobbery in Herbert, confirmed by his aloofness and self-conscious dress-sense. This kind of undergraduate is, to this day, hard to know and hard to like. Herbert as withdrawn young fogey was the father of the country parson with 'his apparel plain, but reverend and clean, without spots, or dust, or smell'.[6] But the man who wrote those words, though still fastidious, had at last settled among the peasants of Wiltshire as their priest.

In his first year at Trinity, in January 1610, he wrote a letter to his mother which confirms Walton's criticisms. The letter announced his intention to write religious, not erotic, poetry, and enclosed two sonnets on that theme.[7] Herbert had himself just recovered from a bout of illness.

> But I fear the heat of my late ague hath dried up those springs by which scholars say the Muses use to take up their habitations. However, I need not their help to reprove the vanity of those many love poems that are daily writ and consecrated to Venus [Shakespeare's *Sonnets* had been published the year before], nor to bewail that so few are writ that look towards God and heaven. For my own part, my meaning, dear mother, is in these sonnets to declare my resolution to be that my poor abilities in poetry shall be all and ever consecrated to God's glory; and I beg you to receive this as one testimony.

Two sonnets follow. They are in the same priggish tone as the preceding prose, in which he takes upon himself the duty to be a puritanical Malvolio and reprove vanity. Neither shows him at his best. He seems to have thought so himself, because he did not include them in *The Temple* with the rest of his collected English religious poetry. The first sonnet is a series of tiresomely hectoring questions, asking God why he allows so much erotic poetry to be written. The second, with the same addressee, is more positive. They are important as an indication of his immature character and of how much he needed to grow as man and poet in order to write poems which went beyond idealism to affirm the ordinary and often disappointing conditions of real life.

My God, where is that ancient heat towards thee,
  Wherewith whole shoals of martyrs once did burn,
Besides their other flames? Doth Poetry
  Wear Venus' livery? only serve her turn?
Why are not sonnets made of thee, and lays
  Upon thine altar burnt? Cannot thy love
Heighten a spirit to sound out thy praise
  As well as any she? Cannot thy dove
Outstrip their Cupid easily in flight?
  Or, since thy ways are deep, and still the same,
  Will not a verse run smooth that bears thy name?
Why doth that fire, which by thy power and might
  Each breast doth feel, no braver fuel choose
  Than that which one day worms may chance refuse?

Sure, Lord, there is enough in thee to dry
  Oceans of ink; for, as the Deluge did
Cover the earth, so doth thy majesty;
  Each cloud distils thy praise, and doth forbid
Poets to turn it to another use:
  Roses and lilies speak thee; and to make
A pair of cheeks of them is thy abuse:
  Why should I women's eyes for crystal take?
Such poor invention burns in their low mind,
  Whose fire is wild, and doth not upward go
  To praise, and on thee, Lord, some ink bestow.
Open the bones, and you shall nothing find
  In the best face but filth; when, Lord, in thee
  The beauty lies in the discovery.

These sonnets have their moments. That last line of the second one, so succinctly conjoining beauty and its discovery in a single moment, is a foretaste of the poetry to come. The image of the deep, still waters of divinity giving smooth passage to verse is memorable, as is the poetic wild fire, horizontally and destructively driven rather than going upwards to God. And in spite of the ostentatious high-mindedness, natural affections peep through in the clouds distilling praise and in 'roses and lilies speak thee'. But these happy moments have to be picked out from the general moral and spiritual haughtiness – which may have been aggravated by sibling rivalry for maternal attention, his brother Edward being an adept love poet. The question marks in the middle of five of the lines of the first sonnet break up the flow and make for a tediously insistent hectoring.

A couple of images in these two sonnets are distinctly and unnecessarily unpleasant: the 'shoals' of burning martyrs in the first one, and the repellent thought in the second one contained in the lines:

> Open the bones, and you shall find
> In the best face but filth.

Readers well acquainted with seventeenth-century poetry have detected in these lines the influence of Donne, the grand master of the gruesome. Herbert loved cleanness. But a more decent and professionally poetic influence of Donne on him is more than likely. Donne's present of sacred poetry to George Herbert's mother, including *La Corona*, had been in her cabinet since July 1607.[8] Her son had had plenty of time to study and appreciate it before sending her his 'New Year's gift' of January 1610: the two sonnets announcing his own intention to devote himself to the same task. Now established in his college, Herbert was catching up with his mother's admirer, resolutely following Donne's example in his decision to write for God and for Magdalen.

The Latin that Herbert had learned so well at Westminster stood him in good stead in his university life. Spoken Latin was at least as much a part of a Cambridge education as written. It was the lingua franca of the Europe-wide republic of letters. In Herbert's day, students were examined and judged by their performances in Latin debate – not by written exams. These disputations were a great feature of Cambridge life. The University Statutes required that every undergraduate should take part in at least four of them, two in college and two before the whole University, to graduate as a Bachelor of Arts. In practice they were more frequent and were laid on as special entertainments for visiting royalty. They were particularly popular with Elizabeth I and James I.

Disputations were conducted within a well-ordered framework. A senior moderator took charge and set the question for debate. The questions were serious and concerned things well worth thinking about.[9] For example: 'Are the arts of peace or war more noble?'; 'Whether it is better to be mediocre in all sciences or outstanding in one?'; 'Are open perjuries more dangerous to the state than hidden ambiguities?' (still a good question); and 'Do virtues inhere by nature?' The moderator assigned one disputant to speak for the question and one against: not necessarily the side that either of them favoured. Then the two disputants set to work. They spoke in turn, each carefully taking up what the other had just said in order to do it justice, then criticizing it and changing the terms of the argument. So it went on until one of them won the argument or time ran out.

A theological dispute, from the title page of Hobbes's Leviathan, *1651.*

A disputation was a severe test of linguistic skill and fluency, not to mention nerves. Its great virtue was intellectual; it inculcated the commonplace maxim that there are two sides to a question; and more than that, it taught its practitioners to get inside the skin of viewpoints which were not necessarily their own. It gave depth and empathy to the critical faculties, even the chance to understand the irregular and the unorthodox from within. This was a point taken up by Richard Steele, disapprovingly, a century later when these ritualized disputes were still going on: 'Those that have been present at public Disputes in the University, know that it is usual to maintain heresies for argument's sake. I have heard a man a most impudent Socinian [one who denied the full divinity of Christ] for half an hour, who has been an Orthodox Divine all his life after.'[10] Disputations fitted nicely into the University syllabus. The main subjects in an undergraduate's first year were rhetoric and dialectic. Dialectic inculcated the ways and means of logical argument, the detection of fallacies and distinction between major and minor propositions. Rhetoric was a training in how to put that argument in a persuasive and interesting way. They combined as the bones and flesh of intellectual work and expression. Together they amounted to a moral, not just an intellectual, education. To succeed in disputations students had to cultivate modesty, candour and sympathy as well as ingenuity.[11]

The experience of disputes could make a man a better, even a more tolerant, Christian. Certainly it had a lasting effect on Herbert. His poems are often structured by debate for and against. Sometimes it is with himself, sometimes between himself and someone else, such as an anonymous friend. Frequently it is between himself and God or the divine Christ, as in 'Dialogue' where he does not hesitate, as he properly might, to take the opposite side and speak for Christ himself.

Dialogue

Sweetest Saviour, if my soul
    Were but worth the having,
Quickly then should I control
    Any thought of waiving.

But when all my care and pains
Cannot give the name of gains
To thy wretch so full of stains,
What delight or hope remains?

What, Child, is the balance thine,
    Thine the poise and measure?
If I say, Thou shalt be mine;
    Finger not my treasure.
What the gains in having thee
Do amount to, only he,
Who for man was sold, can see;
That transferr'd th' accounts to me.

But as I can see no merit,
    Leading to this favour;
So the way to fit me for it
    Is beyond my savour.
As the reason then is thine;
So the way is none of mine:
I disclaim the whole design:
Sin disclaims and I resign.

That is all, if that I could
    Get without repining;
And my clay, my creature would
    Follow my resigning:
That as I did freely part
With my glory and desert,
Left all joys to feel all smart –
    Ah! No more: thou break'st my heart.

The metre has the springy rhythm of debate. The underlying rhythm is a succession of questioning trochees, long–shorts. But the emphatic stresses at the ends of most lines, notably and heavily at the ends of the last four lines of each verse, have the ring of a debater nailing his argument. Though the structure reflects, very strikingly, that of an academic debate, the substance of the argument is far from academic. It is about identity, self-worth and the lack of it. It is not surprising that the chronically self-doubting Coleridge found this poem 'especially affecting to me; because the folly of overvaluing myself in any reference to my future lot is *not* the sin or danger that besets me, but a tendency to self-contempt, a sense of the utter disproportionateness of all I can call *me* to the promises of the Gospel'.[12] Indeed, the argument grinds to a halt at the end of the third verse when the poet declares that it is all beyond him and he gives up (had Herbert perhaps seen a desperate Cambridge undergraduate break down at a University dispute?). Christ replies that that would be all right if the poet were to 'follow my resigning', a resigning which was a giving up of glory and joy for the experience of suffering. At which the poet does indeed give up: not out of desperation but in heartbroken surrender. The whole poem is an example of Herbert's ability to contain the strongest and most urgent emotions in a light and lively framework: in this case, the to-and-fro of a Cambridge oral examination in Latin.

If so, what exactly was the question under debate? It is a personal question certainly and a profound one. It is 'what is the value of being George Herbert?' or, in his own words, is his soul 'worth the having'? It is put at the outset of the poem, as a question under debate should be. Also it is a real question, which is to say that it is unresolved and a matter of doubt. In the first verse the answer is, if anything, 'no'. If it were a clear 'yes' (it *was* worth it) then there would be nothing to argue about.

> Quickly then should I control
> Any thought of waiving.

The debate goes hither and thither. In this instance it is impelled from one side by self-despair, Coleridge's problem. Herbert's efforts to be good, 'all my care and pains', have proved futile, leaving him 'thy wretch so full of stains'. But there is a contrary impulse, an impulse from the other side. It is indicated to the careful reader by the little word 'thy': Herbert is not just a 'wretch so full of stains' but 'thy wretch so full of stains'. He belongs to another, the 'Sweetest Saviour' addressed at the outset. That makes all the difference. In the first verse it is slight, but as the poem develops it gets stronger and stronger.

In the second verse Herbert's adversary in debate, his 'Sweetest Saviour', speaks. In the first verse Herbert had taken the line that there would be no tension and nothing to debate if only he had got control of himself and made some moral progress. Now his adversary proposes that there should be no debate for a quite different reason: it is not for Herbert to be his own moral accountant. He, the Saviour, is in charge of such business. The 'accounts' were 'transferr'd' to him by right of purchase: he was sold for man (Judas' betrayal of Christ to the chief priests for 30 pieces of silver).[13] He gave himself as the price of his ownership of humanity. The mystery of sacrifice and the plainness of buying and selling are compacted together in the Saviour's riposte.

The debate would end there but for Herbert's need to understand, his holding on to his intellectual being. He is frustrated by having the argument taken from his hands and from his own sense of the reasonable by the Saviour's assertion of ownership. He wants to have ownership too, to be an active participant in the deal. But he has nothing of merit to match his Saviour's grace and favour, and no way of making himself fit for it. It is all 'beyond my savour', his 'savoir' or understanding. Reason is with the other, the adversary in debate. The way – the way of life and the way to be fit for such sacrificial love – is not his either. So he gives up. 'I disclaim the whole design.' It is beyond him. More than that, 'Sin disclaims and I resign.' Sin, his warped nature, cannot, or will not, have anything to do with it.

It is a feature of this poem that the end of every verse is emphatically an end, metrically and as a bid to have the last word – and nowhere more so than here with 'I resign.' At this point the Saviour turns the threat round in a manner which is both witty and profound, playing with the word to devastating effect. Resignation, like giving up, can mean two very different things. It can be a passive going-along with things or an aggressive rejection of them. You can give up complacently or you can give up crossly. It is a matter of 'how'. As Herbert's contemporary Bishop Joseph Hall said, 'God loveth adverbs.'[14] So here it is Herbert's tone, choleric and resentful, which his Saviour takes up, disallows and turns round.

> *That is all, if that I could*
> *Get without repining;*
> *And my clay, my creature would*
> *Follow my resigning*

The two 'thats' in the first line need to be equally and echoingly emphasized. In paraphrase, Herbert's Saviour and adversary is saying, 'That would be all right, that would be the end of the matter, if you were giving up in another spirit than this "repining" of yours, this resentful dissatisfaction. I would accept your resignation if it coincided in spirit with my own "resigning".' And what is that? The answer comes:

> That as I did freely part
> With my glory and desert,
> Left all joys to feel all smart

This is the altruism of Christ 'who, being in the form of God . . . made himself of no reputation, and took upon him the form of a servant, and was made in the likeness of men; and being found in fashion as a man, he humbled himself, and became obedient unto death, even the death of the cross'.[15] In the original Greek 'made himself of no reputation' is more starkly 'emptied himself'. This descent from heavenly bliss to earthly pain is an unequalled resigning, a giving up on the epic scale of religious myth which spans the whole of reality from the divine heights to the human depths. It is so complete and pure that it is unanswerable. The reminder of it puts a pressure on Herbert's inmost being which fractures it. His *cri de coeur* breaks off his Saviour's monologue with:

> Ah! no more: thou break'st my heart.

This final line breaks the structure of the poem too. Hitherto the two interlocutors have taken turn and turn about, obeying the rules of fair debate. For all the heat of the argument, it has been a measured affair. But now mannerly good form and poetic symmetry both collapse in a moment of intense feeling, artifice and argument falling away before the self-sacrifice of love. It is a particular skill of Herbert's to make the conclusion of a poem the point which alters the reader's understanding of all that went before.

The pendulum movement of the whole poem, the hither and thither resolved by mutual love, invites comparison with 'Love (III)'. From the point of view of beauty, it suffers from the comparison. There is moral ugliness in 'Dialogue'. In 'Love (III)' the two participants treat one another with gentle reticence and forbearance. 'Dialogue', in contrast, is a stand-off, a confrontation. Instead of the flow of domestic conversation it is set in the adversarial ding-dong of debate in the schools, with the under-tow of memories of family rows. But the portrayal of ugliness, Yeats's 'rag and bone shop of the heart',[16] is as much the poet's business as the portrayal of beauty. The great poets are those who manage both. Herbert's courage enables him to do this.

In 'Dialogue' the apparatus of Christian myth, doctrine and devotion are subordinated to Herbert's arch-topic of love. The reader needs only some experience of love's happiness, storms and conflicts and a willingness to be truthful about them to engage with such poetry. As for Herbert himself, this poem is one of his many attacks on his own religious ambition, his desire for what life repeatedly denies: the closure of a settled and unbreakable sense of self. The end of the matter, at the same time a new beginning from zero, is the broken heart.

In 1612, his third year at Trinity, Herbert wrote two Latin poems on the death of Henry, Prince of Wales and heir apparent, which were published by the University in an official collection of tributes.[17] This was a spectacular start to being a poet in public, though in some contrast with the resolution to be only a religious poet which he had proclaimed to his mother in his first year at Trinity. Very possibly he already had his eye on the ultimate prize, which he achieved seven years later, of becoming the University Orator, pre-eminently in charge of such official eulogies and elegies.

The Prince's death was a national tragedy. Henry was cultivated, popular, brave, promising – and protestant.[18] His father, the King, had made endless efforts to arrange a marriage for him with the princesses of Europe. James was left so distraught by his son's terminal illness, typhoid fever, that he could not bear to be at his deathbed and fled to Theobald's, his house in Hertfordshire, and then to Kensington. Herbert's two poems are a mixture of ostentatious classical tropes and allusions with sincere grief. 'What hopes we had, what hopes could we not rightly have had' for such a prince? Henry was the same age as Herbert himself, nineteen. So the young poet, often ill and always

Henry, Prince of Wales from The Life and Death of our Late most Incomparable and Heroique Henry Prince of Wales, *1641*.

afraid of being ill, was genuinely touched. As he was often to do in his later poems in English, he challenged divine providence. Why had Henry survived the abortive Gunpowder Plot of 1605 only to die so wretchedly and so young? What was it all about? Why – a frequent complaint of Herbert's – had everything changed for the worse so suddenly? The first poem ends with a strong simile of mourning: the flowing river whose lapping shallows can be heard but whose depths are silent.

Ut, fluvio currente, vadum sonat, alta quiescunt.

The second, more conventionally, closes with the Prince's heavenly crown and participation in the harmony of the stars.[19]

A year later, in 1613, Herbert graduated to Bachelor of Arts. A year after that he was made a minor fellow of the college, and a year after that a major fellow. He was now a full member of the institution he inhabited, participating in its business and government. He was obviously well regarded, being made a teaching officer, sublector of the Fourth Class, in 1617. His friend Hacket was in charge of another class. Everything was going well.

4

1618

AMBITIONS

We happen to know a good deal more about Herbert's life in this year than in the preceding five. This provides an opportunity to slacken the pace of biography and get a sense of its varied texture. We see him letter-writing for the University Orator, whose office he was to covet more and more; touching his stepfather for funds to buy books; ill and recovering by riding to Newmarket for fresh air; eating apart from his colleagues in the seclusion of his rooms; lecturing in the college hall; savouring court gossip with his stepfather; pondering the grounds of truth with his brother Edward. It is not that 1618 was a particularly critical year in his life: rather that it was a time when he was just getting on with things. But the seeds of future tensions were there. He was 'setting foot in divinity' with incipient doubts about its usefulness for life. He was writing flowery Latin to praise the Earl of Buckingham while seeking out the plain and simple truth of things with his brother.

In January Herbert did a piece of work for the University Orator, Sir Francis Nethersole. The Orator was an important official: in charge, under the Vice-Chancellor, of the University's external relations with royalty, the court and benefactors – the sort of thing which is familiar nowadays as 'development'. It was an indication of Herbert's excellent reputation that Nethersole chose him to write a letter, on the University's behalf and therefore in Latin, to congratulate the Earl of Buckingham on his elevation to the rank of marquess. Buckingham was a young courtier of extraordinary beauty and elegance, the object of the King's headlong and spectacular infatuation, feared and suspected by practically everybody else as the capricious dispenser of royal patronage. That Buckingham, of all people, should have been the addressee and subject of the austere young Herbert's flowery adulation is incongruous, to say the least. He not only took it on and did it with extravagant courtly panache. It also seems to have given him a taste for this sort of exercise and for the 'academic praise'[1] which it brought him.

He was in cheerful correspondence at this time with his stepfather Sir John Danvers. 'The same heart, which you won long since', he wrote to him early in 1618 thanking him for the gift of a horse, 'is still true to you.'[2] On 18 March he wrote again[3] telling Danvers about his problems, of money and health, and confiding in him his intention to study divinity. This letter is a window into Herbert's inner and outer circumstances, worth quoting in full. It is important to notice that, hard on the heels of the success of his Latin letter to Buckingham, there comes this declaration of a different life-style and a quite different ambition – to understand theology and apply his mind to God and the Church. The tension which this entailed did not yet strike him. The 'friends' to whom he refers mean, first and foremost, his family. The 'journey's end' or 'holy ends' he hints at most likely refer to ordination into the ministry of the Church. Reading divinity was a conscientious preparation for this, which was in any case expected of fellows of Trinity. The style of the letter is confiding but fidgety and a little wheedling. He wants money for theological books. They are many and expensive. So he plays up the high respectability of his reason for asking it, adduces poor health as an auxiliary plea and does all he can to imagine possible objections and pre-empt them. His *amour-propre* is at issue with his needs and his pious religious plans. There are rhetorical questions – and indeed the first half is decidedly rhetorical and elaborate.

Sir,

I dare no longer be silent, lest while I think I am modest, I wrong both myself, and also the confidence my friends have in me; wherefore I will open my case unto you, which I think deserves the reading at least; and it is this, I want books extremely; You know Sir, how I am now setting foot into Divinity, to lay the platform of my future life, and shall I then be fain always to borrow books, and build on another's foundation? What tradesman is there who will set up without his tools? Pardon my boldness Sir, it is a most serious case, nor can I write coldly in that, wherein consisteth the making good of my former education, of obeying that Spirit which hath guided me hitherto, and my achieving my (I dare say) holy ends. This also is aggravated, in that I apprehend what my friends would have been forward to say, if I had taken ill courses, *Follow your book, and you shall want nothing*: you know Sir, it is their ordinary speech, and now let them make it good; for since, I hope, I have not deceived their expectation, let not them deceive mine: But perhaps they will say, you are sickly, you must not study too hard; it is true (God knows) I am weak, yet not so, but that every day, I may step one step towards my journey's end; and I love my friends so well, as that if all things proved not well, I had rather the fault should lie on me, than on them; but they will object again, what becomes of your annuity? Sir, if there be any truth in me, I find it little enough to keep me in health. You know I was sick last vacation, neither am I yet recovered, so that I am fain ever and anon, to buy somewhat tending towards my health; for infirmities are both painful and costly. Now this Lent I am forbid utterly to eat any fish, so that I am fain to diet in my chamber at mine own cost; for in our public Halls, you know, is nothing but fish and white meats: Out of Lent also, twice a week, on Fridays and Saturdays, I must do so, which yet sometimes I fast. Sometimes also I ride to Newmarket, and there lie a day or two for fresh air; all which tend to avoiding of costlier matters, if I should fall absolutely sick: I protest and vow, I even study thrift, and yet I am scarce able with much ado to make one half year's allowance, shake hands with the other: And yet if a book of four or five shillings come in my way, I buy it, though I fast for it; yea, sometimes of ten shillings: But, alas, Sir what is that to those infinite volumes of Divinity, which yet every day swell, and grow bigger. Noble Sir, pardon my boldness, and consider but these three things. First, the bulk of Divinity. Secondly, the time when I desire this (which is now, when I must lay the foundation of my whole life). Thirdly, what I desire, and to what end, not vain pleasures, nor to a vain end. If then, Sir, there be any course, either by engaging my future annuity, or any other way, I desire you, Sir, to be my mediator to them in my behalf.

Now I write to you, Sir, because to you I have ever opened my heart; and have reason, by the patents [promises] of your perpetual favour to do so still, for I am sure you love

Your faithfullest Servant
George Herbert

Later in 1618 he wrote to Danvers again.[4] His brother Henry was in France. Herbert had written him a rather patronizing letter of moral advice[5] and Henry had bought books for him. How might he pay for them? His sister had promised to contribute. Perhaps the annuity he got from his family could be doubled 'upon condition that I should surcease from all title to it, after I enter'd into a Benefice'. Becoming a beneficed clergyman, most likely a country parson, was a clear prospect in his future plans. Then he would be able to put a stop to his 'clamorous and greedy bookish requests'. He felt a little ashamed of his importunities, but once again his future ordination was in the forefront of his mind: not as a sacrificial crisis, it is worth noticing, but as a source of income.

Herbert was in a restless state of mind and at the beginning of a long-drawn-out crisis. The element of vanity and aloofness in his behaviour, reported by Walton, did not help.[6] If ordination, health and money had been his only preoccupations his life would have been manageable enough, if difficult. But the main trouble was that he was beginning to hanker after being the University Orator. Sacred ambitions were in growing tension with secular ones. Whether he was conscious of it or not at the time, there was a contradiction between writing flowery eulogies and the honest truth, between courtliness and Christian simplicity. It would get worse. For the time being he was after them both.

His academic career took a step forward with his appointment as praelector (public lecturer) in rhetoric on 11 June 1618. Rhetoric had none of the negative shadow which it has for us nowadays. It stood high. As his contemporary Ben Jonson, another Westminster alumnus, had said, 'speech is the only benefit man hath to express his excellency of mind above other creatures. It is the instrument of society.' The foundations of the study of rhetoric were securely laid at schools such as theirs, where the pupils learned its various skills in letter-writing, dialogue, drama, speeches, historical narrative, styles and poetry. They came up to the universities well equipped to study Quintilian, the Roman authority whose *The Orator's Education*[7] was an exhaustive treatment of the subject in twelve books. It was the set text for Herbert's lectures to first-year undergraduates, along with Aristotle's *Rhetoric* and the exemplary orations and reflections on oratory of Cicero. Rhetoric was, in effect, a liberal education in itself, designed to form the *vir bonus dicendi peritus*, the good man skilled in speaking. The phrase was Quintilian's and emphasized the ethical purpose of learning rhetoric. Morals and manners of speaking and writing were closely connected. Rhetorical studies were not at all confining: from their basis in Latin literature students, under the supervision of individual tutors, could venture out into the study of history, mathematics, physics and (like Herbert himself) theology and modern languages.[8] Herbert's lectures were given in English and in the hall at Trinity College. The politician and antiquarian Simonds D'Ewes testified that as an undergraduate his knowledge was much increased by attending 'Mr. Herbert's public rhetoric lectures in the University'.[9] With an eye to the court and perhaps to personal advancement, Herbert's lectures included analysis of one of the King's speeches as exemplary in its 'concinnity of the parts, the propriety of the phrase, the height and power of it to move affections'.[10]

At Christmas Herbert was at Charing Cross with his family. The day after Christmas, he and his stepfather amused themselves with writing a letter to Sir Robert Harley in Herefordshire, a cousin by marriage of Herbert's on his mother's side, 'to acquaint you with those passages of news which this time affords'.[11] A rag-bag of court gossip follows. After telling Harley about a Dutch deputation to the King, concerned with trade and fisheries, they wrote a catty (but probably just) sentence about Buckingham: 'My Lord of Buckingham was observed on Christmas day to be so devout as to come to the Chapel an hour before prayers began, of which is doubted whether it have some further meaning.'[12] This is a spectacularly different view of Buckingham from that expressed in the Latin letter to him at the beginning of the same year. Herbert could flatter the King's favourite in fine Latin, but he could also enjoy playing the cynical courtier with appropriate innuendo.

GEORGE AND EDWARD

In 1618 Edward Herbert, George's elder brother, had been back home for more than a year after extensive travels in Europe. He was recovering slowly from an illness which he called 'a quartan [every fourth day] ague'. He had plenty of news and adventures to tell to the family. He had been in Rome, where his religious encounters would have been of particular interest to George. He had called at the English College, the headquarters and seminary for English catholics in Rome,

> where demanding for the regent or master thereof, a grave person not long after appeared at the door, to whom I spake in this manner: 'Sir, I need not tell you my country when you hear my language; I come not here to study controversies, but to see the antiquities of the place; if without scandal to the religion in which I was born and bred up, I may take this liberty, I should be glad to spend some convenient time here; if not, my horse is yet unsaddled, and myself willing to go out of the town.'

Such aggressive courtesy came readily to him. All the same, the two men fell into theological conversation which Edward Herbert concluded, having refused his interlocutor's invitation to dinner, with: 'I thought fit to tell him that I conceived the points agreed upon on both sides are greater bonds of amity betwixt us, than that the points disagreed on could break them; that for my part I loved everybody that was of a pious and virtuous life, and thought the errors on what side soever, were more worthy pity than hate.'[13] These ecumenical overtures getting no further, Edward Herbert got on with his sight-seeing, reflecting bitterly on Rome's empire over men's consciences 'being a greater *arcanum imperii* [state secret] than all the arts invented by statists formerly were'.

Back in London from 1617, Edward cultivated friendships with John Donne and Ben Jonson, as well as having time with his brother George. He aired his religious views in some letters to Sir Robert Harley.[14] 'God's Church', he asserted, 'is all mankind,' and 'God makes no man whom he gives not means to come to him' and receive 'eternal happiness by loving him'. Harley held stricter views and did not entirely agree, but Edward was not to be dissuaded. In 1618 he was working on a book in Latin (because addressed beyond England to a European readership) called *de Veritate*, on Truth, to prove the opinions which he had aired to Harley and in Rome. On 13 May 1619, his health restored, he set out for Paris to act as the English ambassador there, with 'as choice a company of gentlemen for my attendants, as, I think, ever followed an ambassador'. He took the manuscript of *de Veritate*, 'begun by me in England', with him. It survives in the British Library.[15] It is very much a working copy, written in his own hand and much corrected and amended. The date, 20 July 1619, is written at the end of it with his signature. This is only two months after his arrival in Paris, suggesting that most of it was written in England with his brother George to hand.

A further manuscript of the book also survives in the British Library[16] and fastens its connection to George. It is dated 15 December 1622 when Edward was back in Paris after a brief recall to London occasioned by a row with the catholic Duc de Luynes over the protection of French protestants. On its first page, in his own handwriting, it is dedicated:

> To my dearest brother George Herbert and my most learned friend William Boswell [his secretary] with this condition that if there is anything in it which is opposed to good morals or true catholic [universal] faith, they are to expunge it. With which agreement, when at last I shall be placed in eternal light, may this book immediately rejoice in its light.

The pages which follow are a very different affair from the previous manuscript of 1619. They are carefully and beautifully written by an expert scribe, with only a few emendations in the author's own hand: a fine production appropriate to a dedicatory copy. At the very end of the last page 'De Revelatione' is written in large letters, but nothing on the subject follows. It is a promise, more or less fulfilled when *de Veritate* was printed in Paris two years later in 1624, dedicated 'to the whole human race'. The fact is that the grand theological subject of revelation is noticeably absent from the previous manuscripts of *de Veritate*. Even when Edward Herbert gets round to it he treats it, not as God's self-revelation in Christ, but as extraordinary individual experience. It must be a direct answer to prayer and 'recommend some course of action which is good', with 'the breath of the divine spirit immediately felt'. The application is wide: 'Movements of conscience and prayerful impulses have their beginning and end in revelation. In a word, every original impulse of pity and joy which springs in our hearts is a revelation.'[17] His brother George would not have argued with that, such moments being the subject of so many of his poems. For both of them, experience mattered more than theology. And Edward knew what he was talking about. When he was in doubt about publishing *de Veritate* because it 'was so different from anything which had been written heretofore', he betook himself to prayer, which was answered by 'a loud though yet gentle noise from the heavens ... in the serenest sky that ever I saw, being without all cloud'.[18] This is the climax and conclusion of his *Autobiography*.

Edward Herbert's robust self-confidence marks every page of his book. He was a man abundantly pleased with himself, unlike his self-doubting brother George. But he shared with George a persuasion of the value of introspection: 'retire into yourself and enter into your own faculties; you will find there God, virtue, and the other universal and eternal truths.' This chimes with George Herbert's advice in 'The Church Porch':

> By all means use sometimes to be alone.
> Salute thyself: see what thy soul doth wear.
> Dare to look in thy chest, for 'tis thine own:
> And tumble up and down what thou find'st there.

For all that Edward was bumptious and optimistic, George modest and sober, they both saw the interior self as a key to truth.

Dismissing his many and famous predecessors in his quest, Edward Herbert 'cast aside these books, and addressed myself to the construction of my own ideas of truth'. This is not just self-importance. It agreed with the philosophical climate of the time and its emphasis on direct personal experience, 'experiment', as the right way of thinking and the key to universal truth. Universality is, indeed, for him a guarantee of truth and 'the surest mark of divine purpose'. On the other hand 'discursive reason', such as all too many philosophers and theologians go in for, can lead you up hill and down dale and into all sorts of error. Edward Herbert's buoyant optimism springs from his belief in what he calls 'common notions'. Everybody – indeed, everything – is born with them and has them innately. They are derived not from abstract principle but from natural instinct, so we do not need philosophers to tell us about them. They have the character of inherent knowledge, drawing us and the whole creation towards God like iron to a magnet. The Ten Commandments[19] are 'a summary of Common Notions'. We obey them instinctively because they are necessary to our very preservation. Their universality extends beyond human beings into the world of nature: 'It is of the nature of natural instinct to fulfil itself irrationally, that is to say, without foresight. For the elements, minerals and vegetables, which give no evidence of foresight or reason, possess knowledge peculiarly suited to their own preservation.'[20]

A feature of this inclusive way of thinking, of which Edward Herbert was particularly proud, is that it unites the spheres of 'Nature or General Providence with Grace or Special Providence', which theologians like to keep apart. Their 'rash and unconsidered use of discursive reason' results in Calvinism's 'blasphemies against nature ... declaring that it is wholly wicked and corrupt'.[21] True religion consists of five 'common notions', no more and no less: that there is a supreme God; that he ought to be worshipped; that virtue with piety is the essence of religious practice; that we have always been horrified by our own wickedness, which must be expiated by repentance; that we are rewarded or punished after this life. Stick to this and avoid discursive reason and you will not go wrong.

In two important respects, nature and theology, George Herbert's poetry chimes with his brother's ideas. In 'Affliction (I)' – an autobiographical poem to which we shall return – he addresses God and shares Edward's impatience with books and his admiration of the natural world in which plants and animals fulfil themselves by instinct and without anxious thought:

> Now I am here, what thou wilt do with me
> > None of my books will show:
> I read, and sigh, and wish I were a tree;
> > For sure then I should grow
> To fruit or shade: at least some bird would trust
> Her household to me, and I should be just.

In 'Employment (II)' he bursts out with:

> O that I were an Orange-tree,
>> That busy plant!
> Then should I ever laden be,
>> And never want
> Some fruit for him that dressed me.

But it is in his extensive nature-poem 'Providence' that Herbert shows his agreement with his brother's positive doctrine of nature most happily. It is a tour of the whole horizon of the creation in which everything from minerals to man himself fulfils itself by natural instinct. It is an enjoyable poem. To the modern post-Darwinian reader it seems quaintly complacent. But historically its optimistic view of the natural world, at one with the human in the piety of grace and praise, was an enlightened attitude which he shared with his brother. It made Christianity and the natural world accessible to one another. Praise, the expression of harmonious fulfilment, rings through it as jovially as through Haydn's *Creation*.

> Beasts fain would sing; birds ditty to their notes;
> Trees would be tuning on their native lute
> To thy renown: but all their hands and throats
> Are brought to Man, while they are lame and mute.

Everything has a will of its own, yet is in harmonious accord with its Creator's.

> We all acknowledge both thy power and love
> To be exact, transcendent and divine;
> Who dost so strongly and so sweetly move,
> While all things have their will, yet none but thine.

Not only does each and every created thing have a will. It also has wisdom: witness pigeons, with their talent for education.

> Each creature hath a wisdom for his good.
> The pigeons feed their tender offspring, crying,
> When they are callow; but withdraw their food
> When they are fledge, that need may teach them flying.

There is a marvellous balance and continuity everywhere, brought about by everything doing what comes naturally.

> Sheep eat the grass, and dung the ground for more:
> Trees after bearing drop their leaves for soil:
> Springs vent their streams, and by expense get store:
> Clouds cool by heat, and baths by cooling boil.

('Baths' are hot springs, such as the famous therapeutic ones at Bath in Somerset, near to the places where Herbert, then an invalid, spent his latter years.) So everything in the world, thanks to divine ingenuity, attains its ends and works together with everything else.

> All things that are, though they have several ways,
> Yet in their being join in one advice
> To honour thee.

Leisurely celebration of the wonders of creation, in lists of the happy details of its various items, had biblical precedent. A familiar example was the 'The Song of the Three Holy Children' from the Apocrypha, used as a canticle ('Benedicite Omnia Opera') at Morning Prayer. The concord of the two Herbert brothers in their shared belief that everything in the world fulfilled itself by unreflecting instinct testifies to an optimistic moment in intellectual history, as well as in the relations of the two famous members of the sometimes quarrelsome family.

It is more surprising to find George Herbert at one with his brother Edward about theology or 'divinity'. They agreed that it was an unnecessary exercise of discursive reason when we all know perfectly well what we need to do to be right with God. Edward Herbert found that 'my whole book was so different from anything that had been written heretofore, I found I must either renounce the authority of all that had written formerly concerning the method of finding out truth, and consequently insist upon my own way or hazard myself to a general censure concerning the whole argument of my book.'[22] George had a similar experience. Reading divinity was the task he had set himself at Trinity, money to buy the required books the aim of his solicitations to his stepfather in his letter of spring 1618. Apart from the works of St Augustine, grounded in love and the human heart, it turned out to be a disappointing endeavour, even something of a dead end.

In 'Affliction (I)', as we saw, George Herbert complained to God that:

> Now I am here, what thou wilt do with me
>> None of my books will show

and went on to wish he was a tree, growing away and accommodating birds.

It agrees with this disillusionment that in his poem 'Divinity' he put theology on a level with astronomy as a futile speculative exercise: otiose and subject to a certain officious absurdity. The 'spheres' in the first verse are the celestial globes, found in the libraries of the learned, which mapped the heavens. 'Epicycles' in the last verse are the smaller circles, set on the great circle of the heavens, in which the planets move. They were marked on celestial globes. A 'clod' in the first verse is a yokel. Everything we need to know to be saved is clearly put in two italicized lines: love, watchful prayer and doing as one would be done by. Those commonplaces, and participation in the sacrament, are all that is required. They are followed, in lines 19 and 20, by sarcasm directed against mystery-mongers and complexity-lovers.

Divinity

As men, for fear the stars should sleep and nod,
 And trip at night, have spheres supplied;
As if a star were duller than a clod,
 Which knows his way without a guide:

5 Just so the other heav'n they also serve,
 Divinity's transcendent sky:
Which with the edge of wit they cut and carve.
 Reason triumphs, and faith lies by.

Could not that wisdom, which first broach'd the wine,
10 Have thickened it with definitions?
And jagg'd his seamless coat, had that been fine,
 With curious questions and divisions?

But all the doctrine, which he taught and gave,
 Was clear as heav'n, from whence it came.

At least those beams of truth, which only save,   15
    Surpass in brightness any flame.

Love God, and love your neighbour. Watch and pray.
    Do as ye would be done unto.
O dark instructions; ev'n as dark as day!
    Who can these Gordian knots undo?   20

But he doth bid us take his blood for wine.
    Bid what he please; yet I am sure,
To take and taste what he doth there design,
    Is all that saves, and not obscure.

Then burn thy Epicycles, foolish man;   25
    Break all thy spheres, and save thy head.
Faith needs no staff of flesh, but stoutly can
    To heav'n alone both go, and lead.

Although suspicion of speculative or 'discursive' reason is something George and Edward Herbert shared, that penultimate verse is very much George, not Edward Herbert.

5

Deputy to Orator

In June 1619, a month after Edward Herbert had left for Paris with the nearly completed first draft of *de Veritate* in his luggage, George Herbert was working for Orator Nethersole again, this time on severely practical matters. Sir Robert Naunton, a former Orator and now secretary of state, had promised to represent Cambridge's interests at court. Herbert wrote to thank him for doing so by resisting a project to drain the fens and thus reduce the level of the River Cam, so important for the commerce and communications of the colleges and of the town. Further, there had been a disastrous fire in the previous month which had destroyed sixty houses in the east of Cambridge. Herbert thanked Naunton for securing an ordinance forbidding thatched roofs – notorious fire hazards. An Orator's brief was wide, varied and gratifyingly connected to the world and the court. Being Nethersole's assistant and heir apparent aroused thoughts of being his successor. But then there was the other future which Herbert had in mind: reading theology, both for its own sake and with a view to becoming a properly equipped ordained minister of the Church. Which way should he go?

In the autumn of 1619 the great prize of the Oratorship itself was brought within Herbert's grasp by a crisis in international relations. On 19 September 1619 the King knighted Orator Nethersole at Theobald's in Hertfordshire. The honour was to equip him for membership of an urgent diplomatic mission to Prague. James's daughter Elizabeth was married to Frederick, the protestant Elector Palatine. The Bohemian protestants wanted Frederick to be their king. The childless, catholic Holy Roman Emperor opposed them, wanting the crown to go to his catholic cousin Ferdinand. The protestant nobility stormed the palace in Prague and threw the Emperor's regents out of the window – the famous 'defenestration of Prague'. Elizabeth was in the eye of a European storm. Nethersole was to be her secretary, standing at her side, protecting her and her interests.

Theobald's, the scene of Nethersole's knighting and commissioning, was only about 30 miles from Cambridge on the London road, so news of it reached the University quickly. Herbert's excitement is evident in a letter he wrote, right away, to Danvers.[1] Although he was not yet officially Nethersole's deputy, he was so *de facto*: by mutual consent and by virtue of the work he had done – and was currently doing on 'an Oration to the whole University of an hour long in Latin'. The Oratorship was, to all intents and purposes, in the bag. But Herbert was unable to sit back and let it happen. He excused himself to Danvers for not having been to London to see him and thank him for his 'favours' – presumably money. He was working on the Latin oration, 'and my Lincoln journey [to visit his sick sister Frances] hath set me much behind hand.' After these breathless preliminaries, he is on to the Oratorship. The Master of Trinity, now Nevile's successor John Richardson, had written a letter 'in my behalf' which 'expresseth the University's inclination to me'. He encloses the Master's testimonial, which unfortunately is lost, and urges Danvers to get it to Nethersole before he leaves for Prague. Then, realizing that he is perhaps being unnecessarily pressing, he backtracks and allows that 'if you cannot send it with much convenience, it is no matter, for the Gentleman needs no incitation to love me.' Then he expatiates on the glory and prestige of the Oratorship in case Danvers should have underestimated its high importance.

> The Orator's place (that you may understand what it is) is the finest place in the University, though not the gainfullest [Danvers should not consider himself off the hook financially]; yet that will be about 30 *l. per an*. But the commodiousness is beyond the revenue; for the Orator writes all the University letters, makes all the Orations, be it to King, Prince, or whatever comes to the University; to requite these pains, he takes place next the Doctors, is at all their assemblies and meetings, and sits above the Proctors, is Regent or Non-regent at his pleasure, and such like gaynesses, which will please a young man well.

That concluding irony about pleasing 'gaynesses' is a welcome indication that Herbert is just about able to see himself as others saw him
and make light of his own dandified vanity and ambition. 'Regent or
non-Regent' meant that the Orator could choose between full participation in the University's governance and opting out of it. The recital
of these privileges stimulated Herbert into renewed pressure on Danvers to get in touch with Sir Francis Nethersole so that he could get
from him a letter to 'work the heads to my purpose': that is, lobby the
heads of the Cambridge colleges, who nominated for the Oratorship:

> I long to hear from Sir Francis, I pray Sir send the letter you receive from
> him to me as soon as you can, that I may work the heads to my purpose.
> I hope I shall get this place without all your London helps, of which I am
> very proud, not but that I joy in your favours, but that you may see, that
> if all fail, yet I am able to stand on mine own legs. Noble Sir, I thank you
> for your infinite favours, I fear only that I have omitted some fitting cir-
> cumstance, yet you will pardon my haste, which is very great.

Very great haste indeed: the letter is breathless, with no leisure for
rhetorical flourishes. The wheels of academic procedure and election
turn slowly, but Herbert cannot bear to lose any chance of the Oratorship, and Nethersole, his sponsor and friend, would soon be off to
Prague. One senses the effort incurred in finally referring to other
things and even remembering the ordinary courtesies.

Then he had a nasty shock. Nethersole himself, a generous and
good-hearted man, had noticed that Herbert's longing to succeed him
did not sit comfortably with his programme of theological study. The
young man was in danger of taking on too much and getting beyond
himself. He wrote as much in a letter, whether to him or to Danvers.
He certainly had a point, but it flung Herbert into a panic. He wrote
to Danvers on 6 October 1619, asking him to forward a letter, which
he enclosed, to Nethersole and beseech him to answer it by return.[2]

> Sir,
>
> I understand by Sir Francis Nethersole's Letter, that he fears I have
> not fully resolved of the matter, since this place being civil may divert
> me too much from Divinity, at which, not without cause, he thinks,

I aim; but, I have wrote him back, that this dignity, hath no such earthiness in it, but it may very well be joined with Heaven; or if it had to others, yet to me it should not, for aught I yet knew; and therefore I desire him to send me a direct answer in his next letter. I pray Sir therefore, cause this enclosed to be carried to his brother's house of his own name (as I think) at the sign of the Pedlar and the Pack on London-bridge, for there he assigns me.

Nethersole had touched that inflamed part of Herbert's conscience where high office and theological study were in unresolved tension. Herbert did his best to cover it up with a devout reflection: 'This dignity, hath no such earthiness in it, but it may very well be joined with Heaven.' In his poem 'The Elixir'[3] he was to say the same about lowlier jobs:

> All may of thee partake:
> Nothing can be so mean,
> Which with his tincture (for thy sake)
> Will not grow bright and clean.
>
> A servant with this clause
> Makes drudgery divine:
> Who sweeps a room, as for thy laws,
> Makes that and th' action fine.

But, in the context of the letter, this expression of Herbert's fundamental desire to combine the earthly and the heavenly seems very much secondary to his ambition. It looks like putting Nethersole off with sententious piety. In the poem the combination is 'bright and clean'. But a belief can serve different purposes, and in this letter it looks more adventitious than profound. In a postscript he asked Danvers to tell his mother that he had ridden the 200 miles into Lincolnshire and back, 'in the midst of much business', to see his sick sister, so she 'cannot think me lazy'. The possibility of her displeasure could still worry him. He was in a frenzy of solicitation for approval: 'sighing to be approved'.[4]

In the event, all went well. On 21 October 1619, a fortnight after this frantic letter, the University passed a 'Grace' allowing Nethersole to appoint Herbert, who had already deputized so splendidly and variously for him, as his official deputy. More than that, Herbert knew that Nethersole intended to resign the Oratorship itself. He soon did. The election of his successor was to take place three months later.

Two days before the election, on 19 January 1620, Herbert was writing to Danvers yet again.[5] He thanked him for some things he had sent and asked for news of his ailing sister Frances. He had visited her in September and now wondered:

> first, how her health fares, next, whether my peace be yet made with her concerning my unkind departure. Good Sir, make it plain to her, that I loved her even in my departure. Can I be so happy, as to hear of both of these [her health and her forgiveness of his rudeness] that they succeed well? Is it not too much for me? Good Sir, make it plain to her, that I loved her even in my departure, in looking to her son, and my charge. I suppose she is not disposed to spend her eye-sight on a piece of paper, or else I had wrote to her; when I shall understand that a letter shall be seasonable, my pen is ready.

Herbert's anxiety leaps from the page in short, repetitious, questioning sentences, not always lucid. He had left his sister suddenly and rudely, most likely in a hurry to be back in Cambridge and get on with his campaign for the Oratorship. Panic about it resulted in loss of self-control. He now feared to approach his sister directly or before Danvers had told him that the air had cleared. Danvers, it is clear, was a great asset to the quarrelsome Herbert family as a peace-maker. But Herbert's obsession with the Oratorship cannot be restrained. He turns to it yet again at the end of the letter.

> Concerning the Orator's place all goes well yet, the next Friday it is tried, and accordingly you shall hear. I have forty businesses in my hands, your Courtesy will pardon the haste of
>
> > Your humblest Servant,
> > George Herbert

Predictably the news was good. On Friday 21 January 1620, the Senate of the University elected him Orator.

The whole affair had been hard on Herbert's nerves. It was not just a matter of canvassing. It was a crisis of identity, which touched and troubled him at the very sensitive point of what sort of a man he wanted to be. He had 'set foot into Divinity'. Fellows of Trinity such as he were required to take Holy Orders in the Church within seven years of becoming Masters of Arts. Herbert had taken that degree in 1616, so at the time of his election as Orator the deadline for ordination was only one year off. But now he had attained high office which, if the example of previous orators was anything to go by, led to a life at court and to state employment, like Naunton and Nethersole before him. According to Walton:

> At the time of being orator, he had learned to understand the Italian, Spanish and French tongues very perfectly; hoping that, as his predecessors, so he might in time attain the place of a Secretary of State, he being at that time very high in the King's favour, and not meanly valued and loved by the most eminent and most powerful of the Court nobility.[6]

Learning three modern languages on top of the private study of divinity and the glories and demands of public office, he was, for a man seldom in the best of health, overloading himself dangerously. And, despite his airily pious put-off to Nethersole when he had put his finger on the central dilemma, he was still very worried about it.

Decisions once taken do not always clear the mind of the doubts that precede them. At some point in the second half of 1619, when Herbert was writing those frantic letters to his stepfather about getting the Oratorship, he went for advice to the fountain of wisdom, learning and piety, the saintly Lancelot Andrewes. He had known him since Charing Cross and Westminster days. Andrewes had a high regard for Herbert. They had discussed the doctrine of predestination, that great bone of theological contention with the Calvinists. Herbert had sent Andrewes:

> some safe and useful aphorisms, in a long letter, written in Greek; which letter was so remarkable for the language and reason of it that, after reading it, the bishop put it into his bosom and did often show it to many scholars, both of this and foreign nations; but did always return it back to the place where he first lodged it, and continued it so near his heart till the last day of his life.[7]

Early in 1619 Andrewes had been made bishop of Winchester and took up residence there in June. He had not been there long before

Herbert wrote to him asking if he might visit him. Andrewes assented and Herbert undertook the long journey from Cambridge to Winchester and back to consult with the venerable man. If anyone could help him with his problem of combining divinity and oratory it was the great courtier and court preacher, the theologian who began every day with hours of private prayer lasting until noon. The mere fact of undertaking the journey to Winchester and back is an indication of Herbert's inner turbulence at the time and his need for the best advice.

Herbert's avowedly late thank-you letter after his visit survives. Unfortunately, although it is written in his own hand, it is undated. But internal evidence shows that the visit took place in 1619 and that the letter was written in 1620 after Herbert had been appointed Orator. Herbert refers to being busy with the duties of 'Rhetor for that year and of Orator for many more'. So it is a very late thank-you letter indeed: a further testimony to Herbert's turmoil in 1619. It is written in flowery and convoluted Latin which often borders on incomprehensibility. It is difficult, at crucial points, to know exactly what he is talking about. He crams the various rhetorical tropes which Cicero spaced out over the course of long speeches into his complex sentences. Presumably he had decided that such a performance was appropriate for a youthful Orator addressing the famous linguist. It is a pity that he did not pay Andrewes the compliment of imitating his own crisp and clear style. (Even a translation of the whole thing would make tiresome reading. So a précis will serve best.)

Herbert writes from Cambridge where he is 'overwhelmed with academic affairs'. He apologizes for his delay in writing, but hopes that Andrewes will not take that as negligence or a sign of a cooling affection. He had thought carefully about making the visit and had, with characteristic introspection, 'turned the force of my thoughts upon the whole of my life' before deciding to go ahead. Besides, his problem was acute. He wanted very much to be Orator and yet he also wanted a quiet life of study:

If all the hopes and fruits of my studies should have come to this

> Why should I toil so perversely to be famous
> When I could stand in silence for nothing?'

Those last two lines from the Roman poet Martial are a little display of erudition which also carries a *cri de coeur*: why, he wondered, was he attracted to the Oratorship and fame when his life would be so much easier without it? The great problem was not entirely resolved even now. 'Nevertheless', he continues, coming back to the present, 'all of this is turning out in accordance with my wishes, and doors are opened.' He will be too busy to get over to Winchester and see Andrewes again for the foreseeable future.

> Grant me, Father, this request, that I may give in for a little while to the expectations of men, and that I may a little less often dig in the field of Winchester while I busy myself in the rhetorical field. For . . . I think it is an act requiring greater expiation to fail in a public duty than in a private . . . In the former case I am bound by an obligation; in the latter I am also held, but by loose chains, chains which love often relaxes. The former duty is the more necessary to carry out, but the latter is far more pleasant and noble.

The courtly letter ends after further salaams and apology for not having used all Andrewes's titles of honour in the interests of writing rotund and elegant Latin. The contrary pulls of the simple life of a Christian and the glamorous complexities of the court and public life ('O rack me not to such a vast extent')[8] were to be an ongoing theme of Herbert's poetry, itself an intensely private activity akin to prayer. Admiration of him as a poet and a man has too often and too easily resulted, from Izaak Walton on, in idolization. The events of 1619–21 are a corrective. They show him to have been capable of being demanding, ambitious, obsessive, flustered and (in his retort to Nethersole) priggish. They also show him as a deeply conscientious man, self-critical as well as self-concerned in his anxious weighing of public duty against private integrity. And a conscientious man who has taken on too much is in a precarious psychological state.

The crisis in international affairs which took Nethersole off to Prague was, as we have seen, Herbert's point of entry to the Oratorship. On 4 November 1619 James I's son-in-law Frederick was crowned king by the Bohemian protestants. This was an intolerable provocation to the catholic Emperor. In August 1620 he mobilized his forces and moved against Frederick in Prague. At the same time an army from the Spanish Netherlands invaded Frederick's lands to the north in his Rhineland Palatinate. Frederick was caught in a pincer-movement. The Spanish Ambassador in London tried, disingenuously, to persuade the distraught James I that this opened the way to peace: let Frederick renounce his claim to the Bohemian crown and the Palatinate would be restored to him. But the Ambassador refused to promise as much and complained about Secretary Naunton, whom James tamely suspended from office. By the end of the year Prague had fallen and Frederick and Elizabeth fled north to the Palatinate. In 1622 they lost that too. James's pacific foreign policy was in ruins. His only hope of regaining some purchase on the disastrous situation was by improving relations with Spain.

A diplomatic marriage might do the trick: James's son and heir Charles to the Spanish Princess. It was a far-fetched project. The protestant English did not want to end up with a Spanish catholic queen. Only thirty-five years before, so within many people's memory, the Spanish Armada's attempt to invade England and impose catholicism had been defeated with, it was believed, divine assistance; English protestants pored with devout fascination over Foxe's popular *Book of Martyrs* with its sanguinary accounts of martyrdoms in the reign of catholic Queen Mary, married to Philip I of Spain. The Princess, or Infanta, herself said to her brother that she would rather enter a convent than marry a heretic. The Pope was insisting on alarmingly generous terms of liberty and worship for catholics in England as a condition. But the project had two supporters: the Spanish Ambassador in London (less than wholeheartedly) and the Marquess of Buckingham (enthusiastically). The King of Spain and his minister, Olivares, decided to appear to favour it, while secretly opposing it. It all looked pretty hopeless and decidedly fragile, when James's adored Buckingham with Prince Charles in tow came up with a recklessly hare-brained scheme to bring it about. They would ride across France incognito and bring the Infanta back with them as Charles's wife. The King was appalled, but acquiesced.

On 17 February 1623, Charles and Buckingham set out from Dover under the aliases of Jack and Tom Smith, reaching Madrid on 7 March. While they were on their way the University of Cambridge was called upon to play its part in the project. The ambassadors of Spain and the Spanish Netherlands, key players, were admitted as Masters of Arts at a special Congregation of the University of Cambridge on 27 February. This was a blatant attempt to soften up the Spaniards. Herbert gave the accompanying oration. It was important enough to be published straight away with an English translation.[9] Its tone was courtly, cheerful and hopeful: 'What could have happened more pleasing to us than the access of the Officers of the Catholic King, whose exceeding glory is equally round with the world itself?' Herbert took childish pleasure in noticing that James was the name both of the King of England and of the patron saint of Spain: 'both the Spanish and British Nation serve and worship *James. James* is the protecting Saint unto us both.' Putting James I on a sacred level with James the apostle and brother of Christ was going a bit far, but it was the sort of thing that was expected of the Orator, however much Herbert may have bridled at such flattery. Then Herbert touched delicately on the desirability of a Spanish marriage for Prince Charles with the oratorical version of a nudge and a wink: 'The praises also and virtues of the most renowned Princess Isabel, passing daily our neighbouring sea, wondrously sound through all our coasts, and ears.' He closed on a note of high optimism: 'Fame is sown in this age, that it may be reaped in the following; let the first be the care of your Excellencies; we ... vow unto you of the last a plenteous harvest.'

A month later the King visited Cambridge, lodging in Herbert's college. He was not in a good mood, worrying about his 'sweet boys' who were now in Madrid. Herbert's Westminster and Trinity friend John Hacket put on an anti-Jesuit comedy called *Loyola* after the Spanish founder of the Jesuit order. It was meant to amuse the King, but was tactlessly inopportune and failed to do so. The King only 'laughed once or twice toward the end'. Making fun of catholicism was unseasonable at such a delicate moment in international diplomacy. Refreshments followed. The King was escorted 'to the door, entering into the court, where his coach did wait for him: but his Majesty was pleased to stay there, while the Orator Mr. Herbert did make a short farewell speech unto him. Then he called for a copy of the Vice-Chancellor's speech, and likewise for an epigram the Orator made.'[10]

BEATI PACIFICI.

REX FIDEI DEFENSOR

POTENTISS·IACOBVS

DG·MAGNÆ·BRITAN·

GALLIÆ ET HIBERN·

Touch not mine Anoynted.

HONY SOIT QVI MALY PENSE

The right ... and most migh ...
... he Monarch IA ... MES by the Gra ...
... ce of God King of ... great Britaine Fra ...
... ce and Ireland ... Be ... fendor of the Faith ...

*James I in his latter years, with 'beati pacifici' (Matthew 5:9), 'blessed are
the peacemakers', inscribed above him, by Crispin de Passe.*

Herbert's speech attempted to repair some of the damage done by the play, remarking that Cambridge was struck not so much by the Jesuits as 'by your [the King's] writings, which we read with profit every day'. This referred to the King's presentation to Cambridge of a copy of his *Opera Latina* three years before. He had been thanked for it by Herbert on the University's behalf in a fulsome letter saying that it was as good for Cambridge as the Vatican Library for Rome or the Bodleian Library for Oxford: 'this single book is our library.' Herbert's epigram, which the King called for, had been included in the printed version of the speeches which he and the Vice-Chancellor had addressed to the ambassadors on 27 February. So it has survived along with its English translation.

> Dum petit Infantem Princeps, Grantamque Iacobus,
> Quisnam horum maior sit, dubitatur, amor.
> Vincit more suo Noster: nam millibus Infans
> Non tot abest, quot nos Regis ab ingenio.

> *While Prince to Spain, and King to Cambridge goes,*
> *The question is, whose love the greater shows:*
> *Ours (like himself) o'ercomes; for his wit's more*
> *Remote from ours, than Spain from Britain's shore.*

Herbert's courtly wit had done something to rescue the company standing around the King's coach in the Great Court of Trinity College from the embarrassment caused by Hacket's ill-judged play.

In Madrid, meanwhile, it was all farce. The Infanta kept her distance. Charles offended Spanish dignity by trying to take her by surprise by jumping over her garden wall. The Spaniards hoped to convert him to Catholicism and he pretended to go along with them, attending services and theological discussions. James retaliated by sending over two Anglican chaplains 'with all the stuff and ornaments for the service of God'. They were excluded. The Pope raised his terms for the dispensation necessary to allow the marriage: resulting children to be educated under the Infanta's direction until they were twelve, her church to be open to the public, and English catholics to be excused the oath of allegiance to the English crown. Charles was inclined to accept this tall order, with the result that the Spaniards made it taller still and insisted on proclamations suspending the laws against English catholics. Further, the Infanta was to stay in Spain for a year after her marriage. At this point Buckingham lost his temper with the all-powerful minister, Olivares. Charles sulked. James wrote agonized letters to his 'sweet boys' who might 'never look to see your old dad again' and repented 'sore that I ever suffered you to go away'. So it muddled on until Charles signed a treaty which would certainly have been unacceptable to the English Council and Parliament if it had ever got that far, and then found his ardour for the Infanta cooling and his resentment of the Spaniards, who were insisting that he dismiss his protestant servants, increasing. When he threatened to leave for England in September the Spaniards were happy to take him at his word and hustled him off.

The two crestfallen adventurers arrived back at Portsmouth on 5 October. The next day they were in London. The city went wild with jubilation – not just because the Prince was back but more because he had returned without a Spanish catholic bride to be their future queen. Protestantism and England were safe. Bells rang out from the churches. The Strand was thronged with people shouting 'Long live the Prince of Wales!' (They do not seem to have included Buckingham in their acclamations.) The celebrations went on into the evening with bonfires and feasting. Charles refused to give audience to the Spanish ambassadors. He and Buckingham went on to be reunited with their adoring 'dad' at Royston, near Cambridge. The King took them into an inner room and closed the door. Charles vented his fury at the treatment he had received from the Spaniards, and Buckingham, to the King's horror and alarm, sought permission to go and conquer Spain. The courtiers on the other side of the door heard bursts of anger and laughter. When they eventually emerged the King had reconciled himself to the delay of his son's marriage. Perhaps it would allow him, as a persistently fond parent, elbow room for negotiations over the lost Palatinate. 'I like not', he said, 'to marry my son with a portion of my daughter's tears.' Diplomacy was his line. Buckingham's bellicosity had failed.

Only two days later, on 8 October, the authorities of the University of Cambridge were assembled in the University Church, listening to a sermon in the morning and an oration by Herbert in the afternoon. Ten miles away at Royston, Charles and Buckingham had worked themselves into a fury and, to the King's horror, were still insisting on war against Spain.

Herbert's oration had to be made up at high speed and in fraught circumstances. He had played his Orator's part at the outset of the whole sorry business, so would have been following it with interest. And now Charles and Buckingham were back and the dons of Cambridge were assembled in their University Church, robed and ready to hear what their Orator had to say about it all. With Royston near by and the King being an admirer of Herbert, they would have known that the oration would soon come to the royal ears. In any case they had it printed and distributed without delay.

It was a tricky occasion. The Prince and the Duke had returned from the failure of their Spanish adventure digraced, furious and bent on war. Everybody else was delighted to be relieved of the prospect of a Spanish, catholic queen of England. Even the King was grumpily complacent and happy to have his son and his favourite back at any price. The Orator had to navigate these troubled waters.

Herbert drew on fifteen years of training and experience in the rhetorical skills of oratory, from his Westminster schooling to his Cambridge days as praelector in rhetoric and now Orator. He kept to the set pattern of four parts: an exordium or introduction, followed by a narration setting out the circumstances of the matter in hand, argument to justify it, and a final, festive conclusion. Within this framework he showed off a dazzling array of the various rhetorical skills he had learned for so long. He deployed moral adages and proverbs. He foraged history for anecdotes and examples. He was constantly aware of his audience. He quoted a great deal. He made much of the moral topics recommended by Cicero: honour, greatness, glory and friendship. He embellished everything with metaphors, synecdoche (one thing understood from another) and metonymy (an attribute such as a beard standing for wisdom or robes for authority). His speech was altogether a virtusoso display of *copia*, the abundance of resources exhibited in the highest rhetorical style.

He began in celebratory mode. It was wonderful to have Charles back (no mention of Buckingham). The whole nation was restored to health by his return, and as for the wedding ring, it was good to have that back too. The King could now dispose of it where he felt fit and the Cambridge 'nightingales' could sing. The learned audience of 'bookworms and devourers of old documents' could ransack the annals of history in vain to find a Charles, even the famous Charlemagne, to equal theirs. But things do not always turn out as expected. Princes have many concerns and at least their Prince had shown himself to be a man with human passions and he had had some fun. Besides, his aim had been laudable. Marriage is a great and important matter.

At this point Herbert remembered that he was addressing a congregation of celibates, so he reminded them that they were, after all, the results of marriages. He illustrated the point with a picturesque piece of antiquarianism.

> Virginity itself is the fruit of marriage, a point which was made by our ancestors with great elegance, and in a manner superior to the barbarism of their age, when they stained themselves with a kind of painting, and represented on the bodies of their wives the sun, moon, and stars, while on those of unmarried girls they depicted flowers and plants: for, as wives produce virgins, so sun and sky produce flowers; and they are symbols of hope, since from flowers we hope for fruit.[11]

Herbert's invocation of the early Britons refers to a recent theory about national origins and, very precisely, to published pictures of the supposed ancient Britons, adorned just as he described them in his oration. Herbert's fascination with this, and his use of it in his oration, are worth noticing as indications of the historiography of his time and of his own wide scholarly interests. It is worth a digression.

It had long been thought that the first Britons were of Trojan stock. Rome, according to its poet Virgil, had been founded by the Trojan prince Aeneas, driven from his city by the Greeks. Keen on connecting themselves with classical antiquity (and in any case knowing no better), British writers had long believed that Aeneas' great-grandson Brutus had then colonized Albion, which was renamed Britain after him. However William Camden, the great Elizabethan antiquary whom Herbert had known at Westminster, had contradicted all this in his masterpiece *Britannia* of 1586. He believed that the Scottish Picts 'were very natural Britons themselves, even the right progeny of the most ancient Britons [as opposed to Brutus and his Trojan relations]'.

On the strength of this and a slight extension of it, in 1590 there appeared a series of prints of ancient British Picts, their naked bodies painted exactly as Herbert said. They reappeared as engravings of 'Ancient Britons' in John Speed's very popular *Theatre of the Empire of Great Britain* in 1611. But where did these picturesque, tattooed figures come from exactly?

The discovery of America, its native Indians and their obviously very primitive human society was a great stimulus to the historical imagination. The first public appearance of these 'most ancient Britons' was as a supplement of five engravings to Harriot's *A brief and true report of the new found land of Virginia* in 1590. These plates, like those of the Virginian Indians which preceded them in Harriot's book, were engraved from drawings by John White, an English artist and cartographer who had sailed to the east coast of North America in 1585 with Richard Grenville in an expedition sponsored by Sir Walter Raleigh. Harriot assured his public that White 'gave me also these Figures following, found as he did assure me in an old English chronicle'. The ancient Britons were plausible enough companions to the Virginian Indians to share publication with them.[12] One lot of primeval people was, it was fair to assume, much like another.

Herbert had a particular reason for being interested in these pictures. His stepfather, Sir John Danvers, along with William Herbert, Earl of Pembroke (and godfather to Edward Herbert) and the Ferrar family (to whom he was to become increasingly attached), was a member of the Virginia Company, founded in 1606 to promote trade and the propagation of Anglican Christianity. At the time of Herbert's oration in 1623 it was in financial crisis. Herbert had earlier referred to its promising beginnings in a couple of lines of his long poem 'The Church Militant', a poem so poor in conception and execution that it must be juvenilia. The surprising thing to anyone who reads it is that Herbert hung on to it to the end.

> Religion stands on tip-toe in our land,
> Ready to pass to the *American* strand.[13]

Herbert's invocation of White and Harriot's ancient Britons in his oration was a nicely judged conceit, playing on his audience's up-to-date erudition. At this early point in the oration a touch of learned humour was ingratiating. But the wives and mothers painted with the sun, moon and stars, their daughters with flowers and herbs, also appealed to him personally. His own admirable mother, presiding so splendidly over her family and household, with her love of horticulture, beckoned him happily into this picturesque byway, where the classical scholar and his audience were at ease among their elegantly naked pagan forebears.

He returned to his main subject: if marriage in itself was a serious matter, how much more the marriage of a prince? It was to Charles's credit that he took it so seriously as to go to see his potential bride for himself – princes did not always take such trouble. A Spanish bride – it was his pacific father's main motive in letting him go there – would fasten the peace 'which we have been enjoying without cost for so long'.

This was the signal for the most striking, urgent and politically risky part of his oration: a prolonged denunciation of war. War overturns all decent, civilized values: 'In peace, sons bury their fathers; in war, fathers bury their sons. In peace the sick are healed; in war even the healthy die. In peace there is security in the fields; in war, there is none, not even within city walls.' And so on, in terse, punchy contradictions. War is a particular menace to learning and study, those 'delicate and tender' flowers of civilization. War may sometimes be necessary, but it is not for academics to promote it. They should leave such decisions to their prudent and peace-seeking King.

Whether or not Herbert in Cambridge had heard, via one of the eavesdropping courtiers, about the arguments going on at nearby Royston between the King and Buckingham, he had taken the King's side against Buckingham and Charles – decisively and eloquently. If they did not hear about this by word of mouth, they would soon be able to read it for themselves. Spoken on 8 October 1623, Herbert's oration was printed and published by the University immediately. The Orator had very publicly disagreed with the heir apparent and the most powerful man in the land. It was brave and it went down well in Cambridge, but it was not auspicious for his hopes of future preferment, perhaps to be a secretary of state like his predecessors. Herbert seems to have been aware of it at the time – it would certainly have dawned on him later if he was not – and followed his denunciation of war with mollifying remarks about Charles, which have a rather desperate air. He does all he can to associate the foolish Prince with his father's pacific diplomacy. He congratulates him on forsaking the luxury of the court for the dangers of travel. He compares his journeying incognito to King Alfred's disguising himself as a harpist so as to overhear the councils of the Danes (another bit of national history). Besides, travel broadens the mind and enhances one's sense of the character of one's own country. 'All nature loves variety,' and especially man. It was sad for the country when Charles was away, but now he is back and no one should begrudge him his expedition. Should it come to war, he knows the way to Spain. Yet the making of alliances with friends is a more demanding and riskier affair than war and binds people together in stronger bonds. It is the work of great minds. Which brought him back to Cambridge and the Prince's happy return. He ended his oration with cautiously qualified optimism and relief.

> We, my listeners, who long wandered away with our Prince, have arrived home in time for this garland of laurel [the Prince's safe return], under whose shade we can rest for a while – at least, until that cloud be over-passed, which so antagonizes our neighbours [presumably the aggrieved Spaniards]. Here we are in safety from the rain, or rather from the thunder-bolt [war]. Let us only beg him to allow this wreath of ours to take its place among his victorious laurels. I end my speech.

The oration was a masterpiece of its kind, handling the repertoire of rhetorical tropes with elegant and erudite wit. Herbert would have got plenty of 'academic praise'[14] for it as the dons trooped out of the University Church. But was this the kind of thing he wanted to spend his talents on? Readers of his poetry cannot imagine that it really was. In any case, by the sincerity and force of his anti-war stance he had given a hostage to his secular fortunes. If the old King admired him, his heir and that heir's great friend were unlikely to feel the same way.

In any case, and international politics apart, family matters always had a strong claim on Herbert's attention and affection – not least where his mother was concerned. In May 1622 he heard that she was ill at Chelsea. He himself had been ill that February, a particularly bad month for the Cambridge climate. He wrote her a tender but didactic letter on 29 May, saying that he would have liked to go back to London and be with her but:

> my employment does fix me here, it being now but a month to our com-
> mencement [the ceremonial conferring of degrees, in which the Orator
> played a prominent part], wherein my absence by how much it naturally
> augmenteth suspicion, by so much shall it make my prayers the more
> constant and the more earnest for you to the God of all consolation.

He began his efforts to comfort her with a nicely apt domestic simile: the 'bottom' to which he refers is a tidy ball of silk, used in embroidery to prevent tangles: 'I have always observed the thread of life to be like other threads or skeins of silk, full of snarls and encumbrances. Happy is he whose bottom is wound up, and laid ready for work in the New Jerusalem.' There will be needlework in heaven. Herbert can sympathize with his mother's plight. 'For myself, dear mother, I have always feared sickness more than death, because sickness hath made me unable to perform those offices for which I came into the world.' It was true. Illness and its attendant uselessness were a major cause of complaint in his poem 'Affliction (I)'. And in 'Employment (I)' he laments the frustration of unemployment:

> All things are busy; only I
> Neither bring honey with the bees,
> Nor flowers to make that, nor the husbandry
> To water these.
>
> I am no link of thy great chain,
> But all my company is a weed.
> Lord place me in thy consort; give one strain
> To my poor reed.

As Donne said in his sermon about Magdalen, psychological depression plagued her: always difficult to distinguish from physical illness. So in the rest of the letter Herbert covers, methodically, the distresses of 'estate' (economy), of the body and of the soul. As for estate, he reminds her that 'the blessings in the Holy Scripture are never given to the rich, but to the poor'. Bodily pains are compared to the agonies of the Christian martyrs, 'burnt by thousands'. 'Lastly, for those afflictions of the soul: consider that God intends that to be as a sacred temple for himself to dwell in, and will not allow any room there for such an inmate as grief, or allow that any sadness shall be his competitor.' He is appealing to her strong sense of a well-run and happy household. If that is a shade superficial, he brings in the Christian belief that in Christ 'God puts his shoulder to our burden.' He quotes St Paul: '*the Lord is at hand, be careful for nothing. What can be said more comfortably?*' He concludes modestly with:

Dear madam, pardon my boldness, and accept the good meaning of
Your most obedient son,
George Herbert.

6

Francis Bacon

Herbert's Oratorship brought him into close contact with a greater and more famous philosopher than his brother Edward: Francis Bacon, author of *The Advancement of Learning*. That work was published in English in 1605 when Herbert was in his first year as a scholar at Westminster School. Bacon was a graduate of Trinity College Cambridge like himself and, as a lawyer, had risen to the supreme legal office of chancellor of England. Three letters and two poems which Herbert as Orator wrote to him survive.

The first letter, written in June 1620 along with the similar one to Sir Robert Naunton mentioned in Chapter 5, thanked Bacon for his support in resisting plans for the drainage of the fens, which threatened to lower the depth of the River Cam and so threaten Cambridge's route of supply for heavy goods such as building materials: not least to Trinity College, which stood on its right bank.[1]

The second addressed a less everyday subject. In 1620 Bacon published a projection of the work he had done in *The Advancement of Learning*, his *Instauratio Magna*, the founding and renewal of all human sciences, no less. He gave a copy to the University of Cambridge and Herbert wrote on the University's behalf to thank him for it. He did so in fine style, congratulating Bacon on doing something more important than the discovery of the New World: the scattering of the shadows of traditional philosophy by his penetrative intellect, which established it on the firm ground of the natural world. He also wrote two Latin poems in praise of the book.[2] The first celebrates the graceful style with which Bacon despatches his traditionalist opponents, and posterity's luck in having such a lead to follow. The second is a sprightly production, subsequently much printed and read. It

Francis Bacon, Herbert's friend and 'veritatis pontifex' (Works,
p. 436) by Simon de Passe.

begins with an abrupt wake-up call. 'Who is this then? He does not go around with an ordinary aspect. Don't you know, you ignoramus? Then listen!' Twenty-five lines of compliments follow: Bacon is the leader of thought, the Pope of truth, lord of the inductive method (proceeding from observed particulars to generalizations instead of, vice versa, deductively), master of facts, liberator of the sciences, and so on and so on – all apt and well judged – until it all ends with 'I'm exhausted! Posterity, take over!' (O me probe lassum! Iuvate, Posteri!').

Herbert's third letter to Bacon, dated January 1621, thanks him for help against another threat to Cambridge's well-being: the attempts of the London Stationers' Company to get the monopoly of printed books and break Cambridge's publishing rights, granted long since by Henry VIII.[3]

During this time, Bacon was at the height of his career as statesman and on the edge of its collapse. On 22 January 1621 he celebrated his sixtieth birthday with a lavish banquet at York House and on 27 January was created Viscount St Alban by the King. Then a group of parliamentarians engaged in an anti-corruption campaign picked on him. Only three months and a week later, on 3 May, he was found guilty by the House of Lords of taking bribes (a common fault, but woe to him who was found out), dismissed from his office of chancellor, fined the enormous sum of 40,000 pounds (not collected, in the event) and put in the Tower of London for three days. He retired to his country house at Gorhambury and spent the rest of his life there, writing, gardening and experimenting. As Herbert had done when in difficulty, he wrote to Lancelot Andrewes. Bacon's letter looks like a response to a sympathetic inquiry by Andrewes after his welfare, for it makes clear that Bacon had got a grip on his traumatic plight. He takes consolation from the examples of great men of antiquity who had borne similar disgrace: Demosthenes, Cicero and Seneca. There were comforts in reading. And he was resolved to write: to take the *Instauratio Magna* further, get on with a book about law which would steer a course between philosophical speculation and practical particularities, and write more of his famous essays. He also mentioned a project which he had nursed for some time: the translation of The *Advancement of Learning* into Latin, 'the general language'. Then it would be 'a citizen of the world, as English books are not'. He had tried to get this done soon after its publication, but without success. But in 1623, two years after his calamity, it was published in an expanded version as *de Dignitate et Augmentis Scientiarum*, 'Concerning the Dignity and Increase of the Sciences'.

George Herbert had a hand in it. He was a friend. Aubrey relates that Bacon 'came often to Sir John Danvers at Chelsea'. They shared an enthusiasm for gardening and had mutual friendships. Also, Herbert was now recognized as an eminent Latinist. Archbishop Tenison recalled in his *Baconiana* of 1679 that Bacon had *The Advancement of Learning* 'translated into the Latin tongue, by Mr. Herbert, and some others, who were esteemed masters in the Roman eloquence'. When Bacon published his *Translation of Certain Psalms into English Verse* two years later in 1625 he dedicated it 'To his very good friend Mr. George Herbert' with the following epistle:

> The pains that it pleased you to take about some of my writings I cannot forget; which did put me in mind to dedicate to you this poor exercise of my sickness. Besides, it being my manner for dedications, to choose those that I hold most fit for the argument, I thought that in respect of divinity and poesy met (whereof the one is the matter, the other the style of this little writing), I could not make better choice. So, with signification of my love and acknowledgment, I ever rest your affectionate friend.

'The pains' clearly refer to some particular and considerable help given by Herbert to Bacon in his literary work. The translation of *The Advancement of Learning* is the obvious reference.

The important and neglected question is what there is in common between Bacon's book, which Herbert would certainly have read whether or not he helped translate it, and Herbert's poetry – 'divinity and poesy met' – which Bacon certainly knew well enough to make that true judgement. *The Advancement of Learning* is a review of all the knowledge that human beings can attain, with recommendations of how it can be improved and extended. Thought must begin with facts, not principles, nor words which 'are but the images of matter: and except they have life of reason and invention, to fall in love with them is all one as to fall in love with a picture'.[4] The difference between this and Herbert's love of language is more apparent than real. Herbert's ceaseless drive towards 'simplicity' is an insistence that words should correspond to the truths of experience and not go off on their own. Bacon believed that 'the use of *history mechanical* [engineering] is of all others the most radical and fundamental towards natural philosophy.'[5] How things work is what matters. Theology, in consequence, does not get much of a look in: 'The contemplation of God's creatures and works produceth (having regard to the works and creatures themselves) knowledge, but having regard to God, no perfect knowledge, but wonder, which is broken knowledge.'[6] That last phrase is excellent. 'Broken knowledge' is a frequent feature of Herbert's poetry. Bacon took it further: 'As for perfection or completeness in divinity, it is not to be sought.'[7]

Perhaps Herbert had thought that that 'completeness in divinity' was attainable when as a young fellow of Trinity in 1617 he wrote to Sir John Danvers, asking for money to buy theological books and 'lay the platform of my future life'. But, as we have seen, in the later poem 'Divinity' he shared Bacon's scepticism about theological ratiocination – along with the biblical image of Christ's seamless coat deployed by Bacon in *The Advancement of Learning*: 'So we see the coat of our Saviour was entire without seam, and so is the doctrine of the Scripture in itself; but the garment of the Church was of divers colours [like Joseph's coat at Genesis 37:3] and yet not divided.'[8] After dismissing astronomy in its first verse (Bacon was interested in it only as an aid to navigation and reserves his opinion of Copernicus),[9] Herbert turned to theology in the same spirit.

> Could not that Wisdom, which first broach'd the wine,
>> Have thicken'd it with definitions?
> And jagg'd the seamless coat, had that been fine,
>> With curious questions and divisions?

Herbert went further than Bacon: the coat had been 'jagg'd', slashed and shredded, by the 'curious questions and divisions' of the theologians.

On the great matter of language the two friends were in basic agreement, with one qualification. Bacon's grand intellectual project made him distrustful of rhetoric, the subject of Herbert's Cambridge lectures.

Taught too early, it gave rise to 'childish sophistry and ridiculous affectation'.[10] The young Herbert was not entirely innocent of that, as his letter to Lancelot Andrewes shows. And it can reasonably be inferred that distaste for the sophistry and affectation required of an Orator eventually turned him against the office which he had sought so eagerly. His poetry, on the other hand, is a sustained search for lucidity and the simple truth. And Bacon was more favourable to poetry than his material realism might suggest. It bothered him that it confused the actual with the imaginary, but that did not stop him writing some, more famous in his day than it is now, and translating biblical psalms into English verse. He allowed that it gave 'some satisfaction to the mind of man in those points wherein the nature of things doth deny it, the world being in proportion inferior to the soul'.[11] In other words, it was a comfort. And that was Herbert's hope for his poetry when he entrusted it on his deathbed to Nicholas Ferrar: that 'it may turn to the advantage of any dejected poor soul'. Poetry was a moral benefit according to Bacon and 'serveth and conferreth to magnanimity, morality, and to delectation'. He admired 'the agreement and comfort it hath in music' – a decidedly congenial point for Herbert. And, as we have seen, he admired Herbert's achievement of 'divinity and poesy met' when he dedicated his own *Translation of Certain Psalms into English Verse* to him.

Above all, Bacon and Herbert agreed on the primacy of charity over knowledge and everything else. They had learned it from St Paul's supreme chapter 13 of his First Epistle to the Corinthians. Knowledge, as St Paul said, could 'puff up' – 'ventosity or swelling' were Bacon's words – and needed a corrective: 'This corrective spice, the mixture whereof maketh Knowledge so sovereign, is Charity.' Bacon used the 'charity' of the King James Version for the same Greek original, *agape*, where Herbert preferred the warmer monosyllable 'love'. Whether divinity or philosophy was the task in hand, 'only let men beware that they apply both to charity, and not to swelling; to use and not to ostentation.' So Bacon's insistent practicality is part and parcel of his charitable desire for the easing of human sufferings by scientific knowledge. Bacon is as eloquent in his way as Herbert on the theme of love – here using that word as synonymous with 'charity'.

All other affections, though they raise the mind, yet they do it by distorting and uncomeliness of ecstasies or excesses; but only love doth exalt the mind, and nevertheless doth settle and compose it; so in all other excellencies, though they advance nature, yet they are subject to excess; only charity admitteth no excess: for so we see, aspiring to be like God in power, the angels transgressed and fell . . . by aspiring to be like God in knowledge, man transgressed and fell . . . but by aspiring to a similitude of God in goodness or love, neither man nor angel transgressed, or shall transgress.[12]

This is a passage which would have delighted Herbert, not least by its noticing of how love 'doth settle and compose' the mind, as in his masterpiece 'Love (III)' and in so many other instances. Likewise, Bacon's acute psychology let him see that 'if a man will begin with certainties, he shall end in doubts; but if he will be content to begin with doubts, he shall end in certainties':[13] the pattern of poem after poem by Herbert.

Bacon died in 1626, a martyr to his belief in experimentation, having caught cold while stuffing a chicken with snow to try out refrigeration. Herbert contributed a Latin elegy to the memorial volume to him which was published that year. We need to know a couple of things, one from classical mythology and the other from Bacon's biography, before we can appreciate the Latin properly. Flora is the classical goddess of flowers. Herbert reduces her plural name to the singular 'Flos', 'Flower', with her initial capital letter 'F' showing that she is the personification of them all. Philomel, in classical mythology, was the princess who was raped, had her tongue cut out so she could not tell anybody (*lingua* in the last line has three meanings: 'tongue', 'language' and 'speech'), and was turned by the gods into a swallow – hence the swallow's plaintive little cry. Here it is in its original[14] (to show Herbert's mastery with Latin metre) and my translation.

In Obitum Francisci Vicecomitis Sancti Albani

Dum longi lentique gemis sub pondere morbi
Atque haeret dubio tabida vita pede,
Quid voluit prudens Fatum, iam sentio tandem:
Constat, *Aprile* uno te potuisse mori:

Ut *Flos* hinc lacrymis, illinc *Philomela* querelis,
Deducant *linguae* funera sola tuae.

On the Death of Francis, Viscount St Albans

While you groan under the weight of a long, slow illness,
　　And life hangs on with a wavering, wasting foot,
I understand at last what prudent Fate willed:
　　Certainly you could only die in April,
So that here Flora with her tears, there Philomela with her plaintive cries,
　　Might lead the lonely funeral of your speech.

In the Latin original, preferably read aloud, the rhythm made by the metre brings the poor old invalid vividly before us, his hesitant foot being simultaneously the 'foot' of Herbert's metrical diction:

Dum longi lentique gemis sub pondere morbi
Atque haeret dubio tabida vita pede

It is a classic elegiac couplet. In the first line every other syllable, five of them in all, is heavy, as the old man shuffles and hobbles amazingly into view. It moves by metres, and the metre here is iambic – that is to say, it is like walking: short–long, short–long and so on. The vowels, particularly the three 'o's, are open and sonorous as a great bell. But Herbert does not repeat this entirely successful rhythmical trick. The second line has two short syllables at the start, 'atque' only means 'and'. The last two syllables of 'tabida', meaning decaying and sounding like it, are short too. The same with 'lentique'. The tremulous hesitancy of the old man's foot required a slightly lighter touch. The vowels are weaker in sound. In the next two lines the poet has a happy thought. Bacon had to hang on so that he could die in April, that wonderful month of flowers and birdsong for a keen gardener like him. The last two lines tell why it had to be so with natural classical allusion.

Instead of the grand funeral which would have been his in his days of power, Bacon was buried quietly in St Michael's parish church in St Alban's. In these last two lines Herbert describes the modest, rural funeral of a great writer, among flowers and calling swallows, with lighter rhythms than in his sadder first two lines.

Ut *Flos* hinc lacrymis, illinc *Philomela* querelis,
Deducant *linguae* funera sola tuae.

There are only four stressed syllables out of the total of fourteen in the first line. The last line has the same number of stresses but in a shorter span of twelve syllables in all. Lightness results. Once again the effect is beautifully vivid: the tears of dew on the flowers and the lamenting calls of the swallows surround the funeral of a master of language who might once have been buried in courtly pomp. Herbert's elegy for his old friend breathes tender personal affection. It is only six lines long, but within its smallness contains a peripateia or turn-around: the first two lines are hesitant and sad. The second two clear the air: Bacon's death in April made sense – 'constat' is the most definite and decided of words. So the last two lines are free for the flowers and birdsong of spring and the acceptance of death.

Interlude: The Williams Manuscript

After Herbert's celebrated oration on Prince Charles's return in late 1623 he spent less and less time in Cambridge. He was briefly a member of Parliament, stayed with his mother at Chelsea and then, after her death, with his stepfather's brother at Dauntsey in Wiltshire. These were listless years which will be examined in the next chapter. But they were productive of poetry. Whatever else was going on in his life, he wrote. And a precious relic from the earlier part of this time survives in Dr Williams's Library in London.[1]

It is a small notebook, such as were commonly bought from stationers' shops, measuring a little less than 6 inches by 4, its 120 leaves of paper bound in leather. Herbert got a scribe to copy seventy-eight of his English poems into it: less than half of the number which were to make up *The Temple*, in which all but six of them reappear. The scribe wrote out the poems in what is called a 'secretary hand', curly but clear. Herbert himself wrote out the Latin poems which follow in his own, more angular, italic hand: perhaps because his scribe was not a good Latinist, and/or because he set a high value on them. He also made emendations to the English poems, which allows us to see the poet at work, correcting and revising. Comparison with the final versions in *The Temple* reveals that further self-editing intervened. The Williams Manuscript brings us very close to Herbert.

Internal evidence makes it possible to date it around 1623 or soon after. The Latin poems include three addressed to Urban VIII, who became pope in 1623: bantering epigrams, happy that a poet rather than a contentious theologian holds the office. Herbert's ecclesiastical sympathies were wide. Another Latin poem, on 'The Triumph of Death', uses themes deployed in the 1623 oration: denunciation of the horrors of war and an interest in their origin among primeval mankind. The unresolved disillusionment with academic life expressed in 'Affliction (I)', included in the Williams Manuscript, serves to confirm that it should probably be dated at the end of Herbert's Cambridge years. He is stuck in academe in his college gown, with his tedious book. He is particularly fed up with the 'simp'ring' with which he had to answer praise of the oratorical flattery which, for his own part, made him 'rage'.

On the fly-leaf of the notebook its eighteenth-century owner John Jones wrote (in abbreviated Latin which I translate) that he got it from 'the library of the famous and learned H.M. of Huntingdon who died in 1730'. 'H.M.' was Hugh Mapletoft, the son of Judith Collett who had been brought up in the religious community at Little Gidding: that extended family given to prayer, good works and the calligraphy that produced the surviving manuscript of *The Temple*. Herbert was deeply interested in Little Gidding in his latter years and corresponded with Nicholas Ferrar, the head of the community and his particular friend. This connection preserved the notebook. It is now known as 'The Williams Manuscript' because it is jealously preserved in Dr Williams's Library in Bloomsbury.

After a blank page, Herbert's poem '*The Dedication*' is written out in the scribe's hand with no corrections by the author. No great poem, it is interesting in two ways: it announces that the following poems are Herbert's 'first fruits', work to date and not complete (more to come); and in the final couplet it expects other people to read it in manuscript (printing is not implied), for good or ill.

The Dedication

> Lord, my first fruits present themselves to thee;
> Yet not mine neither: for from thee they came,
> And must return. Accept of them and me,
> And make us strive, who shall sing best thy name.
> > Turn their eyes hither, who shall make a gain:
> > Theirs, who shall hurt themselves or me, refrain.

There follow the seventy-eight poems of which all except six were to reappear in *The Temple*, Nicholas Ferrar's publication of Herbert's English poetry immediately after the poet's death. Many of them are in

1. The magnificent tomb in Montgomery Church erected by George Herbert's mother Magdalen for herself (though she was to be buried in Chelsea Old Church) and her husband Richard. Her own family is as spectacularly displayed as her husband's, and is given priority in the inscription.

2. Magdalen Herbert, George Herbert's mother, by Federico Zuccaro. John Donne praised her 'loving facetiousness and wit' as well as her 'holy cheerfulness and religious alacrity'. 'God gave her such comeliness,' he wrote, 'as, though she were not proud of it, yet she was so content with it as not to go about to mend it by any Art.'

3. The Elizabethan summerhouse at Eyton-upon-Severn, a surviving remnant of George Herbert's maternal grandmother's estate. It was to Eyton that Magdalen Herbert brought her family in 1597 after her husband's death.

4. Edward Herbert, George's brother, diplomat and fellow poet, posing in front of a view of the Severn valley as a Spenserian knight and melancholy lover, by Isaac Oliver.

5. Lancelot Andrewes, Dean of Westminster and later bishop of Winchester, the greatest linguist and preacher of his day, and George Herbert's senior friend.

6. The School Room at Westminster School c. 1840, unchanged since George Herbert's day.

7. Charles, Prince of Wales, by Daniel Mytens, *c.* 1624, soon after returning with Buckingham from their Spanish adventure.

8. George Villiers, Duke of Buckingham, James's adored favourite, by Paul van Somer, 1624.

9. *A Young Daughter of the Picts* by Jacques le Moyne de Morgues *c.* 1580, as referred to by Herbert in his 1623 Cambridge Oration: 'on the bodies of unmarried girls ... [our ancestors] painted flowers and plants'.

The Church.

Perfection The Elixir

Lord teach mee to referr
All things I doe to thee
That I not onely may not erre
But also pleasing bee.

A man that looks on glass
On it may stay his eye:
Or if he pleaseth through it pass
And then the heaun espy.

Hee that does ought for thee
Marketh y[t] deed for thine:
And when the Divel shakes y[e] tree
Thou saist, this fruit is mine.

All may of thee partake:
Nothing can be so low, meane
wth w[ch] his tincture (for thy sake
will not grow bright & clean

10. 'The Elixir' from the Williams Manuscript, written by a scribe and corrected
by Herbert in his own hand.

A servant, wth this clause,
Makes drudgery divine.
Who sweeps a room, as for thy lawes,
Makes that, and th'action fine.

But these say, hither, perfer toub,
Happy are they that dare
Lett in the Light to all their actions
And show them all they are.

This is y^e famous stone
That turneth all to gold
For y^t wch God doth touch & owne
Cannot for less be told.

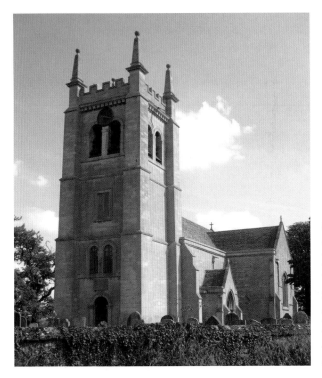

11. Leighton Bromswold Church, restored by George Herbert and Nicholas and John Ferrar: the tower traditional and medieval in shape but classical in detail (round-headed windows and instead of finials, obelisks supporting balls).

12. The spacious and luminous interior of Leighton Bromswold Church, with reading pew and pulpit of equal height, as Herbert had stipulated.

a different order in *The Temple*. But the first sixteen poems are in the same order in the Williams Manuscript as in *The Temple*, and so are the last nine: so the eventual framework of *The Temple* was already set, with 'Love (III)' coming last in both with 'Finis' written below it, flanked by flourishes, suggesting that Herbert already knew that it was somehow ultimate. Despite that 'Finis', five blank pages follow, waiting for further poems. So 'Finis' did not mean that he was finished with poetry by any means, just that 'Love (III)' was always to be the crown of his work so far as he was concerned. Posterity has agreed. The presence of 'Love (III)' in the Williams Manuscript resists any attempt to argue for an even, upwards development in Herbert's poetry-writing. After the five blank pages comes that immature poem 'The Church Militant', well separated from the preceding poems as a thing apart from them. Another batch of four blank pages follows, on the last of which is written in pencil by John Jones (he was given to this sort of behaviour) the correct speculation: 'The following supposed to be Mr. Herbert's own writing. See the Records in the Custody of the University Orator at Cambridge.' 'The following' are two sets of Herbert's Latin religious poems: 'Lucus' (The Grove) and another on the incidents of Christ's passion, 'Passio Discerpta'. They are all written in his own italic hand and end with 'Finis' and 'Soli Deo Gloria' (to God alone be glory). This suggests that Herbert set a particular value on his Latin poetry, over and above the English which he gave to a scribe.

Herbert's corrections of his own work are far and away the most interesting thing about the Williams Manuscript. They let us see him at work, refining and perfecting. The first important one of these is in lines 77–9 of 'The Sacrifice' where Christ is brought before King Herod. Herbert's scribe had written:

> Herod & all his bands do set me light
> Who teach all hands to war, fingers to fight
> To whose pow'r thunder is but weak and slight.

Herbert struck out the last line and substituted:

> And only am the Lord of Hosts and might.

This is tighter. The previous line had quoted Psalm 144:1: 'Blessed be the Lord my strength, which teacheth my hands to war and my fingers

to fight.' Herbert's amendment takes its cue from that military metaphor, rather than unnecessarily introducing thunder and making a
looser comparison. A less exigent poet would have been content with
the line as it stood.

When his sonnet 'Redemption' ('Having been tenant long to a rich
Lord...') came under his scrutiny, he went for the couplet which described
how the tenant, in search of his landlord to arrange a cheaper rent,

> Sought him in Cities, Theatres, resorts,
> In grottoes, gardens, Palaces and Courts

Herbert left 'sought him' but cancelled the rest and substituted:

> [Sought him] accordingly in great resorts;
> In cities, theatres, gardens, parks, and courts

Not only is this tidier: one line for the search in general, another for
its various destinations. It is also a great improvement to the rhythm
and its essential eagerly forward movement. 'Theatres' had made it
stumble in the first version. Moved to an early place in the next line,
it actually kicks it on. The casualty is 'grottoes', but they were a feature of gardens, as in his stepfather's at Chelsea, and so strictly
speaking redundant. 'Parks' for hunting, such as St James's Park in
Herbert's young days, is better. So Herbert did not just cast an eye
over his work to date. He listened to it and, when his ear caught a
false note or beat, reached for his pen. The title 'Redemption' in *The
Temple* is a later improvement: a pun on the two meanings integral to
the poem, legal and Christian. In the Williams Manuscript it is entitled,
less interestingly, 'The Passion'. Herbert liked titles which were more
teasing to the reader at first, but turned out to be enigmatic keys to the
poem and integral to its imagery. This is one of them.

It often took more than one go to get a poem right. The Williams
Manuscript version of the second part of the beautiful double-poem
'Easter' reads:

I   I had prepared many a flower
> To strow thy way and Victory,
> But thou wast up before mine hour
> Bringing thy sweets along with thee.

The sun arising in the east   5
Though he bring light and th' other scents:
Can not make up so brave a feast
As thy discovery presents.

Yet though my flowers be lost, they say   9
A heart can never come too late.
Teach it to sing thy praise, this day,
And then this day, my life shall date.

Herbert made only one correction at the time. He changed 'And brought' in line 4 to 'Bringing'. An improvement? Not noticeably so. In the final version, as it appears in *The Temple*, he changed it again into 'And brought'st': a slight rhythmical and grammatical improvement. But that final version is a radical rewriting of the poem as he had left it in the Williams Manuscript. Here it is. I have underlined the words and phrases surviving from the previous Williams version. They occur in each of the three verses and amount to a plan or structure for this rewritten version, verse by verse: a first verse about the poet preparing flowers for Christ, pre-empted by Christ being the earlier riser; a second verse about the sun, similarly put in the shade by Christ's light; a last verse about the day (Easter Day).

I got me flowers to straw thy way;
I got me boughs off many a tree:
But thou wast up by break of day
And brought'st thy sweets along with thee.

The Sun arising in the East,
Though he bring light, & th' East perfume;
If they should offer to contest
With thy arising, they presume.

Can there be any day but this,
Though many suns to shine endeavour?
We count three hundred, but we miss:
There is but one, and that one ever.

The sound of this final version is much improved. Herbert's lucid intelligence and musical ear has got to work – more and more confidently as he goes on. The short–long iambics of the first two verses are made more gracefully lyrical and serve the contrasts between 'I' and 'they' on one hand and 'thou' and 'thee' on the other. The metre is varied by the long–short trochees of the first two lines of the last verse, which hold up the flow with a moment of wonder (Bacon's 'broken thought'). The removal of 'victory' in the second line of the Williams version was a good idea. Its military connotations were an intrusion on the pastoral peace. Instead we get the 'boughs off many a tree'. 'Boughs' makes a hidden near-rhyme with 'flowers' in the previous line, and refers to Christ's entry into Jerusalem in the Gospels.[2] It also reflects the country custom of having the church 'strawed, and stuck with boughs' which Herbert approved in *The Country Parson* (Chapter XIII). Likewise, taking out the 'feast' from the second verse of the Williams version rids the poem of a grand intruder from the court into its country setting.

'By break of day' in the first verse is much better than 'before mine hour' in the Williams version – in aural resonance and visual delight. There is a sort of naive rapture in beginning both the first two lines of the poem with the same phrase 'I got me . . .' The last verse of the final version puts its predecessor in the Williams Manuscript in the shade with its ringing affirmation of 'one' and 'ever'. Vaughan Williams's setting in his *Five Mystical Songs* catches it triumphantly.

A lot of work, done at some time after 1623, went into transforming the lame poem in the Williams Manuscript into the lyrical crescendo of joy in the final form of the poem. It was work of the mind, the ear and the heart and was both critical and creative. Yet it does not obtrude. We can appreciate its 'art concealing art' only because the older version has survived.

The Williams Manuscript version of the poem now known as 'The Elixir' and sung (unnecessarily altered) as the hymn 'Teach me, my God and King' may startle readers familiar with those later versions. Here it is, with the scribe's version in ordinary roman type, Herbert's crossings-out underlined and his revisions in italic type.

Perfection   The Elixir

Lord teach me to refer
All things I do to thee
That I not only may not err
But also pleasing be

A man that looks on glass
On it may stay his eye
Or if he pleaseth, through it pass
And then the heav'n espy.

<u>He that does aught for thee</u>
<u>Marketh that deed for thine:</u>
<u>And when the Devil shakes the tree,</u>
<u>Thou say'st, this fruit is mine.</u>

All may of thee partake
Nothing can be so <u>low</u>   *mean*
Which with his tincture (for thy sake)
Will not <u>to Heaven grow</u>   *grow bright & clean*

A servant with this clause
Makes drudgery divine:
Who sweeps a <u>chamber</u> for thy laws   *room, as*
Makes that and th' action fine

<u>But these are high perfections.</u>   *This is the famous stone*
<u>Happy are they that dare</u>   *That turneth all to gold:*
<u>Let in the Light to all their actions</u>   *For that which God doth*
                   touch and own
<u>And show them as they are.</u>   *Cannot for less be told.*

And here is the final version as printed in 1633 and subsequently.

The Elixir

Teach me, my God and King,   I
In all things thee to see,
And what I do in any thing,
To do it as for thee;

2   Not rudely, as a beast,
    To run into an action;
But still to make thee prepossessed,
    And give it his perfection.

3   A man that looks on glass,
    On it may stay his eye;
Or if he pleaseth, through it pass,
    And then the heav'n espy.

4   All may of thee partake:
    Nothing can be so mean,
That with his tincture (for thy sake)
    Will not grow bright and clean.

5   A servant with this clause
    Makes drudgery divine:
Who sweeps a room as for thy laws,
    Makes that and th' action fine.

6   This is the famous stone
    That turneth all to gold:
For that which God doth touch and own
    Cannot for less be told.

No other poem of Herbert's has been so much revised as this: first the Williams Manuscript's scribe's version; then Herbert's thorough revision of it; then Herbert's final version in *The Temple*, which is different again. The versions in modern hymn books differ yet again by omitting verse 2 and also substituting 'this' for 'his' (meaning 'its') in verse 4 – a minor change with major implications, as we shall see. It is worth navigating through all this because in the process we shall get very close to the poet at work.

It is best to start, as Herbert himself may well have done, with his greatest alteration in the Williams Manuscript: his crossing out of the last verse written by his scribe and its substitution by his new one beginning 'This is the famous stone …' What famous stone? The alchemists, predecessors of modern chemists, were preoccupied with finding primal matter, the original generating substance out of which

God had created such secondary elements as sulphur and salt.[3] It was, they therefore believed, immensely transformative. In particular, it could transform base metals (and even anything else) into gold. It was known variously as 'the philosopher's stone', 'the elixir' and 'the tincture'. It might be solid or liquid or vaporous: not having found it, they could not be sure. Their nomenclature was consequently confused. They dug for it in mines and broke down the minerals they found in their laboratories by fire. Needless to say, it eluded their search, but the hope of finding such an original, unitary and transformative thing was invincible. Edward Herbert claimed to have seen an example of its effect (not the thing itself) on his travels.

> From Venice, I went to Florence . . . having seen the rarities of this place likewise, and particularly that rare chapel made for the house of Medici [in San Lorenzo], beautified on all the inside with a coarser kind of precious stone, as also that nail which was at one end iron, and the other gold, made so by virtue of the tincture into which it was put, I went to Siena . . .[4]

No doubt he told his brother about this wonder. George Herbert used the word 'tincture' in its fourth verse throughout the versions of his poem. But he preceded it with 'his': 'his [that is, its] tincture'. Whereas Edward Herbert had thought that the tincture was some extraneous matter into which the nail he credulously admired in Florence had been put, George Herbert's 'his' asserts that the tincture belonged to the object it transformed – was even inherent to it. To many alchemists a tincture was 'the quintessence, spirit or soul of a thing'.[5] So in the fourth verse of the poem:

> All may of thee partake:
> Nothing can be so mean,
> Which with his tincture (for thy sake)
> Will not grow bright and clean.

The tincture is not some sort of externally applied polish but the inner quality which cleaning brings out and restores.

Alchemy comes into its own in the triumphant last verse which Herbert substituted for the cancelled one which his scribe had written out:

This is the famous stone
That turneth all to gold:
For that which God doth touch and own
Cannot for less be told.

That done, Herbert went to the top of the page and put there a new, alchemical title, 'The Elixir', next to the existing one, 'Perfection'. In *The Temple* 'Perfection' has disappeared and the title is 'The Elixir' alone. It is an improvement because the whole poem is about the transformation of the ordinary by the spirit which 'makes drudgery divine'. God does not only touch things. He owns them. They are his 'prepossessed' property in the more exact and philosophical sense of 'property' as part of a being. This was his brother Edward's belief: that things had within them, as their essence, a knowledge tending to God.

Herbert made two other revisions. In his final 1633 version he left out the third verse in the Williams Manuscript. So we lose the nice little vignette of the devil shaking the tree like a thief trying to get its fruit down. He seems to have felt that, for all its charm, it was unnecessary. A spare simplicity was Herbert's constant aim. The second revision in the Williams Manuscript is to the fourth verse.

All may of thee partake.
Nothing can be so low
Which with his tincture (for thy sake)
Will not to Heaven grow

becomes:

All may of thee partake.
Nothing can be so mean
Which with his tincture (for thy sake)
Will not grow bright and clean.

Growing to heaven went out. It was something that Herbert learned to be suspicious about – ambitious and risky. In his later masterpiece 'The Flower' he depicts himself 'off'ring at heav'n, growing and groaning thither' as if it was his own, only to be beaten down by God's anger. The excision of spiritual climbing from 'The Elixir' can be seen as a preliminary to the drama of 'The Flower'. In any case, heaven is not the business of 'The Elixir'. There heaven can be espied, not reached. The business of 'The Elixir' is getting things on earth well done, 'bright and clean' – and that is the phrase which takes its place, with 'low' changed to 'mean' to rhyme with it. In any case 'low' needs to go along with the vertical spatial metaphor of growing upwards. Besides all which, 'bright and clean' is an aptly shining-sounding phrase which beats its predecessor hollow by virtue of its combination of domestic practicality and the onomatopoeic brilliance of its vowels.

In quality the poems in the Williams Manuscript extend from the best to the worst of Herbert's work. 'Love (III)' is there at the end with 'Finis' written under it. It would have the same distinguished position and subscription in the first 1633 printed edition of *The Temple*, which Herbert's friend Nicholas Ferrar saw through the press within a year of Herbert's death. And so it remains. There is only one difference from the Williams Manuscript: 'doth' for 'does' in line 14. But after five blank pages comes 'The Church Militant', that tedious and clunky piece of (presumably) juvenilia which Herbert not only preserves but works on a little. Great poems such as 'Affliction (I)', 'Prayer (I)', 'Church Music' and 'Church Monuments' are there. So are six poems which Herbert rightly dropped from *The Temple* and Hutchinson (as rightly) reclaimed for his complete edition of Herbert's *Works*.[6]

Strikingly, the main outlines of the structure of *The Temple* are there in the Williams Manuscript. The opening sequence of sixteen poems from '*The Dedication*' to 'Holy Baptism' is there, with some adjustments of order in the middle of it. So is the closing sequence of five poems from 'Death' to 'Love (III)'. In between the order of poems is shuffled and switched backwards and forwards, hither and thither. It would seem that Herbert had a plan for a book of poems in his mind at least from 1623. The Williams Manuscript may have been a way of seeing how it looked. If so, there was an element of overall organization, even strategy, in the writing of the poetry, making it more than incidental – an element, for in the main and middle part of *The Temple* it is not discernible. The entrance and the exit were there and held it all.

The Williams Manuscript is a window on to Herbert as poet at a particular point, probably the end of his Cambridge days, in the course of his life. Before that he must certainly have revised and corrected the poems that are written there in the scribe's rhythmical hand. After that, as well as composing as many poems and more, he revised yet again. He was always at it. This may well be the reason why, when his great editor Hutchinson searched through seventeenth-century manuscript commonplace books for Herbert's poems he reported that 'in no case have I seen any reason to suppose that they were not transcribed from one or other of the printed editions, even when that fact is not explicitly stated.'[7] The strong implication is that Herbert kept his poems to himself out of perfectionism: a sense that they were not all what they might be and that scrutiny would suggest improvements.

Truth is what mattered to him as much as love: truth with its twin hallmarks of accuracy and sincerity. It meant work. Herbert was impatient with the just-about-all-right. He wants words that have the clarity which lets the actuality show through:

> ... for life is straight,
> Straight as a line, and ever tends to thee,
> To thee, how art more far above deceit,
> Than deceit seems above simplicity.
> Give me simplicity, that I may live,
> So live and like, that I may know thy ways.[8]

Simplicity in any art does not, to put it mildly, come easily. Children have it, so 'childhood is health'.[9] Adults have to regain it by subjecting themselves to rigorous critical examination. In 'Little Gidding' (Herbert's ideal society as well as his) T. S. Eliot witnessed to:

> A condition of complete simplicity
> (Costing not less than everything)

Here, where the simple truth is sought and eventually discovered, Herbert as man and poet converge. The poetry is an exercise in understanding the man, himself, by the discovery of the right words. The man is the maker of things which, when they are made right, are 'something understood'.[10]

*

'Affliction (I)' (which we shall look at more closely at the beginning of the next chapter) is one of the finest poems in the Williams Manuscript and might well have been left alone; but when it came out in the 1633 printing Herbert had made improvements. In the Williams Manuscript lines 15–16 read:

> Thus argued into hopes, I was preserved
> Before that I could fear.

But 1633 reads:

> Thus argued into hopes, my thoughts reserved
> No place for grief or fear.

The first four words are fine: arguing ourselves into hopeful views is just the kind of thing we do, and Herbert puts it so clearly and succinctly that we recognize it at once. But the following words in the Williams version are by no means so lucid. What is 'that' doing? Does it stand for something he 'could fear'? And if so, what? Or can it be omitted as an unnecessary adjunct to 'before'? By contrast, 1633 is a pellucid description of a common, if reckless, movement of the human mind.

Another example from the same poem: in the Williams Manuscript lines 29–30 read:

> Sorrow was all my soul; I did not know
> That I did live, but by a pang of woe.

Once again, it starts strongly and well. And this time what follows would satisfy a mediocre poet on a mediocre day. But 'pang of woe' is something of a poetic platitude and not quite equal to the thing itself. In 1633 Herbert has substituted a little stroke of genius.

> Sorrow was all my soul; I scarce believed,
> Till grief did tell me roundly, that I lived.

Personified grief can tell him the truth 'roundly': with the unsparing bluntness of a verbal body-blow, an abrupt recall to reality of the self-pitying soul.

PART TWO

7

Lost in a Humble Way

DISILLUSIONMENT

'Affliction (1)' is an autobiographical narrative. Herbert wrote no fewer than five poems under this title, getting to grips with his various griefs and grievances by ordering them into verse. This is the longest and greatest: eleven six-line verses making up a narrative which covers several years. It starts happily but darkens into a crisis marked by illness, the death of friends and discontent with the academic life which had got him 'entangled in the world of strife': all those disputations, not to mention the snares of national relations with Spain. He feels that he has been tricked into it by God – not reflecting on his own frantic efforts to become University Orator – and is at the end of his tether. 'My friends die' is a justified complaint. 'Friends' meant family: which had been sadly reduced by death during his time at Cambridge. His brothers Charles and William had died in 1617, his brother Richard in 1622 and his sister Margaret Vaughan in 1623. It is never possible to date the poems in *The Temple* with any precision, but all this suggests that the poem was written late in his time at Cambridge and in his early thirties. It is in the Williams Manuscript. As we have seen, Herbert worked on it subsequently, making two telling amendments but otherwise only minor corrections. It deserves and rewards careful reading.

Affliction (I)

When first thou didst entice to thee my heart,   1
     I thought the service brave;
So many joys I writ down for my part,
     Besides what I might have

Out of my stock of natural delights,
Augmented with thy gracious benefits.

2   I looked on thy furniture so fine,
            And made it fine to me;
Thy glorious household-stuff did me entwine,
            And 'tice me unto thee.
Such stars I counted mine; both heav'n and earth
Paid me my wages in a world of mirth.

3   What pleasures could I want, whose King I served
            Where joys my fellows were?
Thus argued into hopes, my thoughts reserved
            No place for grief or fear.
Therefore my sudden soul caught at the place,
And made her youth and fierceness seek thy face.

4   At first thou gav'st me milk and sweetnesses;
            I had my wish and way:
My days were straw'd with flow'rs and happiness;
            There was no month but May.
But with my years sorrow did twist and grow,
And made a party unawares for woe.

5   My flesh began unto my soul in pain,
            Sicknesses cleave my bones;
Consuming agues dwell in ev'ry vein
            And tune my breath to groans.
Sorrow was all my soul; I scarce believed,
Till grief did tell me roundly, that I lived.

6   When I got health, thou took'st away my life,
            And more; for my friends die:
My mirth and edge was lost; a blunted knife
            Was of more use than I.
Thus thin and lean without a fence or friend,
I was blown through with ev'ry storm and wind.

Whereas my birth and spirit rather took   7
      The way that takes the town;
Thou didst betray me to a ling'ring book,
      And wrap me in a gown.
I was entangled in a world of strife,
Before I had the power to change my life.

Yet, for I threaten'd oft the siege to raise,   8
      Not simp'ring all mine age,
Thou didst with academic praise
      Melt and dissolve my rage.
I took thy sweet'ned pill, till I came where
I could not go away, nor persevere.

Yet lest perchance I could too happy be   9
      In my unhappiness,
Turning my purge to food, thou throwest me
      Into more sicknesses,
Thus doth thy power cross-bias me, not making
Thine own gift good, yet me from my ways taking.

Now I am here, what thou wilt do with me   10
None of my books will show:
I read, and sigh, and wish I were a tree;
      For sure then I should grow
To fruit or shade; at least some bird would trust
Her household to me, and I should be just.

Yet, though thou troublest me, I must be meek;   11
      In weakness must be stout.
Well, I will change the service, and go seek
      Some other master out.
Ah my dear God! Though I am clean forgot,
Let me not love thee, if I love thee not.

That last verse is extraordinary: three abrupt changes of mood within it, each of them proposing a different way of coping with the catalogue of disappointments which has bundled and jolted readers through the preceding ten stanzas. The first two lines settle for a bitter and sarcastic stoicism, spoken through gritted teeth. The next two lack that sort of irony and are outspoken: the poet decides to have done with God altogether. The shock of this thought clears the air for the honesty of the amazing final couplet. 'Ah my dear God!' is an ardent, urgent address to the one whom he still loves – and by doing so loves his own life – in spite of everything:

> . . . though I am clean forgot.
> Let me not love thee if I love thee not.

Love and pretence, love and hypocrisy, are irreconcilable. As St Paul had written, 'Let love be without dissimulation.'[1] That at least is clear: love must not and cannot be compromised.

A piece of private writing, remote from Herbert in time and place, has the same exacting demand for obstinate love and gives some insight into the extraordinary toughness of Herbert's last two lines. On 25 September 1855 the Danish theologian Søren Kierkegaard, unsparingly his individual self to the last, made his last entry in his journal before he died in a Copenhagen hospital.[2] It mixes naive imagery and penetrating speculation into a parable and offers a vantage point for reading Herbert's poem again.

> What does God want? What pleases him even more than the praises of angels is a man, who in the last lap of his life, when God is transformed as though into sheer cruelty, and with the cruellest imaginable cruelty does everything to deprive him of all joy in life, and who continues to believe that God is love and it is from love that God does this. Such a man becomes an angel. And in heaven he can surely praise God. But the apprentice time, the school time, is always the strictest time. Like a man who thought of journeying through the whole world to hear a singer who had a perfect voice, so God sits in heaven and listens. And every time he hears praise from a man whom he brings to the point of uttermost disgust with life, God says to himself, This is the right note. He says, Here it is, as though he were making a discovery.

Herbert's last line is, surely and precisely, Kierkegaard's 'right note'. It has the ring of honest truth and, more than that, of honest love which has no other ends in view. It insists on it as the *unum necessarium*, the one thing necessary: for it is the only way of relating to another which avoids both servility and manipulation. It is the fulfilment of freedom. As Kierkegaard wrote a few lines later, 'only freedom can do it.'

We should, after all that, begin the poem at the beginning. Herbert has a long, eventful tale to tell, so it needs a lively rhythm to carry the reader along. He chooses the most natural English metre: the iambic pentameter (five feet), the walking or heartbeat rhythm of short and long: 'When <u>first</u> thou <u>didst</u> en<u>tice</u> to <u>thee</u> my <u>heart</u>' and so on. In the first four lines he gives them a lift and a flourish by alternating them with shorter three-feet lines in the same springy metre: 'I <u>thought</u> the <u>ser</u>vice <u>brave</u>'. Then he ends the stanza with a couplet in renewed iambic pentameter, tying it up loosely: that was that, but just for the time being. The metre is elastic enough to carry sad as well as happy memories. But the happy ones are ominously qualified from the start. The sinister 'entice', repeated as "tice' in the second verse (where it replaces the still more extreme 'bewitch' in the Williams Manuscript), has the colour of crafty seduction. It casts an ominous shadow over the 'joys' which follow. The attentive reader should expect some bad news to come.

But not for a while. The first three verses and the first four lines of the fourth, climaxing with 'There was no month but May', are full of good cheer. Herbert contemplates his former, jolly self with amused detachment. He 'thought' he was on to a really good thing with the benefits of divine grace on top of his natural pleasures: a common religious failure of imagination. The God who has enlisted him is a very rich patron. Herbert, used to being in great houses, can enjoy his fine furniture as if it were his own. That household is the universe,³ stars and all. He is on double pay, from heaven as well as earth, and in 'a world of mirth'.

The third verse introduces a quietly threatening note into the merriment. What could possibly go wrong with God in charge and joys his daily companions? But he was 'argued' into hopes, persuaded against what might have been his better judgement. And he knows himself to be headlong and impetuous ('my sudden soul' is paralleled by his admission elsewhere that some people thought him 'eager, hot, and undertaking,/But in my prosecutions slack and small').⁴

The next, fourth verse is a turning point. 'At first' takes up the similar 'When first' of the beginning, but with a note of foreboding. God had then been like an indulgent mother, giving him 'milk and sweet-nesses' and letting him have his own way all the time – or perhaps, like the witches in fairy tales, God had only pretended to be so, since we know already that he is up to enticement. Very stealthily, 'unawares', sorrow, like bindweed, insinuated itself into his life.

In the fifth verse this sorrow is everywhere, 'all my soul'. Pain is described with the same vivid actuality as pleasure before – particu-larly how the soul itself is overwhelmed by the agony of the flesh and is in no way separate from it. The sufferer is addressing the reader with forceful, grim directness when he says:

> . . . I scarce believed,
> Till grief did tell me roundly, that I lived.

He recovered. But only to find himself, in the sixth verse, in one of those dismal phases of life when deaths are all around. 'My friends die.' He felt useless, worse than 'a blunted knife', and exposed as to an icy wind which cuts through the clothes.

> Thus thin and lean without a fence or friend,
> I was blown through with ev'ry storm and wind.

Was he recalling Shakespeare's King Lear in the storm with the naked Edgar? Not necessarily. The sense of acute discomfort, of a 'thin and lean' man (as he was)[5] out alone in bad weather, needs no other source than going about out of doors in England.

The rest of the poem is set in Cambridge. From there he looks back regretfully to Charing Cross and Whitehall. His 'birth and spirit', as aristocrat and intellectual, were better suited to 'the way that takes the town', but he finds himself reading a 'ling'ring' book (slow and sticky reading), wrapped in an academic gown, and 'entangled' in the 'strife' of an argumentative society with its adversarial debates, not to mention having to make a respectable oration out of the exploits of Charles and Buckingham over the Spanish marriage. He was kept at it, and his resentment dissolved, by the gratification of 'academic praise'. He was stuck. The notorious Cambridge climate with its fogs and north-east winds made him ill. Drawing his metaphor from the games of bowls which were his recreation at Chelsea and Trinity, he complains that:

Two Cambridge academics, from John Speed, The Theatre of the Empire of Great Britain, *1611: 'Thou didst betray me to a ling'ring book/And wrap me in a gown.'*

> Thus doth thy power cross-bias me, not making
> Thine own gift good, yet me from my ways taking.

The broken rhythms there figure his inner dislocation. 'Now I am here,' in his room in Trinity, with books which are useless to show the way ahead, wishing he was a tree (as elsewhere: 'Oh that I were an Orange-tree,/That busy plant!')[6] in which 'some bird' might nest and give him a sense of participation in life at large. And so to the last verse where we began. The only thing which stays steady under such disappointments, bereavements, bewilderment of spirits and sickness is love. It is disinterested in the strong and correct sense of being unbiased by personal interest or concern – and it is the negative pressure of all those misfortunes which shows, positively, that it is so.

WITHDRAWAL

Herbert's great Latin oration on Prince Charles's return was a fulfilment of his worldly ambitions, a tour de force of wit and diplomacy. He was famous and admired and could reasonably have looked forward to a secure and distinguished career as a Cambridge don, perhaps culminating in the mastership of his college. Or, like other Orators before him, he could expect high office at court. For complex reasons, nothing of the sort was to come about. For the next seven years, which were to see his mother's illness and death and the hesitantly slow development of his commitment to life as a clergyman, he drifted about as a guest in the houses of his friends and relations. Poetry was his anchor. 'The Answer' was his response to the friends and acquaintances who wondered why he had not made more of the brilliant promise of his earlier years. They bear down on the poem like 'the legions of cruel inquisitive They' which Auden pictures persecuting Edward Lear in his limericks.[7] It is an intimately personal and Shakespearean sonnet. The tree, which he longed to be like, has become autumnal and winter is upon him.

The Answer

My comforts drop and melt away like snow:
I shake my head, and all the thoughts and ends,
Which my fierce youth did bandy, fall and flow
Like leaves about me; or like summer friends,
Flies of estates and sunshine. But to all
Who think me eager, hot, and undertaking,
But in my prosecutions slack and small;
As a young exhalation, newly waking,
Scorns his first bed of dirt, and means the sky;
But cooling by the way, grows pursy and slow,
And settling to a cloud, doth live and die
In that dark state of tears: to all that so
    Show me, and set me, I have one reply,
    Which they that know the rest, know more than I.

The conclusion, coming after the prolonged Shakespearean simile of vapour becoming cloud, is evasive. 'The rest' might mean all sorts of things: the remainder of his life, answers to his critics which he has withheld from the poem, the Latin poems and oration which he had published, even the ultimate heavenly rest. He does not say. But what he implies, sarcastically, is that 'they', being such know-alls, must know the answer better than he does. As for himself, his own answer and consolation was in crafting his unintelligible and unhappy state into one of his best and most psychologically realistic poems. The comforts of religion are absent.

In November 1623 he was nominated to Parliament for his native borough of Montgomery. This was by way of a family duty: Edward Herbert had served as member for the shire in 1605 and the borough was taken on by their brother Henry in 1627. Being an MP in those days was an occasional obligation and not, as it is now, a political career. Between 1614 and 1621 there had been no Parliaments at all; nor would there be between 1629 and 1640. The Parliament of 1624 was stormy. The King wanted to ease the repressive measures against English catholics in the interests of getting his son Charles married. The attempted Spanish Match had failed disastrously, but it was time to try again. This time the bride in view was, once again, a catholic: the French Princess Henrietta Maria. A catholic alliance would balance his daughter Elizabeth's marriage to the protestant Elector Palatine. It was a matter of foreign policy and the negotiations involved Edward Herbert as ambassador in Paris. Parliament once again took the protestant side and refused to co-operate. It was also pressing the King for more control of the valuable monopolies which were at his disposal. To the bitter disappointment of all in Herbert's circle, the charter of the Virginia Company was revoked. As well as these frustrations, the powerful puritans in Parliament brought forward a bill for 'the better observance of the Sabbath', which offended the King's genial paternalism. He resisted it as 'allowing no recreation to the poor men that labour hard all the week long, to ease themselves on the Sunday'.[8] Fed up with all this insubordination, James got rid of the Parliament by proroguing it after less than a year.

The only record of Herbert's participation in this short Parliament is as a member of a committee to consider 'petitions concerning Learning and Religion': in effect, complaints against schoolmasters and heads of colleges. John Richardson, the Master of Trinity, Herbert's own college, had unspecified complaints laid against him twice, but they were twice dismissed – no doubt to Herbert's relief. Far more serious and shocking petitions were alleged against Thomas Anyan, the President of Corpus Christi College, Oxford. He was found to have wasted college money, attempted bribery, failed to discipline a drunken fellow and another who had spoken slightingly about the Archbishop of York's preaching and, disgracefully, gone in for 'unnatural lust with some tavern boys'. The committee decided that he was 'fit to be removed from his now place, and unfit to hold any other, in respect of those foul matters, proved to the Committee, and reported to this House, against him'.[9] The King refused to have anything to do with the case and passed it on to Lancelot Andrewes, Visitor of Corpus as bishop of Winchester. In the event, Anyan survived as president for the next five years, a beneficiary of unparliamentary procedures and episcopal procrastination.

There is no record of Herbert in Parliament after 1624. In his later years, encouraging the gentry to get themselves 'a calling' and not be idle, he took a positive view.

> When there is a Parliament, he [the typical gentleman] is to endeavour by all means to be a Knight or Burgess there; for there is no school to a Parliament. And when he is there, he must not only be a morning man, but at committees also; for there the particulars are exactly discussed, which are brought to the House but in general.[10]

Herbert had done his bit, and admired the attention to 'particulars' of his own committee. But his fastidious temperament would have been put off by its grubby business. In any case, he had other things to attend to. Away in Montgomeryshire, in 1623 his sister Margaret Vaughan had died a widow, leaving three young daughters. She had made her brother Edward their guardian, but he was away in France. Their grandmother Magdalen, who had kept an eye on them when she was well, was now ill. George and Henry Herbert were left to do what they could for the orphans. They eventually, and happily, ended up in George's household at Bemerton Rectory in 1630.

Cambridge gave him, as Orator, six months' leave of absence on 11 June 1624 'on account of many businesses away'.[11] There is no evidence that Herbert returned to Cambridge after the expiry of his leave, though he would remain Orator for another four years and was still a fellow of Trinity – according to the statutes of which he should by now have been made deacon in the Church of England. Instead, he had, if briefly, taken on the responsibilities of an MP. A year of probation was required before being made deacon, but Herbert was suddenly eager to skip it and, on 3 November 1624, got the Archbishop of Canterbury's dispensation: he could be made (and presumably was made) deacon by John Williams, Bishop of Lincoln, right away. That done, he could no longer, as a clergyman, be an MP and most routes of secular employment were closed to him. As with his becoming an MP, too, much should not be made of this: required of him as a fellow of Trinity, it was no kind of an heroic decision. The remarkable thing is that Herbert was in a hurry for it – and then did nothing much about it for a year and a half, and then took on only the very occasional duties and stipend of a canon of Lincoln. Being an active, fully committed clergyman as rector of Bemerton was six years away. This haste followed by inanition is another instance of his being in other people's eyes:

> . . . eager, hot, and undertaking,
> But in my prosecutions slack and small.

Luckily in John Williams he had a powerful and discriminating ecclesiastical patron to keep an eye on him. Williams was a cultivated exemplar of traditional Anglican churchmanship who favoured learned and moderate men.

JOHN WILLIAMS

When the young Herbert arrived at Trinity in 1609, Williams was a fellow of St John's College next door and ordained into the Church. Short and dapper, he had a usefully pragmatic business sense and an endearing tendency towards lavish hospitality. A childhood accident, hitting 'a big ragged stone' when he jumped from a wall, had made him 'chaste perforce' and 'a stranger to wanton lusts'.[12] He was a life-long, cheerful bachelor. As junior proctor of the University he was in charge of the conduct of disputations: a context in which he and Herbert would have come to know each other well. He was chosen to preach before the King at Newmarket in 1611. The sermon went down well and Williams commented that 'I had a great deal of court holy water, if I can make myself any good thereby.'[13] He could and did – and the witty combination of sacred and secular in that remark was typical of him. He was on the up and in 1621 had become a high-level pluralist: dean of Westminster and bishop of Lincoln, successor to Bacon as lord keeper of the Seal. He did his best to dissuade Prince Charles and Buckingham from their Spanish adventure of 1623, rightly warning them that they would be 'subject to be stayed on many and contrary pretences; [and] made a plot for all the contemplations of that state and that religion to work on'. So it turned out, and King James ruefully reflected that 'if he had sent Williams into Spain with his son, he had kept heart's ease and honour.'[14]

It was as bishop of Lincoln, with Herbert's friend John Hacket as his chaplain, that Williams ordained Herbert as deacon and secured a little income for him from a share, involving no pastoral duties, in the rectory of Llandinam, a few miles from Montgomery. Two years later Williams did Herbert another favour, making him a canon of Lincoln Cathedral with the prebend (a further source of income without pastoral duties) of Leighton Bromswold in Huntingdonshire. The restoration of the church there was to become a great concern of Herbert's. Williams was himself a keen restorer: in his younger days as rector of Walgrave in Northamptonshire; then at Westminster Abbey and Buckden, his episcopal palace near Huntingdon; and again at Lincoln College Chapel in Oxford where brilliant stained glass remains today as a testimony to the taste and patronage of its episcopal Visitor. Herbert took his cue as church-restorer from his patron.

Westminster School was another bond between them. As dean of Westminster from 1620, Williams modelled himself on his predecessor Lancelot Andrewes, assiduously teaching the boys himself, dining with them and questioning them closely about their studies. He loved the music in the Abbey and 'procured the sweetest music for organ and voice that was ever heard in an English quire'.[15] Orlando Gibbons, the composer and best organist of the day, was in charge of it. Williams took particular pains to hang on as dean of Westminster

John Williams, Herbert's congenial patron, as Bishop of Lincoln and Keeper of the Great Seal, by an anonymous engraver, 1621–5.

when he was made lord keeper of the Great Seal: being 'loath to stir from that seat where he had command of such exquisite music'.[16] It was a love shared by Herbert. Gardening was another mutual enthusiasm, inherited by Herbert from his mother and indulged by Williams at Walgrave and Buckden where 'he loved stirring and walking, which he used two hours or more, every day in the open air, if the weather served: especially if he might go to and fro, where good scents and works of well-formed shape were about him.'[17]

Williams and Herbert shared convictions as well as tastes. The beauty of holiness had to include order, 'the best rampire [rampart] the wit of man can invent' according to Williams.[18] In Herbert's poem 'The Family',[19] order is the master-musician that 'plays the soul'. And order is a constant theme of his *Country Parson*. For all his cultured magnificence, Williams was diligent in his duties of preaching and pastoral care. He had an inclusive mind. After a Sunday during which he had taken an ordination service he put on a performance of *A Midsummer Night's Dream* at Buckden in 1631 and got into trouble with the puritans for it. Yet he was sympathetic to puritan devotion, while differing from it by liking churches to be richly furnished and services to be on traditional lines. Herbert felt the same and extended his sympathy into being 'a lover of old customs, if they be good, and harmless; and the rather, because country people are much addicted to them, so that to favour them therein is to win their hearts, and to oppose them therein is to deject them'.[20] Among the proverbs which he collected was 'With customs we live well, but laws undo us.'[21] Williams was astute and assiduous in spotting and fostering men who would make good priests. He recommended John Donne to be dean of St Paul's in 1621, a brilliant appointment if ever there was one.[22] Hacket wrote that 'they were godly men whom he obliged, and such as had waited long in the Universities and fit to be called forth for their talents.' Herbert was pre-eminently one such, conscientious but pragmatic, who valued his Church's stance between the extremes of dogmatic Calvinism and elaborate catholic ritual.

This is celebrated in his happily complacent poem 'The British Church'. It is not one of his great pieces, but a cheerful one probably from the last decade of his life (it is not in the Williams Manuscript). The dating of letters mentioned in the first verse refers to the calendar in use at the time which began the year with the feast of the Annunci-ation or 'Lady Day'. 'She on the hills' in its third verse is Rome; 'She in the valley' is lakeside Geneva, the home of Calvin and Calvinism and the cynosure of those Anglican puritans who disapproved of the use of the modest white surplice in worship. The metaphor of 'Mother' for the Church was age-old. Here it frames the poem at its start and finish – for which Magdalen Herbert is surely to be thanked. Her-bert's Church was thoroughly feminine and maternal. 'The mean' in the last verse connotes the middle place or, in music, the middle voice.

The British Church

I joy, dear Mother, when I view
Thy perfect lineaments, and hue
   Both sweet and bright.
Beauty in thee takes up her place,
And dates her letters from thy face,
   When she doth write.

A fine aspect in fit array,
Neither too mean, nor yet too gay,
   Shows who is best.
Outlandish looks may not compare:
For all they either painted are,
   Or else undress'd.

She on the hills, which wantonly
Allureth all in hope to be
   By her preferr'd,
Hath kiss'd so long her painted shrines,
That ev'n her face with kissing shines,
   For her reward.

She in the valley is so shy
Of dressing that her hair doth lie
   About her ears:
While she avoids her neighbour's pride,
She wholly goes on th' other side,
   And nothing wears.

But, dearest Mother, (what those miss)
The mean thy praise and glory is,
And long may be.
Blessed be God, whose love it was
To double-moat thee with his grace,
And none but thee.

An early satire of John Donne's (3: 'Kind pity chokes my spleen ...'), which Herbert may have known, made similar points more sharply. Where is 'true religion'? One man looks to Rome 'because he doth know/That she was there a thousand years ago'. Another looks to Geneva where religion is 'plain, simple, sullen, young,/Contemptuous yet unhandsome'. Yet another, a reactionary stay-at-home Anglican, thinks that 'she/Which dwells with us is only perfect' (compare the complacency of Herbert's last line). The best thing is to 'doubt wisely' because:

On a huge hill,
Cragged and steep, Truth stands, and he that will
Reach her, about must, and about must go;
And what the hill's suddenness resists win so.

Donne, Herbert and Williams were James I's kind of clergymen. William Laud, Bishop of London and a humourless, busy disciplinarian who detested Williams as his chief rival for advancement, was not. He was ultra-orthodox and a born enforcer. 'I keep Laud back from all place of rule and authority,' James I had perceptively remarked, 'because I find that he hath a restless spirit, and cannot see when things are well but loves to toss and change, and to bring things to a pitch of reformation floating in his own brain.'[23] When the old King died in 1625 Williams preached his funeral sermon, comparing him advantageously to Solomon and Augustus. As dean of Westminster he ought, by long tradition, to have taken a leading part in the coronation of the new King Charles I. But Charles, prompted by Buckingham, ordered Williams to absent himself from the Abbey and chose Laud to supplant him. With Laud's star rising, the days of tolerant and inclusive Anglicanism were numbered. Herbert was to die in the same year that Laud became archbishop of Canterbury, thereafter assisting Charles I on the path to civil war.

LEIGHTON BROMSWOLD

There were no pastoral duties attached to the money Herbert got, thanks to Williams, from Llandinam and Leighton Bromswold. In his Cambridge days he had had too much to do. Now he had too little. During the years between his work on the parliamentary committee and his becoming rector of Bemerton, that is from 1624 to 1630, he seems to have been pretty much adrift. Late in 1625 he was at Chelsea with his mother and stepfather, along with John Donne who was taking refuge from the plague in London. The Cambridge oration on the death of James I in that year was given by Herbert's deputy. This is striking, because his sincere admiration of the learned and pacific King would certainly have resulted in a moving and brilliant performance. Walton reports that at the time he was staying with 'a friend in Kent',

> where he lived very privately and was such a lover of solitariness as was judged to impair his health more than his study had done. In this time of retirement he had many conflicts with himself, whether he should return to the painted pleasures of a court life or betake himself to a study of divinity and enter into sacred orders (to which his dear mother had often persuaded him).[24]

Walton seems to have forgotten that Herbert was already a deacon, the step next to the priesthood, albeit an inactive one. On 13 July 1626 Herbert was back in London. The Duke of Buckingham (he had been raised to the highest rank of the peerage in 1623) had been made chancellor of the University of Cambridge. Herbert, as its Orator, gave the required Latin speech at the Duke's installation at York House: his last performance in that role and not a congenial one. It does not survive. As a canon of Lincoln his only duties were to preach once a year on Whitsunday or get a deputy to do it, and to recite Psalms 31 and 32 every day. Verses of these would have answered to Herbert's listless condition at the time, by both their complaint and their reassurance:

> I am clean forgotten, as a dead man out of mind: I am become like a broken vessel.

My time is in thy hand.

And when I made haste, I said: I am cast out of the sight of thine eyes.
Nevertheless, thou heardest the voice of my prayer when I cried unto thee.

Although Herbert's installation to his canonry of Lincoln was by proxy, his induction at Leighton Bromswold in the same year (1626) had to be done in person.[25]

The geography of Leighton Bromswold is telling. It lies in the rolling, open agricultural country of Huntingdonshire. Six miles to the south was Williams's episcopal palace at Buckden. He had recently taken up residence there after the disappointment of his London court life by the accession of the antipathetic Charles I, and set about restoring its dilapidated buildings and gardens: characteristically making the best of things. The eupeptic poet Abraham Cowley, another Westminster and Trinity man, wrote of Williams that:

> You put ill-fortune in so good a dress
> That it out-shines other men's happiness.[26]

Another disappointed friend of Herbert's from Cambridge days, Nicholas Ferrar, had recently bought the Manor of Little Gidding, 5 miles to the north of Leighton Bromswold. The Virginia Company, in which he and his family were deeply and actively involved, had been wound up after many failures and turned into a royal colony in 1624. Ferrar resolved to retire with his extended family of some thirty in all to Little Gidding and lead a life of prayer, study and charity in Christian community there, like a little college. Things were in a sorry state, particularly the nearby chapel which had been used as a pigsty. Ferrar's energetic mother set about clearing it, while he himself was made deacon by Laud at Westminster Abbey on 26 February 1626 so that he could conduct services.

By the time of Herbert's installation at Leighton Bromswold the community at Little Gidding was settled. There is no record of the event, but it is hard to believe that Nicholas Ferrar would not have ridden the short distance down the lanes to Leighton Bromswold for Herbert's installation by their mutual friend Bishop Williams from nearby Buckden. The church at Leighton was another dilapidated structure. Whoever Herbert stayed with for the occasion, Ferrar or

Williams, could offer helpful experience of that kind of trouble and its remedies. The restoration of Leighton Church and its funding became a long-standing preoccupation and achievement of Herbert and Ferrar, to be completed only at the end of Herbert's life.

After the ceremony, Herbert left Leighton to the care of its vicar, Maurice Hughes, and returned to his brother Henry's house at Woodford in Essex. His health was poor and he needed looking after. Walton calls his illness 'a sharp quotidian [daily] ague'.[27] He put himself on a vegetarian diet, but that only brought on 'rheums, and other weaknesses, and a supposed consumption'. It was probably at Woodford that he translated *A Treatise of Temperance and Sobrietie* by Luigi (aka Alvise) Cornaro. Cornaro was a considerable and interesting patron of the arts and architecture in Padua, where his classical theatre and music room can still be seen. He was also a garrulously solipsistic octogenarian and dietician, who recommended scrupulous attention to weights and measures in the kitchen.[28] Herbert sent a copy to Nicholas Ferrar, who shared this interest.

Herbert had much to ponder at Woodford and his chosen way of pondering things was poetry. There are particular reasons for supposing that one of his strongest English poems 'The Cross' was written in the wake of his induction to Leighton Bromswold. It is plainly autobiographical, set at a time when he at last had an opportunity to settle in a place where he and 'all my wealth and family' might 'sing and serve thee' – only to be thwarted by illness.

The Cross

What is this strange and uncouth thing?
To make me sigh, and seek, and faint, and die,
Until I had some place, where I might sing,
        And serve thee: and not only I,
But all my wealth and family might combine
To set thy honour up, as our design.

And then when after much delay,
Much wrestling, many a combat, this dear end,
So much desir'd, is giv'n, to take away
        My pow'r to serve thee; to unbend

Herbert's Leighton, among the windmills on the left, with Nicholas Ferrar's Little Gidding among the other windmills at top left, and Bishop Williams's Buckden

(Bugden) to the south-east, by the enclosure; from
John Speed, The Theatre of the Empire of Great
Britain, 1611.

All my abilities, my designs confound,
And lay my threat'nings bleeding on the ground.

    One ague dwelleth in my bones,
Another in my soul (the memory
 What I would do for thee, if once my groans
    Could be allowed for harmony):
I am in all a weak disabled thing,
Save in the sight thereof, where strength doth sting.

    Besides, things sort not to my will,
Ev'n when my will doth study thy renown:
Thou turnest th' edge of all things on me still,
    Taking me up to throw me down:
So that, ev'n when my hopes seem to be sped,
I am to grief alive, to them as dead.

    To have my aim, and yet to be
Further from it than when I bent my bow;
To make my hopes my torture, and the fee
    Of all my woes another woe,
Is in the midst of delicates to need,
And ev'n in Paradise to be a weed.

    Ah my dear Father, ease my smart!
These contrarieties crush me: these cross actions
Do wind a rope about, and cut my heart:
    And yet since these thy contradictions
Are properly a cross felt by thy Son,
With but four words, my words, *Thy will be done.*

So what was 'this strange and uncouth thing' which confronts the reader so suddenly? The obvious answer is the title: it is the cross. The modern reader supposes that it refers to the cross of Christ. But that is the meaning which Herbert settles for only at the very end of the poem. Up to then it has the old meaning of a contradiction, the sort of thing in ordinary life which makes one, by elision, 'cross'. There is a further possible answer to the question so aggressively put in that first line. The church at Leighton (cruciform, as it happens and as

Walton reports: 'for the form an exact cross')[29] was certainly in an uncouth state. Some of its roof had fallen in and it had not been fit to accommodate common worship for years, during which time the vicar had held services in the manor house. The sight of it, for which Herbert was responsible as its prebend, was enough to make anyone 'sigh, and seek [think up plans], and faint, and die'. But then those first two despondent lines are followed by the hope that Herbert might have 'some place' in which he could worship and his 'wealth and family' could get together 'to set thy honour up as our design'. It is not a logical transition, but it does coincide with what was to happen to Leighton Church: Herbert and his family, particularly his mother and brother Henry, got together to raise the funds necessary to restore it. His aspiration that he and they might worship there, in a Little Gidding of their own to match the example of the Ferrar family near by, was not to be fulfilled. God confounds Herbert's hopes and plans, his 'threat'nings' as he calls them, and leaves them 'bleeding on the ground'. They are instantly frustrated by the illness in his bones and soul which he complains about in the third verse. The Father is still a torturer, but his Son is the reconciled and reconciling victim who, in the last verse, makes Herbert's crosses his own.

Along with the transformative use of 'cross' in this final verse there is a double use of the sentence '*Thy will be done*': by Christ to God in the agony of facing his divinely ordained death; by Christians in their daily prayer 'Our Father'. Christ accepted the cup of suffering in the garden of Gethsemane with the words '*thy will be done.*'[30] The Christian's familiar daily prayer goes 'Our Father, which art in heaven, hallowed be thy name, thy kingdom come, thy will be done.' This needs to be borne in mind when reading the last three, resolving lines of the poem. They are intricate and come suddenly after the agonizing metaphor of the heart bound and cut by ropes.

> And yet since these thy contradictions
> Are properly a cross felt by thy Son,
> With but four words, my words, *Thy will be done.*

Here is a resolution which does not reveal itself immediately. Being double, it takes two goes. The reader has to participate, if only as reader, in the poet's struggle.

A first reading of these three lines might well take Christ to be the speaker of those final 'four words' (a poet counts his words carefully). But that raises a difficulty: the whole sentence is incomplete. Since Christ felt his cross with the 'four words, my words, *Thy will be done*' . . . what? But read it again and one notices that the four words are uttered by the poet. They are 'my words', from that daily prayer 'Our Father which art in heaven . . . *thy will be done.*' Read like that, the sentence is complete: Herbert can say for himself 'Thy will be done' because Christ too feels God's 'contradictions' and gives him the words he needs to reconcile himself to them. Both readings matter. The reader goes through both. Herbert set the difficulty and solved it. The puzzling incompleteness of the first, faulty reading is resolved and completed by the second. What Christ said is appropriated by the poet, grammatically and dramatically. The divine victim and the afflicted poet are reconciled in words which themselves reconcile them both, Christ and poet, to one another and the pains inflicted on them by their terrible mutual Father. It could not be more complete. This is something warmer than bleak Stoic resignation. It is the warmth of participation and compassionate companionship which cannot abolish suffering but breaks up the terrible isolation of all the previous verses with a reciprocal presence.

When Herbert was inducted to Leighton Bromswold his mother was ill and had less than a year to live. She was worried about his health, particularly because she had heard that he intended to undertake the taxing work of rebuilding the church. So clearly the project was in his mind and known to his friends and family very soon after his induction. Walton tells us, in a passage so vividly actual as to suggest authenticity, that she:

> being informed of his intentions to rebuild that church, and apprehending the great trouble and charge that he was likely to draw upon himself, his relations, and friends, before it could be finished, sent for him from London to Chelsea (where she then dwelt), and at his coming said, 'George, I sent for you to commit simony [trading in ecclesiastical offices], by giving your patron [Williams] as good a gift as he has given you; namely, that you give him back his prebend; for, George, it is not for your weak body and empty purse to undertake to build churches.'[31]

Magdalen's characteristics of wit and maternal worry are evident. Herbert told her that he would think about it overnight and then asked her that 'she would, at the age of thirty three years, allow him to become an undutiful son; for he had made a vow to God that, if he were able, he would rebuild that church'. He had to remind her that he was old enough now to make up his own mind. The ailing old lady conceded, put herself down as a subscriber to the work and promised to solicit the Earl of Pembroke, as head of the Herbert family, to be another. The project was under way. But George was hardly ever there himself. The business of restoration was left to Nicholas Ferrar, Nicholas's brother John and the capable layman who was a mutual friend of them and Herbert, Arthur Woodnoth. Though anxiously possessive to the end, Magdalen knew her son well enough to realize that, for all his frail health, he needed things to occupy his mind.

Leighton Bromswold Church, Herbert's 'cross' by virtue of being both a cruciform building and the onerous burden of restoration which he had shouldered, still stands as he left it. Pevsner calls it 'a wonderful church, thanks to the Early English architects, and a highly interesting church, thanks to the patrons of the first half of the seventeenth century'.[32] Its interior furnishings show what Herbert thought a church should be. It is an uplifting place to go into: spacious and filled with light from its clear windows. 'The interior', says Pevsner, 'is one of large unbroken surfaces.' The overall impression is of luminous accessibility. The wooden furnishings, which Herbert and Ferrar got made in oak by a good country carpenter, are particularly revealing. The nave is divided from the chancel very minimally. There is no difference in floor level between them. The dividing screen is low, no more than chest high, and pierced by open, round-headed arches. The stalls in the chancel face one another from either side, college-wise. Their seats are long, simple benches. The desks in front of them, like the screen, are not solid but an open balustrade. They are surmounted by knobs, modestly ornamental but also useful to help the aged and infirm pull themselves to their feet. The stalls in the nave are of the same pattern but without the knobs and arranged in the usual way to face east. In particular they face two identical canopied pulpits on either side of the screen. This is an unusual feature and of particular interest. In fact, one of them is not a pulpit for preaching at all, but the place for reading the prayers which made up most of the service. Walton made a point of how, together, they embody Herbert's liturgical ideas.

> By his order the reading pew and the pulpit were a little distance from each other, and both of an equal height; for he would say, they should neither have a precedency or priority of the other; but that prayer and preaching, being equally useful [note the modestly pragmatic adjective], might agree like brethren, and have an equal honour and estimation.[33]

There was a quiet polemic to this deliberate arrangement. To the radical puritans of Herbert's day, preaching had no equal and they constructed elaborate pulpits, adorned with biblical texts, to match their conviction. By making a prayer desk of the same height and design as the pulpit, Herbert was declaring himself a moderate Anglican in the mould of John Williams, Leighton's diocesan bishop. Pulpits are the perches of power, whence preachers dominate their audiences. Prayer, by contrast, is an open and attentive submission in which all are equal and waiting. Equality is the keynote throughout at Leighton Church: not only of prayer and preaching but also the social equality of everyone on the same level and accessible to one another physically and visually – the furniture of reciprocity.

Externally, the great feature of the early seventeenth-century restoration of the church is the tower. It dominates the countryside for miles around, looks medieval from afar but from nearer to is dramatically classical. 'It exhibits no gothic yearnings,' says Pevsner, 'except that from a distance its general shape is traditional.' It bears the date 1634, a year after Herbert's death. It is held by plain clasping buttresses, its door and bell-openings are round arched and – the crowning classical touch – where the middle ages would have put finials at the top corners, there are obelisks with balls on top. The whole tower was the generous contribution of 'the most noble, religious, worthy good Duke of Lennox'.[34] This was James Stuart, cousin of James I. The magnificent portrait of him with his adoring hound by Van Dyck shows a thoughtful aristocrat with long curly hair, dressed in sober black, his stockings rumpled: a serious man. He had a widowed mother, the Dowager Duchess, and owned the manor house at Leighton Bromswold which abuts on the eastern edge of the churchyard. A stately gatehouse of 1616, still there, is all that was achieved of the Lennoxes' plans for a great mansion. Wealth, class and neighbourhood made them an obvious target for the raising of funds to restore the church. When, late in his life, George Herbert wrote to Nicholas Ferrar to thank him for taking charge of the practicalities of restoration he added an excited postscript.

> As I had written thus much, I received a letter from my brother, Sir Henry Herbert, of the blessed success that God had given us by moving the Duchess's heart to an exceeding cheerfulness in signing 100 pounds with her own hands (and promising to get her son to do as much) with some little apology that she had done nothing in it (as my brother writes) hitherto. She referred also to my brother to name at first what the sum should be, but he told her Grace that he would by no means do so, urging that charity must be free. She liked our book [probably of plans with a list of donors] well, and has given order to the tenants at Leighton to make payment of it. God Almighty prosper the work. Amen.[35]

These successful negotiations between Henry Herbert and the Duchess took place in London. Henry Herbert was master of the revels at the court and had much to do with the great architect of the age, Inigo Jones, who designed sets and costumes for the masques in the Banqueting House at Whitehall which Henry Herbert arranged. So it is even possible that Jones had a hand in the design of the tower at Leighton Bromswold, which bears the marks of the austere, classical clarity of his Queen's House at Greenwich. More than anything else that remains of George Herbert, his poetry apart, the church at Leighton Bromswold can make him a living presence to its visitors.

EMPLOYMENT AND UNEMPLOYMENT

Herbert's last performance as Orator of the University of Cambridge was on 13 July 1626 at York House in the Strand – a step away from his old home at Charing Cross. He had not gone to Lincoln, three weeks earlier, to be installed as prebendary of Leighton, but left it to a proxy. He may well have been ill. There are signs that he was more and more at Chelsea with his mother and stepfather. He was there the year before, along with John Donne, and it was there that he wrote a letter to his Deputy Orator Robert Creighton, Professor of Greek in the University. It is interesting in several ways.

He and Creighton were friends and contemporaries at Westminster School, so the letter is cordial. But it is in Latin and therefore official. Indeed, it is in effect Herbert's testament to his successor and the harbinger of his own resignation seven months later.

The letter is an interesting declaration of Herbert's stylistic preferences. He begins by admitting that 'for many years' he has been living and speaking in English, not the high-level Latin of the academy – though the clarity which he so insistently recommended to Creighton was also his watchword for his English poetry. He declares his own stylistic preferences with the authority of the expert. He advises Creighton to bear in mind that he should please the University rather than indulge his own inclinations. He should not be abjectly obsequious to the great, merely modest. An oration should be clear, lucid and transparent ('clara sit, perspicua, pellucens'): obscurity is inappropriate. Orations and letters, the two duties of an Orator, are different genres. Letters should be sparing of doctrine ('parce doctrina'). Herbert rehearses Quintilian's insistence on 'the good man skilled in speaking' ('oratio perfecta, uti vir'). The oratory should be like the man; four-square, serious, noble, perspicuous and succinct. It all makes Herbert feel like an old man. 'God!' ('Jupiter!'), he exclaims, 'how many years it is since I could carry off the highest Latin!' It had been four years in fact since his masterpiece on the return of Buckingham and Prince Charles in 1623. He ends with a quotation from Plato (*Republic* 328e) in Greek as a compliment to Creighton: 'I enjoy talking to old men, for they have gone before us, as it were, on a road that we too may have to tread, and it seems to me that we should find out from them what it is like.' He was feeling his age: only thirty-four, but for a man in poor health and without effective remedies, that was later middle age in his century.

Early in June 1627 his mother died at Chelsea. It was a heavy blow. He had been with her most of the time for the last three years and the bond between them was strong. Their mutual friend John Donne,

Dean of St Paul's, was unable to preach at her funeral because of engagements in the city. Instead he preached in commemoration of her at Chelsea Old Church on 1 July, dwelling on her 'loving face-tiousness and sharpness of wit', her 'holy cheerfulness and religious alacrity', the way she hustled her family to church 'with that cheerful provocation, *For God's sake let's go, for God's sake let's be there at the confession*.' She had been ill and depressed for some years. Donne related in his sermon that:

> for her, some sicknesses, in the declination of her years, had opened her to an overflowing of melancholy; not that she ever lay under that water, but yet, had sometimes, some high tides of it; and, though this distem-per would sometimes cast a cloud, and some half damps upon her natural cheerfulness, and sociableness, and sometimes induce dark, and sad apprehensions, nevertheless, who ever heard, or saw in her, any such effect of melancholy as to murmur, or repine.[36]

Within a month of her death her bereft son composed *Memoriae Matris Sacrum*: the set of nineteen elegies for her which were pub-lished along with Donne's Sermon of Commemoration for her in the same year (1627). Fourteen were in Latin, five in Greek. As a result, they are little read nowadays. But at the time the archaism was hon-orific, a fitting tribute to an aristocratic and learned lady from a son who was a master of classical languages. The eighteenth elegy refers to moonlight on the lapping waters of the Thames, a reference to Chelsea. The whole set was a major work, exerting all Herbert's skill to sort out his feelings about the absence of the most important source of human love and support in his life. His poetry was his chief resource for coping with life as 'a business, not good cheer': getting it down on paper, objectifying its miseries into words – Latin words at that – and patterns which gave its chaos form and its ugliness beauty.

Memoriae Matris Sacrum means 'sacred to a mother's memory'. Like his English poems, these elegies are varied in form and metre, intimate and graceful, often bursting with strong emotion. His moth-er's absence is as painful to him as God's. More than once he calls his mother 'severa', strict. The seventh of the poems starts as a nightmare in iambic pentameters. He imagines her as a bloodless, cloudy ghost, her breasts as clouds filled with air and rain, not milk, deceiving her open-mouthed child.

> Uberaque aerea hiscentem fallentia natum

The primal, physical need of a baby was there still – and wretchedly denied. But he finds comfort in fantasy: a country cottage with a little garden where he and she will be alone, feeding daily on herbs:

> Hic ego tuque erimus, variae suffitibus herbae
> Quotidie pasti.

Herbert is going back beyond the splendours of Chelsea and heaven to the primal idyll of mother and child. The second poem of the cycle is imbued with a more mature affection and a more objective love. He imagines her usual day. She rises to dress in a simple style: no elaborate hair-do, just a simple ribbon (a change from her effigy at Montgomery and the portrait at Weston Park, both from her younger days). She says her prayers devoutly, then sees to her household: the food for lunch, gardening and sewing. Sometimes a grandee from the country might turn up, ready to discuss hunting or cattle-rearing or whatever the occasion demanded. She was up to that. Then there was her writing, beautiful in form, even more beautiful in content, thoughts and their expression marvellously matched:

> Sententiae cum voce mire convenit.

She could not have done better – for her son or for generations of his readers. The very words and letters which he is inscribing on his paper are a debt to her care for his education:

> ... literae hoc debent tibi
> Queis me educasti.

And if that was not enough, her love of music and the poor were further graces of character which he admired and practised.

The fifth poem in the cycle is, by contrast, a sad meditation on transience and decay. Herbert calls on the gardens, which were the delight of their mistress, to wither. They have provided the flowers on her coffin which cannot stay fresh, but rather produce thorns of painful anxiety in the mind. Presumably, they were roses. And in the dying gardens, everything must go back to its roots and the earth which fathered it, or live only until evening when the hearse will shine with the drops of dew. The withered plants slowly shrink back into their roots and their native mounds or beds:

> Cuncta ad radices redeant, tumulosque paternos.

This was an image which Herbert used again in his English poetry. In the second verse of 'The Flower' it stands for the temporarily withdrawn heart:

> Who would have thought my shrivel'd heart
> Could have recover'd greenness? It was gone
> Quite under ground; as flowers depart
> To see their mother-root, when they have blown;
> Where they together
> All the hard weather,
> Dead to the world, keep house unknown.

An interesting change of gender has happened between the writing of the Latin poem and the later English one, which is not in the Williams Manuscript. In the Latin poem the flowers return to their roots in their *paternos* beds, which I translated as 'native'. It can mean that, but also 'ancestral' or 'paternal'. But in 'The Flower', the English poem, Herbert has 'their *mother*-root' (my italics) – a coinage of his own. Maternity has taken over, bringing with it a reassuring domesticity to modify the sadness. The reader's visual imagination may conjure up a vignette: a little cottage under snow, with a lighted window and a curl of smoke from the chimney indicating inward warmth. And now in 'The Flower' it is the 'mother-root'. For other poets, erotic love was usually the most interesting and identity-forming kind of human relationship. For Herbert it was the bond between mother and child.

Soon after his mother's death the crown granted the vacant manor of Ribbesford, by the River Severn in Worcestershire, to Edward and George Herbert and a cousin of theirs. Henry Herbert bought them out for 3,000 pounds, with the result that George was suddenly a man of means. The windfall gave him his independence. So he resigned from the Cambridge Oratorship, which Robert Creighton took up on 28 January 1628. But with his mother and his Cambridge duties gone, what was Herbert, so keen on being usefully employed, to do with his life? It was a long-standing problem, going back to the end of his Cambridge days when he wrote 'Affliction (1)', and he found no help with it from his books. It was not just a matter of having things to do but, more crucially and more profoundly, of what, or rather who, he should be. Around the same time he wrote two unhappy poems under the title 'Employment'.

The first of these is, as so often, an argument with the God who governs human lives, yet refuses or fails to impart to them the grace and happiness which is his to give. It would be to God's advantage as well as Herbert's if the divine disposer would arrange for the poet to have a satisfyingly productive life, such as he believed to prevail throughout the natural world, before he died and came up before God's 'great doom' or judgement. The poem becomes a prayer for this benefit. The last two lines turn from nature to music, Herbert's great love, and his longing to play in God's consort with his 'poor reed' or rustic pipe. The metre is a loose and lively iambic, good for pleading. The lines are varied between four beats (twice) and five, followed by a little two-beat line. It is set to be winning, a prayer which will get what it asks for by being pleasing. So it has the levity of a song, for all its complaining.

Employment (I)

If as a flower doth spread and die,
Thou wouldst extend me to some good,
Before I were by frost's extremity
Nipt in the bud;

The sweetness and the praise were thine;
But the extension and the room,
Which in the garland I should fill, were mine
In thy great doom.

For as thou dost impart thy grace,
The greater shall thy glory be.
The measure of our joys is in this place,
The stuff with thee.

Let me not languish then, and spend
A life as barren to thy praise,
As is the dust, to which that life doth tend,
But with delays.

All things are busy; only I
Neither bring honey with the bees,
Nor flowers to make that, nor the husbandry
To water these.

I am no link of thy great chain,
But all my company is a weed.
Lord place me in thy consort; give one strain
To my poor reed.

'Employment (II)' is a curious piece. It begins with a genial invitation to join in a lively session of witty chat, rather than hunkering down into one's fur-lined robes (the weather is, by implication, cold). The conversation turns out to be full of surprises which give it a listless, fidgety quality as thought hops from one topic to another like a flea. So we may imagine it going from one participant to the other, swapping proverbial saws verse by verse. The repartee darkens as it goes on. Man is a 'mortal fire', in need of tending; our earth is the lowest of the elements; life is a business, not a party; the stars have to bide their time; it would be good to be an orange tree, always in fruit. The last verse of all is an astonishing piece of bitter pessimism, unrelieved by any Christian comfort and worthy of Shakespeare at his most drastic.

Employment (II)

He that is weary, let him sit.
My soul would stir
And trade in courtesies and wit,
Quitting the fur
To cold complexions needing it.

Man is no star, but a quick coal
   Of mortal fire:
Who blows it not, nor doth control
   A faint desire,
Lets his own ashes choke his soul.

When th'elements did for place contest
   With him, whose will
Ordain'd the highest to be best;
   The earth sat still,
And by the others is oppressed.

Life is a business, not good cheer;
   Ever in wars.
The sun still shineth there or here,
   Whereas the stars
Watch an advantage to appear.

Oh that I were an Orange-tree,
   That busy plant!
Then should I ever laden be,
   And never want
Some fruit for him that dressed me.

But we are still too young or old;
   The Man is gone
Before we do our wares unfold:
   So we freeze on,
Until the grave increase our cold.

What began so cheerfully ends with a shudder of utter bleakness. It is never the right time. We are like market traders who lose a customer while they are busy laying out their wares. 'So we freeze on' – and will be colder still when we are dead. The poem is a measure of Herbert's bewilderment and depression.

His widowed stepfather, Sir John Danvers, kept a kindly eye on him. But life went on. A year after Magdalen's death Sir John married Elizabeth Dauntsey, her dowry being the estate of Lavington in Wiltshire. There he set about making gardens on an even more lavish and elaborate scale than at Chelsea. What was to become of his stepson George? With his own new property in Wiltshire in mind, Danvers turned to his elder brother Henry, who was living with their widowed mother at Dauntsey in the north of that county: according to Walton 'a noble house which stands in a choice air'. Walton reports that Henry Danvers 'loved Mr. Herbert so very much that he allowed him such an apartment in it as might best suit with his accommodation and liking'.[37] It was a handsome piece of family generosity and an excellent arrangement, enhanced by the company of Henry Danvers's aged mother, whom John Aubrey described as having 'prodigious parts for a woman. I have heard my father's mother say that she had Chaucer at her fingers' ends. A great politician, great wit and spirit, but revengeful: knew how to manage her estate as well as any man; understood jewels as well as any jeweller. Very beautiful, but only short-sighted.'[38] 'Politician' here means an astutely politic person, good at intrigue. When her son was away at his other house, Cornbury in Oxfordshire, she was more than capable of keeping Herbert the lodger entertained, not least with recitations from Chaucer: a model for Herbert's lucid and easy English style. The old lady was perhaps something of a substitute for Herbert's mother.

Dauntsey House, now with an elegantly plain Georgian façade, still stands quietly by the River Avon among pleasant pastures. It is cheek by jowl with the village church: an epitome of the structure of the English establishment and an ideal place for Herbert. His host was a great man. Henry Danvers was in his mid-fifties when Herbert came to live with him, an old bachelor and an old soldier. He had a black patch on his cheek where he had been shot in the face while serving in Ireland with the Earl of Essex in Queen Elizabeth's days. He could look back on an adventurous life, marked with numerous narrow escapes from death. In his youth he had served as page to Sir Philip Sidney and had been knighted for his valour at the siege of Rouen (1591–2). In his twenties he and his brother Charles, also a military man, had attacked a troublesome neighbour called Henry Long and shot him dead in the scuffle. The two brothers took refuge with Shakespeare's patron, the Earl of Southampton, and then fled to France to serve under Henri IV. There they were noticed by the Earl of Shrewsbury who interceded with Queen Elizabeth's right-hand man, Sir Robert Cecil, on their

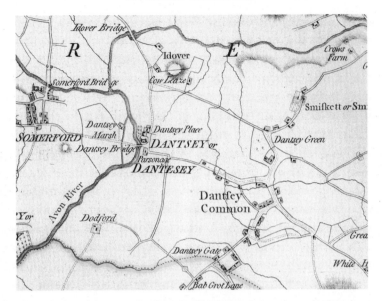

Dauntsey Place, where Herbert lodged with Henry Danvers, Earl of Danby in 1628, secluded among pastures by the River Avon, from Andrewes and Dury's map of Wiltshire, 1773.

behalf. He described them as 'two discreet fine gentlemen, who carry themselves here with great discretion, reputation and respect: God turn the eyes of her Majesty to incline unto them.' With the help of two ladies of the court, Sir Philip Sidney's widow (now Essex's wife) and their own politically astute mother (then married to a cousin of the Queen), they were pardoned in 1598 and came back to England. Their connections at court had served them well, but the Essex connection proved fatal for Charles Danvers, who joined in Essex's conspiracy and abortive rebellion in 1601 and was beheaded on Tower Hill. Henry kept clear of it and resumed his military career, serving in Ireland again and getting shot in the thigh. James I made him Baron Danvers of Dauntsey and keeper of St James's Palace, a short walk across the park from Herbert's Charing Cross home. In their younger days he had helped Charles, as prince of Wales, with his art collection, ensuring that paintings by Rubens were from the master's own hand and not studio productions. When Charles came to the throne he made Henry earl of Danby in 1626.

Now the old soldier could take up the arts of peace. He was the founder of the Botanic Garden at Oxford, modelled on the Jardin des Plantes in Paris which had been constructed during his last year of exile in France. The Oxford garden's magnificently rusticated gateway by Nicholas Stone, who had made statues for his brother's garden at Chelsea, still stands at the bottom of the High Street. Henry Danvers also shared the other great passion of George Herbert's circle: building and restoration. During Herbert's stay at Dauntsey, Henry was planning the restoration of the next-door church, the work being done soon after Herbert had moved on. In 1630 he erected a fine tower, which has very striking resemblances to the slightly later tower of 1634 at Herbert's Leighton Bromswold. It is medieval in shape but the finials on top of it are obelisk-like and crowned by balls. Like Leighton it has plain, clasping buttresses, but its windows are sparsely gothic and it has gargoyles. On its west face Danby's coat of arms is carved and set in an elaborately classical stone frame, surmounted by a broken pediment with a bearded male bust at its centre – more probably a depiction of Danby himself than of any allegorical personage. A tablet below records 1630 as the date when the building of the tower began. On the south face there is a sundial and on the north, looking over the gardens of the house, an elaborate clock. It is part of the whole stone fabric, supported by a winged cherub and surmounted by Old Father Time with his scythe. Altogether, it is more of a mixture than the tower at Leighton – a stage on the way to it, one could say. The same judicious blending of gothic with classical marks Henry Danvers's restoration of the woodwork inside. The screen, stalls and pews used as much as possible of what was there already and combined it with neo-medieval and classical work of his own devising. The screen is higher than that at Leighton and supports the medieval cornice on top of it; but, as at Leighton, classical balusters provide wide openings. The desks in front of the stalls are similarly open. This sort of renewal with respect for tradition was very much to Herbert's mind and taste, as is the plainness and openness.

The fine simplicity of Henry Danvers's tomb in the church is Herbertian in spirit too. It is a large sarcophagus made of the best white and dark-grey marble, unadorned except for the excellent carving of his name and heraldry. Its eastern face, difficult of access now because of the intrusion of the organ machinery, has this epigram carved into it:

> Sacred marble, safely keep
> His dust who under thee must sleep
> Until the graves again restore
> Their dead, and Time shall be no more:
> Meanwhile, if he (which all things wears)
> Do ruin thee; or if the tears
> Are shed for him, dissolve thy frame,
> Thou art requited; for his Fame,
> His Virtues, and his worth shall be
> Another Monument for Thee.
>
> G: Herbert:

Danby died in 1644, eleven years after Herbert, but people were often inclined to prescribe their epitaphs, and their monuments, before they died. Magdalen Herbert at Montgomery is a case in point. However, it is reasonable on grounds of quality to assign the poem to Herbert's apocrypha or 'doubtful poems'. The image of the monument worn out and ruined by time was used by Herbert in 'Church Monuments' to much greater effect. There the monuments themselves, though meant to be perpetual memorials of the human dust within,

> shall bow, and kneel, and fall down flat
> To kiss those heaps, which now they have in trust.

It only takes those two lines of genuine Herbert, particularly the graphic no-nonsense of 'fall down flat', to show up the dullness of the epitaph and its preposterous image of the hefty sarcophagus dissolved by the tears of the mourners. There is the 'signature' at the bottom, but that could very well be a sign of Herbert's fame in the years between his death and Henry Danvers's, during which at least six editions of *The Temple* were printed. The pseudo-'G: Herbert:' who wrote the poem knew of the real Herbert's association with Henry Danvers, and that his own effort would be enhanced by the attribution.

Dauntsey was comfortable for Herbert: his own apartment in the house and the church for his prayers and meditations. He had interesting company in old Elizabeth Danvers with her 'great wit and spirit' and her poetry learned by heart, and in Henry Danvers with his schemes for improving the church. There was ample time for writing. But was he useful?

In 1624, he had been in a hurry to be made a deacon, the first step in a Church career. He could have stopped there, as his friend Nicholas Ferrar had done. And a deacon Herbert remained while he was at Dauntsey four years later. But then Ferrar had found fulfilment in running his neo-monastic family at Little Gidding – not to mention the responsibility for the work at Leighton Bromswold which he and his brother John had undertaken on Herbert's behalf. Herbert felt bad about this later and, 'understanding that his prebend of Leighton lay within two miles [actually six] of Nicholas Ferrar, earnestly entreated him to accept of that prebendship, as most fitted for him, at so near a distance'.[39] Ferrar refused his offer, shrewdly realizing that Herbert's connections made him, as prebendary, a valuable fundraiser for the work.

The obvious answer to Herbert's dilemma was to progress from being a deacon to the priesthood. But this was something he could not contemplate lightly. The priesthood had awesome powers and duties. When the bishop made a man a priest he placed his hands on the man's head and uttered daunting words:

> Receive the Holy Ghost for the office and work of a Priest in the Church of God, now committed unto thee by the imposition of our hands. Whose sins thou dost forgive, they are forgiven; and whose sins thou dost retain, they are retained. And be thou a faithful dispenser of the Word of God, and of his Holy Sacraments; in the name of the Father, and of the Son, and of the Holy Ghost. Amen.

The middle sentence there is not a mere quotation of Jesus' words empowering his disciples after his resurrection.[40] It is a reactivating of them. A priest was given power to forgive and power to withhold forgiveness. In a thoroughly Christian society this meant nothing less than either restoring people who had transgressed its rules to that society or leaving them out in the cold. Further, a priest had two other important social duties. He was to be a 'faithful dispenser of the Word of God, and of his Holy Sacraments'. Dispensing the Word of God meant preaching – in seventeenth-century England the pre-eminent means of social communication by the exposition of God's truth in the Bible. There were two 'Holy Sacraments', both of them socially creative and determinative. Baptism admitted children into membership of the Christian society. Holy Communion sustained them in it, the priest feeding them with the consecrated bread and wine which were 'the spiritual food of the most precious body and blood of thy son our saviour Jesus Christ', making its recipients 'very members incorporate in the mystical body of thy Son, which is the blessed company of all faithful people'.[41]

The actualities and practicalities of the Anglican priesthood were more variable. The clergy, like the magistrates – and many men combined both roles – were deeply embedded in England's social fabric: sometimes all too much so. Some were given to drink, negligence and generally scandalous behaviour which brought the ministry into disrepute.[42] At the same time, it was possible in 1624 for Joseph Hall, the future Bishop of Norwich, to tell the Convocation of Clergy gathered in St Paul's Cathedral that 'stupor mundi clerus Britannicus', ' the clergy of Britain are the wonder of the world'.[43] Herbert's friend John Hacket asserted that 'in the long reign of Queen Elizabeth and King James, the clergy of the reformed Church of England grew the most learned in the world.'[44] The growth of the universities of Oxford and Cambridge brought this about so effectively that in London, for instance, three-quarters of the parish clergy were graduates. The clergy often took their profession so seriously as to meet together in voluntary groups and share their experiences and studies, an activity which Herbert was to call in his *Country Parson* 'good correspondence with all the neighbouring pastors'.[45] Men of great distinction, such as Hooker, Andrewes and Williams, graced the ministry. James I was keen that John Donne should be ordained, and so he was in 1615. Like Herbert, Donne had been disappointed in his hopes of secular advancement, but was still hesitant about becoming a priest. His reasons seem to have been social rather than intellectual. A friend of his called Tilman was ordained in 1619, having previously written a poem about his doubts, which were founded in a sense of his own unworthiness, passions and mutability. Donne wrote a counter-poem 'To Mr. Tilman after he had taken orders'.[46] It addressed his own misgivings about ordination more than Tilman's and these were repetitively social. He wrote of 'lay-scornings of the ministry':

> Why do they think unfit
> That gentry should join families with it?
> As if their day were only to be spent
> In dressing, mistressing and compliment.

He encouraged Tilman with:

> Let then the world thy calling disrespect,
> But go thou on, and pity their neglect.
> What function is so noble, as to be
> Ambassador to God and destiny?
> To open life, to give kingdoms to more
> Than kings give dignities; to keep heaven's door?
> Mary's prerogative was to bear Christ, so
> 'Tis preachers' to convey him, for they do
> As angels out of clouds, from pulpits speak;
> And bless the poor beneath, the lame, the weak.

Herbert, well above Donne in social class, could have felt Donne's 'scornings' and 'disrespect' with more justification. But his hesitations were more like Mr. Tilman's. He confronted the question very seriously and with searching integrity.

Using poetry to clear his mind as usual, he set it all out in his poem 'The Priesthood'. His temporary answer to the problem of whether to be priested was to wait and see. The mood changes from verse to verse as he worries away. In the first verse he is, as people said of him and as he had publicly been when he went all out for the Cambridge Oratorship, 'eager, hot, and undertaking':[47] 'fain would I draw nigh.' Then follows the argument which runs, or rather meanders, through the rest of the poem. Three of its verses begin with the word 'But' and one with the equivalent 'Yet'. Herbert's wandering musings are held together by the two contrasted metaphors announced at the beginning of the second verse: God is fire and he is 'but earth and clay'. At first this looks promising. Earth and fire together make pottery, such as the finely decorative blue-and-white Chinese wares of his own time, displayed on the tables of people 'who make the bravest shows'. But it is, on reflection, a dead end: 'feeder, dish and meat' are all of the earth earthy and perishable. Priests serve up God to people in Holy Communion.

Their hands convey him who conveys their hands.
O what pure things, most pure must those things be,
Who bring my God to me.

Abashed by holiness, Herbert is reminded of the terrifying biblical
story of the hapless Uzzah who, noticing that the Ark of the divine
presence was tottering while it was being carted about, put out his
hand to steady it and was promptly killed by God for his pains.[48]
Herbert will not make the same mistake, though the Church is shaky
with 'old sins and new doctrines'. At last the biblical parable of God
the potter[49] surfaces. Herbert handles it with sly wit. One day God
might feel like showing off his skill by working with particularly
unpromising material. He will wait for that moment, having observed
that 'the distance of the meek doth flatter power': a neat and shrewd
proverb, such as he loved, of his own invention.

The Priesthood

Blest Order, which in power dost so excel,
That with th' one hand thou liftest to the sky,
And with the other throwest down to hell
In thy just censures; fain would I draw nigh,
Fain put thee on, exchanging my lay-sword
      For that of th' holy Word.

But thou art fire, sacred and hallowed fire;
And I but earth and clay: should I presume
To wear thy habit, the severe attire
My slender compositions might consume.
I am both foul and brittle; much unfit
      To deal in holy Writ.

Yet have I often seen, by cunning hand
And force of fire, what curious things are made
Of wretched earth. Where once I scorned to stand,
That earth is fitted by the fire and trade
Of skilful artists, for the boards of those
      Who make the bravest shows.

But since those great ones, be they ne'er so great,
Come from the earth, from whence those vessels come;
So that at once both feeder, dish and meat
Have one beginning and one final sum:
I do not greatly wonder at the sight,
        If earth in earth delight.

But th' holy men of God such vessels are,
As serve him up, who all the world commands:
When God vouchsafeth to become our fare,
Their hands convey him, who conveys their hands.
O what pure things, most pure must those things be,
        Who bring my God to me!

Wherefore I dare not, I, put forth my hand
To hold the Ark, although it seem to shake
Through th' old sins and new doctrines of our land.
Only, since God doth often vessels make
Of lowly matter for high uses meet,
        I throw me at his feet.

There will I lie, until my Maker seek
For some mean stuff whereon to show his skill:
Then is my time. The distance of the meek
Doth flatter power. Lest good come short of ill
In praising might, the poor do by submission
        What pride by opposition.

Herbert was a shrewd and ironical observer of the human comedy. He had had frequent occasions to notice that keeping at a submissive distance from the great and good pleases them: and works as well as, if not better than, getting in close and confronting them. Applying this aperçu to the problem that has been bothering him throughout the poem is a happy sign that, for the time being, Herbert has mastered his anxieties and is back on form, treating anxiety with a light wit.

It was not long before he had a more substantial reason to be happy. The Danverses were a large and ramifying family. Henry Danvers had cousins a day's ride south of Dauntsey at Baynton Manor. It was situated on the northern edge of Salisbury Plain, very close to Lavington

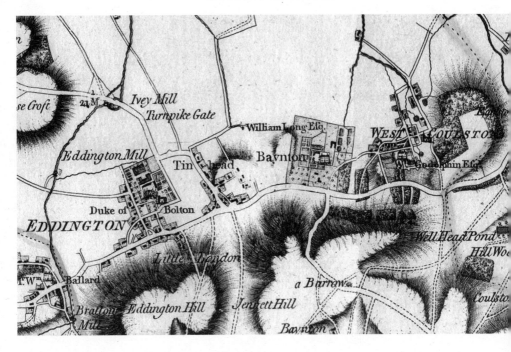

Baynton, from Andrewes and Dury's map of Wiltshire, 1773. Edington Church is in the middle of the village. Baynton, Jane Danvers's home is to the east (right). Going further east, Sir John Danvers's house and

where Herbert's remarried stepfather Sir John Danvers was busy on his new gardens. There in Baynton lived the family of Charles Danvers, who had died in 1626 leaving no fewer than fourteen children, including eight unmarried daughters and only one married. According to Walton, Charles Danvers had had a particular fondness for George Herbert.

> This Mr. Danvers, having known him long and familiarly, did so much affect him that he often and publicly declared a desire that Mr. Herbert would marry any of his nine daughters (for he had so many), but rather his daughter Jane than any other, because Jane was his beloved daughter: and he had often said the same to Mr. Herbert himself; and that if he could like her for a wife, and she him for a husband, Jane should have a double blessing; and Mr. Danvers had so often said the like to

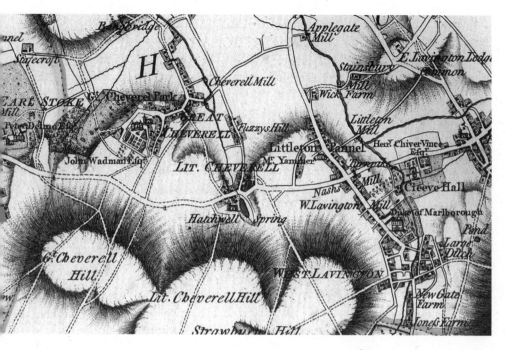

garden was situated in West Lavington, where 'Duke of Marlborough' (a later owner) is inscribed on the map. The steep ascent to Salisbury Plain runs along the south.

Jane, and so much commended Mr. Herbert to her, that Jane became so much a Platonic as to fall in love with Mr. Herbert unseen.

This was a fair preparation for a marriage; but alas, her father died before Mr. Herbert's retirement to Dauntsey; yet some friends of both parties procured their meeting; at which time a mutual affection entered into both their hearts, as a conqueror enters into a surprised city, and Love, having got such possession, governed, and made there such laws and resolutions as neither party was able to resist; insomuch that she changed her name to Herbert the third day after this interview.[50]

There follows a rapturous paragraph on the Herberts' concord and mutual love. However, that three-day courtship was impossible: the marriage was legally set up by an 'allegation', or declaration of intent, and a bond ten days before the wedding; and the banns would have been publicly called over the three preceding Sundays. Walton's calling Jane 'so much a Platonic as to fall in love with Mr. Herbert unseen' needs to be balanced against John Aubrey's view of her. He had excellent Wiltshire connections and was related to Jane and the other Danverses of Baynton. With a characteristic nod and a wink he wrote: 'His marriage, I suppose, hastened his death. My kinswoman was a handsome *bona roba* and ingenious.'[51] Aubrey's phrase '*bona roba*' is a surprise to Herbert's more pious devotees. Literally translated it is 'good stuff'. When Aubrey used the same phrase to describe the famous beauty Venetia Digby, 'a most beautiful and desirable creature', it summed up his description of her as having 'a perfectly healthy constitution; strong; good skin; well-proportioned; much inclining to a *Bona Roba* (near altogether)'.[52] Richard Lovelace's poem 'La Bella *Bona Roba*' of 1649 is purely and robustly physical:

> I cannot tell who loves the skeleton
> Of a poor marmoset, naught but bone, bone.
> Give me a nakedness with her clothes on:
>
> Such whose white satin upper coat of skin,
> Cut upon velvet rich incarnadine,
> Has yet a body, and of flesh, within.'[53]

The phrase comes up twice in Shakespeare's *Henry IV Part 2* (Act III, scene ii). When Justice Shallow recalls his days and nights as a lad at Clement's Inn he boasts that 'we knew where the *bona robas* were, and had the best of them all at commandment.' Jane Nightwork, in particular, came to his mind. 'She was then a *bona roba* . . . and had Robin Nightwork by old Nightwork before he came to Lincoln's Inn.' So Jane was not only 'handsome' and 'ingenious', meaning witty and generally talented and capable. She was something more: a woman of lively and alluring sexual charms. So Herbert was lucky in love. He had once declared 'I will not marry,'[54] and in *The Country Parson* still maintained 'that Virginity is a higher state than Matrimony',[55] but now he had found a wife who was clever, very good-looking, ten years younger than him and more robust in health.

Aubrey says that Herbert himself 'was a very fine complexion and consumptive', which matches Walton's more lyrical description: 'He was for his person of a stature inclining towards tallness; his body very straight, and so far from being cumbered with too much flesh that he was lean to an extremity. His aspect was cheerful, and his speech and motion did both declare him a gentleman.' Herbert's description of the ideal Christian physique and physiognomy in 'The Size' matches his own appearance.

> A Christian's state and case
> Is not a corpulent, but a thin and spare
> Yet active strength: whose long and bony face
> Content and care
> Do seem to equally divide,
> Like a pretender, not a bride.

Herbert the lean 'pretender', meaning suitor or wooer, looked very different from his bride Jane, the *bona roba*.

George Herbert and Jane Danvers were married in Baynton Manor's parish church of St Mary, St Katherine and All Saints at Edington on 5 March 1629. Edington Church gets Pevsner's admiration in his *Wiltshire*: 'A wonderful and highly important church. It is so varied in its skyline and so freely embattled that it looks like a fortified mansion, and the solemn lines of the downs rising immediately South are the perfect foil.'[56]

Seventeenth-century weddings were no less festive than nowadays: flowers, presents and dancing included. Shakespeare testifies to their being 'full of state and ancientry' (old customs).[57] With the Danverses' ramifying county connections there would have been plenty of guests, both in the church and at the party in Baynton Manor House (now vanished) afterwards. Henry Danvers from Dauntsey, with his black patch and his wounded leg, and his brother Sir John, Herbert's handsome stepfather with his new wife, would have been there – and all those brothers and sisters, not to mention cousins and uncles and aunts. The daunting altar rail at which the bride and groom knelt for the final prayers is still there: 'Jacobean, flat, openwork balusters alternating with normal turned ones', writes Pevsner, 'but the top as spiky as a stockade – a design not accommodating to communicants'. The floor on which it stands is of chequered marble, such as Herbert described in 'The Church-floor', allegorizing its black and white as

Humility and Patience. And it is situated at the same 'gentle rising' leading 'to the Choir above', which he allegorized as Confidence. Outside, in the lanes and fields around it was the time for daffodils, 'lent lilies' as they are called in the West Country. Although Herbert believed that it was a season for a certain 'sweet abstinence',[58] he and Jane were married in Lent.

8

Bemerton: Being a Country Parson

For the last three years of his life Herbert was rector of the two villages of Fugglestone and Bemerton in Wiltshire. They lie beside water meadows in the valley of the little River Nadder, whose stream flows down to Bemerton and Salisbury from the grounds of Wilton, the great mansion of the Herberts, earls of Pembroke. There in the 1580s the poet Mary Sidney, married to the second Earl, had held court and made it a centre of literary culture much frequented by her brother Sir Philip Sidney. In George Herbert's time it was occupied by her sons, 'the incomparable pair of brethren' to whom the First Folio of Shakespeare was dedicated: first William, who died just before George Herbert became rector of Bemerton, then Philip. The little church at Fugglestone, with its steep tiled roof surmounted by a polygonal bell turret, stands at the eastern edge of Wilton's grounds. From there the Nadder flows on to Bemerton. Herbert's rectory, an ample house of chequered stone and flint, has lawns going down to the river's edge on its southern side and the church, a simple and smaller building with a wooden bell turret, only a few paces away on its northern side with the road squeezed between. From Bemerton the Nadder flows on to Salisbury, past the mill at Fisherton where John Constable set his easel to paint Salisbury Cathedral beyond the water meadows, its spire rising into turbulent sky. From Wilton to Salisbury it is 3 miles, with Bemerton halfway between them: the family mansion at one end and the cathedral at the other.

It is all more built up now on the north of the Nadder, but to its south the landscape is unchanged. There are water meadows, a complicated irrigation system of channels, banks and sluices. Opening the sluices allowed the land to be fertilized by 'drowning' in winter. This suggested

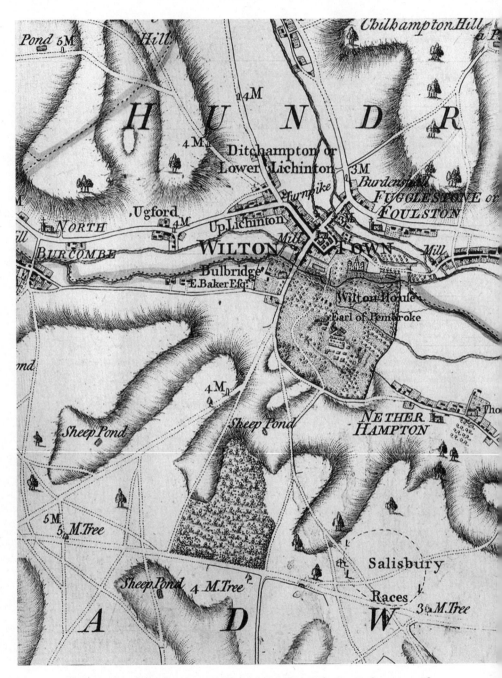

Wilton, Fugglestone, Bemerton and Salisbury, from Andrewes and Dury's map of Wiltshire, 1773.

20 M. to Devizes
Avon Br.
North Hill Farm
25 M
Old Sarum Castle
Stratford House
Thos. Pitt Esq.
Old Castle House
D
Stratford Mill
STRATFORD DEAN
Bishop Down Farm
Bishop Down Hill
1M
1 M. from Salisbury
26 M. to Marlborough
Mismass Hill
hampton
81M.
Direction Post
1M
SALISBURY
BEMERTON
Brickiln
Gallows Gate
The College
Henry Penr. Wyndham Esq.
Paper Mill
Turnpike
Green Croft
Milford Hill
Pleasure House
FISHERTON ANGER
Mill
es Esq.
Milford
Harnham Mill
St. Martins Ch.
WEST HARNHAM
The Cathedral
Muttons Bridge
Harnham Bridge
Parsonage
East Harnham
The New Canal
Harnham Hill
1 M. from the Council House in Salisbury
1 Mile Tree
Brilford Br.
Direction Post
R
1M
T
H
2 Mile Tree

a metaphor to Herbert: the streams of God's grace were diverted from the Jews to the Christian Church 'by the Apostles' sluice' for use in baptism.[1] The winter soaking of the meadows by the Nadder meant that there was rich grazing for sheep in the early spring. This resulted in further fertilization: as Herbert observed in 'Providence' (line 69): 'Sheep eat the grass and dung the ground for more.' Then the sheep were driven on to the chalk downs rising steeply beyond the meadows, and the grass, which they had manured, was allowed to grow into hay which, once harvested, left the meadows to be grazed by cattle in the summer. This was intensive farming requiring intensive labour to sustain it, all under the management of the earls of Pembroke. These meadows, with frequent traces of the old system still visible, remain.[2]

So do the main architectural features of Herbert's landscape. The Tudor east front of Wilton, which Herbert knew, is still there. Fugglestone Church with its low, tiled roof is approached along an avenue of yews. Bemerton Church and Rectory are still as they were, narrowly separated by the road, now metalled but then muddy, which goes on to Salisbury and the shining landmark of the cathedral spire.

The appointment of a rector for Bemerton with Fugglestone was usually in the hands of the earls of Pembroke. The living became vacant in December 1629 when its rector, Walter Curll, was enthroned as bishop of Bath and Wells. Curll was a pluralist who had held Bemerton, where he never lived, along with several other Wiltshire parishes, a Salisbury prebend and the bishopric of Rochester. He was also a chaplain to James I, whom he had pleased by preaching for peace in Europe when it was threatened in the early 1620s, and against puritan dissent in the Church. Because the King, Charles I, had appointed Curll to Bath and Wells, he was automatically entitled to appoint his successor at Bemerton. But this was no problem. William Herbert, Earl of Pembroke,[3] had a word in the King's ear and 'requested the King to bestow it on his kinsman, George Herbert; and the King said, "Most willingly to Mr. Herbert, if it be worth his acceptance." And the Earl as willingly and suddenly sent it to him without seeking.'[4]

Charles seems to have forgotten or forgiven, if he had been offended by it, Herbert's oration of 1623 – or else Walton is inventing. Bemerton, with its good-sized if neglected rectory and its situation between Wilton and Salisbury, was the ideal place for the newly married Herberts – and the solution to George's anxieties about living a useful life. Nevertheless, according to Walton, he had a nervous crisis over accepting the appointment and 'endured (as he would often say) such spiritual conflicts as none can think, but only those who have endured them'.[5] His worries about the priesthood, expressed earlier in the poem with that title, had resurfaced in the face of actuality. But after a month of delay he accepted. Nicholas Ferrar sent Arthur Woodnoth, a cousin of his and an able man of business (of whom more later), over to Baynton to collect Herbert and take him to Bemerton without further conscientious shilly-shallying.

Herbert's arrival at Bemerton is an occasion of uncontrollable excitement for Walton, who lays on a glamorous drama, a good deal of which is fiction. We need to remember that he wrote *The Life of Mr. George Herbert* in 1670, thirty-seven years after Herbert had died, when the monarchy and the Church of England were restored after the Commonwealth and Cromwell's rule. Like others at the time, Walton looked back to the old days before the war and the republic with pious nostalgia. They provided him with models for his own time – none more exemplary than Herbert.

According to Walton, when Herbert and Woodnoth arrived at Wilton, 'the King, the Earl, and the whole Court were there, or at Salisbury.' Herbert, Walton goes on, told them that he had not yet really made up his mind about Bemerton. He was taken aside by William Laud, then Bishop of London and rising in royal favour, and persuaded that his refusal would be a sin. At which point:

> a tailor was sent for to come speedily from Salisbury to Wilton to take measure, and make him canonical clothes against the next day; which the tailor did; and Mr. Herbert being so habited, went with his presentation to the learned Dr Davenant, who was then Bishop of Salisbury, and he gave him his institution immediately (for Mr. Herbert had been made a deacon some years before) and he was also the same day (which was April 26, 1630) inducted into the good and more pleasant than healthful parsonage of Bemerton.

The date is right and it is likely that, with Bemerton Rectory in a mess from being uninhabited for so long, Herbert and Woodnoth stayed at Wilton. But some of the people in Walton's tableau, particularly the

King and Laud, are highly unlikely. Aubrey testifies that 'King Charles
Ist did love Wilton above all places: and came thither every summer.'[6]
But this was spring and Wilton was in mourning for William Herbert,
who had died suddenly on 10 April.

Two days later more bad news came to Wilton. On 12 April William Herbert's brother Philip, successor to the house and the earldom,
lost his contest against Laud for the Chancellorship of Oxford University by only nine votes: 'too hard for my lord chamberlain' as a
contemporary wrote five days later.[7] It would have been particularly
galling for an aristocrat like Philip Herbert to be defeated by Laud, a
jumped-up son of a Reading cloth merchant whom the old King,
James I, had distrusted for his 'restless spirit'. This busy little parvenu
would not have been a probable or welcome guest at Wilton a fortnight after triumphing over its lord. Laud had given offence all round.
He was also on bad terms with John Davenant, Bishop of Salisbury,
whom he had hauled up before the Privy Council for preaching that
Lent to the court on the forbidden subject of predestination. Davenant was simply warned not to do it again. So Laud would have been
an embarrassing presence at Salisbury as well as at Wilton. More than
all that, he would have been awkward company and no congenial
adviser for Herbert, since he was the unrelenting enemy of Herbert's
friend and patron John Williams, Bishop of Lincoln. Walton inveigled
Laud into Herbert's induction because, when he writes about it, Laud
was an Anglican martyr: impeached by Parliament, imprisoned in the
Tower of London for four years and beheaded on Tower Hill on
10 January 1645. Bridging back over the intervening years of the puritan Commonwealth, Walton contrived a grand tableau in which
Laud, one saint (and martyr) of the old order, attending upon the
royal martyr Charles I, brings about the institution of another Anglican saint, Herbert. It made gratifying reading for Anglicans of the
restored monarchy and Church in 1670, but does not stand up to
scrutiny.

Herbert's arrival at Bemerton, whatever actually happened then
and there, was a less dramatic and grandly attended occasion than
Walton depicts. There remains the speedy tailor. It seems grudging to
be suspicious about him, but also unlikely that the dress-conscious
Herbert would have allowed himself, still less would have been

allowed by his wife and Woodnoth, to set out for Bemerton without the necessary outfit.

Walton provides a touching and less far-fetched anecdote about Herbert's induction. The ceremony included the new incumbent being shut into the church alone to ring the bell as an announcement to the parishioners that he was there and ready for worship. The people waiting outside could then enter. Walton relates that:

> He stayed so much longer than an ordinary time before he returned to those friends that had stayed expecting him at the church door, that his friend Mr. Woodnoth looked in at the church window, and saw him lie prostrate on the ground before the altar; at which time (as he after told Mr. Woodnoth) he set some rules to himself for the future manage of his life, and then and there made a vow to labour to keep them.[8]

Certainly his friends would have been due an explanation for being kept hanging about in the churchyard. Realism, however, is not a guarantee of truth. Walton knew *The Temple*, which had been through nine editions when he wrote, and quotes from it. There he could read 'The Priesthood' in which Herbert contemplated that dignity with much misgiving:

> Only, since God doth often vessels make
> Of lowly matter for high uses meet,
>   I throw me at his feet.
>
> There will I lie, until my Maker seek
> For some mean stuff whereon to show his skill:
> Then is my time.

What Woodnoth saw when he looked through the window could have been Herbert actualizing his own poem. Equally, Walton could have used the poem as a source for his, or Woodnoth's, anecdote. It is impossible to know. And perhaps it is not necessary to do so. Life and poetry mix together with Herbert. *The Temple* is where we know him best, and the anecdote is best read as an illustrative vignette for it.

That night, according to Walton, Herbert had a long talk with Woodnoth. Walton relates it as an uninterrupted speech by Herbert: the spoken counterpart to his dramatic tableau at Wilton. Fabricated speeches by the protagonist were a stock in trade of classical and renaissance biography. Walton's is a collage of reminiscences of Herbert's poetry along with a quotation from the Book of Common Prayer, to which he and Herbert were devoted. Indeed, Walton virtually acknowledges as much by following the speech with a paragraph in which he discusses the two poems that he has used in composing it: 'The Pearl' and 'The Odour'. As with the incident of Herbert prostrate before the altar, Herbert's speech to Woodnoth is a combination of Woodnoth's reminiscence with Herbert's poetry, and quotation of the Book of Common Prayer added to the mixture. We are left to unscramble it. The speech is serene and begins with:

> I now look back upon my aspiring thoughts, and think myself more happy than if I had attained what then I so ambitiously thirsted for; and I can now behold the Court with an impartial eye, and see plainly that it is made up of fraud, and titles, and flattery, and many other such empty, imaginary, painted pleasures – pleasures that are so empty as not to satisfy when they are enjoyed. But in God and his service is a fullness of all joy and pleasure, and no satiety.

This passage chimes so well with Herbert's 'The Pearl' as probably to be derived from the poem.

The Pearl. Matt. 13.45.

> I know the ways of Learning; both the head
> And pipes that feed the press, and make it run;
> What reason hath from nature borrowed,
> Or of itself, like a good housewife, spun
> In laws and policy; what the stars conspire,
> What willing nature speaks, what forc'd by fire;
> Both th' old discoveries, and the new-found seas,
> The stock and surplus, cause and history:
> All these stand open, or I have the keys:
>   Yet I love thee.
>
> I know the ways of Honour, what maintains
> The quick returns of courtesy and wit;
> In vies of favours whether party gains,

When glory swells the heart, and mouldeth it
To all expressions both of hand and eye,
Which on the world a true-love-knot may tie,
And bear the bundle, wheresoe'r it goes:
How many drams of spirit there must be
To sell my life unto my friends or foes:
                    Yet I love thee.

I know the ways of Pleasure, the sweet strains
The lullings and the relishes of it:
The propositions of hot blood and brains;
What mirth and music mean; what love and wit
Have done these twenty hundred years, and more;
I know the projects of unbridled store:
My stuff is flesh, not brass; my senses live,
And grumble oft, that they have more in me
Than he that curbs them, being but one to five:
                    Yet I love thee.

I know all these, and have them in my hand:
Therefore not sealed, but with open eyes
I fly to thee, and fully understand
Both the main sale, and the commodities;
And at what rate and price I have thy love;
With all the circumstances that may move:
Yet through these labyrinths, not my grovelling wit,
But thy silk twist let down from heav'n to me,
Did both conduct and teach me, how by it
                    To climb to thee.

The title refers to Christ's little parable in St Matthew's Gospel of 'a merchant man seeking goodly pearls: who, when he had found one pearl of great price, went and sold all that he had, and bought it'.[9] The poem is a good deal longer than the parable because Herbert expands its terse 'all that he had' into detailed lists of the good things exchanged for the pearl. They are arranged, verse by verse, under the categories of learning, honour and pleasure – all dear to Herbert's heart. Affection for the fine things that have been traded in for the pearl glows through each verse's rich inventory and keeps it buoyantly afloat: in the first, education and learning in its wide Baconian scope; in the second, just a touch more satirically, the stratagems of the court; in the third pleasure of the senses, not least his beloved music. By giving them so much space and describing them so vividly, Herbert first changes the distribution of weight in the parable, then restores it all the more dramatically with 'Yet I love thee' (love is the pearl) at the end of the first three verses and 'To climb to thee' at the end of the last. This last verse recapitulates what has gone before in appropriately mercantile terms. It beautifully combines a couple of classical and biblical stories: Ariadne's thread which guided Theseus through the labyrinth and Jacob's ladder joining heaven to earth in Genesis 28.

Walton goes on to have Herbert resolve to 'live well, because the virtuous life of a clergyman is the most powerful eloquence to persuade all that see it to reverence and love': a point insisted upon in 'The Windows' where the divine light must shine though the preacher's life and not just his words:

> Doctrine and life, colours and light, in one
> When they combine and mingle, bring
> A strong regard and awe: but speech alone
> Doth vanish like a flaring thing,
> And in the ear, not conscience ring.

The collect, or seasonal prayer, for Easter Day in the Book of Common Prayer has at its centre 'we humbly beseech thee, that, as by thy special grace preventing [going before] us thou dost put into our minds good desires, so by thy continual help we may bring the same to good effect.' It is quoted in Herbert's/Walton's speech: 'And I beseech that God, who hath honoured me so much as to call me to serve him at his altar, that as by his special grace he hath put into my heart these good desires and resolutions; so he will, by his assisting grace, give me ghostly strength to bring the same to good effect.' The speech concludes with:

And I beseech him that my humble and charitable life may so win upon others as to bring glory to my Jesus, whom I have this day taken to be my Master and Governor; and I am so proud of his service, that I will always observe, and obey, and do his will, and always call him Jesus, my Master; and I will always contemn my birth, or any title or dignity that can be conferred upon me, when I shall compare them with my title of being a priest, and serving at the altar of Jesus my Master.

Here Walton is drawing on 'The Printers to the Reader', the preface to *The Temple* by Herbert's friend Nicholas Ferrar which was included in its first edition of 1633 and all subsequent editions: 'he used in his ordinary speech, when he made mention of our Lord and Saviour Jesus Christ, to add, *My Master*.'

Herbert's choice of the word 'master' for his saviour was obviously a striking usage to Ferrar and Walton. It was characteristically everyday and pragmatic – not just honorific. There were masters everywhere. They taught apprentices their trade and schoolboys their lessons. They were in charge of ships, colleges, departments of state and hospitals. In having Herbert's speech to Woodnoth close with it, Walton is further referring to the poem entitled 'The Odour'. In it Herbert made 'master' the word to run through the whole composition, savouring and investigating its connotations as he went.

The Odour. 2. Cor. 2.15

How sweetly doth *My Master* sound! *My Master!*
As amber-grease leaves a rich scent
Unto the taster:
So do these words a sweet content,
An oriental fragrancy, *My Master*.

With these all day I do perfume my mind,
My mind ev'n thrust into them both;
That I might find
What cordials make this curious broth,
This broth of smells, that feeds and fats my mind.

My Master, shall I speak? O that to thee
My servant were a little so,
As flesh may be;
That these two words might creep and grow
To some degree of spiciness to thee!

Then should the Pomander, which was before
A speaking sweet, mend by reflection,
And tell me more;
For pardon of my imperfection
Would warm and work it sweeter than before.

For when *My Master*, which alone is sweet,
And ev'n in my unworthiness pleasing,
Shall call and meet,
My servant, as thee not displeasing,
That call is but the breathing of the sweet.

This breathing would with gains by sweet'ning me
(As sweet things traffic when they meet)
Return to thee.
And so this new commerce and sweet
Should all my life employ and busy me.

Walton says that Herbert 'seems to rejoice in the thoughts of that word, Jesus, and say that the adding these words, my Master, to it, and the often repetition of them, seemed to perfume his mind and leave an oriental fragrancy in the very breath'.[10] It is just as well that Walton rarely attempts literary criticism. 'Oriental fragrancy' is an accurate quotation from the poem. But 'that word, Jesus' is entirely and deliberately absent from it. 'My Master' is not added to it, but dominates on its own. Most of all, 'thoughts' are not at issue but feelings – and physically sensuous ones at that.

The title 'The Odour' makes that point at the outset. It refers to several biblical texts about good smells. In St Paul's Second Epistle to the Corinthians the apostle writes, 'Now thanks be unto God, which always causeth us to triumph in Christ, and maketh manifest the savour of his knowledge by us in every place. For we are unto God a sweet savour of Christ . . . the savour of life unto life.' And in his Epistle to the Ephesians (5:2) he exhorts his readers to 'walk in love, as Christ also hath loved us, and hath given himself for us an offering and a sacrifice to God for a sweet-smelling savour'. The third verse of the biblical love-song, *The Song of Songs,* begins: 'Because of the savour of thy good ointments thy name is as ointments poured forth.' So there was plenty of canonical precedent and the flagrant sensual pleasure of the poem is not in the least illicit or untoward. Its combination with religious propriety is very much Herbert – and a legacy to his admirer, the poet Richard Crashaw. The phrase '*My Master*' occurs five times. Herbert loves its sound: the deliciousness of its mumbled 'm' opening into the long 'a', followed by the dental crush of 'ster'. It is like biting into a peach. Also in italics, but with no capital letter, is '*servant*': the last four verses are about the poet's aspiration ('breathing') that he might himself be a pleasing fragrance for Christ to enjoy, a pomander for him to sniff happily when warmed by forgiveness. Ambergris (Herbert's 'amber-grease') is 'a wax-like substance of ashy colour, found floating in tropical seas, and as a morbid secretion in the intestines of the sperm-whale. Used in perfumery, and formerly in cookery'.[11] The five senses, touch, taste, hearing, smell and sight, were a popular theme in seventeenth-century art and literature. In the first verse Herbert manages to include all of them except sight, arguably the most refined, and makes much of smell, arguably the basest.

Mystical and sensuous throughout, the poem uses the word 'sweet' – that favourite word of Herbert's which holds sense and grace together – no fewer than five times. The verses contract then expand. They breathe: inhalation in the first two lines, down to a holding of the breath in a two-foot-line pause, then exhalation in the last two lines. Its happiness is in the achievement of the reciprocity between himself and God which was Herbert's life's aim and fulfilment.

Walton has Herbert make another such speech to his wife when he and Woodnoth returned to Baynton three days later, telling her that, as 'a minister's wife', she had 'no precedence or place but that which she purchases by her own humility'. Walton assures the reader, implausibly, that Jane took this talking-to cheerfully. Indeed, this coy little anecdote looks like another of his saccharine inventions.[12]

There was a good deal to do at Bemerton before the Herberts could settle there. According to Walton, Herbert had to 'to rebuild almost three parts of his house, which was fallen down or decayed by reason of his predecessor's living at a better parsonage ... sixteen or twenty miles away'.[13] In view of the time it took to put things to rights – probably some six months – this looks like an exaggeration. But

Aubrey corroborates: 'The old house was very ruinous. Here he built a very handsome house for the Minister, of brick, and made a good garden and walks.' This is not right either. The rectory at Bemerton still stands and predates Herbert. It is handsome, but constructed of flint and stone in chequerwork, not brick. Herbert did not build it himself, but repaired it, and this was all done within the year. Walton records an inscription, since vanished, 'on the mantel of the chimney in the hall': a jingle by Herbert, closing with a reference to Shakespeare's play, to mark the completion of the work.

To My Successor

> If thou chance for to find
> A new house to thy mind,
>   And built without cost;
> Be good to the poor
> As God gives thee store,
>   And then my labour's not lost.

The rectory is only six paces, door to door, from the church, which is a very simple affair with no aisles and only six or seven paces wide. The chancel, where Herbert is buried 'under no large, nor yet very good, marble grave-stone, without any Inscription' (Aubrey – it has not survived), has a cornice of rustic medieval woodwork. In the west window underneath its little bell tower, good stained glass depicting Ferrar and Herbert has recently been inserted.

HERBERT AS PASTOR

The Herberts were settled at Bemerton six months or so after George Herbert's induction, perhaps with restoration work still going on. Arthur Woodnoth stayed with them in the autumn next year. His letter to Nicholas Ferrar about his visit survives.[14] He was, as we shall see, a neurotic, forever worrying about whether he should be a clergyman or remain a layman, get married or remain a bachelor. When he can bring himself to forget his self-concern for a while, he gives glimpses of Herbert's life at Bemerton. He accompanied Herbert to nearby Wilton and 'whilst he was with the Countess I obtained an hour's loneliness in which I endeavoured a more serious [!] consideration of all things.'[15]

Herbert had firm views about the conduct of clergy in 'Noble Houses'. He had chaplains particularly in mind when he wrote about it in the second chapter of *The Country Parson*. Herbert was not the Pembrokes' chaplain, but the sort of behaviour that he recommends has a wider application, including to himself as an ordained relative.

> After a man is once Minister, he cannot agree to come into any house, where he shall not exercise what he is, unless he forsake his plough, and look back.[16] Wherefore they are not to be over-submissive, and base, but to keep up with the Lord and Lady of the house, and to preserve a boldness with them and all, even so far as reproof to their very face, when occasion calls, but seasonally and discreetly.

The Lord and Lady of Wilton, a magnificent Tudor edifice with a household of 120 people, were a constant part of Herbert's life at Bemerton. As we have seen, William Herbert, Earl of Pembroke, died only a few days before Herbert's induction, which he had arranged. His brother Philip succeeded him. Aubrey describes Philip as a 'gallant and handsome' man who:

> did not delight in books, or poetry: but exceedingly loved painting and building, in which he had singular judgement, and had the best collection of any peer in England, and was the patron to Sir Anthony van Dyck: and had most of his painting. His Lordship's chief delight was in hunting and hawking, both which he had to the greatest perfection of any peer in the realm.[17]

His magnificent classical building at Wilton was completed after George Herbert's time, during which Philip Herbert was engaged on the garden: 'the third garden of the Italian mode' after Sir John Danvers's at Chelsea and Lavington.

Van Dyck's vast 1634–5 group-portrait of Philip and his family still dominates Wilton's magnificent Double Cube room. The Earl sits among his resplendent progeny, Lord Chamberlain's wand of office in hand, and points towards Mary Villiers, orphan of the Duke of Buckingham and bride of Philip's son Charles. She is dressed in shining white

Wilton House, the seat of the senior Herberts, Earls of Pembroke, from Survey of Lands for the first Earl of Pembroke, *1566.*

silk set spectacularly against the red silk worn by her elegant husband. What Philip does not do is to pay the least attention to his wife, who is sitting beside him, her hands folded in her lap, gazing miserably at the viewer. Van Dyck's painting of her is thinner and noticeably less brave than in the rest of the picture. This is Anne Clifford, the Countess and object of George Herbert's visit with Woodnoth.

She was Philip's second wife: little, pretty and strong-willed. None of the young people standing around are her children, but rather Philip's by his first wife along with two of their spouses. Her own marriage to Philip was childless and acrimonious, ending in bitter separation. She had a lot to be unhappy about. Her husband before Philip was the Earl of Dorset, with whom she had lived in uneasy splendour at Knole in Kent. He was profligate and unfaithful. She had a tremendous row with him about her money and estates, a constant preoccupation of hers, followed by a period of depression. Dorset died in 1624. She married Philip in 1630, the year of Herbert's arrival at Bemerton. Her life at Wilton proved to be no better than her life at Knole. 'The marble pillars of Knole and Wilton', she wrote in her diary, 'were to me oftentimes but the gay arbours of Anguish.'[18] Unlike her second husband she was a great reader, particularly of poetry, and an intellectual: according to John Donne 'she knew well how to discourse of all things, from predestination to slea-silk [fine sleave-silk, used in embroidery].'[19] Like her neighbour George Herbert, she was a good lutanist, learned but not a puritan, devoted to the Book of Common Prayer and the restoration of churches, and no stranger to sorrow: as a 'dejected poor soul' such as Herbert hoped would be comforted by his poetry, she may well have benefited from reading some of his poems, given to her by him in manuscript. She was certainly lucky to have such a congenial and solicitous kinsman near by. Herbert's hour with her while Woodnoth was sunk in his solipsistic 'serious considerations' could have been spent counselling her, or on the many things they had in common.

Walton printed a letter which Herbert wrote to the Countess in the 1675 edition of his *Life*. It is a thank-you for a present of metheglin, a spiced or medicated kind of mead sent to thank Herbert for his services to her. This was a Welsh speciality, a nice reference to their mutual ancestry. His letter is courtly and at the same time comforting, conveying 'a Priest's blessing, [which] though it be none of the Court-style . . . can do you no hurt'. There is ironical self-consciousness and class-consciousness, as well as a touch of scepticism in that artfully contrived sentence. Herbert refers to Anne's mother, her mentor and exemplar who had died in 1616 but whose memory was a comfort to her daughter in her marital troubles. So evidently there had been a recent counselling session at Wilton. With a witty twist in a postscript, Herbert refers to his family at Bemerton as Anne's 'colony': the Pembrokes had participated in the Virginia Company along with so many of George Herbert's family and friends.

Madam,

What a trouble hath your goodness brought on you, by admitting our poor services? Now they creep in a vessel of *metheglin*, and still they will be presenting or wishing to see, if at length they may find out some thing not unworthy of those hands at which they aim. In the mean time a Priest's blessing, though it be none of the Court-style, yet doubtless Madam, can do you no hurt: wherefore the Lord make good the blessing of your mother upon you, and cause all her wishes, diligence, prayers and tears, to bud, blow and bear fruit in your soul, to his glory, your own good, and the great joy of

Madam,
Your most faithful Servant
In Christ Jesu,
George Herbert.

Dec. 10. 1631
    Bemerton.

Madam, Your poor
colony of servants
present their hum-
ble duties.

Once rid of her two husbands (she broke up with Philip in the late 1640s) Anne lived a good and busy life on her North Country estate, much occupied with restoring its churches, before dying at the age of eighty-six.

Herbert's dealings with the Countess are matched, at the other end of the social scale, by an anecdote of Walton's, telling of an encounter with 'a poor old woman'. The woman started to tell her rector about her problems but 'was surprised with a fear, and that begot a shortness of breath, so that her spirits and speech failed her'. Herbert took her hand, called her 'mother', calmed her down and promised to see to her needs.[20]

Woodnoth's letter to Nicholas Ferrar, describing his visit to Wilton with Herbert, affords glimpses of life at Bemerton Rectory. They include Herbert's reading, Jane Herbert's pharmacy and the strong links with Little Gidding. Herbert was reading *The Simplicity of the Christian Religion* by the radical Florentine reformer Savonarola ('he saith he doth understand Italian a little') and recommended it to Woodnoth. Woodnoth in turn brought him a biblical concordance compiled in the writing room at Little Gidding: a welcome present, facilitating Herbert's fondness for hopping from verse to verse of his Bible. Potions were a domestic concern. Jane Herbert asked Woodnoth to get Ferrar to send her 'the receipt [recipe] of the balsam and any other, it would be very acceptable (the Oil of Elder she has)'. She would also like to have one of the Little Gidding Story Books: tales of the saints with moral advice to the reader. Clearly Jane was doing all she could to be the good parson's wife.

The man who conducted Herbert to Bemerton, peeped through the church window to see him lying on the ground before the altar, and later accompanied him on a visit to Wilton, stretched Herbert's pastoral patience and skill to the uttermost. Arthur Woodnoth was good at the practicalities, but he was a worrier and more or less forced Herbert to give him the spiritual advice for which he was insatiably greedy.

Woodnoth, a source for Walton's *Life* of Herbert, was the nephew of old Mrs. Ferrar, Nicholas Ferrar's mother and the energetic matriarch of the community at Little Gidding. He was a goldsmith and banker in London, who had worked with Herbert's stepfather, Sir John Danvers, on the affairs of the Virginia Company until the King took it over. After that, he helped Sir John with the management of his money and estates. They now included Lavington near Baynton, which had come to him with his second marriage. Sir John was spending away on the gardens at Lavington as freely as he had done at Chelsea when he had married Herbert's mother.

Able businessman as he was, Woodnoth was ill at ease with his profession and worried about how to keep strictly to honest bargaining. A very pious man, he was extremely fond of his relations at Little Gidding and went there often. The combination of young women and piety was a magnet. He was forever tormenting himself and other people by worrying about becoming a clergyman. Those whom he consulted about this problem generally and reasonably thought that he was better and more useful as a layman. George Herbert came in for some of these agonized conversations. As an answer to Woodnoth's anxieties he wrote a poem for him entitled 'The Bunch of Grapes'. It refers to the sign that stood over Woodnoth's London goldsmith's business in Foster Lane in the City of London. The poem's content, as well as its title, show that it is addressed to Woodnoth's concerns about the course and aim of his life. Herbert had had the same problem and knew for himself that plans to live 'in a straight line'[21] are soon diverted and swerved out of course by inner thoughts as much as outward events. But that, Herbert's poem insists, is just what reading the Bible should lead you to expect.

Before it thickens with the biblical references which will be elucidated, the poem begins suddenly in the everyday present with splendid attack. Where has joy gone? Joy is, metaphorically, one of the farmer's animals which he had carefully locked up in its stall, only for it to be let out by 'some bad man': the usual suspect when we have lost something.

The Bunch of Grapes

Joy, I did lock thee up: but some bad man
   Hath let thee out again:
And now, me thinks, I am where I began
   Sev'n years ago: one vogue and vein,
   One air of thoughts usurps my brain.
I did towards Canaan draw; but now I am
Brought back to the Red Sea, the sea of shame.

For as the Jews of old by God's command
   Travell'd and saw no town;
So now each Christian hath his journeys spann'd:

> Their story pens and sets us down.
>   A single deed is small renown.
> God's works are wide, and let in future times;
> His ancient justice overflows our crimes.
>
> Then have we too our guardian fires and clouds;
>   Our Scripture-dew drops fast:
> We have our sands and serpents, tents and shrouds;
>   Alas! our murmurings come not last.
>   But where's the cluster? Where's the taste
> Of mine inheritance? Lord, if I must borrow,
> Let me take up their joy, as well as sorrow.
>
> But can he want the grape, who hath the wine?
>   I have their fruit and more.
> Blessed be God, who prosper'd *Noah's* vine,
>   And made it bring forth grapes good store.
>   But much more I must him adore,
> Who of the Law's sour juice sweet wine did make,
> Ev'n God himself being pressed for my sake.

Precisely because the Bible takes the lead in the poem, a good deal of explanation is required for readers not as thoroughly soaked in the Bible as Herbert and Woodnoth were. The basic presupposition is that the Hebrew Old Testament is a prophetic template for the Christian New Testament, and so for Christian life at large. Herbert believed this traditional view of the Bible strongly. In his poem 'The Holy Scriptures (II)' he rejoices in skipping from verse to verse of his Bible because, put together, they 'make up some Christian's destiny'.

> Thy words do find me out, and parallels bring
> And in another [that is, a story other than my own] make me understood.

The same conviction structures 'The Bunch of Grapes'. Life is a journey, the Bible its travel guide: particularly its long account of the wanderings of the Jews between their Exodus from Egypt until their arrival at the border of Canaan, their Promised Land. Before they eventually got there they had to go back to the start and then on again. The third verse is packed with references to incidents on the way: 'fires and clouds' God's protection of the Jews in Numbers 14:14; 'dews' Numbers 11:4–9 where dew accompanies the mysterious but delicious 'manna' sent down by God when the Jews were hungry; 'sands' the wilderness generally; 'serpents' sent by God to punish the rebellious Jews in Numbers 21 and I Corinthians 10:9; 'tents' Numbers 16:26–7; 'shrouds' with which Moses veiled his face in God's dazzling presence in Exodus 34:34–5; 'murmurings' of the discontented Jews in Numbers 14:1–2.

It all comes to a climax with the big question 'But where's the cluster?' Where is the bunch of grapes? This question looks back to the Jews' first and frustrated arrival on the borders of the land. They sent spies into Canaan to look it over. The spies came back with a splendid and promising sample: a bunch of grapes so enormous that it took two men to carry it on a staff.[22] Unfortunately, the spies also saw massive giants in the Promised Land. Their news of these monsters caused the Jews to refuse to go on into their inheritance. So God punished them by sending them back through the wilderness to the Red Sea, where they had begun. So much for the old story. The question 'where is the bunch of grapes now?' is answered by Herbert with the Christian Holy Communion service: grapes were first turned into wine by old Noah,[23] then wine was changed into his own redemptive blood by Christ at the Last Supper, ever after to be drunk by Christians at Holy Communion. So the sign over Woodnoth's own shop hid the key to unlock its proprietor's perplexity. It is a witty solution, its typological complexities handled accordingly.

Woodnoth should have been pleased and reassured. His personal worries were settled into the great scheme of things by a poem in which Christian consolation gradually surfaces with the aid of biblical typology. Herbert's pastoral advice to this 'dejected poor soul'[24] is finely tuned. There is the comfort of linking individual perplexity to the structure of tradition, refashioned into the pleasure of a poem, which treats its epic foundation-story with the light humour appropriate to personal conversation.

It is clear from Woodnoth's long and informative letter to Ferrar that his main concern while at Bemerton was to take advantage of Herbert's skill and sympathy as a pastor and counsellor. Peevishly, Woodnoth complains to Ferrar that his time with Herbert was interrupted 'both in respect of his weakness and other friends' presence'. Woodnoth wanted Herbert all to himself and resented both Herbert's being ill and the presence of other people. But he was generously rewarded. Herbert took great pains over his problems, to which Ferrar had already given much attention.

Woodnoth wanted advice about his continual worry: whether to carry on as a man of business or be ordained. He opened the subject as soon as he arrived at Bemerton on a Tuesday evening. Herbert did not feel up to it there and then. It was a hardy perennial and difficult to handle. Woodnoth was invaluable to Herbert and Ferrar as a highly competent businessman and a contact in London who bought materials there for the Little Gidding scriptorium and helped with fundraising for the restoration of Leighton Bromswold Church. He was also an essential brake, as his agent and manager, on Sir John Danvers's reckless spending. Of course, his religious aspirations had to be respected. To put it bluntly, he was both very useful and something of a spiritual pest. Herbert asked for a postponement, and took Woodnoth with him to Evening Prayer in the church. Next morning he gave Woodnoth a paper which he had written overnight 'that I might the better consider of it, which he first read and then delivered me'. The paper, written in Herbert's fine and clear hand, survives.[25] It has a note at the top by Ferrar: 'Mr. Herbert's reasons for Arth. Woodnoth's Living with Sir John Danvers'. That catches Herbert's drift, but the paper itself is subtler and less conclusive. It begins solemnly, and with a certain exasperation: 'In the name of God. Amen.' It goes on to set out the options facing Woodnoth in seven numbered paragraphs.

Herbert starts by reflecting that although ordination is a higher calling than business, and therefore preferable, Woodnoth is now deeply engaged in looking after 'Sir John's affairs'. 'Change shows not well' and constancy is one of the 'things that are lovely and of good report' recommended by St Paul.[26] Woodnoth should put himself in God's hands and consider himself free to decide for himself, having no family to support. Waiting on God is no bad situation. God himself waits on us, knocking at the door of our hearts and (a typically happy turn of thought and phrase) 'to be without doors with him, is no ill company.' As for Woodnoth's complaint of lack of complete success

Herbert's autograph letter to Woodnoth, written overnight at Bemerton, then read and delivered to Woodnoth in the morning.

in looking after Sir John Danvers, he should consider that giving up doing so would make things worse and give him subsequent pangs of conscience. Woodnoth should consider that his good intentions, however muddled, are enough for God. Although Solomon actually built the temple, his father David had intended to, which was as good. 'Do this and be a man as David, after God's heart.' Finally, Herbert pleads that the great thing is to get on with something. 'When we exhort people to continue in their vocation, it is in opposition to idleness. Work rather than do nothing.'

Herbert may well have hoped that this paper, read out and then handed over to him, would keep Woodnoth quiet for a while. It failed to do so. Herbert tried to reinforce what he had written by telling Woodnoth that 'we were much troubled about words, for the name of a Divine would satisfy all when in truth I might do the office though I wanted the title, for to be as prompter of good to Sir John was to be a good angel to him,[27] nay was to do that which God himself did.' Woodnoth pleaded for more advice, but Herbert replied that 'he was full with this' and it was time for church. After dinner they went to Wilton together, Woodnoth sticking to Herbert like a burr. There it was that Woodnoth sat and brooded on his plight while Herbert had his hour with the Countess of Pembroke. Another problem came to Woodnoth's mind: should he get married? He had Anna Collett in mind. She was Nicholas Ferrar's niece and a devout member of his household. It was a propitious match for Woodnoth, but hopeless because, after much agonizing, she decided on celibacy. Herbert was wisely evasive about all this, while confessing that his own marriage had been a benefit to his precarious health (contrary to Aubrey's speculation that it 'hastened his death').[28]

Constancy, sticking to your occupation and obligations, was at the heart of Herbert's paper, which Woodnoth took away with him to Little Gidding. It is also the title and subject of one of Herbert's later poems, not included in the Williams Manuscript, and therefore from around the time when Herbert had dealings with Woodnoth. It is certain enough that Herbert wrote 'The Bunch of Grapes' for Woodnoth, referring to the sign above his shop and his spiritual perplexities. Considering that psychological comfort was a conscious motive of Herbert's poetry, 'Constancy' could well be another poem for Woodnoth, matching the advice in Herbert's paper and answering Woodnoth's concern about the honesty of his lay calling. Whereas 'The Bunch of Grapes' is a witty and erudite piece of biblical typology, 'Constancy' is made up of the straightforward moral common sense of 'The Church Porch' at the outset of *The Temple*. It is illustrated with vignettes of everyday life: in verse 2, the steady horseman; in verse 3, the shrewd but honest dealer ('What place or person calls for, he doth pay' brings Woodnoth's business dealings to mind); in verse 6, the sensitive friend who allows for the vagaries of invalids and (alas) women; in verse 7, the nicely observed bowls player who ineffectually 'writhe[s] his limbs' with the bias of his bowl or 'wood';[29] and the marksman with his eye on his target. God gets a bare mention in the third line of the poem but shares it with neighbour and self.

Constancy

1
      Who is the honest man?
He that doth still and strongly good pursue,
To God, his neighbour, and himself most true:
      Whom neither force nor fawning can
Unpin, or wrench from giving all their due.

2
      Whose honesty is not
So loose or easy, that a ruffling wind
Can blow away, or glittering look it blind:
      Who rides his sure and even trot,
While the world now rides by, now lags behind.

3
      Who, when great trials come,
Nor seeks, nor shuns them; but doth calmly stay,
Till he the thing and the example weigh:
      All being brought into a sum,
What place or person calls for, he doth pay.

4
      Whom none can work or woo
To use in any thing a trick or sleight;
For above all things he abhors deceit:
      His words and works and fashion too
All of a piece, and all are clear and straight.

5
      Who never melts or thaws
At close temptations: when the day is done,
His goodness sets not, but in dark can run:
      The sun to others writeth laws,
And is their virtue; Virtue is his Sun.

6
      Who, when he is to treat
With sick folks, women, those whom passions sway,
Allows for that, and keeps his constant way:
      Whom others' faults do not defeat;
But though men fail him, yet his part doth play.

7
      Whom nothing can procure,
When the wide world runs bias from his will,

> To writhe his limbs, and share, not mend the ill.
>   This is the Marksman, safe and sure,
>   Who still is right, and prays to be so still.

'Constancy' is a good-natured poem, counselling an unsettled man to settle down and work out his honesty in the routines of everyday life. Herbert's whole handling of Arthur Woodnoth and his problems show his tactful practicality – a great virtue in a pastor or counsellor. His hospitality, his conversation and his writings for this trying man in prose and verse were all of a piece: they urged Woodnoth to see his dilemma with sober objectivity and did nothing to fan the flames of his solipsistic piety.

Herbert's orphaned nieces, Dorothy and Magdalene Vaughan, came to live in Bemerton Rectory with George and Jane. They seem to have been left in Wales for the seven years since their widowed mother's death in 1623. George's elder brother Edward was their guardian, a duty which he performed and evaded by trying to get his brothers to take on one niece each. Soon after coming to Bemerton, George wrote to his brother Henry, at court as Master of the Revels, about the situation.[30] He told him that he had rejected Edward's proposal on good grounds.

> I wrote to him that I would have both or neither; and that upon this ground, because they were come into an unknown country, tender in knowledge, sense and age, and knew none but one [he means himself] who could be no company to them. Therefore I considered that if only one came, the comfort intended would prove a discomfort. Since that I have seen the fruit of my observation, for they have lived so lovingly, lying, eating, walking, still together, that I take a comfort therein.

But there was a third Vaughan sister, Katherine, the 'youngest and least looked unto': so overlooked that she had been left in Wales with her schoolmistress, 'and you know what those mercenary creatures are.' The schoolmistress was probably hanging on to Katherine as a modest source of income. The child had occasional visits from Edward Herbert's daughter Beatrice, 'my cousin Bett', who lived with the Newport family at Eyton. But that was a good way away, and the little girl had no one to 'repair to at good times, Christmas, &c.'. George urges her on Henry, who had been hospitable to him in his wandering years. 'If you think of taking her, as once you did, surely it were a good deed, and I would have her conveyed to you.' Herbert does not press his brother: 'I judge you not.' Henry should do 'that which God shall put into your heart'. And 'if you take her not, I am thinking to do it.' His finances were much reduced by repairing his rectory, but he would not let that stand in the way of charity and:

> Truly it grieves me to think of the child, how destitute she is, and that in the necessary time of education. For the time of breeding is the time of doing children good; and not as many who think they have done fairly, if they leave them a good portion after their decease. But take this rule, and it is an outlandish one [a friendly reference to Henry's love and collection of 'outlandish', or foreign, proverbs], which I commend to you as now being a father, 'the best bred child hath the best portion.' Well; the good God bless you more and more; and all yours; and make your family, a houseful of God's servants. So prays

Your ever loving brother,

G. Herbert.

My wife's and nieces' service.

To my very dear brother Sir Henry Herbert, at Court.

Charity and education were central to Herbert's creed. He was glad of the chance to put them into practice. In the event, Katherine joined her sisters at Bemerton. Dorothy died there in 1632, half a year before Herbert himself, leaving a hundred pounds to each of her sisters and to her uncle George, with smaller legacies to the Danvers family at Baynton – a sign that they too had become part of her life. In his will Herbert was to leave Dorothy's two surviving sisters, Magdalene and Katherine, his own legacy from Dorothy plus 400 pounds. The fostering was an acknowledged success.

Like his dealings with Woodnoth, his handling of the situation of his little niece and his younger brother show Herbert's pastoral patience, insight and delicacy. As in his poetry, he had the capacity to treat the recalcitrant matter of human life with a firm yet light touch. There is control and letting-be, the devising of frames for experience which lets it speak for itself while making it something manageable and, whether morally or poetically, elegant.

A PRIEST TO THE TEMPLE OR THE COUNTRY PARSON

The Countess, the old woman, Woodnoth and the Vaughan nieces were individual beneficiaries of Herbert's pastoral care. His major prose work, *A Priest to the Temple or The Country Parson, his Character, &c.*, describes it at large. It was finished in 1632, the middle of his time at Bemerton, and was clearly meant for publication. In the event, it was posthumously published in 1652, when seven editions of *The Temple* had made Herbert famous. Hence, probably and by way of an advertisement, the first title *A Priest to the Temple*. (*The Temple* itself was not Herbert's own title for his collected poems but Ferrar's.) The second title *The Country Parson* is much less pompous and much more workaday. This suits the pragmatic contents of the book, in which Herbert always refers to 'the country parson' or just 'the parson'. So I will refer to it as that. The possibility that it was begun just before he got to work as a country parson and while his rectory was still being refurbished is suggested by 'The Author to the Reader' which states that:

> I have resolved to set down the form and character of a true pastor, that I may have a mark to aim at: which also I will set as high as I can, since he shoots higher that threatens the moon, than he that aims at a tree. Not that I think, if a man do not all which is here expressed, he presently sins and displeases God, but that it is a good strife to go as far as we can in pleasing him, who hath done so much for us.

In other words, the book is a statement of intentions, 'a mark to aim at', not a record of achievements. But it is all in the present tense, full of observed reality, and all practical. Chapter XXVI is entitled 'The Parson's eye'. That eye was shrewd. Herbert is drawing on experience and is far from theoretical when he notices that country people can be mean, preferring to borrow a spade from a neighbour and 'wear out that' (spades were made of wood, some tipped with metal), rather than buy their own, even when they could afford one. They met their match in a parson whose wits had been sharpened by his education.

> Country people are full of these petty injustices, being cunning to make use of another, and spare themselves: and scholars ought to be diligent in the observation of these, and driving of their general school rules ever to the smallest actions of life; which while they dwell in their books, they will never find; but being seated in the Country, and doing their duty faithfully, they will soon discover.

There was no specialist training in seminaries in the Church of England in those days. The parson learned his trade by doing it and by interaction with his parishioners.

The book is divided into thirty-seven short chapters describing a parson thoroughly embedded in his parish and committed to it. His parish duties were good for Herbert. The subjective internal demands which he laid upon himself so heavily were balanced by the objective, practical and external demands of his job. He had something other than himself to get his teeth into. There was plenty to do: 'The Country Parson desires to be all to his Parish, and not only a Pastor, but a Lawyer also, and a Physician.'[31]

Having dealt with the nobility in the second chapter of *The Country Parson*, he gets among the peasantry in the third chapter. Their labour contributed to the parson's income by way of the tithe, or 10 per cent tax, on agricultural produce. The parson should go easy on this.

> Because country people live hardly, and therefore as feeling their own sweat, and consequently knowing the price of money, are offended much with any, who by hard usage increase their travail, the country parson is very circumspect in avoiding all covetousness, neither being greedy to get, nor niggardly to keep, nor troubled to lose any worldly wealth.

He should also know his people, respect them and speak their language. 'He condescends even to the knowledge of tillage, and pasturage [the grazing of sheep and cattle], and makes great use of them in teaching, because people by what they understand, are best led to what they understand not.'[32]

He could be strict, particularly with his parishioners' behaviour during church services. In a passage in Chapter VI which amounts to a vivid genre picture of a country congregation, the parson is disciplinary: 'by no means enduring talking, or sleeping, or gazing, or leaning, or half-kneeling'. The people should make the spoken responses required of them by the Prayer Book 'not in a huddling, or slubbering fashion, gaping, or scratching the head, or spitting even in the midst of their answer'. They should be as responsively alert as Herbert himself in his poetry.

Chapter X describes life in an ideal parsonage. The parson's wife is busy bringing up their children and 'curing, and healing of all wounds and sores with her own hands'. The children are expected to visit other sick children, tend their wounds and give them money. The servants are given time to read or taught to do so. Psalm 101 is inscribed on the wall as a model of domestic morality:

> Mine eyes look upon such as are faithful in the land: that they may dwell with me . . .
>
> Whoso leadeth a godly life: he shall be my servant.

Herbert's concerns with cleanliness and careful diet give his picture of the contents of the parsonage some of the luminous domesticity of a contemporary Dutch Interior.

> The furniture of his house is very plain, but clean, whole, and sweet [fragrant], as sweet as his garden can make; for he hath no money for such things, charity being his only perfume, which deserves cost when he can spare it. His fare is plain, and common, but wholesome, what he hath is little, but very good; it consisteth most of mutton, beef, and veal, if he adds anything for a great day, or a stranger, his garden or orchard supplies it, or his barn or back-side [the store at the back of the house].

The insistence on cleanness and diet is a reminder that these were important prophylactics when medicines were few. There were the drugs sold by apothecaries, but Herbert held that:

> home-bred medicines are both more easy for the parson's purse, and more familiar for all men's bodies. So where the apothecary useth either

for loosing, rhubarb, or for binding, bolearmena [an earth product], the parson useth damask or white roses for one, and plantain, shepherd's purse, knot-grass for the other, and that with better success . . . Accordingly, for salves, his wife seeks not the city, but prefers her garden and fields before all outlandish gums. And surely hyssop, valerian, mercury [the plant, not the metal], adder's tongue, yarrow, melilot, and Saint John's wort made into a salve; and elder, camomile, mallows, comfrey and smallage made into a poultice, have done great and rare cures.[33]

The mellifluous lists of herbs has a poetry of its own and shows the horticultural knowledge Herbert had learned from his mother, along with his own love of the simple and homely in language.

The rectory had an open door, especially at the great festivals, when the parson should see to it that no one should 'want a good meal suiting to the joy of the occasion'. Love bade them welcome, diffident as many of them would have been as they crossed the threshold.

Like the rectory, the church should be an open and orderly place, 'swept, and kept clean without dust, or cobwebs, and at great festivals strawed, and stuck with boughs, and perfumed with incense'. Again, there is an echo in the poetry. In 'Easter' Herbert gets himself ready for the risen Christ:

> I got me flowers to straw thy way;
> I got me boughs off many a tree:
> But thou wast up by break of day,
> And brought'st thy sweets along with thee.

Whatever strict puritans said, the parson should treasure such ceremony. He should also value the informal to-and-fro of catechizing. There was an official Church catechism, with set questions and answers, as well as an abundance of unofficial printed ones. But this was not enough because it could be said 'by rote, as parrots, without ever piercing into the sense of it'. 'The saying of the Catechism is necessary, but not enough; because to answer in form may still admit ignorance: but the questions must be propounded loosely and widely, and then the answerer will discover what he is.'[34]

Free and candid dialogue, that stock in trade of Herbert's poetry, is essential to the discovery of self and secure identity. Herbert had a model for it in his classical education: 'Socrates did thus in philosophy, who held that the seeds of all truths lay in everybody, and accordingly by questions well ordered he found philosophy in silly trades-men ... To this purpose, some dialogues in *Plato* were worth the reading, where the singular dexterity of *Socrates* in this kind may be observed and imitated.'[35] The parables of Christ, his Master, in the Gospels were precedents and models for Herbert's own skill as a maker of images which gave inward experience an everyday correspondent. It was deployed in his catechizing along with his Socratic tactics. Even the great mystery of salvation could be brought home by a rustic parable, worked out in dialogue.

> As, when the parson once demanded after other questions about man's misery; since man is so miserable, what is to be done? And the answerer could not tell; he asked him again, what would he do, if he were in a ditch? This familiar illustration made the answer so plain, that he was even ashamed of his ignorance; for he could not but say, he would haste out of it as fast as he could. Then he proceeded to ask, whether he could get out of the ditch alone, or whether he needed a helper, and who was that helper? That is the skill, and doubtless the Holy Scripture intends thus much, when it condescends to the naming of a plough, a hatchet, a bushel, leaven, boys piping and dancing; showing that things of ordinary use are not only to serve in the way of drudgery, but to be washed, and cleansed, and serve for lights even of heavenly truths.

There is a nice shaft of observation there when Herbert notices the embarrassment of his interlocutor: 'even ashamed of his ignorance'.

One way and another, clerical life was a fulfilment, a coming to rest and social use of Herbert's resources: as gardener, scholar, poet and counsellor. The happy sense of having at last found the job which suited him informs Chapter XXXII, 'The Parson's Surveys' in which he looks about him at surrounding society. As he knew for himself, there is nothing worse than the listlessness of lacking employment. Its effects on other people too – the examples he gives are scarcely from his own reactions to being jobless – were plain to see. 'For when men have nothing to do, then they fall to drink, to steal, to whore, to scoff, to revile, to all sorts of gamings. Come, say they, we have nothing to do, lets go to the tavern, or to the stews, or what not.'

So he 'represents to every body the necessity of a vocation'. Married people have their work cut out in looking after their families and doing what they can for their neighbours. The gentry should not evade their duty of serving as justices of the peace just because they look down on the 'mean persons' currently in post or because it is a troublesome chore. The study of law, including 'the Statutes at large' and attendance at Assizes, is recommended to the sons of the gentry, who would do well to go further and stand for Parliament: 'no School to a Parliament'. If elected they should be ready to sit on committees and get to grips with their detailed business as Herbert himself had done, albeit briefly. Apart from all that, Herbert 'commends the Mathematics, as the only wonder-working knowledge' and, drawing on his family's enthusiasm for the Virginia Company, 'if the young gallant think these courses dull, where can he busy himself better, than in those new plantations, and discoveries, which are not only a noble, but also as they may be handled, a religious employment?' Failing that, there is always travel in Europe with the practical aim (which would have pleased his friend Francis Bacon) of observing 'the Artifices and Manufactures there' so as to set them up in England. Busy himself at last, Herbert is carried away by the opportunities for doing good which are available to the gentry at large.

The final chapters of the book settle down into the parish and the parson's care for his people. Here his own personal experiences of self-discipline, doubt, difficulty and recovery stand him in good stead for helping others.

> It fares in this as it doth in physic: he that hath been sick of a consumption, and knows what recovered him, is a physician so far as he meets with the same disease, and temper; and can much better, and particularly do it, than he that is generally learned, and was never sick. And if the same person had been sick of all diseases, and were recovered of all by things that he knew, there were no such physician as he, both for skill and tenderness. Just so it is in divinity . . .

So the agonies which Herbert made into poetry had more than a literary value. They could be turned by sympathy to the advantage of his parishioners when they were troubled in their spirits. The Herbert

13. Henry Danvers, Earl of Danby, *c.* 1630, a wound on his cheek covered by a black patch, by van Dyck. In 1628, at a low point in Herbert's life, Danby was his host at Dauntsey House.

14. The tower of Dauntsey Church, cheek by jowl with the House (refaced in the eighteenth century). Danby 'allowed him [Herbert] such an apartment in it as might best suit with his accommodation and liking' (Walton). On the tower is Danby's coat of arms in an elaborately classical frame, dated 1630 (15).

16. Philip Herbert, Fourth Earl of Pembroke, with his family, George Herbert's neighbours and kinsmen at Wilton House, c. 1634–35, in one of van Dyck's masterpieces.

17. A detail from 16, showing Philip's disgruntled wife Anne Clifford, George Herbert's friend, less brilliantly painted than any other figure in the picture.

18. The Tudor east entrance of Wilton, still largely as it was when Herbert visited from Bemerton.

19. St. Peter's, George Herbert's church at Fugglestone, on the edge of the Wilton estate.

20. George Herbert's church at Bemerton, with his rectory some six paces to the right, photographed in 1919.

21. A lady believed in Cooke family tradition to be Jane Danvers, wife of George Herbert and later of Sir Robert Cooke.

22. Nicholas Ferrar, founder of the Little Gidding community and George Herbert's friend, by Cornelius Janssens. It was to Ferrar that Herbert, as he was dying, sent the 'little book' of his poetry, soon published under the title 'The Temple'.

The Original of Mr George Herbert's Temple;
as it was at first Licenced for the presse.

The Temple.
Psal: 29: 8.

In his Temple doth every man
speake of his honour.

The Dedication

Lord, my first fruits present themselves to thee;
Yet not mine neither; for from thee they came;
And must returne. Accept of them, and mee,
And make us strive, who shall sing best thy Name.
Turne their eyes hither, who shall make a gaine;
Theirs, who shall hurt themselves, or mee, refraine.

B: Lany Procan:

Tho: Bainbrigg

William Beale

Tho: Ffreman

23. The title page of the Bodleian Manuscript of 'The Temple' (so entitled by Ferrar above the dedication); Archbishop Sancroft's ownership above and the signatures of the Cambridge licensing authorities below.

24. George Herbert in academic/clerical dress by
Robert White, probably after a lost painting by Cornelius
Janssens. All other known images of Herbert are based
on this drawing.

who had been aloof and distant in his younger days had turned into a social being, glad to be part of the life of his village.

Customs had survived from the days before the protestant reformations which radical and doctrinaire spirits deplored. Herbert valued them as good social glue, particularly the springtime Rogationtide procession. Priest and people walked together through the fields and around the parish boundaries, marking the bounds and praying for God's blessing on the springing crops. Herbert is eloquent, even fierce, in his support of it.

> The country parson is a lover of old customs, if they be good and harmless; and the rather, because country people are much addicted to them, so that to favour them therein is to win their hearts, and to oppose them therein is to deject them . . . Particularly, he loves Procession, and maintains it, because therein are contained four manifest advantages. First, a blessing of God on the fruits of the field; secondly, justice in the preservation of bounds; thirdly, charity in loving walking, and neighbourly accompanying one another, with reconciling of differences at that time, if there be any; fourthly, mercy in relieving the poor by a liberal distribution and largess, which at that time is, or ought to be used. Wherefore he exacts of all to be present at the perambulation, and those that withdraw, and sever themselves from it, he mislikes, and reproves as uncharitable, and unneighbourly; and if they will not reform, presents them [to the bishop's court]. Nay, he is so far from condemning such assemblies, that he rather procures them to be often, as knowing that absence breeds strangeness, but presence love. Now love is his business, and aim; wherefore he likes well that his parish at good times invite one another to their houses, and he urgeth them to it: and sometimes, where he knows there hath been or is a little difference, he takes one of the parties, and goes with him to the other, and all dine or sup together.

'Love is his business': as poet, as pastor. The rapt mysticism of 'Love (III)' has its counterpart in the customs and domestic supper parties of the people of Bemerton. It was a great integration for him that love, his ideal, had become his job, his 'calling' in his own word. It was a business, a constant matter of repair and maintenance.

In that spirit, the last chapter of *The Country Parson* is not any kind of a grand finale but a discussion of gossip, the questionable life-blood of communities, and what to do about it. It is entitled 'Concerning detraction': detraction being the taking away of somebody's reputation. It is a tricky subject, balancing principles of truth and falsehood against social harmony. Herbert begins with observed and commonplace actualities: 'The country parson perceiving that most, when they are at leisure, make others' faults their entertainment and discourse, and that even good men think, so they speak truth, they may disclose another's fault, finds it somewhat difficult how to proceed in this point.'

Simply stamping it out is impossible and would anyway allow evils to spread. Herbert divides the subject, 'faults are either notorious or private', and proceeds to discuss the first category without (disappointingly) getting round to the second. Notorious faults are, by definition, in the public realm and may be talked about, but 'not with sport, but commiseration'. The law reinforces social disapprobation with its punishments, and Herbert, hardened from childhood by such spectacles at Charing Cross, is complacent about whipping, branding and the stocks. Sensing his readers' unease at this, he interjects: 'But some may say, though the law allow this, the gospel doth not, which hath so much advanced charity.' 'But this', he rejoins, 'is easily answered.' The executioner is only doing his job and is not offending against charity unless he has 'a tincture of private malice in his joy and haste of acting his part'. Likewise, anyone who justly accuses someone else is doing the right thing, 'except he also do it out of rancour'. When Herbert declares that 'it concerns the Common-Wealth, that rogues should be known, and charity to the public hath the precedence of private charity', we realize that the man whose poetry presents him as a tender-hearted private person has found his place, as a country parson, in public governance and has accepted its more brutal aspects with a deliberate lack of tenderness which is only somewhat relieved by the last words of the book: 'Nevertheless, if the punished delinquent shall be much troubled for his sins, and turn quite another man, doubtless then also men's affections and words must turn, and forbear to speak of that, which even God himself hath forgotten.' Cultural relativists may accept all this coolly as what was to be expected of a responsible member of Stuart society. Other modern readers may reflect that Herbert was descended from rough and tough border barons and that there was a moral cost as well as moral benefit to being the rector of Bemerton.

SALISBURY AND THE WAY THERE

There were only three years between Herbert's institution at Bemerton and his death, but they were well occupied and happy. As well as his visits to Wilton on the western edge of his parish to see the distressed Countess, he went twice a week to Salisbury on its east. There he went to Sung Evensong in the cathedral, his 'heaven on earth' according to Walton, preceded by a 'private music-making' in somebody's house, probably that of Giles Tomkins, half-brother of the composer Thomas Tomkins, who was in charge of the choir and favoured at court as a good all-rounder on strings, lute and keyboard. Herbert's love and talent for music is evidenced by Walton, Aubrey and his own poems.[36] Walton tells of three encounters on the way to Salisbury.[37] One was with 'a gentleman who is still [in 1670] living in that city' to whom Herbert gave 'rules for the trial of his sincerity, and for a practical piety'. After that they met often on the road alongside the River Nadder. Another was with 'a neighbour minister' to whom Herbert recommended catechizing and an exemplary life of 'visible humility and charity'. The third encounter related by Walton is more sympathetic than these didactic occasions.

> In another walk to Salisbury he saw a poor man with a poorer horse that was fallen under his load; they were both in distress, and needed present help, which Mr. Herbert perceiving, put off his canonical coat, and helped the poor man to unload, and after to load his horse. The poor man blessed him for it, and he blessed the poor man; and so was like the good Samaritan, that he gave him money to refresh both himself and his horse, and told him, that if he loved himself, he would be merciful to his beast. Thus he left the poor man, and at his coming to his musical friends at Salisbury, they began to wonder that Mr. George Herbert, who used to be so trim and clean, came into that company so soiled and discomposed; but he

told them the occasion; and when one of the company told him he had
disparaged himself by so dirty an employment, his answer was, that the
thought of what he had done would prove music to him at midnight, and
that the omission of it would have upbraided and made discourse in his
conscience, whensoever he would pass by that place. 'For if I be bound to
pray for all that be in distress, I am sure that I am bound, so far as it is in
my power, to practise what I pray for. And though I do not wish for the
like occasion every day, yet let me tell you, I would not willingly pass one
day of my life without comforting a sad soul, or showing mercy; and I
praise God for the occasion. And now let's tune our instruments.'

The story rings true. The riverside road was muddy. Blessing people
was a topic to which Herbert gave a chapter (XXXVI) of *The Country Parson*, writing that 'In the time of Popery, the Priest's *Benedicite*,
and his holy water, were over highly valued; and now we are fallen to
the clean contrary, even from superstition to coldness, and atheism.'
And Herbert's almost obsessive love of cleanliness pervades his writings as much as his love of music.

PREACHING AND PRAYER

Taking the few steps from the rectory to the church, Herbert preached
his first sermon to his parishioners. It was, according to Walton, florid,
learned and eloquent. Sensing that this was no way to address the vil-
lagers, he concluded by saying that in future he would be 'more plain
and practical'. Walton may, yet again, be inventing a scene, this time
in the interests of marking the transition of the orator to the preacher.
But it agrees with what Herbert has to say in 'The Parson preaching',
Chapter VII of *The Country Parson*. The sermon should be precisely
targeted at the various groups in the congregation: 'This is for you,
and this is for you.' He believed in eye-contact, 'a diligent and busy
cast of his eye on his auditors, with letting them know, that he observes
who marks, and who not'. It was a mutual business of interchange.

Sometimes he tells them stories, and sayings of others ... for them also
men heed, and remember better than exhortations; which though earnest, yet often die with the sermon, especially with country people; which

are thick and heavy, and hard to raise to a point of zeal, and fervency, and need a mountain of fire to kindle them; but stories and sayings they will well remember.

Above all, the sermon was to be 'not witty, or learned, or eloquent, but holy', and for that to be achieved it had to be sincere. Herbert uses a dinner-table metaphor for this: 'dipping and seasoning all our words and sentences in our hearts, before they come into our mouths, truly affecting, and cordially expressing all that we say; so that the auditors may plainly perceive that every word is heart-deep'.

No sermon by Herbert survives but all the indications, in his prose and his verse, are that it would be very different from those of his mentor Lancelot Andrewes or his friend John Donne at St Paul's. They were court and metropolitan preachers and Herbert understood that preaching, however universal and eternal in matter, was also a very local thing. 'A crumbling a text into small parts' in the manner of Andrewes was not for his rustics. Nor should the sermon go on beyond an hour for fear it might weary its rustic hearers and turn them 'from not relishing, to loathing'.

Sermons are monologues. In many ways Herbert preferred dialogue: the Socratic to-and-fro of freely conducted catechizing for half an hour on Sunday afternoons. As in his poetry, he was after the reciprocal. The primary response was to God as the creator, governor and redeemer of human lives. So prayer was best of all: private in his poetry, public in his church. Every day he went there with his household, ten or so people in all, for Morning Prayer at ten o'clock and Evening Prayer at four. These services consisted of the Psalms, all read through every month, readings from the Old and New Testaments, and prayers: all nourishment for Herbert's life and poetry. Walton relates that they were joined by 'most of his parishioners and many gentlemen in the neighbourhood'.[38] 'And some of the meaner sort of his parish did so love and reverence Mr. Herbert, that they would let their plough rest when Mr. Herbert's saints' [sanctus] bell rung to prayers, that they might also offer their devotions to God with him, and would then return back to their plough.'

Prayer was as communal a part of church life as preaching and catechizing. As such, Herbert preferred it to private devotion, which is striking in view of the unmatched quality of the latter in his poetry. In 'The Church Porch' (stanza 67), he asserted that public prayer was better than private, or than the domestic gatherings of 'six and seven' at home.

> Though private prayer be a bold design,
> Yet public hath more promises, more love:
> And love's a weight to hearts, to eyes a sign.
> We all are but cold suitors; let us move
> > Where it is warmest. Leave thy six and seven;
> > Pray with the most: for where most pray, is heaven.

Public prayer was better because it was socially stronger and warmer, even cosier. There was a polemical edge to this. The puritan wing of the Church preferred preaching. At the Hampton Court Conference, called by James I to sort out religious differences at the start of his reign, Richard Bancroft, Bishop of London, had pleased the King by protesting that there was too much emphasis on preaching, 'which motion His Majesty liked very well, very acutely taxing the hypocrisy of our times, which placeth all religion in the ear, through which there is an easy passage; but prayer, which expresseth the heart's affection, and is the true devotion of the mind, as a matter putting us to over-much trouble'.[39] In Norfolk, full of preaching and puritanism, the clergy were told in 1638 that 'prayer is the end to which God's house is erected, *domus mea, domus orationis est* ['my house is the house of prayer', Luke 19:46]. Though there be many other religious duties to be exercised in God's house, yet there is none other mentioned but prayer.' And Norfolk's Archdeacon Francis Mason declared in 1613, 'we repent and pray; we thank God and pray; we confess our sins and pray; we preach and pray; we receive the sacraments and pray.'[40]

It helps to understand the force of this controversy if we reflect on the psychological, and even physical, difference between preaching and prayer. In preaching, the clergyman in his pulpit is very active, even hyperactive in the case of 'plain and powerful' Mr. Rogers of Dedham in Essex, who drew crowds by such stunts as 'his taking hold with both hands at one time of the supporters of the canopy over the pulpit, and roaring hideously, to represent the torments of the damned'.[41] The hearers, by contrast, sat there being terrified, bored or instructed. All power was with the preacher. But in prayer all were equal in the alert passivity of waiting. People knelt (a posture distrusted by the puritans) like subjects before a monarch, their hands held together before them in expectant loyalty. In this posture the richer laity were represented on their tombs, awaiting their eventual resurrection. In contrast, the great preachers and instructors of the day often appear frontally upright, confronting the viewer commandingly over the cushions of their pulpits. The form of prayer which Herbert and his congregation used twice a day was responsorial, going from minister to people and back again. Herbert even had the people joining with him in the collects, or seasonal prayers, which were assigned by the book to the minister.[42] Preaching was a one-way traffic which Herbert made as two-way as he could. Prayer was communal, a traffic between minister and people, all together waiting on God. Herbert's desire for a balance between them was, as we saw, realized in his refurbishing of Leighton Bromswold Church, where 'the reading pew [for prayers] and pulpit were ... both of an equal height.'[43]

Herbert wrote two poems about prayer, of which the first is the best: an ecstatic and delicious list of its qualities.

Prayer (I)

Prayer the Church's banquet, angels' age,
     God's breath in man returning to his birth,
     The soul in paraphrase, heart in pilgrimage,
The Christian plummet sounding heav'n and earth;
Engine against th' Almighty, sinner's tow'r,   5
     Reversed thunder, Christ-side-piercing spear,
     The six-days world transposing in an hour,
A kind of tune, which all things hear and fear;
Softness, and peace, and joy, and love, and bliss,
     Exalted Manna, gladness of the best,   10
     Heaven in ordinary, man well drest,
The milky way, the bird of Paradise,
     Church-bells beyond the stars heard, the soul's blood,
     The land of spices; something understood.

Prayer is 'the Church's banquet': according to *The Oxford English Dictionary* a banquet is 'now usually a ceremonial or state feast, followed by speeches' but in Herbert's time 'a slight repast between meals, a course of sweetmeats, fruit and wine' – the Church's main meal being the Holy Communion. Prayer is also 'angels' age', limitlessly transcending human time. As God breathed life into man when he created him,[44] so man breathes that life back to God in prayer. This trope of reversal is repeated in the images which follow such as the upward-soaring plummet, the Manna (food which God dropped down to earth from heaven)[45] going up there again; and the 'reversed thunder'. A sort of giddy exhilaration results from this topsy-turvydom. Awe-inspiring music and sensual pleasures are mixed with the humdrum image of man in his Sunday best. Things come down to earth when the exotic images reach a climax, when 'the land of spices' is abruptly followed by the numinous-cum-matter-of-fact phrase at the close: 'something understood'.

The images, each of them a delicious surprise, come tumbling out headlong – five in a row in line 9 and twenty-six in all. The sheer joy of it all in a sonnet devoted to the sober topic of prayer astonishes its readers. The mystical and the sensual are old partners, and this poem's ecstasy brings to mind images of rapt saints at prayer from the art of the catholic counter-reformation – Zurbarán and Bernini for example. But the happy wit of this scrapbook of little pictures makes for something less grand, a more accessible and somehow English sublimity. 'Something understood' ties everything up into the pragmatic benefit of praying: that it settles the mind.

DISSATISFACTIONS

While he was busy in Bemerton, Herbert was worried about his prebend at Leighton Bromswold and the restoration of the church there. He tried to arrange for the prebend to be transferred to Nicholas Ferrar, but Ferrar would not accept the idea.[46] In the summer of 1632, the last of Herbert's life, work on the church was in full swing and nearing completion: eighteen masons and labourers and ten carpenters at work, with John Ferrar going over from Little Gidding three times a week to supervise and Arthur Woodnoth keeping the accounts.[47] 'God prosper the work,' John Ferrar wrote to his brother Nicholas, 'and send money in. Amen.' Meanwhile in Bemerton,

> Mr. Herbert, seeing he could not draw Gidding nearer him, he would draw nearer to his Brother Nicholas Ferrar & not long before his death, was upon exchanging his living for one, merely for the situation, as being nearer his dear brother, though in value much inferior to his own; but he said that he valued Mr. Ferrar's near neighbourhood more than any living.[48]

Once again, the usual view needs revision. Herbert was not in a state of complete and settled contentment. He had the employment that he had longed for in the previous, irresolute years and an excellent wife. The Vaughan girls were happy to be with them. But, for all the benefits of being at Bemerton with Salisbury's music on one side and Wilton's civilized entertainment on the other, he was still not sure that he was in the right place: somewhere nearer to Ferrar would surely be better. As it was, they could communicate only by letters. Herbert's ardent nature and mercurial temperament were never entirely satisfied or at rest for long.

'The Pilgrimage', one of his later poems, is about disappointment. Pilgrimage survived the reformation of religion, not as a practice but as a picture for the homesickness of the devout soul, longing for a fulfilment beyond the conditions of earthly life. The Epistle to the Hebrews described the Old Testament heroes of faith as 'strangers and pilgrims on the earth' and the First Epistle of Peter extended this double appellation to Christians: 'I beseech you as strangers and pilgrims, abstain from fleshly lusts.'[49] As an allegory of travel, pilgrimage was to get its most thorough and popular treatment in John Bunyan's *The Pilgrim's Progress from this World to that Which is to Come* of 1678. Bunyan may have been indebted to Herbert's poem for his much more thorough allegorical treatment of the theme. But, apart from that, Herbert's poem is a very different, altogether briefer and, above all, more pessimistic affair than Bunyan's.

The Pilgrimage

I travell'd on, seeing the hill, where lay
    My expectation.
  A long it was and weary way.
  The gloomy cave of Desperation
I left on th' one, and on the other side
    The rock of Pride.

And so I came to Fancy's meadow strow'd
    With many a flower;
  Fain would I here have made abode,
  But I was quicken'd by my hour.
So to Care's copse I came, and there got through
    With much ado.

That led me to the wild of Passion, which
    Some call the wold;
  A wasted place, but sometimes rich.
  Here was I robb'd of all my gold,
Save one good Angel, which a friend had ti'd
    Close to my side.

At length I got unto the gladsome hill,
    Where lay my hope,
  Where lay my heart; and climbing still,
  When I had gain'd the brow and top,
A lake of brackish waters on the ground
    Was all I found.

With that abash'd and struck with many a sting
    Of swarming fears,
  I fell, and cried, Alas my King!
  Can both the way and end be tears?
Yet taking heart I rose, and then perceiv'd
    I was deceiv'd:

My hill was further: so I flung away,
    Yet heard a cry

> Just as I went, *None goes that way*
> *And lives*: If that be all, said I,
> After so foul a journey death is fair,
> And but a chair.

Like Dante, the traveller is already on his way when the poem begins in midstream with 'I travelled on . . .' Herbert's way with allegory is deft, lightened by a picturesque realism which pleases its readers and lets them expect the happy ending which, in the end, they will be denied. The emblematic incidents along the way are realized with vivid economy.

After 'the gloomy cave of Desperation' and 'the rock of Pride' comes the welcome relief of the poet's paradise: 'Fancy's meadow' with its flowers. The pilgrim would like to stay there, but time is getting on and his journey lies through a less agreeable place: 'Care's copse'. He battles his way, as walkers have to, through its undergrowth 'with much ado'. This takes him to the open wold. This is 'the wild of passion', ambiguous as a place of waste (Shakespeare's 'lust in action' as an 'expense of spirit in a waste of shame' comes to mind), but 'sometimes rich' with yellow gorse. Here the traveller is robbed, keeping only 'one good Angel, which a friend had tied/Close to my side'. An angel was a gold coin, so called from the figure of an angel stamped on it – which allows the pun. Most real of all is the climactic anticlimax when 'the gladsome hill' which had attracted the traveller's hope and heart at the outset turns out to be bitterly disappointing. It has a brackish pond on its top which releases a swarm of stinging midges ('swarming fears'). All these allegorical figures are at the same time actual and real parts of an English landscape.

The poet-pilgrim keeps trying to make the best of one difficulty after another. The poem's form makes them palpable. Short–long iambic is the inevitable metre for walking. Herbert uses it throughout but varies it by making each verse out of lines with three different lengths: five-beat, two-beat, two four-beats, another five-beat and another two-beat. This, with frequent enjambment (disregard of line-endings), puts a spring in his step. There is no mere aimless ambling, such as a scheme made only of five-beat pentameters would accommodate: there is a destination. To each verse there is its drama: a getting-along, a getting somewhere, a leaving it. Trials are met and overcome as hope drives him on. He reaches the summit of his hope at last: the top of 'the gladsome hill' on which he had set his heart. It turns out to be a wretched pond, bug-ridden with fears. He falls to the ground, exhausted and desperate. Even this does not stop him. He gets up and sees that he was wrong: 'my hill was further.' 'So I flung away,' getting going again with a defiant flourish. The last discouragement is the mysterious 'cry', ringing in his ears as he goes, '*None goes that way and lives.*' His destination lies beyond death, beyond dissolution. Undiscouraged, he goes on with bitter determination.

> After so foul a journey, death is fair,
> And but a chair.

Death will be a welcome relief, a sitting down at last. At its very end, the poem reveals itself as an account of the everyday heroism of bashing on through one disappointment after another. The pilgrim has accepted the worst and is grimly undeluded.

'The Pilgrimage' is a strenuous contradiction of Herbert's image as a placid man and a placid poet. Even in his final Bemerton years, no sooner had he settled into his employment with his family, including his three orphaned Vaughan nieces, than he was feeling that he would be better of in a living near the Ferrars at Little Gidding. He was still the restless man who had worried and angled for the Cambridge Oratorship and then walked away from it.

Herbert's health had never been good, or at least never good for long. Diagnosis was (and is) not possible and cure, for the many diseases at large, practically unavailable. Tuberculosis, as Aubrey supposed, is probable. Herbert did what he could in the preventative line: keeping clean, dieting, fresh air and exercise – and writing poetry to settle his spirits. In 'The Forerunners' he reconciles himself to the onset of old age and the waning of his powers, even the poetic powers which the poem itself, by contradiction, displays. Its beginning and end refer to the forerunners of a royal progress, here a metaphor for the approach of death, marking the doors of houses which they were to requisition with white chalk. Dementia is Herbert's worst fear: the 'disparking', like deer driven from their deerpark, of his brain's 'sparkling [note the bright internal rhyme] notions'. The poet's spiritual and mental work is to get himself on terms with his forebodings, and he does it in the face of his love of thinking and composing, with a light and humorous touch: his pride, like his mother's, of cleaning up his grubby little children and taking them to church, the parental scolding of 'Fie, thou wilt soil thy broidered coat.' He makes light of his own familiar obsession with cleanness. This levity with a frightening or sublime subject is very much Herbert, particularly in his last poems. He can do it because in his heart, the centre of his being, the God who made and redeemed him, is still his.

The Forerunners

The harbingers are come. See, see their mark;
White is their colour, and behold my head.
But must they have my brain? must they dispark
Those sparkling notions which therein were bred?
    Must dullness turn me to a clod?
Yet have they left me, *Thou art still my God.*

Good men ye be, to leave me my best room,
Ev'n all my heart, and what is lodged there:
I pass not, I, what of the rest become,
So *Thou art still my God*, be out of fear.
    He will be pleased with that ditty;
And if I please him, I write fine and witty.

Farewell sweet phrases, lovely metaphors.
But will ye leave me thus? when ye before
Of stews and brothels only knew the doors,
Then did I wash you with my tears, and more,
    Brought you to Church well drest and clad:
My God must have my best, ev'n all I had.

Lovely enchanting language, sugar-cane,
Honey of roses, whither wilt thou fly?
Hath some fond lover tic'd thee to thy bane?
And wilt thou leave the Church, and love a sty?
    Fie, thou wilt soil thy broider'd coat,
And hurt thyself, and him that sings the note.

Let foolish lovers, if they will love dung,
With canvas, not with arras, clothe their shame:
Let folly speak in her own native tongue.
True beauty dwells on high: ours is a flame
     But borrow'd thence to light us thither.
Beauty and beauteous words should go together.

Yet if you go, I pass not; take your way:
For, *Thou art still my God*, is all that ye
Perhaps with more embellishment can say,
Go birds of spring: let winter have his fee;
     Let a bleak paleness chalk the door,
So all within be lovelier than before.

DEATH

As he approached the age of forty Herbert's ill-health was a matter of concern to his friends at Little Gidding. In 1633 Nicholas Ferrar sent Edmund Duncon, a Norfolk clergyman who was staying with him, to see how Herbert was. Duncon found him in bed, but glad to have a visitor. Herbert asked Duncon to pray with him, using 'the prayers of my mother, the Church of England. No other prayers are equal to them!' They said the Litany together. Then, according to Walton,

> Mrs. Herbert provided Mr. Duncon a plain supper and a clean lodging, and he betook himself to rest. – This Mr. Duncon tells me; and tells me that at his first view of Mr. Herbert, he saw majesty and humility so reconciled in his looks and behaviour, as begot in him an awful reverence for his person, and says, 'his discourse was so pious, and his motion so genteel and meek, that after almost forty years, yet they remain still fresh in his memory.'[50]

If this is hagiography, it is eye-witnessed and supported by his brother Edward's testimony that 'about Salisbury, where he lived beneficed . . . he was little less than sainted.'[51] Duncon returned to Bemerton five days later. Herbert was dying and knew it.

He had come to terms with an early death in his poem 'Life': death as integral to all life. The 'posy' of the first line is simultaneously the bunch of flowers which he is gathering and the poem, or 'poesy', which he is writing. No further comment is needed.

Life

I made a posy as the day ran by:
Here will I smell my remnant out, and tie
           My life within this band.
But Time did beckon to the flowers, and they
By noon most cunningly did steal away,
           And wither'd in my hand.

My hand was next to them, and then my heart:
I took, without more thinking, in good part
           Time's gentle admonition:
Who did so sweetly death's sad taste convey,
Making my mind to smell my fatal day;
           Yet sug'ring the suspicion.

Farewell dear flowers, sweetly your time ye spent,
Fit, while ye liv'd, for smell or ornament,
           And after death for cures.
I follow straight without complaints or grief,
Since if my scent be good, I care not if
           It be as short as yours.

Herbert's 'fatal day' was imminent when Duncon visited him at Bemerton. He had a little book to hand, a manuscript of his English poems. 'With a thoughtful and contented look' he gave it to Duncon with the words, already quoted in this book,

'Sir, I pray deliver this little book to my dear brother Ferrar, and tell him that he shall find in it a picture of the many spiritual conflicts that have passed betwixt God and my soul, before I could subject mine to the will of Jesus my Master; in whose service I have now found perfect freedom;[52] desire him to read it; and then, if he think it may turn to the advantage of any dejected poor soul, let it be made public; if not, let him burn it; for I and it are less than the least of God's mercies.'[53]

Soon after this legacy to posterity, Herbert made his will – on the Monday before his death. He left everything to his wife, less legacies to his nieces, servants and Leighton Bromswold Church. He remembered his curates: John Hayes got a Bible Commentary and Nathaniel Bostock 'St. Augustine's works' – St Augustine was Herbert's favourite and most congenial theologian, the philosopher of love and the author of the autobiographical Confessions which were a stimulus for Herbert's autobiographical poetry. Arthur Woodnoth was executor and Sir John Danvers overseer of the will. The day before that, Herbert had had a sudden return of strength, called for his lute and sang his poem 'Sunday' to its accompaniment. His last day was distressing. The family were around his bed in the upstairs room looking over the garden and the river.

> As they stood thus beholding him, his wife observed him to breathe faintly and with much trouble; and observed him fall into a sudden agony, which so surprised her, that she fell into a sudden passion, and required of him to know what he did; to which his answer was, 'That he had passed a conflict with his last enemy, and he had overcome him by the merits of his Master Jesus.' After which answer he looked up and saw his wife and nieces weeping to an extremity, and charged them, 'If they loved him, to withdraw to the next room, for nothing but their lamentations could make his death uncomfortable.' To which requests their sighs and tears would not suffer them to make any reply, but they yielded him a sad obedience, leaving only with him Mr. Woodnoth and Mr. Bostock.

It must have been very upsetting for Herbert's womenfolk, this last manifestation of his old habit of self-withdrawal. He told Bostock to get his will out of its cupboard and handed it over to Woodnoth, that useful and troublesome man. He then said he was ready to die, and with the words 'Lord, now receive my soul' expired 'without any apparent disturbance'. He was a month short of his fortieth birthday.

Herbert had written a poem about death. It is the greatest possible contrast to his friend Donne's famously superb bravado in his Holy Sonnet 'Death, be not proud'. Donne's posture in the face of death is hostile and contemptuous. Death's dominion is a sham. He thrusts his apparently all-powerful enemy right down the social scale into base servility:

Thou art slave to fate, chance, kings and desperate men,
And dost with poison, war and sickness dwell

and ends triumphantly with 'Death, thou shalt die.' Shakespeare had written in the same vein, but more circumspectly: 'And death once dead, there's no more dying then.'[54] Dylan Thomas was to match Donne's reckless grandiloquence in the high rhetoric of his poem 'And death shall have no dominion.'[55] Herbert, unlike all of these, meets Death on the level and addresses it with good-tempered familiarity. His poem reads like a meeting with an old acquaintance, not seen for a while, or a village encounter with a parishioner who had previously been looking dreadfully ill and emaciated, 'nothing but bones', but now appears a lot better. 'Thy mouth was open, but thou couldst not sing' treats horror with a childlike, direct realism.

Death

Death, thou wast once an uncouth hideous thing,
     Nothing but bones,
   The sad effect of sadder groans:
Thy mouth was open, but thou couldst not sing.

For we consider'd thee as at some six
     Or ten years hence,
   After the loss of life and sense,
Flesh being turn'd to dust, and bones to sticks.

We look'd on this side of thee, shooting short;
     Where we did find
   The shells of fledg'd souls left behind,
Dry dust, which sheds no tears, but may extort.

But since our Saviour's death did put some blood
     Into thy face;
   Thou hast grown fair and full of grace,
Much in request, much sought for as a good.

For we do now behold thee gay and glad,
     As at dooms-day;

When souls shall wear their new array,
And all thy bones with beauty shall be clad.

Therefore we can go die as sleep, and trust
Half that we have
Unto an honest faithful grave;
Making our pillows either down, or dust.

The structure of the poem turns on differences between times – before Christ and after, when death was remote and when close – and the difference of perception which those times entailed. When death was still 'some six/Or ten years hence' all we could see was rubbish: 'dust' and 'sticks', the 'shells of fledge souls left behind' – empty eggshells. That was in the past. But now – and here Herbert changes from the few years of our own personal lives to the long narrative of Christian history – Christ's own redemptive dying for love has changed the look of everything. 'Our Saviour's death did put some blood/Into thy face.' The colloquial phrase is wonderful in the lightness it brings to the heaviest human concern: death now has some colour in his cheeks. It is even 'much in request', the recipient of many invitations. As a result, we can look forward to a happy doomsday resurrection when death's grizzly bones will be clothed with beautiful flesh. And for the present, 'we can go die as sleep' on soft pillows of 'either down or dust'. The metre, suiting the sentiment, is lively and relaxed.

Doomsday itself, the subject and title of the next poem in *The Temple*, is no Michelangelo scene of overwhelming terror but a cheerful reunion of bodily limbs, beginning with:

Come away,
Make no delay.
Summon all the dust to rise,
Till it stir, and rub the eyes:
While this member jogs the other,
Each one whisp'ring, *Live you brother?*

Walton gives no account of Herbert's burial at Bemerton, but Aubrey, moved by a family connection with the occasion, does so in terms which remind one of Thomas Hardy:

He lies in the chancel, under no large, nor yet very good, marble grave-stone, without any inscription ... He was buried (according to his own desire) with the singing service for the burial of the dead, by the singing men of Sarum [that is, Salisbury]. Francis Sambroke (attorney) then assisted as a Chorister boy; my uncle, Thomas Danvers, was at the Funeral.

9

Herbert's Days and Years

DAYS

A biography cannot but distort the real life of its subject by a drastic reduction of time. What took forty years to live through can be read in less than half as many hours. But although the delusive acceleration of reality entailed in writing and reading about life and lives cannot be dissolved, it can sometimes be counteracted. With Herbert we can slow things down to something more like the pace of real time by restoring them to the cycle of the seasons, matched and enhanced for him by the cycle of the Christian year, itself set in motion by biography: Christ's life from his midwinter birth at Christmas to his Easter death and resurrection in the spring. This calendar was a sort of living, regular poem. As such, it marked out and sustained Herbert's life, articulated it and fastened it to his faith. And we can decelerate still more by concentrating on the single day, what it contained and how it was arranged. There is a realism in that which is neighbour to the therapeutic moral value of living day to day. Herbert's familiar psalmist expostulated in vain, 'Lord, let me know mine end, and the number of my days: that I may be certified how long I have to live.'[1] Christ remedied that anxiety with:

> Take therefore no thought for the morrow: for the morrow shall take thought for the things of itself. Sufficient unto the day is the evil thereof.[2]

Herbert took that advice and passed it on in 'The Discharge', meaning discharge from anxiety about his future.

> Only the present is thy part and fee,
> And happy thou,
> If, though thou didst not beat thy future brow,
> Thou couldst well see
> What present things require of thee.
>
> They ask enough; why shouldst thou further go?
> Raise not the mud
> Of future depths, but drink the clear and good.
> Dig not for woe
> In times to come; for it will grow.

And with a typically domestic metaphor for the ways of divine providence:

> God chains the dog till night: wilt loose the chain,
> And wake thy sorrow?

Days marked out by prayer were his inheritance from home and, particularly richly, from Westminster School. In his latter years at Bemerton he was notably regular in his daily saying of Morning and Evening Prayer with his family in the church over the road.

Herbert's two poems 'Matins' and 'Evensong' are not about those regular occasions. They are additional devotions. They have old, pre-reformation titles: Matins being the service in the catholic Breviary which could be said at daybreak, Evensong (or Vespers) its sunset service. Herbert's fondness for these old names, dropped from the Book of Common Prayer since 1552, is a signal of his difference from more radical protestants, who were suspicious of such relics of popery. But he is not substituting them for the Morning Prayer and Evening Prayer in the Church of England's Book of Common Prayer. 'Matins' and 'Evensong' are private prayers: the first said when waking up before going over to the church with his family; the second after church and in the evening, at the time of his going to bed. Such additional prayers were common in his circle. They proliferated at Little Gidding, said in the house in addition to the services in the church, and are to be found among Lancelot Andrewes's long and poetically beautiful *Preces Privatae* (the great linguist prayed in Latin).[3] Herbert's two poems are perfectly suited to the moods of their times of day. 'Matins' is set at the transition from the passivity of sleep to the activity of work: a crescendo. 'Evensong' marks the transition from the day's business, inadequately done in his view, to repose in the divine love: a diminuendo.

'Matins' is appropriately light and fresh. Its short verses mimic the growing consciousness of waking up: first a short three-beat line, then two four-beat ones, and finally a five-beat line – all in simple, forward-moving iambs. God, with his world, is up already, before the poet. The two of them must 'make a match': an agreed agenda for the day. 'Match' also had connotations of love and marriage. This triggers the next two verses, brightened by a little list of bright metaphors for the human heart, in which God is the poet's wooer. After these two verses about the individual heart comes one about man generally: rich but oblivious of the creator of his opportunities. In the last verse the poet speaks for himself, ready to learn about love in this new morning light and ending with the lovely image of the last line.

Matins

I cannot ope mine eyes,
But thou art ready there to catch
My morning-soul and sacrifice:
Then we must needs for that day make a match.

My God, what is a heart?
Silver, or gold, or precious stone,
Or star, or rainbow, or a part
Of all these things, or all of them in one?

My God, what is a heart,
That thou shouldst it so eye, and woo,
Pouring upon it all thy art,
As if that thou had'st nothing else to do?

Indeed man's whole estate
Amounts (and richly) to serve thee:
He did not heav'n and earth create,
Yet studies them, not him by whom they be.

Teach me thy love to know;
That this new light, which now I see,
May both the work and workman show:
Then by a sun-beam I will climb to thee.

'Evensong' also begins with a short three-beat line, but it starts with a trochee, its slowing-down stress on the first syllable being the mirror-opposite of an iamb. This is a signal that the whole poem will have the character, appropriate to bedtime, of a quietening-down instead of the getting-going of 'Matins'. It is a lullaby.

Evensong

Blest be the God of love,
Who gave me eyes, and light, and power this day,
Both to be busy and to play.
But much more blest be God above,
Who gave me sight alone,
Which to himself he did deny:
For when he sees my ways, I die:
But I have got his son, and he hath none.

What have I brought thee home
For this thy love? have I discharg'd the debt,
Which this day's favour did beget?
I ran; but all I brought was foam.
Thy diet [provision of food], care, and cost
Do end in bubbles, balls of wind;
Of wind to thee whom I have crost,
But balls of wild-fire to my troubled mind.

Yet still thou goest on,
And now with darkness closest weary eyes,
Saying to man, *It doth suffice:*
Henceforth repose; your work is done.
Thus in thy ebony box
Thou dost enclose us, till the day
Put our amendment in our way,
And give new wheels to our disorder'd clocks.

> I muse, which shows more love,
> The day or night: that is the gale, this th' harbour;
> That is the walk, and this the arbour;
> Or that the garden, this the grove.
> My God, thou art all love.
> Not one poor minute scapes thy breast,
> But brings a favour from above;
> And in this love, more than in bed, I rest.

The eight-line verses first climb towards the middle, then relax and fall towards the end. There is dreamy complexity in the second half of the first verse, based on two scriptural reminiscences worth noting. First, 'If thou, Lord, wilt be extreme to mark what is done amiss, O Lord, who may abide it':[4] so God denies himself sight so as to spare man. Second, 'God so loved the world, that he gave his only-begotten Son, to the end that all that believe in him should not perish, but have everlasting life':[5] so God let go of his Son so that man could have him. A son/sun pun is included, the light of God's sun having been darkened when his Son died on the cross.[6] After all those crammed allusions, the poem distils into lucidity. In the second verse the poet reviews his unsatisfactory day. In the third the kindly and forgiving Father-God tucks him up in bed with the reassuring words in italics. Two homely metaphors grace this third verse: the 'ebony box' of night and the 'new wheels for our disorder'd clocks' in the morning: God putting things into safe-keeping in his box of rare and precious oriental wood, and mending clocks. The last verse slips sleepily hither and thither among matching opposites, such as help the process of dropping off: day and night, gale and harbour, walk and restful arbour, ordered garden and wild grove. 'My God, thou art all love' is the thought which ensures sleep and – the final word – 'rest'.

For some reason a little poem with the forbidding title 'Sin' is placed between 'Matins' and 'Evensong' in *The Temple*. Perhaps the reason is that sin, in its negative sense of failure to do good, is to be the topic of the second verse of 'Evensong', where it characterizes the non-achievements of the day gone by. The poem emerges to be not so much forbidding as a surprising rehabilitation of the devil. He is not as bad as our sins, or as he is painted. In the Bible, after all, Satan is one of God's courtiers or ex-courtiers and his public prosecutor:[7] 'some good in him, all agree'. Sin, on the other hand, is 'flat opposite to th' Almighty', lacking not only *virtue* but also *being*: a doctrine Herbert had learned from St Augustine who wrote that 'whatever is, is good. Evil is not any substance; for if it were a substance, it should be good.'[8] Herbert even comes near to demythologizing the devil: he is 'our sins in perspective'. A 'perspective' (pronounced with the stress on the first syllable) could be a fantastic or distorted picture viewed aslant: the skull in Holbein's *Ambassadors* in the National Gallery is a prime example of the viewer as:

> ... one coming with a lateral view,
> Unto a cunning piece wrought perspective.[9]

The image of the devil is God's way of sparing us the horror of the direct sight of our sins, which would drive us mad. The poem is a prime example of Herbert's ability to treat dark things with a light touch.

Sin (II)

> O that I could a sin once see!
> We paint the devil foul, yet he
> Hath some good in him, all agree.
> Sin is flat opposite to th' Almighty, seeing
> It wants the good of *virtue* and of *being*.
>
> But God more care of us hath had:
> If apparitions make us sad,
> By sight of sin we should grow mad.
> Yet as in sleep we see foul death, and live:
> So devils are our sins in perspective.

The weekdays turned upon Sundays: their beginning and their summation. Herbert was enthusiastic about Sundays. They were the days when his vocation came into its own.

The Country Parson, as soon as he awakes on Sunday morning, presently falls to work, and seems to himself so as a Market-man is, when the Market day comes, or a shopkeeper, when customers use to come in . . . Then having read divine Service twice fully, and preached in the morning, and catechized in the afternoon, he thinks he hath in some measure, according to poor and frail man, discharged the public duties of the Congregation. The rest of the day he spends either in reconciling neighbours that are at variance, or in visiting the sick.[10]

He wrote a nine-verse poem entitled 'Sunday' which, according to Walton, he sang to his lute on his deathbed. Not one of his greatest achievements, it is, all the same, full of happy metaphors. Sunday is 'the couch of time; care's balm and bay'. Sundays are the pillars 'on which heav'ns palace arched lies'. And, reverting to his love of horticulture,

> They are the fruitful beds and borders
> In God's rich garden.

The last verse is exhilarated, treating Sundays as a kind of hopscotch in which jumping from number to number, seven being the highest, ends on the place marked 'rest' or 'home':

> Thou art a day of mirth:
> And where the week-days trail on ground,
> Thy flight is higher, as thy birth.
> O let me take thee at the bound,
> Leaping with thee from sev'n to sev'n,
> Till that we both, being toss'd from earth,
> Fly hand in hand to heav'n!

YEARS

The Christian year begins in late autumn with the four Sundays of Advent, which were a preparation for the great feast of Christmas. Christmas was a twelve-day holiday. The Elizabethan master of doggerel, Thomas Tusser, in his *Five Hundred Points of Good Husbandry* insisted on generous hospitality.

> Good husband and housewife, now chiefly be glad
> Things handsome to have, as they ought to be had.
> They both do provide, against Christmas do come,

To welcome their neighbours, good cheer to have some.
Good bread and good drink, a good fire in the hall,
Brawn, pudding and souse [pickled pork] and good mustard withal.
Beef, mutton and pork, and good pies of the best,
Pig, veal, goose and capon and turkey well-dressed,
Cheese, apples and nuts, and good carols to hear,
As then in the country is counted good cheer.

Morris dancers were welcomed into the house, which was decorated with holly and ivy, and there were games of cards – both of these entertainments favoured by Magdalen Herbert in the Charing Cross days. At court there were plays, dances and exchanges of presents. It was all too much for the puritans in Parliament who were to legislate against Christmas in the 1640s and 1650s. But Herbert was strong on hospitality and sympathetic to old country customs. Christmas was a 'good time' for him. (As we have seen, he worried that his orphaned niece in Wales had nowhere to go for it.)[11]

His double-poem 'Christmas' is a masterpiece, starting on a puritan note with the hunt for 'pleasures' leading him 'quite astray', but ending in joy. The birth of Christ, God come to earth, is its turning point. This taking of the festival into its religious heart, done with an actuality which is both natural and supernatural, attains the depth of significance which is always sought by good-natured Christians.

The first poem is a narrative sonnet, starting in the everyday with a hunting incident. This slides into allegory when the lost huntsman discovers that the inn where he has put up is the inn of Christ's birth at Bethlehem. At this crux, Herbert achieves a breathtaking but modest mythopoeic stroke with the lines:

> O Thou, whose glorious, yet contracted light,
>> Wrapt in night's mantle, stole into a manger

In the second poem that light comes to flood the mind. It is a pastoral lyric and starts with the shepherds who first witnessed Christ's birth. Then it swells into a crescendo of cosmic glories in which light and music 'twine'. Both poems move on sprightly feet, gaining extra momentum from their sprung changes of direction midway: at line 9 of the sonnet and line 27 of the lyric.

Christmas

All after pleasures as I rid one day,
      My horse and I, both tir'd, body and mind,
      With full cry of affections, quite astray,
I took up in the next inn I could find.
5   There when I came, whom found I but my dear,
      My dearest Lord, expecting till the grief
      Of pleasures brought me to him, ready there
To be all passengers' most sweet relief?
O Thou, whose glorious, yet contracted light,
10   Wrapt in night's mantle, stole into a manger;
      Since my dark soul and brutish is thy right,
To Man of all beasts be not thou a stranger:
      Furnish and deck my soul, that thou mayst have
      A better lodging than a rack or grave.

15 The shepherds sing: and shall I silent be?
          My God, no hymn for thee?
My soul's a shepherd too; a flock it feeds
          Of thoughts, and words, and deeds.
The pasture is thy word: the streams, thy grace
20   Enriching all the place.
Shepherd and flock shall sing, and all my powers
          Out-sing the day-light hours.
Then we shall chide the sun for letting night
          Take up his place and right:
25 We sing one common Lord; therefore he should
          Himself the candle hold.
I will go searching, till I find a sun
          Shall stay, till we have done;
A willing shiner, that shall shine as gladly,
30   As frost-nipt suns look sadly.
Then we will sing, and shine all our own day,
          And one another pay:
His beams shall cheer my breast, and both so twine,
Till ev'n his beams sing, and my music shine.

The exhilarating freedom of invention in both these poems conceals their debt to the Bible. The first poem depends on the first chapter of St John's Gospel which was read out at Holy Communion on Christmas Day. There the incarnation of God's Word is described in cosmic, mythical terms as the descent of light into the world's darkness. The poem then moves, in its last five lines, into St Luke's narrative of Christ's birth which was read at Morning Prayer. There Christ's mother 'wrapped him in swaddling clothes and laid him in a manger; because there was no room for them in the inn'.[12] Deftly combining St John and St Luke, Herbert makes St Luke's swaddling clothes into 'night's mantle', 'wrapt' around St John's 'glorious, yet contracted light'. Later tradition supplied, by implication,[13] the beasts around the manger (Herbert's 'rack' with its dark connotations of judicial torture in the last line, before the even more ominous 'grave').

The second poem (written, since absent from the Williams Manuscript, later than the first) goes the other way about, starting with St Luke's shepherds and ending with St John's light. St Luke tells of the proclamation of Christ's birth by angels to shepherds 'abiding in the field, keeping watch over their flocks by night'.[14] Having seen the newborn Saviour 'lying in a manger' (as in the first poem) they went back to their work 'glorifying and praising God':[15] singing, as Herbert plausibly and characteristically presumes. Scripture was, for Herbert, not flatly authoritative but a stimulus to his imagination which takes off from it magnificently. Magnificent – but at the same time homely. The field in which the shepherds kept watch is a water meadow, such as still pastures sheep by the River Nadder at Bemerton: it is fed by 'streams, thy grace/Enriching all the place' (lines 19 and 20). An English December evening comes vividly to the reader's eye with 'frost-nipt suns look sadly' (line 30). Local landscape is part of the ecstasy. This is something that Henry Vaughan was to learn from Herbert and which Stanley Spencer was to paint.

Most engagingly earthly of all is the allegorical hunting parable at the beginning of the first poem. It reminds us that Herbert was an aristocrat and knew well that aristocratic sport, indulged at Christmas. This allegory (his body is the horse, his mind the rider) is handled with Herbert's usual light realism. The hunt, which stands for the perpetual human hunt 'after pleasures', has been long and tiring and the rider has lost it while it was in 'full cry', and got 'quite astray'. Then comes 'the next inn which I could find', the place of rest and revelation. Starting from the vivid realism of this beginning, the two poems together describe a heart's conversion: from predatory hunter to self-giving musician, from rapacity to praise, from darkness to light. It all ends in the brilliant confusion of the last line: music with light, singing sunbeams with shining song.

Light and music cheered those darkest days of the English winter, when 'frost-nipt suns look sadly', and Christmas went on over twelve days of holiday. These carried over into the season of Epiphany which celebrated the manifestation of Christ to the world. From then on the calendar was formed by the attraction of the greatest festival of all: Easter. The number of Epiphany Sundays varied. This was because the first Christian Easter of Christ's death and resurrection coincided with the Jewish Passover, and that was determined by the Passover full moon, its extreme limits being 21 March and 25 April. This calendrical conundrum having been solved by careful calculation, the Church was ready to enter on the five weeks of Lent in which it prepared itself, by prayer and fasting, for Easter itself.

Herbert's poem, 'Lent', is a good-natured piece of rambling argumentation in his earlier style. Its tone of sensible persuasion is set in its first verse with the cheerful paradox of Lenten fasting called a feast and the usual designation of the Church as mother:

> Welcome dear feast of Lent: who loves not thee,
> He loves not Temperance or Authority,
> > But is composed of passion.
> The Scriptures bid us *fast*; the Church says *now*:
> Give to thy Mother, what thou wouldst allow
> > To ev'ry Corporation.

It goes on to recommend fasting as good for health and intellectual vivacity ('quick thoughts'); as an imitation of Christ's forty days of fasting in the wilderness (but not his full stretch, just 'let's do our best'); and as an opportunity for the Christian to starve out sin and feed the poor, 'and among those his soul'.

Easter is the foundation of Christianity. It dominates the Bible's New Testament. In the canonical Gospels long, sequential accounts of

Christ's last days are so dominant that the Gospels have been called by their scholars 'passion narratives with prologues'. In this they follow St Paul, the writer who preceded them. He had nothing to say about Christ's journeyings and miracles, and very little indeed about his teaching. All he had to say about his birth was that it happened. Christ crucified was the be-all and end-all of his faith and gospel. It was the point on which history turned: from the long years of living under the Old Testament's divine law to the new age of living under divine grace: from servitude to freedom. This revolution had happened because of the great sacrifice. Christ, God's embodiment, had died the death of an outcast outside the law and under its curse. This tragically explosive revelation, with the resurrection which followed it, brought in a world reborn into love and grace.

Strong emphasis on Easter was carried over from the Bible into the Church. It was given extensive liturgical coverage over a week: much more than any of the other festivals. The Book of Common Prayer had all four of the long passion stories in the Gospels read out *in extenso* over Holy Week. Special celebratory anthems were appointed for Easter Day, with biblical readings for the following Monday and Tuesday – altogether a solemn nine days' festival.

All this was no arbitrary ecclesiastical imposition. The power of Easter, and particularly Good Friday as its crucible, answered profound and problematical human anxieties. It was Christianity's answer to 'the only problem': affliction and particularly the unmerited affliction of the innocent. It was not a logical answer, but something with more psychological power. It confronted suffering humanity with the unsurpassed suffering of the divine sacrifice: the *non sicut*, nothing like, of Lancelot Andrewes's great Good Friday Sermon, which lies behind Herbert's long and superbly sombre 'The Sacrifice', at the outset of his Easter sequence. Human suffering was encompassed and included in the divine. In a world of diseases without cures and deaths without analgesics, not to mention the horrors inflicted by human cruelty, the contemplation of the cross and the hope of resurrection were the only remedy.

Herbert followed 'The Sacrifice' with six poems which attempt, one after the other, to respond appropriately to its depth and reach. He keeps on trying, but it cannot be done. And this confronts him, again and again, with a problem which is at the same time psychological or spiritual and also a problem of poetry and its writing. The two go together, life and art, and any solution must cope with them both. The question was: how to write a poem in which the poet's voice makes an adequate response to the voice of Christ's long monologue in 'The Sacrifice', with its insistent questioning of the reader? It depends upon the poet finding a point of view, a positioning of the imagination, which does justice to its most daunting subject. To pre-empt the argument, this comes about when Herbert gets clear of subjectivity and his own limited psychological resources, and achieves objectivity – and with it, the unassumingly great poetry of 'Redemption'.[16]

The series of responses begins with 'The Thanksgiving'. Practical as ever, Herbert proposes a list of good resolutions which might achieve a balance between himself and his redeemer. Writing poetry, naturally comes first.

> Shall I then sing, skipping thy doleful story,
>   And side with thy triumphant glory?
> Shall thy strokes be my stroking? thorns, my flower?
>   Thy rod, my posy? cross, my bower?
> But how then shall I imitate thee, and
>   Copy thy fair, though bloody hand?

So that will hardly do. He turns to more concrete good works: giving his money to the poor, not marrying (though eventually he did), giving up his profane friends, building a chapel or a hospital, mending 'common ways'. He will withdraw from public life (and indeed was to do so) and give himself over to music. Perhaps wit will be some use:

> If thou shalt give me wit, it shall appear,
>   If thou hast giv'n it me, 'tis here.

The headlong list of good intentions is engagingly ironical at the expense of his piety. Last of all, he will read the Bible, learn Christ's 'art of love' and turn it back on him. 'O my dear Saviour, Victory!' Surely that is an adequate response. A balanced relation of reciprocal love, even if proclaimed with bravado, must be the solution. But the last two lines which follow it say not. Christ's passion is beyond even that. He had postponed consideration of it in the middle of the poem: 'of that anon'. Now, finally, he confronts it – and is at a loss:

> Then for thy passion – I will do for that –
> Alas, my God, I know not what.

This anticlimax, following upon the headlong list of good intentions, is at the same time a climax: simultaneously of the irreducible mystery of the passion and of the poet's serial failures.

'The Reprisal' which follows takes that up immediately:

> I have consider'd it and find
> There is no dealing with thy mighty passion.

Confession is now proposed as a way to get on terms with the mystery. Instead of positioning itself over against Christ, confession (in its meaning of acknowledgement) will take his side:

> Yet by confession will I come
> Into thy conquest: though I can do nought
> Against thee, in thee will I overcome
> The man, who once against thee fought.

This lacks force: more of an ingenious manoeuvre than a heartfelt resolution.

The next poem, 'The Agony' does have force and gets it by the objectivity of seeing Christ's agony. It is methodically set up in its first verse, which establishes 'sin and love' as the two great things to which philosophers (intellectuals of all sorts in seventeenth-century usage) should put their minds, rather than geography, politics or astronomy. The next two verses deal with the 'two vast, spacious things', each in turn.

The Agony

> Philosophers have measur'd mountains,
> Fathom'd the depths of seas, of states, and kings,
> Walk'd with a staff to heav'n, and traced fountains:
> But there are two vast, spacious things,
> The which to measure it doth more behove:
> Yet few there are that sound them; Sin and Love.

> Who would know Sin, let him repair
> Unto Mount Olivet; there shall he see
> A man so wrung with pains, that all his hair,
> His skin, his garments bloody be.
> Sin is that press and vice, which forceth pain
> To hunt his cruel food through ev'ry vein.
>
> Who knows not Love, let him assay
> And taste that juice, which on the cross a pike
> Did set again abroach; then let him say
> If ever he did taste the like.
> Love is that liquor sweet and most divine,
> Which my God feels as blood; but I, as wine.

Each verse has its own mood. The first is ironically quizzical. The second and central verse presents the sheer pain of Christ's agony with overwhelmingly bloody realism. The third describes the release of divine love with sensuous pleasure, the blood become wine. 'The Agony' is a return to base after the previous searchings of conscience. Again the Bible is at its source. In Christ's agony on Mount Olivet before his arrest 'his sweat was as it were great drops of blood falling on the ground.'[17] Herbert turns this into the excruciating couplet:

> Sin is that press and vice, which forceth pain
> To hunt his cruel food through ev'ry vein.

The conclusion of the third and last verse astonishes by complete contrast. It savours the pleasure of taste:

> Love is that liquor sweet and most divine,
> Which my God feels as blood; but I, as wine.

The horror of the preceding verse is changed for a delicious wine-tasting. It derives from the climax of St John's account of the crucifixion: when Christ died 'one of the soldiers with a spear pierced his side, and forthwith came there out blood and water.'[18] This was traditionally understood to be the origin of the wine mixed with water, changed into Christ's blood, in the cup from which the worshippers drink in Holy Communion. That final couplet holds the mystery of sacrificial exchange in a simple conjunction of opposites: blood and wine, pain and pleasure.

The next two poems revert to subjectivity. Herbert set great store on accusatory self-analysis, 'tumbling' the contents of his inmost 'chest'.[19] It was the spiritual aspect of his obsession with cleanliness. The effect of it on his poetry is variable and in these two poems, 'The Sinner' and 'Good Friday', it is depressing. The results of the self-examination in 'The Sinner' are overwhelmingly negative and scarcely redeemed by the concluding prayer, referring to God writing his law on tablets of stone:[20]

> And though my hard heart scarce to thee can groan,
> Remember that thou once did write in stone.

The poem fails to ignite. The next, 'Good Friday', is a double-poem and particularly disappointing. The title leads readers to expect something monumental on the level of 'The Sacrifice'. Instead, in the first part, they get three short verses of unanswered questions in the style of the previous 'The Thanksgiving' but more artificial, followed by two which match sins with sorrows. The second part beseeches God to use his heart as a writing box (boxes being a favourite metaphor) in which he can inscribe the instruments of the passion, leaving no room for sin. If this metaphor testifies to the closeness of writing and devotion for Herbert, it is too consciously literary and too-clever-by-half for the tragic day of its title.

'Redemption', which follows 'Good Friday' in the sequence, is an altogether greater achievement – indeed, a masterpiece (it is quoted in full in Chapter 1 and considered in the Interlude). Herbert manages to resolve his turbulent anxiety into an objective narrative, one of his 'allegories in miniature' admired by Louis MacNeice as 'an out-and-out allegorical sonnet in everyday diction and with images drawn from something so prosaic as real estate'.[21] Herbert has got his problem at arm's length and put it into the short space of a sonnet which at last answers to the mystery of the passion – artistically and psychologically at the same time. It is the moment his readers have been waiting for through the twists and disappointing turns of the preceding poems.[22] The long storm, which has gone on fitfully and listlessly through the previous five poems, has blown itself out. The reader is left with the poet to simply *see* the mystery of sacrificial redemption, aghast and without officious commentary.

In the last poem of the passion series, 'Sepulchre', Christ's body is laid in its tomb:

> these stones in quiet entertain thee,
> And order.

Humanity will continue in its destructive course but divine love is invincible.

> Yet do we still persist as we began,
> And so should perish, but that nothing can,
> Though it be cold, hard, foul, from loving man
> Withhold thee.

It is a conclusion with a rueful serenity comparable to the final chorus of Bach's *St John Passion*. The passion series at the outset of *The Temple* establishes, through tormented irony and repeated attempts to penetrate its mystery, the sovereignty of the love which will bring closure with the welcoming and persistent host of 'Love (III)'.

Easter Day announces a switch of feeling to the opposite pole after a week of mounting grief – so sudden that it is hard to adapt to it. Herbert was, incidentally, to be helped in this difficulty by a cheering idea: Christ's burial clothes were left behind for us to use as handkerchiefs to dry our eyes: thrifty divine housekeeping! Herbert was to make this homely conceit into the last verse of 'The Dawning', a later poem:

> Arise sad heart: if thou dost not withstand,
> Christ's resurrection thine may be:
> Do not by hanging down break from the hand,
> Which as it riseth, raiseth thee:
> Arise, arise;
> And with his burial-linen dry thine eyes:
> Christ left his grave clothes, that we might, when grief
> Draws tears, or blood, not want a handkerchief.

'Easter' is a double-poem, like 'Good Friday' but far better and in another, exultant key. It is musical – such celebratory music that in the second verse it can include even the anguish of Christ's crucifixion: the 'stretched sinews' of his body are the strings of a lute, his wooden cross its soundboard. The gruesomeness of the metaphor, painfully actualizing pain, is met in a bitter-sweet conjunction by the brilliant music of the metre: pentameters twice followed by lively little two-beat lines and capped by two more swinging pentameters.

The first verse lifts up the reader with its image of Christ and poet rising together, hand in hand. It is followed by an abstruse (to us) reference to alchemy: 'calcining' was the purifying reduction of some ordinary substance to powder in the hope of then changing it into gold – here the gold of being morally good or 'just'. Abstruse too is the musical reference in the first poem's last verse to music being 'but three parts vied and multiplied' with the prayer for the Spirit to join in with lute and voice. 'The basis of harmony', notes Helen Wilcox, 'is the triad or common chord, made up of three concordant notes, each a third apart.'[23] But Herbert wants more than that: a super-music of the Spirit.

The first poem of the pair has plentiful enjambment, the end of one line carrying straight into the beginning of the next, thus keeping things up and running. The second poem evokes landscape, the brilliance and fragrance of a spring morning – but only to compare it unfavourably with the glorious light and accompanying 'sweets' (the herbs and spices of his burial) of Christ's resurrection.

Easter

Rise heart; thy Lord is risen. Sing his praise
            Without delays,
Who takes thee by the hand, that thou likewise
            With him mayest rise:
That, as his death calcined thee to dust,
His life may make thee gold, and much more, just.

Awake, my lute, and struggle for thy part
            With all thy art.
The cross taught all wood to resound his name,
            Who bore the same.
His stretched sinews taught all strings, what key
Is best to celebrate this most high day.

Consort both heart and lute, and twist a song
            Pleasant and long:

Or, since all music is but three parts vied
                    And multiplied,
O let thy blessed Spirit bear a part,
And make up our defects with his sweet art.

I got me flowers to straw thy way;
I got me boughs off many a tree:
But thou wast up by break of day,
And brought'st thy sweets along with thee.

The Sun arising in the East,
Though he give light, and th' East perfume;
If they should offer to contest
With thy arising, they presume.

Can there be any day but this,
Though many suns to shine endeavour?
We count three hundred, but we miss:
There is but one, and that one ever.

The last lines achieve resolution and rest by means of a kind of mathematical tour de force: there are (very roughly) 300 days in the year, but they are reduced to one eternal day: Christ's overcoming of death erases time's most formidable marker.

'Easter' is followed in *The Temple* by 'Easter Wings'. It is a pattern poem, crafted to look like the wings of birds flying eastward across the page to the rising sun. This point was lost on Thomas Buck, the printer of the first edition. For some reason he tilted it ninety degrees so that the wings fly vertically straight upwards. Both the previous manuscripts have it horizontal: which must be right, because Herbert worked on the Williams Manuscript, making several corrections in his own hand of which the most striking were the substitution of 'harmoniously' for 'do by degree' in line 8 and 'victories' for 'sacrifice' in line 9: both distinct improvements. The original horizontal arrangement shows a day-by-day movement through time rather than an escape heavenwards. Time runs through both verses. They are little narratives. The metre reduces from five feet to four to three – all in the past tense – and reaches a narrow present crisis in the two feet of the middle lines. At this point it

escapes and expands by reversal into a free future. 'Imp', by the way, is
a term of falconry, meaning 'to engraft feathers in a damaged wing to
restore or improve its power of flight' (*OED*).

Easter wings

Lord, who createdst Man in wealth and store,　　　　　　　I
　　Though foolishly he lost the same,
　　　　Decaying more and more,
　　　　　　Till he became
　　　　　　　Most poor:　　　　　　　　5
　　　　　　With thee
　　　　　O let me rise,
　　　As larks, harmoniously,
　And sing this day thy victories.
Then shall the fall further the flight in me.　　　　　　10

My tender Age in sorrow did begin:　　　　　　　　　11
　　And still with sicknesses and shame
　　　　Thou didst so punish sin
　　　　　　That I became
　　　　　　　Most thin.　　　　　　　　15
　　　　　　With thee
　　　　　Let me combine,
　　　And feel this day thy victory:
　For if I imp my wing on thine,
Affliction shall advance the flight in me.　　　　　　20

Form, feeling and thought are perfectly combined in the archetypal
Christian dramatic pattern: fall followed by redemption, sin overcome by Christ's Easter victory. The alliteration in line 10 achieves the
reversal with uplifting subtlety.

From 'The Sacrifice' to 'Easter Wings' (seven poems) the structure of
the collection of poems in *The Temple* is sequential, deliberate and
clear. The Easter season, from passion to resurrection, is the foundation
of the whole of Herbert's religion. After Easter comes Whitsunday. Herbert's somewhat laboured poem about that will be considered in the
next chapter. After Whitsunday comes Trinity Sunday and the twenty-five

'Sundays after Trinity' which bring the year back to begin again at Advent.

Herbert's poem for 'Trinity Sunday' is a perfectly crafted miniature. The ponderous theological complexities of three divine 'persons' unified in monotheism are not for him. Practical as always, he is interested in what each of them does: the Father as maker, the Son as redeemer, the Spirit as moral supplier. The three of them give him his structure of three little verses. The three 'persons' in the first verse get a line each. The middle verse moves through past, present and future: another trio. The last verse is made of three threes: three parts of the poet's body, St Paul's three chief virtues,[24] and three human states of being resolved by the last – 'rest with thee', which neatly ties up the poem with relaxed reciprocity.

Trinity Sunday

Lord, who hast made me out of mud,
    And hast redeem'd me through thy blood,
    And sanctifi'd me to do good;

Purge all my sins done heretofore:
    For I confess my heavy score,
    And I will strive to sin no more.

Enrich my heart, mouth, hands in me,
    With faith, with hope, with charity;
    That I may run, rise, rest with thee.

Herbert's clever arithmetic, spare craftsmanship and sincere devotion has made a bright prayer-toy out of abstruse and cumbersome theology.

PART THREE

10

Heirs and Imitators

'The current of his feeling failed; he became his admirers.'[1]

PUBLICATION

The only poetry of Herbert's to be published in print in his lifetime was in Latin and Greek. He kept his English poems in manuscript.

It was the same with his friend since childhood, John Donne. The greater part of Donne's poetry was not published in print until 1633, two years after his death. He had long preferred manuscript to print, writing to a friend in 1612 that 'we take as it comes whatever the printing presses bring forth with inky travail, but what is written by hand is much more to be venerated.'[2] A manuscript might be 'venerated' for its greater beauty, but also for its unique personal character as having rare social value. Printed publication, by contrast, was considered *infra dig*. This infuriated Michael Drayton, the much published and prolifically professional writer on public themes, who denounced 'this time, when verses are wholly deduced to chambers, and nothing esteemed in this lunatic age but what is kept in cabinets and must only pass by transcription'.[3] (One thinks of Donne's *La Corona* sequence in Magdalen Herbert's cabinet.) And a certain Richard Nicolls went head-on at what he saw as the snobbery of manuscript:

Many idle humourists [followers of fashion] whose singularity allows nothing good that is common in this frantic age, esteem of verses upon which the vulgar in a stationer's [bookseller's] shop hath once breathed as of a piece of infection, in whose fine fingers no papers are wholesome, but such as pass by private manuscriptation.[4]

There were also practical considerations in favour of manuscript. It kept the work in the author's control. Donne was worried about the manuscript of his *Biathanatos* – with reason: as its title suggested, it was a defence of suicide. In 1619 he wrote about it to his friend Sir Robert Carr in some anxiety. 'Reserve it for me, if I live, and if I die, I only forbid it the press and the fire: publish it not, but yet burn it not; and between those, do what you will with it.'[5] He was even more anxious about his prose *Paradoxes* and his erotic *Songs and Sonnets* getting out of his control and into print.

The privacy of manuscript was appropriate to Herbert's fastidious nature and the intimate self-disclosure of his English poetry. It was, after all, his way of exercising the discipline of self-examination with all the honesty and precision at his command: he was writing for God. Manuscript also suited his practice as a poet given to scrupulous revision. He might have circulated poems in manuscript as Sir Philip Sidney had done, but he seems to have avoided even that. There are no traces of their pre-publication versions in the commonplace books into which people habitually copied poems they liked. Apart from the two poems which were written for Arthur Woodnoth, 'The Bunch of Grapes' and 'Constancy', he seems to have kept his poetry to himself.

At the same time he had readers in mind – eventually. The last two lines of 'The Dedication', which is in his early Williams Manuscript, are:

> Turn their eyes hither, who shall make a gain:
> Theirs, who shall hurt themselves or me, refrain.

The dilemma, private or public, hung in the air until the very end. Herbert's directions to Ferrar about the little book which was to be published as *The Temple* marked a qualified turnaround. The private man and poet was, at the point of death, ready to be public – but left the decision and the responsibility to someone else.

The little book that he had entrusted to Edmund Duncon got safely to Little Gidding, where Nicholas Ferrar was its first known reader.

He was deeply affected. According to his brother John, 'The which when N. F. had many and many a time read over and embraced and kissed again and again, he said, he could not sufficiently admire it, as a rich jewel and most worthy to be in the hands and hearts of all true Christians that feared God and loved the Church of England.'[6] Right away he set his nieces to work in the Writing Room to make a fair copy of the manuscript in order to submit it to the authorities of Cambridge University, who since 1534 had the right, shared only by Oxford, to license publications for the press. The little book itself has vanished without trace. But the fair copy survives in the Bodleian Library at Oxford (hence 'the Bodleian Manuscript') and 'fair', not to say magnificent, is the word for it. It is not little, but a folio, measuring $12^{1}/_{2}$ by $7^{1}/_{3}$ inches. It bears no trace whatever of Herbert's own clear and rather angular handwriting, but is an ostentatious masterpiece of calligraphy. The writing is large, curvaceous and florid. There are plenty of loops and swoops of the pen, thickened by extra pressure on the quill. They distract the reader's eye. Fortunately, each letter is carefully formed and the turbulently ornate text is framed by the double ruled lines around it.

The title page of the Bodleian Manuscript witnesses to four stages in the book's making and transmission. The first stage, set in the middle of the page, is 'The Dedication'. This is a poem of Herbert's announcing the reciprocal relations of author, God and readers.

The Dedication

> Lord, my first fruits present themselves to thee;
> Yet not mine neither: for from thee they came,
> And must return. Accept of them and me,
> And make us strive, who shall sing best thy name.
>> Turn their eyes hither, who shall make a gain:
>> Theirs, who shall hurt themselves or me, refrain.

There are two interesting things about it. 'First fruits' is no way to describe a final and complete collection, but fits an earlier one. And in fact 'The Dedication', as we have seen, had appeared at the start of just such an earlier and smaller collection: the Williams Manuscript. The other point of interest is that, as noted earlier, the last two lines show that Herbert envisaged future readers of his poems, probably in manuscript and less probably in print – but not just yet.

The second stage appears above '*The Dedication*'. In a different and less fine, but careful, hand is written:

The Temple

Psal: 29:8
In his Temple doth every man
Speak of his honour.

The handwriting is Nicholas Ferrar's. So he was responsible for the title, *The Temple*, by which Herbert's English poems have been known ever since. It has led critics, such as T. S. Eliot, to expect an architectural unity in the collection which, apart from its beginning and end and some instances in between, is usually lacking. (It was also the cue for Herbert's seventeenth-century imitators, Christopher Harvey and Ralph Knevet, who wrote *The Synagogue, or, The Shadow of the Temple* and *A Gallery to the Temple* – see below.)

The third stage in the compilation of the title page is a string of five signatures below '*The Dedication*'. These name the officials of the University of Cambridge who, according to the University's privilege, licensed the manuscript to be printed. The first signature is 'B: Lany Procan:' – the Master of Pembroke College who was vice-chancellor ('Procancellarius') between the autumns of 1632 and 1633. The signatures of three other masters of colleges follow, followed by that of an obscure minor official, Thomas Freeman. The date shows that the women in the Little Gidding Writing Room worked fast as well as splendidly. So did the printers when they got their copy. *The Temple* was out within the year of Herbert's death, 1633.

Finally, in the top right-hand corner of the title page is the name 'W. Sancroft'. Below it, in a ruled space left by the Little Gidding scribes, there is written in the same hand, 'The Original of Mr. George Herbert's Temple; as it was first Licensed for the press'. 'W. Sancroft' was William Sancroft, who entered Emmanuel College, Cambridge in 1633, the year of Herbert's death and the first printing of *The Temple*. His uncle was master of the college and he himself eventually became a fellow and then master. He was a life-long collector of manuscripts and no doubt got hold of this one while in Cambridge: a copy of the manuscript of every book printed at Cambridge had to be left there with the Vice-Chancellor. Sancroft had a hard time during the Commonwealth but went on to great things, working with Wren on the rebuilding of St Paul's. He got a good word from Dryden in *Absalom and Achitophel*[7] and a bad one from Gilbert Burnet in his *History of his Own Times*[8] and ended up as archbishop of Canterbury. When he died, a large part of his collection including the Bodleian Manuscript was bought by another collector, the antiquary and churchman Thomas Tanner, who bequeathed it with the rest of his collection to the Bodleian Library where it has been ever since.[9] It is thanks to Sancroft and Tanner that we still have the Little Gidding manuscript.

There was a spot of bother over the licensing to print. The Vice-Chancellor was averse to a couple of lines in Herbert's youthful church history poem 'The Church Militant' which seemed to cast aspersions on the state of the Church in England:

> Religion stands on tip-toe in our land,
> Ready to pass to the *American* strand.

Ferrar refused to drop them and, according to Walton, 'the Vice-Chancellor said, "I knew Mr. Herbert well, and know that he had many heavenly speculations, and was a divine poet; but I hope the world will not take him to be an inspired prophet, and therefore I license the whole book."'

Thomas Buck and Roger Daniel, the Cambridge printer-publishers, got to work and produced a beautiful little book. The credit for it should most probably go to Daniel, who was keen on not confining their joint publications to remunerative school books and branching out into 'other books which would more honour the University press': including poetry, of which he published a good deal in the 1630s, such as Milton's *Lycidas*. Buck, on the other hand, was less innovative and more interested in the finance.[10] The title page of the first edition of *The Temple* is bordered by lace-like ornament.

There are three additions to the Bodleian Manuscript's title page in this first printed edition. The subtitle, 'Sacred Poems and Private Ejaculations', was perhaps added to placate the Vice-Chancellor by announcing it as a personal, 'private' text. The poet is named. So are

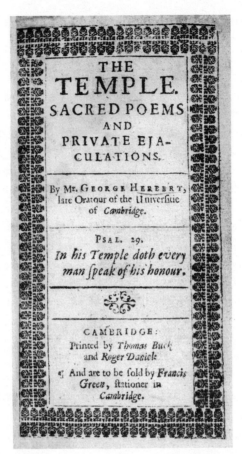

the printers and the University of Cambridge. It was a local production for the place where Herbert was famous as a former Orator. Being a little duodecimo book (pocket sized), it was cheap and sold well: so well that, in the four editions which followed within three years, Buck and Daniel had arranged an outlet with a bookseller, '*Francis Green*, stationer in *Cambridge*'. Their investment in the book had paid off handsomely.[11]

After the title page comes 'The Printers to the Reader'. This is a short biographical introduction by Nicholas Ferrar: the earliest life of Herbert. Ferrar offers Herbert's book to the world 'in that naked simplicity, with which he left it'. He notes, succinctly, Herbert's noble birth, his Cambridge career and his choice of the priestly life rather than 'the honour of State-employments'. The hagiography begins when he relates that Herbert's 'faithful discharge' of his clerical duties 'was such, as may make him justly a companion to the primitive Saints, and a pattern or more for the age he lived in' – an idea to be seized upon and much embroidered and amplified by Walton. Ferrar recalls Herbert's colloquial way of referring to Jesus as 'My Master' in his 'ordinary speech', his love of the Bible and his conformity to the liturgical disciplines of the Church. He gives a paragraph to Herbert's failed attempt to get him to take over the Leighton Bromswold prebend and the eventual restoration of the church there. He ends with Herbert's motto, 'Less than the least of God's mercies'.

The Temple was an instant success. It became the model and stimulus of subsequent English religious poetry. By the time Walton wrote Herbert's *Life* in 1670 there had been no fewer than ten editions of *The Temple*: he was writing about a famous man, a widely read and admired poet. Thomas Traherne, for instance, would quote Herbert's renunciation of 'curling with metaphors a plain intention'[12] when he refused 'curling metaphors that gild the sense'. He was following Herbert's lead as a master of colloquial English ('I like our language')[13] when he adopted 'an easy style drawn from a native vein'.[14] Herbert's achievement of candour and simplicity invited imitation. He had made poetry look as if anyone could do it so long as they did not put on airs: the deceptive appearance of an art which concealed art. In any case, there was nothing disreputable about poetic imitation. On the contrary, it was a standard literary pursuit, learned at school with Latin poetry and widespread in the literary world.

IMITATORS

We know of three imitators of Herbert soon after the publication of *The Temple*. Their various successes and failures show what they admired in their master and model and what there was about him that they could not match. Christopher Harvey (1597–1663) was a priest and schoolmaster in the Midlands. Cardell Goodman (1608–54) was, like Herbert, a beneficiary of the patronage of John Williams: first as a fellow of St John's College, Cambridge and then as rector of

Freshwater on the Isle of Wight. Ralph Knevet (1601–71) was tutor
to the Paston family in Norfolk before becoming rector of Lyng in
that county. He was given to imitation and wrote a continuation of
Spenser's unfinished *The Faerie Queen*. Knevet's and Goodman's imi-
tations of Herbert remained in manuscript until they were published
in the twentieth century. Harvey's, on the other hand, enjoyed printing and frequent reprintings by virtue of hanging on to Herbert's
coat-tails: more precisely being bound together with *The Temple* from
1640 until the nineteenth century.

Harvey's title page proclaims his imitation without reserve. Taking
his cue from Ferrar's title *The Temple* for Herbert's poems, he calls his
own *The Synagogue, or, The Shadow of the Temple*. In Christian
thought the Church superseded the Jewish synagogue, so Harvey has
got history back to front while acknowledging subordination. But his
subtitle rescues this, more or less, by advertising his book as a shadow
cast by Herbert's. The sub-subtitle is borrowed verbatim from *The
Temple*: 'Sacred Poems and Private Ejaculations'. The quotation from
Pliny vindicates the exercise.

Harvey was a modest man. His first poem is called '*A stepping-stone
to the threshold of Mr. Herbert's* Church-porch' and praises his master and model:

> In building of his temple Master *Herbert*
> Is equally all grace, all wit, all art.

It is a fair summing-up of Herbert's achievement – if atrociously
rhymed (even given that 'Herbert' was pronounced 'Herbart' at the
time). Harvey's own poetry shows that he had a lot to be modest
about. His strategy was to add a set of five poems to precede his own
version (duller and shorter than Herbert's) of 'The Church Porch'.
The reader is invited to 'take a turn or two' through 'The Church-yard',
over 'The Church-stile', through 'The Church-gate', noticing 'The
Church-walls' as he goes, and finally confronting 'The Church' itself.
All are moralized, and pedestrian in both senses of the word. In his
second edition Harvey added another set of seven poems about things
inside the church: the font, the reading pew, the Prayer Book, the
Bible, the pulpit, the communion table and the communion plate.

Herbert taught Harvey to write personal poetry in colloquial

THE
SYNAGOGVE,
OR,
THE SHADOW
OF THE
TEMPLE.
SACRED POEMS,
AND
PRIVATE EJA-
CVLATIONS.
In imitation of Mr. GEORGE
HERBERT.

Stultissimum credo ad imitandum non optima
queq; proponere.
Plin. Secund. lib. 1. Epist. 5.
Not to imitate the best example is the greatest folly.

LONDON,
Printed by I. L. for *Phil. Stephens*, and *Chrysto-*
pher Meredith, at the golden Lion in St.
Pauls Church-yard. 1 6 4 0.

language and a variety of forms. In 'Confusion' he does it well, hitting
on the metaphor of a tangled work box.

> Oh! How my mind
>   is gravel'd!
>   not a thought
> That I can find
>   but ravel'd
>   all to nought.
> Short ends of threads,
>   and narrow shreds
>   of lists [bordering strips],

> Knots, snarled ruffs,
>> loose broken tufts
>>> of twists,
> Are my torn meditations ragged clothing.

But Herbert's economy, over-imitated, could result in the clogged-up and barely intelligible prayer to Christ at the end of 'Invitation':

> Thou, that by saying, *let it be*, didst make it,
> Canst, if thou wilt, by saying *give't me*, take it.

Imitation of Herbert's splendidly abrupt opening lines, such as 'How fresh, O Lord, how sweet and clean' or, at a slightly lower level, 'Mark you the floor?', proves a trap when Harvey makes this trope into a mannerism as with:

> The Bible? That's the book. The Book indeed.

or

> The Font I say. Why not?

There are poems worth rescuing in *The Synagogue*, but overall it is *the* work of an inferior intelligence, cheerfully derivative but often cack-handed.

Cardell Goodman's poems did not get into print until three centuries after he wrote them. He too acknowledged his debt to Herbert as *the* religious poet and his superior.

> I need not tell you whence I took my pattern for these meditations; the author is so well known to you that you will soon discover the mark I aim at, though every shaft I deliver fall many bows short of it . . . and herein my aim is, not to be a fellow but a follower at distance of my leader. It shall be honour enough for me to be accounted his Echo, endeavouring to say something after him, though I reach no farther than to the repetition of half words and sentences.[15]

Goodman could be vivid. In 'The Race' the Fellow of St John's College could well be complaining about the usual behaviour of the undergraduates. He does it with an actuality comparable to Herbert's and in vividly indignant terms of which his master might have approved.

> Is this the way to heav'n
> To snort it out till past elev'n,
> And then to rouse and feed
> Height'ning the lusty blood
> With wanton sauce, instead of cleanly food?

So the minor emotion of annoyance with the young is the driver for a good-enough piece of minor poetry. In 'Poverty Inriched' Goodman has learned something more substantial from Herbert: the primacy of love focused on an objective and common symbol: a wedding ring with a 'poesy' engraved inside it.

> I chose the endless ring of Love,
>   Looking in which
> The poesy was, 'Love makes me rich':
> I well perceiv'd my choice was best;
> He that hath this, hath all the rest.

Knevet had neither of these qualities and only startles by his bad lines and inept metres. He prefaced his *A Gallery to the Temple*[16] with praise of Herbert as the man who had 'added new life to the withered branches' of religious poetry and equalled the biblical Psalms of David. 'It was he who rightly knew to touch David's harp: and though Heaven affords me not so much favour that I may come near him in the excellency of his high enthusiasms, yet I am comforted in that I am permitted to follow him in his devotions.' The clumsiness in such prose is immediately apparent in Knevet's first poem, 'The Incarnation'. It is an imitation of Herbert's 'The Sacrifice' with the refrain 'Was ever love like thine?' instead of Herbert's 'Was ever grief like mine?' It trudges through the Gospel story in stanzas such as:

> The brutish Sadducees thou didst confute,
> And mad'st the Scribes and Pharisees as mute
> As mushrooms, when they did 'gainst thee dispute:
>   Was ever love like thine?

The iambic pentameters that Herbert had used to convey the solemn tread of tragic irony are turned to triviality by Knevet's lack of intelligence and feeling. Elsewhere, Knevet's failure to learn anything from Herbert about metre and rhyme is evident in his 'The Pilgrimage'. Comparison with Herbert's poem of the same title is invited. Knevet seems to have found it too short and pessimistic. His poem is 215 lines long, Herbert's a mere 36. Knevet meanders through encounters with allegorical ladies, one after the other: Fortune, Pleasure, Knowledge and finally Grace, on to its happy ending. Herbert drove himself through an allegorical landscape: the 'cave of desperation', 'Fancy's meadow', 'Care's copse' and 'the wild of Passion' to:

> the gladsome hill,
> Where lay my hope,
> Where lay my heart

– only to find there a brackish, midge-infested pond. Herbert's allegory is as vivid as it is succinct. The end is bitter: the goal of pilgrimage is unattainable in the land of the living. The final verses of each poem tell it all:

> Here was such fullness of delight,
> That forepast joys,
> I counted toys.
> And former labours forgot quite;
> Here of my God I did request,
> To set up my repose, and rest. (Knevet)

> My hill was further: so I flung away,
> Yet heard a cry
> Just as I went, *None goes that way*
> *And lives:* If that be all, said I,
> After so foul a journey death is fair,
> And but a chair. (Herbert)

CRASHAW AND VAUGHAN

Herbert's power over poets who admired him is more rewardingly evident in two other and much better poets of the two decades following his death: Richard Crashaw and Henry Vaughan. Crashaw was not so much an imitator of Herbert as a religious poet with his own distinctive voice, for whom Herbert was an inspiration. Vaughan was an imitator who, eventually finding his own ecstatic voice, wrote poems of extraordinary beauty. Together they suggest that imitation may be good training, as was commonly believed at the time, but that inspiration consists of an individual voice telling of things which, however hackneyed or unregarded, have not been told quite like this before. There needs to be something new and, even if modestly, startling.

Richard Crashaw went up to Cambridge in 1631 and was a fellow of Peterhouse from 1636 until Cromwell's take-over in 1644. Crashaw then transferred his allegiance to the Roman Catholic Church and flourished in its tradition of fervid devotion until his early death at Loreto, with its shrine of the alleged Holy House of Jesus' infancy, in 1649. Like Arthur Woodnoth, he had been a frequent visitor to Little Gidding, drawn there by his voracious religious appetite and his enthusiasm for saintly women: in his case, particularly Nicholas Ferrar's niece, Mary Collett, sister to the object of Arthur Woodnoth's affections. In 1646, when he was in Rome, a London printer published his *Steps to the Temple: Sacred Poems, with other Delights of the Muses*. The title was a homage to Herbert. The anonymous writer of the Preface introduced Crashaw with 'Here's *Herbert's* second, but equal, who hath retrieved Poetry of late, and returned it up to its primitive use; let it bound back to heaven gates, whence it came.'

The claim, like Crashaw's poetry, was ambitious. Included in the collection was Crashaw's own homage to Herbert. It accompanied a gift of *The Temple* to a lady – a 'fair', or 'fairest' – whose 'morning sighs' and white hands interest the writer.

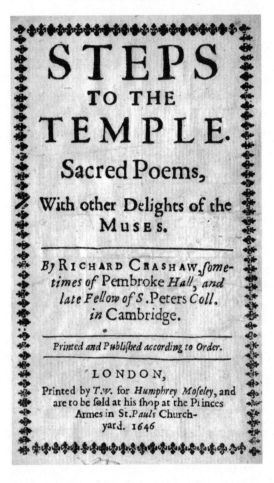

On Mr. G. Herbert's Book entitled The Temple of
Sacred Poems, Sent to a Gentlewoman

> Know you fair, on what you look;
> Divinest love lies in this book:
> Expecting fire from your eyes,
> To kindle this his sacrifice.
> When your hands untie these strings,
> Think you have an Angel by th' wings.
> One that gladly will be nigh
> To wait upon each morning sigh.

To flutter in the balmy air,
Of your well perfumed prayer.
These white plumes of his he'll lend you,
Which every day to heaven will send you:
To take acquaintance of the sphere,
And all the smooth faced kindred there.
And though *Herbert's* name do owe
These devotions, fairest: know
That while I lay them on the shrine
Of your white hand, they are mine.

The innocent mixture of erotic and religious excitement is typical of
Crashaw. The lady opening the strings on the parcel has 'an angel by
th' wings'. Her prayer is 'perfumed', and her reading will send her up
to heaven. Rapture is Crashaw's stock in trade, his devotion to the
mystic St Teresa of Avila inspiring two of his best poems.[17] The first is
a hymn with the superb beginning:

> Love, thou art Absolute sole lord
>   Of *Life* and *Death*

The second is a poem drawing on the popular image of St Teresa,
taken from her *Autobiography* and soon to be made famous by
Bernini, swooning under the penetration of an angel's spear. Again
there is an 'attack' which could well owe something to Herbert's
example in Crashaw's lines:

> Live here, great *Heart*; and love and die and kill;
> And bleed and wound; and yield and conquer still.
> Let this immortal life where'er it comes
>   Walk in a crowd of loves and *Martyrdoms*.

The tone is not Herbertian. Herbert had indulged this kind of grandiose hysteria in his early days when he had written the two sonnets for
his mother which begin with:

> My God, where is that ancient heat towards thee,
> Wherewith whole shoals of *Martyrs* once did burn,
> Beside their other flames?

He developed a lighter and more modest diction in his later verse. All the same, Herbert had opened the whole field of religious verse for Crashaw. The younger poet did not imitate him. In religion, Crashaw's Catholic Baroque is a far cry from Herbert's temperate Anglicanism: never further than in his 'Epigram: Luke 11': a Gospel text where a woman cries out to Jesus, 'Blessed is the womb that bare thee, and the paps which thou hast sucked.' Crashaw's epigram is addressed to Jesus' mother Mary, confusing her nursing of him with his wounded side on the cross:

> Suppose he had been tabled at thy teats,
>   Thy hunger feels not what he eats:
> He'll have his teat ere long (a bloody one)
>   The Mother then must suck the Son.

William Empson observed drily that 'to think of it as ambiguous may be the right mode of approach . . . a wide variety of sexual perversions can be included in the notion of sucking a bloody teat which is also a deep wound . . . the sacrificial idea is aligned with incest.'[18] Herbert may have provoked Crashaw's complete failure of taste by likening, in his poem 'The Bag', the wound in Christ's side to a mailbag to which messages to God could be entrusted:

> If ye have anything to send or write,
>   I have no bag, but here is room:
>   Unto my Father's hands and sight,
>   Believe me, it shall come.
>   That I shall mind what you impart,
> Look, you may put it very near my heart.

But the gruesomeness inherent in Herbert's metaphor is kept firmly under control, and made acceptable, by the kindly courtesy and homely grace of Christ's utterance.

Henry Vaughan imitated Herbert more closely in the letter and the spirit than Crashaw did. But he also, having served his apprenticeship, found his own voice, marked by a quiet rapture of visionary beauty, nurtured by his natural surroundings. As well as being Herbert's heir, he was Wordsworth's precursor.

Vaughan was a layman, living in secluded retirement from the turmoil of the Civil War and the Commonwealth: bad days which

Herbert had escaped by death. On his title pages he called himself 'Henry Vaughan Silurist'. The obscurity of 'Silurist' was intentional. His remote corner of south-east Wales in the valley of the River Usk was a very different environment from Herbert's, whether at Charing Cross or Trinity College, or indeed Bemerton. According to the Roman historian Tacitus, Vaughan's country was once inhabited by a doughtily separatist British tribe called the Silures.

Vaughan acknowledged Herbert's achievement in his two books: *Silex Scintillans* of 1650 and *Olor Iscanus* of 1651. *Silex Scintillans* means 'The Glittering Flint'. Above the title he put an engraved emblem to explain it: a flinty heart being struck by a thunderbolt driven by God's arm so that it exudes flames and tears. This is a pictorialized

quotation of Herbert's 'The Altar' which stands at the entrance of *The Temple*:

> A HEART alone,
> Is such a stone,
> As nothing but
> Thy pow'r doth cut.

Below Vaughan's title comes a further borrowing from Herbert, as with Harvey: the subtitle 'Sacred Poems and Private Ejaculations' is word for word the same as the subtitle of *The Temple*. Again like *The Temple*, Vaughan's *Silex Scintillans* begins with '*The Dedication*' to God. Herbert's 'Dedication' addressed the deity with 'from thee they [the following poems] came, And must return', Vaughan with '"Twas thine first, and to thee returns' – the first of hundreds of such quotations.[19]

Vaughan's preface to *Silex Scintillans*, after much lamentation over the literature of the day and its 'most gross and studied *filthiness*', went on to praise Herbert: 'The first, that with any effectual success attempted a diversion of this foul and overflowing stream, was the blessed man, Mr. George Herbert, whose holy life and verse gained many pious converts, (of whom I am the least) and gave the first check to a most flourishing and admired wit of his time.' The 'wit' has not been identified. It could be John Donne, whose erotic *Songs and Sonnets* had now been published posthumously and revealed the other side of the eminent divine. Vaughan apparently attributes Donne's conversion to religious verse to Herbert's 'first check'.

Vaughan was dismissive of Herbert's previous imitators:

> After him followed diverse, – *Sed non passibus aequis* [but with steps which match not his]; they were more of fashion than of force: and the reason of their so vast distance from him, besides differing spirits and qualifications (for his measure was eminent) I suspect to be, because they aimed more at verse, than perfection . . . for not flowing from a true, practic piety, it was impossible they should effect those things abroad, which they never had an acquaintance with at home.

Vaughan is unfair to Harvey and the others in implying that they were, as poets, strangers to 'a true, practic piety'. This was not the problem. He was nearer the mark in speaking of their 'differing spirits and qualifications'. It was these that made them versifiers rather than good poets: 'more of fashion than of force'.

Olor Iscanus ('The Swan of the Usk' – another local reference) has a richly illustrated title page, with a swan on a river between trees and bees,[20] and bears a motto adapted from Virgil's *Georgics*: *Flumina amo Silvasque inglorius*: 'I am a man without fame or glory, loving rivers and woods.' The collection begins with a Latin poem, 'To Posterity' in which Vaughan described himself as a countryman, deeply indebted to Herbert, enduring rough times. In translation:

> Wales gave me birth, in the place where Father Usk launches down from the windswept mountains to wander in broad valleys. Then Herbert, a man most expert in learning, the master of Latin scholarship, took me under his serene protection, and under his guidance I progressed for six years. This one man bestowed a double bounty: learning and love; with both mind and hand he would strive for my welfare, and neither mind nor hand grew weary.

Herbert mattered as much to Vaughan as his rural retreat and his Bible.[21] Together, they saw him through the 'gloomy shadow' of his times. Herbert is a constant presence in Vaughan's poetry: he took up his subjects, even his titles, and quoted him abundantly.

Vaughan was not immune from the dangers of imitation, not least its debilitating effect on 'force'. He was so overwhelmed by Herbert's example that he often seems to have thought that quoting him over and over again was the best way to write religious poetry. The result was predictably, precisely and all too often secondary to the point of being second rate. For example, in 'Obedience', Herbert used the writing of a legal conveyance of ownership or '*deed*' as a metaphor for writing a poem passing his life over to God. He excluded any kind of reservation from the transaction.

> If that hereafter Pleasure
> Cavil, and claim her part and measure,
> As if this passed with a reservation,
> Or some such words in fashion;
> I here exclude the wrangler from my treasure.

OLOR ISCANUS

SELECT
Poems, and translations
by
Hen: Vaughan Silurist

Flumina amo Silvasq; inglorius

Ro: Vaughan sculp

In the last verse he wrote:

> How happy were my part,
> If some kind man would thrust his heart
> Into these lines . . .

Vaughan made use of both these pieces of Herbert's poem in the first verse of his own 'The Match', which addresses Herbert directly as his friend.

> Dear friend! Whose holy, ever-living lines
> Have done much good
> To many, and have checked my blood,
> My fierce, wild blood that still heaves, and inclines,
> But is still tamed
> By those bright fires which thee inflamed;
> Here I join hands, and thrust my stubborn heart
> Into thy *deed*,
> There from no *duties* to be freed,
> And if hereafter *youth*, or *folly* thwart
> And claim their share,
> Here I renounce the poisonous ware.

Herbert's original is concentrated. Vaughan's response to it is more diffuse, wandering through poetry, blood and fires before settling into the legal metaphor, and then straying away into youth, folly and poison instead of Herbert's one word 'Pleasure'.

Vaughan fell into his own trap. He thought that Herbert's imitators were weak 'because they aimed more at verse than perfection', that their efforts were debilitated by not 'flowing from a true, practic piety'. Yet his own self-consciousness as Herbert's heir hobbled him. Fortunately he knew and found the way of escape from the entanglements of imitation. Indeed, Herbert had shown it to him. He must speak directly from his own life, from his own heart and with his own voice. And it is Vaughan's own voice that rings out at the beginning of his famous poem 'The World':

> I saw eternity the other night
> Like a great ring of pure and endless light,

> All calm, as it was bright,
> And round beneath it, Time in hours, days, years
> Driv'n by the spheres
> Like a vast shadow mov'd, in which the world
> And all her train were hurl'd.

That first line announces amazing vision with disarmingly informal directness. The casual 'the other night' flips the whole universe into the convincing actuality of the lines which follow. The extremities of darkness and light combine with mystical intensity into a cosmic vision.

Vaughan loved the night. In another of his masterpieces, 'The Night', it is celebrated as the time of:

> God's silent, searching flight:
> When my Lord's head is fill'd with dew, and all
> His locks are wet with the clear drops of night;
> His still, soft call;
> His knocking time; the soul's dumb watch,
> When spirits their fair kindred catch.

There is nothing in Herbert like this vision of the night sky as epiphany: the stars seen as 'clear drops of night' sparkling in God's drifting hair, the silence his 'still, soft call'.

To take another example: childhood. It mattered to Herbert as a practical model of love: 'Write thee great God, and me a child.'[22] Herbert's 'one calling, *Child!*' at the end of 'The Collar' is the voice of parental solicitude restoring sanity and order. Childhood mattered to Vaughan in quite another way. It was a mystical magnet to his sad soul, a blessed state to which he longed to return. A poem aptly entitled 'The Retreat' is as clearly readable as it is regressively heartfelt. The only external reference which a reader might need to know is to Deuteronomy 34: 'And Moses went up from the plains ... and the Lord showed him ... the plain of the valley of Jericho, the city of palm-trees ... and the Lord said unto him, This is the land which I sware unto Abraham, unto Isaac, and unto Jacob, saying, I will give it unto thy seed.' Palestine becomes Wales and the future shown to Moses is changed to the longed-for past of Vaughan's childhood.

Happy those early days! when I
Shin'd in my Angel-infancy.
Before I understood this place
Appointed for my second race,
Or taught my soul to fancy aught
But a white, celestial thought,
When yet I had not walkt above
A mile, or two, from my first love,
And looking back (at that short space,)
Could see a glimpse of his bright-face;
When at some gilded cloud or flower
My gazing soul would dwell an hour,
And in those weaker glories spy
Some shadows of eternity;
Before I taught my tongue to wound
My conscience with a sinful sound,
Or had the black art to dispense
A several sin to ev'ry sense,
But felt through all this earthly dress
Bright shoots of everlastingness.
   O how I long to travel back
And tread again that ancient track!
That I might once more reach that plain,
Where first I left my glorious train,
From whence the enlightened spirit sees
That shady City of Palm Trees;
But (ah!) my soul with too much stay
Is drunk, and staggers in the way.
Some men a forward motion love,
But I by backward steps would move,
And when his dust falls to the urn
In that state I came return.

Again, this proto-romantic nostalgia is Vaughan's very own, not a borrowing from Herbert. Its beauty is powered by his regressive and nostalgic psychology.

Finally, a comparison of their two poems about Whitsunday, the feast of the Holy Spirit (Herbert's 'Whitsunday' and Vaughan's 'The Shower'), shows Vaughan as a poet who can sometimes outstrip Herbert.

Herbert is the more biblical. In the personal prayer of his first verse the Spirit is 'like a dove' as at Jesus' baptism.[23] The main part of the poem uses the account of Pentecost in the Acts of the Apostles, chapter 2: the Spirit descending on Jesus' gathered Apostles in tongues of fire, enabling them to preach the gospel in all the languages under the sun. Herbert decided that these fiery tongues were the stars and the sun: a somewhat laboured conceit which he manages to treat lightly enough. He then laments his own spiritless times and prays for renewal. This time, it is Herbert who takes on too much material, Vaughan who concentrates and keeps to the point. First Herbert.

Whitsunday

Listen sweet Dove unto my song,
And spread thy golden wings in me;
Hatching my tender heart so long,
Till it get wing, and fly away with thee.

Where is that fire which once descended
On thy Apostles? Thou didst then
Keep open house, richly attended,
Feasting all comers by twelve chosen men.

Such glorious gifts thou didst bestow,
That th' earth did like a heav'n appear;
The stars were coming down to know
If they might mend their wages, and serve here.

The sun, which once did shine alone,
Hung down his head, and wisht for night,
When he beheld twelve suns for one
Going about the world, and giving light.

But since those pipes of gold, which brought
That cordial water to our ground,
Were cut and martyr'd by the fault
Of those, who did themselves through their side wound,

Thou shutt'st the door, and keep'st within;
Scarce a good joy peeps through the chink:
And if the braves of conqu'ring sin
Did not excite thee, we should wholly sink.

Lord, though we change, thou art the same;
The same sweet God of love and light;
Restore this day, for thy great name,
Unto his ancient and miraculous right.

Now Vaughan. Compared with Herbert's 'Whitsunday', his 'The Shower (II)' is shorter (ten lines rather than twenty-eight); more unified (a single flow rather than a series of episodes and verses); and simpler (five rhyming *a a* couplets instead of *a b a b* quatrains). He sticks to the image of the Holy Spirit as a dove and ignores the tongues of fire – being less set on the Church's Whitsunday and more individually himself. Instead of rambling through history like Herbert, he settles on a single and vivid moment in his own life: an evening shower in his native Wales. His rapture lives up to his exclamation marks. A natural event takes the place of Herbert's humorously miraculous descent of the sun to earth. Vaughan's abundant italics assist reading, so are retained. I have added numbers to the lines to help reference.

Waters above! eternal springs! 1
The dew that silvers the *Dove's* wings!
O welcome, welcome to the sad: 3
Give dry dust drink; drink that makes glad!
Many fair *evenings*, many *flowers* 5
Sweeten'd with rich and gentle showers
Have I enjoyed, and down have run 7
Many a fine and shining *sun*;
But never till this happy hour 9
Was blest with such an *evening-shower*!

This is a great achievement.[24] Nature and supernatural grace are together as happily as in Herbert at his best: a complete integration of feeling with fashioning. The framework is not as simple as it sounds. There are ten lines made up of five rhyming couplets. Starting at line 5 he enjambs four lines and does the same with the last two. This is in contrast to the first four lines, 1–4, which are each complete in themselves and firmly concluded with exclamation marks and a colon in line 3 which could just as well be an exclamation mark too. The effect of these first four lines is of arrest in static wonder, held to it by the repetitions of 'welcome', 'drink' and 'many'. The last five lines, by contrast, move along with no more interruption than a modest semi-colon, which could as well be a mere comma, to the conclusion – at which final point the reader realizes that the cosmic excitement of the opening lines has been about a natural, and very local, event: a shower of rain after a drought.

Herbert, the:

> Dear friend! whose holy, ever-living lines
> > Have done much good
> To many,

had done more than anyone to teach Vaughan the trick of the last line which transforms the whole poem and the combination of the quotidian with the sublime. It entailed a progress through imitation and quotation to the source in the self and the actual and, from there, the finding of the individual voice. That, with its necessary leave-taking, is the greatest debt that one poet can owe another: a blessing from 'that blessed man, Mr. *George Herbert*'.

PUBLICATION OF
THE COUNTRY PARSON

The publication of Vaughan's poems in 1650 and 1651, with his praises of Herbert, was quickly followed by the publication in London in 1652 of *A Priest to the Temple, or, The Country Parson.*

The first words of the long-winded title capitalized on the success of *The Temple.* It was printed as part of a book called *Herbert's Remains* which also included his collection of proverbs, *Jacula Prudentum*, and three of his Latin poems. The book had a fulsome and dramatic subtitle, drawing on Herbert's fame as poet and orator.

As *The Temple* was Herbert's fruitful legacy to the religious poets of the next decades, so *The Country Parson* was his bequest in prose

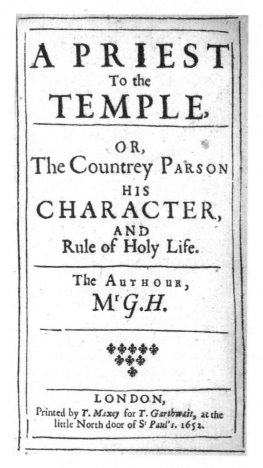

A PRIEST
To the
TEMPLE,

OR,
The Countrey PARSON
HIS
CHARACTER,
AND
Rule of Holy Life.

The AUTHOUR,
Mr *G.H.*

LONDON,
Printed by *T. Maxey* for *T. Garthwait,* at the
little North door of St *Paul's.* 1652.

to his colleagues and followers in parochial ministry. It was edited by
Barnabas Oley, a fellow of Clare Hall, Cambridge. He had been there
since 1617, so he would have known Herbert in his years as fellow of
Trinity and University Orator. Oley had got the manuscript from
Edmund Duncon, the man to whom Herbert had entrusted his manu-
script of *The Temple* on his deathbed.

England in 1652–3 was in ferment. King Charles I, a reader of *The
Temple* during his captivity,[25] had been beheaded in 1649, and the
country was at war. In 1651 his son Charles II invaded England from
Scotland. He got as far as Worcester where he was defeated by
Cromwell and fled. Cromwell, a puritan secure in his belief that he
was God's agent, was the only hope for stability in the land, where the

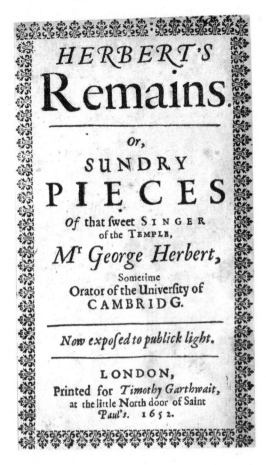

army and Parliament were at one another's throats: Parliament wanting to sustain the clergy of the traditional Church of England, Milton and other religious Independents hoping for disestablishment.

But amid the flux Herbert's memory and his works were fostered in Oley's Clare Hall: Nicholas Ferrar's old college, now with Ralph Cudworth as its master. Cudworth was one of the group known as the Cambridge Platonists who shared Herbert's beliefs in Christianity as a primarily moral religion, worked out in tolerance, virtue, holiness and love. In a sermon preached to the members of the House of Commons in 1647 Cudworth had told them that true religion was not 'merely' an assenting to 'a few barren notions, in a form of certain dry and sapless opinions'. Nor was it a matter of finicky ritual observance, such as Archbishop William Laud enforced, 'as if Religion were nothing else but a dancing up and down'. It was a life well lived, not 'acquaintance with systems of divinity'. While his colleague Oley was working on Herbert's manuscript, Cudworth was writing about the causes of good and evil being eternal, not simply due to arbitrary divine decrees as the Calvinists, with biblical warrant, insisted. His first work was *A Discourse concerning the True Notion of the Lord's Supper*. He understood the rite, like Herbert, as 'a feast of amity and friendship between God and men' reaffirming 'an inviolable league of friendship'.[26]

So Cudworth was in warm agreement with principles dear to Herbert: the humanely social heart of the Lord's Supper and the subordination of doctrine to life. He would have been glad to read in *The Country Parson*, which was being edited in his college, that for Herbert the Lord's Supper was 'a feast of charity' to which arguments about sitting or kneeling for it were insubstantial. And he would have appreciated Herbert's downgrading of theological speculation to a level with astronomy in the poem 'Divinity' in *The Temple*.

> *Love God, and love your neighbour. Watch and pray.*
> *Do as you would be done unto.*

That was all you needed to know and do. So the parson's life could be summed up in a few words: 'Love is his business and aim.'[27] Reconciling quarrelling parishioners by getting them to 'dine or sup together' was a practical example of it, and 'there is much preaching in this friendliness.' And as for preaching itself, it was for Herbert a matter of God:

> making thy life to shine within
> The holy preacher's.[28]

So Oley's editing of *The Country Parson* was done in a collegiate haven from the crisis in national life and in a place where Herbert, already famous and admired for his poetry, was appreciated. Oley added a 'Prefatory View' to Herbert's text. Having praised the lives of Thomas Jackson, the saintly President of Corpus Christi College, Oxford,[29] and Nicholas Ferrar as men 'admirable in separating from the vile, what was precious in every sect or person under heaven',

Oley moved on to Herbert. In effect, he writes the second biography: after Ferrar's and before Walton's. It is Oley who records that in Cambridge people were still shaking their heads over their excellent Orator's subsequent life: 'he might, so I have heard, as other Orators, have had a Secretary of State's place.' Oley contributed to the myth of Herbert's self-sacrificial ordination, ignoring the advantages of Bemerton's closeness to Wilton and Salisbury, when he wrote that he ' lost himself in a humble way'.

Oley's main concern was to defend Herbert's devotion to the Book of Common Prayer against its detractors in his own, later day. He emphasizes Herbert's regular use of its Morning and Evening Prayer, 'knowing that the sophism used to make people hate them, was a solid reason to make men of understanding love them; namely, because taken out of the Mass Book: taken out, but as gold from dross, the precious from the vile'. Oley recalled that Herbert called 'for the Church Prayers a while before his death, saying, None to them, none to them' – they were, he meant, unsurpassed. He testifies to Herbert's reverence for a custom which had survived the reformation and meant so much to his friend John Donne.[30] Herbert 'at the stroke of a passing bell when an ancient charity used (said he) to run to Church and assist the dying Christian with prayers and tears (for sure that was the ground of that custom)'. This agrees with Herbert's defence of old-fashioned priestly blessings in Chapter XXXVI of the text Oley was editing. Oley relates that Herbert attended the sung service in Salisbury Cathedral 'a few days before his death' and quotes an arresting saying of his: 'God has broken into my study, and taken off my chariot wheels.'

Oley may well have gleaned these bits and pieces of memorabilia from Nicholas Ferrar, a former member of his college. *The Country Parson* was not the instant publishing success of *The Temple*. It had to wait until after the restoration of the monarchy for further editions in 1671, 1675 and 1701. But it was often quoted and praised in the eighteenth century. From then on, and particularly in the nineteenth century, it has been a model and resource for the profession which it addressed: 'a mark to aim at' as Herbert called it.

SUCCESSOR, FAMILY AND FRIENDS

Herbert's widow Jane had to leave Bemerton after he died, probably taking the two surviving Vaughan sisters to her old and crowded family home at Baynton Manor. Walton relates that she mourned her husband for six years, supplying her with suitable expressions of grief, 'till time and conversation had so moderated her sorrows that she became the happy wife of Sir Robert Cooke of Highnam in the county of Gloucestershire'. She lived for some fifteen years longer, surviving her second husband by whom she had a daughter. Walton says that he was 'an affectionate husband; yet she would, even to him, often take occasion to mention the name of Mr. George Herbert and say "That name must live in her memory till she put off mortality." '[31] Aubrey, as usual, has something less suspiciously edifying to report. His Jane, the *bona roba*, is a robustly practical woman. Noting Herbert's writings, *The Temple* and *The Country Parson*, he adds that 'He also writ a folio in Latin, which, because the parson of Hineham could not read, his widow (then wife of Sir Robert Cooke) condemned to the uses of good housewifery.'

The Earl of Pembroke appointed a distinguished high-church pluralist to succeed Herbert at Bemerton. Thomas Laurence had been his brother William's chaplain. He was a chaplain to Charles I, also a former fellow of All Souls and Master of Balliol College, then Lady Margaret Professor of Divinity at Oxford with its accompanying canonry of Christ Church. He attracted puritan and parliamentary hostility by his sermon before the King in 1637 in which he exalted priestly dignity and defended the real presence of Christ in Holy Communion. Laud advised him to be 'mindful of the waspishness of these times' in vain. When the parliamentary committee for Wiltshire looked into life at Bemerton in 1646 it was horrified. Herbert had been 'a lover of old customs, if they be good and harmless; and the rather because country people are much addicted to them, so that to favour them therein is to win their hearts, and to oppose them therein is to deject them'.[32]

Laurence shared his predecessor's view and took it to some lengths. The committee found that Laurence had often been absent from

Bemerton, but when he was there he allowed skittling, bowling and dancing on Sundays after Evening Prayer. Like Herbert, he was hospitable and enjoyed music – if at a lower level than Herbert's 'private music-makings' in Salisbury. Laurence entertained musicians in the rectory. The committee noted reprovingly that 'there did usually come a poor fellow that was a fiddler to the Doctor's [Laurence was a Doctor of Divinity] house on the Sabbath days, and play to his children, to whom the Doctor usually gave sixpence and his dinner.' The committee came down heavily on all this, aggravated by Laurence's reverent liturgical conduct – railing off the communion table and bowing towards it. They forced him to let out the rectory in order to pay a drastic fine which impoverished him. Laurence had been kind to a parliamentary colonel imprisoned in royalist Oxford. In return, the colonel got him a modest chaplaincy in Huntingdonshire, where he died in 1657.[33]

Nicholas Ferrar died in 1637 and was buried at Little Gidding without a monument. Charles I visited the remaining community in 1642, en route for the north, and again in 1646 when he was on the run after his defeat at the battle of Naseby (the 'broken king' of T. S. Eliot's 'Little Gidding'). John Ferrar conducted him over the fields to a house near by for greater safety. The Ferrar family stayed on at Little Gidding, and in 1714 John's grandson and great-grandson rebuilt the church, the latter having been rector of Little Gidding from 1691 to 1706. It is no longer, as pilgrims to it like to suppose, the church of Nicholas Ferrar's and George Herbert's day, but a monument to the Ferrar family and its famous community. Their memorial tablets were installed in the new building and a table tomb for Nicholas himself erected in front of the door. That door is at the centre of its remarkable façade. T. S. Eliot thought it 'dull', unimpressed by its monumentality. Others may find that it deploys the vocabulary of Vanbrugh's and Hawksmoor's English Baroque on a small scale with striking success. There are obelisks: a large and imposing one crowns the centre of the façade, with little ones on either side. The doorway below is derived from Michelangelo's windows of the Palazzo Farnese in Rome.[34] On either side of the doorway's keystone is engraved the biblical text 'This is none other than the House of God & the Gate of Heaven.'[35]

Herbert's elder brother Edward, Lord Herbert of Cherbury, did what he could to keep out of the Civil War on grounds of ill-health and devoted himself to literature. He wrote *The Life and Reign of King Henry the Eighth*, *de Causis Errorum* (on the causes of errors) and poetry. He was much concerned for his libraries in London and at Montgomery and managed to keep hold of them. He left his books in Greek and Latin to Jesus College, Oxford, where they remain. On his deathbed in 1648 'he would have received the sacrament. He said indifferently of it that *if there was good in anything 'twas in that*, or *if it did no good 'twould do no hurt.*' The Archbishop of Armagh, who was ready to oblige him, was so offended by this flippant remark that he refused: 'for which', wrote Aubrey, 'many blamed him. [Edward] then turned his head to the other side and expired very serenely.'[36] His autobiography was eventually published by Horace Walpole's private press at Strawberry Hill in 1764. His brother Thomas, the sailor, had died some years before, melancholy and disappointed of promotion, having written a poem 'The Storm'.

The Danvers brothers took different sides in the Civil War. Henry Danvers supported the King, died aged seventy in 1644, and was buried in the fine marble tomb at Dauntsey with its verses ascribed to his protégé George Herbert.[37] John Danvers, Herbert's congenial step-father, supported Parliament to the extent of signing the King's death warrant in 1649, but according to Aubrey was also 'a great friend to the King's party and a patron to distressed and cashiered Cavaliers'.[38] He died in 1655. The walls of his 5-acre garden at Lavington still stand, and the torso of one of the many statues with which he adorned it has recently (in 2013) been dug up.

John Williams, Ferrar's and Herbert's patron and friend, became archbishop of York in 1641, having been rehabilitated after a period of imprisonment in the Tower of London. He had been sent there by the Court of Star Chamber for disclosing secrets of the Privy Council in characteristically relaxed and lively conversation, aggravated by suborning witnesses. Herbert's admirer the Duke of Lennox (who built the tower of the church at Leighton Bromswold) tried to mitigate the ruinous fine imposed on Williams along with imprisonment. It did not help that some jocular letters to him from the Headmaster of Westminster were found in his house at Buckden in which their enemy Archbishop Laud was styled 'the little urchin' and 'the little meddling hocus-pocus'. Returned to the House of Lords, he did all he could to reconcile puritan and establishment differences within the Church. His efforts were rewarded by a further spell in the Tower at the behest of the House of Commons. On the outbreak of the Civil War Williams left York to fight for the King in Wales. With his customary realism, he soon saw that he was in a hopeless military position and made terms with his parliamentary opponent. He never returned to England but died a broken man in his native country in 1650, haunted by thoughts of his beheaded King: a sad end for the man of whom the great historian of seventeenth-century England, S. R. Gardiner, wrote, 'if Williams had been trusted by Charles instead of Laud, there would have been no Civil War and no dethronement.'[39]

Arthur Woodnoth eventually got married, never got ordained, went on looking after Sir John Danvers's affairs and died in 1645. Edmund Duncon, the man who took the 'little book' of Herbert's poetry to Little Gidding, married and became a country clergyman, moving around during the Civil War and dying at Friern Barnet in Middlesex in 1673, aged seventy-two, having told his memories of Herbert to Izaak Walton.

11

Herbert's Readers

While Vaughan, Crashaw and the others were revelling in Herbert's legacy, the great philosopher Thomas Hobbes was having his doubts. His friend the poet Sir William Davenant (no relation to Herbert's Bishop of Salisbury) published the first part of his epic poem *Gondibert* in 1650 with a preface praising Hobbes. Stimulated by this, Hobbes set about categorizing the whole field of poetry in his *The Answer of Mr. Hobbes to Sir Will. Davenant's Preface before Gondibert*. Predictably for such an unsparing realist, Hobbes took against artificiality generally and figure poems in particular:

> In an Epigram or a sonnet, a man may vary his measures, and seek glory from a needless difficulty, as he that contrived verses into the form of an Organ, a Hatchet, an Egg, an Altar, and a pair of Wings; but in so great and noble a work as an Epic Poem, for a man to obstruct his own way with unprofitable difficulties, is great imprudence.

The last two items in that list show that Hobbes had Herbert's 'The Altar' and 'Easter Wings' in his sights.

John Dryden, the first Poet Laureate, was even harder on the genre. In 1676 he wrote *Mac Flecknoe*, a satire against the poet of its title and the playwright Thomas Shadwell. In lines 203–10 he advised Shadwell to give up trying to write in good, straightforward iambics and revert to the fiddly forms of the previous generation.

> Thy Genius calls thee not to purchase fame
> In keen Iambics, but mild Anagram.
> Leave writing plays, and choose for thy command
> Some peaceful province in acrostic land:

> There thou mayest wings display and altars raise,
> And torture one poor word a thousand ways.
> Or if thou wouldst thy different talents suit,
> Set thy own songs and sing them to the lute.

Dryden's scorn is aimed at the same targets as Hobbes had picked out, with an added shot at Herbert's musicality. But the insinuation that the writing of figure poems could only be a kind of quaint fiddling about falls and fails with Herbert. 'The Altar', 'Paradise' and 'Easter Wings' are all heartfelt poems, not at all distorted by their appearance or dependent on it (they work aurally as well as visually) for their effect. All the same, they gave Herbert a bad name, confirmed by Joseph Addison in the 7 May 1711 issue of his popular magazine the *Spectator*: 'This fashion of false Wit was revived [from antiquity] by several poets of the last Age, and in particular may be met with among Mr. Herbert's Poems.' Addison may have been alerted by editions of *The Temple* which appeared in 1703 and 1709. But after that Herbert was out of fashion and there was only one more edition before the very end of the century.

Herbert did not, however, entirely lack admiring readers in the eighteenth century, the depressive poet William Cowper being the most striking example. In the *Memoir of the Early Life of William Cowper, Esq. written by himself* he recalled a sad time around 1752 when he was twenty-one years old.

> Day and night I was upon the rack, lying down in horrors and rising in despair. I presently lost all relish to those studies I had been closely attached to; the classics had no longer any charm for me. I had need of something more salutary than mere amusement, but had none to direct me where to find it. At length with Herbert's poems, gothic and uncouth as they were, I yet found in them a strain of piety which I could not but admire. This was the only author I had any delight in reading. I pored upon him all day long and though I found not there what I might have found, a cure for my malady, yet it never seemed so much alleviated as while I was reading him.

Cowper's reading fulfilled Herbert's hopes for his poetry, expressed to Edmund Duncon on his deathbed, that 'it may turn to the advantage of any dejected poor soul'.[1]

The revival of Herbert began modestly with the publication in 1799 of *The Temple* together with Walton's *Life* and Harvey's *The Synagogue* by a London printer called Edwards. In 1806 Edwards printed *The Temple* and *The Country Parson*, followed by another edition of the same, with Walton's *Life* added in 1809. In 1816 he published Cowper's *Memoir*, sixteen years after the poet's death. His publications prepared the ground for Herbert's enthusiastic admirer and reviver, Samuel Taylor Coleridge.

From 1817 onwards Coleridge, like Cowper, got 'substantial comfort' from reading Herbert.[2] It helped him with his 'tendency to self-contempt . . . a sense of the utter disproportionateness of all I can call *me*, to the promises of the Gospel'. 'Love (III)' must have been among the 'hundred' of Herbert's poems 'that in one mood or other of my mind [particularly no doubt his glooms] have impressed me'. Coleridge also recognized Herbert as a poet of happiness. He found 'The Flower' 'a delicious poem' and 'especially affecting'. It is about recovery from depression, a narrative of the overcoming of religious ambition and its defeats by the common-sense remedy of acknowledging one's inevitable mutability and mortality. These interior movements of the mind are presented in terms of outdoor domesticity: it is set in gardening, that favourite activity of Herbert's, as of his mother and stepfather. Coleridge noticed in the poem's phrase 'And relish versing' 'a sincerity, a reality' which he found in 'many other of Herbert's homely phrases'. The penultimate verse, where this phrase occurs, is a wonderful combination of sensuality and spirituality:

The Flower

How fresh, O Lord, how sweet and clean
Are thy returns! ev'n as the flowers in spring;
To which, besides their own demean,
The late-past frosts tributes of pleasure bring.
Grief melts away
Like snow in May,
As if there were no such cold thing.

Who would have thought my shrivel'd heart
Could have recover'd greenness? It was gone

Quite under ground; as flowers depart
To see their mother-root, when they have blown;
Where they together
All the hard weather,
Dead to the world, keep house unknown.

These are thy wonders, Lord of power,
Killing and quick'ning, bringing down to hell
And up to heaven in an hour;
Making a chiming of a passing-bell.
We say amiss,
This or that is:
Thy word is all, if we could spell.

O that I once past changing were,
Fast in thy Paradise, where no flower can wither!
Many a spring I shoot up fair,
Off'ring at heav'n, growing and groaning thither;
Nor doth my flower
Want a spring-show'r,
My sins and I joining together.

But while I grow in a straight line,
Still upwards bent, as if heav'n were mine own,
Thy anger comes, and I decline:
What frost to that? what pole is not the zone,
Where all things burn,
When thou dost turn,
And the least frown of thine is shown?

And now in age I bud again,
After so many deaths I live and write;
I once more smell the dew and rain,
And relish versing: O my only light,
It cannot be
That I am he
On whom thy tempests fell all night.

These are thy wonders, Lord of love,

> To make us see we are but flowers that glide:
> Which when we once can find and prove,
> Thou hast a garden for us, where to bide.
> Who would be more,
> Swelling through store,
> Forfeit their Paradise by their pride.

The theme is as old as poetry itself, as old indeed as humanity's ability to reflect on its mortality and the puzzle of constant change. Herbert tackles it with the ancient metaphor of human life, the growth and decay of vegetation, given to him by his garden and his Bible.

> Thou turnest man to destruction: again thou sayest, Come again, ye children of men.
>
> As soon as thou scatterest them they are even as a sleep: and fade away suddenly like the grass.
>
> In the morning it is green, and groweth up: but in the evening it is cut down, dried up, and withered.[3]

For the hot biblical day, morning to evening, he substitutes the English seasons of spring, the time of writing, and the previous winter. Both are vivid: the shrunken, underground survival of plants in winter, the smell of dew and rain in spring. Such is life, and in the first three verses he is content just to describe it from the happy vantage-point of springtime recovery. It is so happy that even the past ordeal of winter is given a cheerful aspect. The flowers, after blooming, have only gone back to mother and 'keep house unknown' together: a cosily reunited family. Submission to the divine ordinance of mutability is the poem's destination. Such is life.

But why? Stable happiness – presumably the 'Lord of power' could arrange it quite easily – would surely be better than all these ups and downs, which serve only the purpose of demonstrating divine power over human lives, with no apparent benefit or advantage to them. This is particularly galling to the conscientiously religious man 'Off'ring at heav'n, growing and groaning thither' and always ready to repent with tears. But 'Thy anger comes, and I decline,' frost-bitten and frustrated. Turn and turn about, the beautiful penultimate verse returns Herbert to his present springtime with sensuous actuality, the sincerity and reality that Coleridge admired. The reader is with the poet, present at his act of thinking. This is the lyrical climax of the poem. It allows and illuminates the deliberate bathos of the last verse, which is addressed, not to the 'Lord of power' any more, but to the 'Lord of love'. Love reconciles him to reality. Love wants him to be happy. And it is the condition of that happiness that he, the poet, should affirm his mutability and mortality: 'To make us see we are but flowers that glide.' 'Glide' means passing along and slipping away. We, poet and reader too, must 'find and prove' that fact by trial and error – from experience. Then, and not by the way of religious ambition with its 'Offring at heav'n', its 'upward bent' and wanting to 'be more' than mortal flesh and blood, is Paradise regained and assured. It is a truthful poem: not just in the sense that it quietly insists on a fundamental and necessary truth, but also that it follows the errant intellectual and emotional stages on the way to it with an accuracy which allows them to be themselves as they were before he got to the resolution – or even wrote the poem.

'Every time I read Herbert anew,' Coleridge wrote in a notebook, 'the more he grows in my liking. I admire him greatly.' One had, Coleridge felt strongly, to know and feel for the man to appreciate his poetry. 'G. Herbert is a true poet, but a poet *sui generis*, the merits of whose poems will never be felt without a sympathy with the mind and character of the man.' Sympathy with Herbert is not difficult. The poetry does it, endearing him to his readers by its candour and grace, the sense that 'every poem in the book is true to the poet's experience.'[4] But Coleridge wanted to make the qualification for being a good reader of Herbert more exclusive. One should be 'a *Christian*, and both a zealous and an orthodox, both a devout and a *devotional* Christian. But even this will not quite suffice. He must be an affectionate and dutiful child of the Church.'

Coleridge's reason for this alarming injunction is that 'religion is the element in which he lives, and the region in which he moves.' So it is. But it is worth noticing that some 10 per cent of his poems are not religious and that those that are frequently subject religious belief to searching and unsparing criticism. In any case, time has not endorsed Coleridge's verdict. T. S. Eliot swatted it down as 'a gross error'.[5] The most sympathetic and understanding critics of Herbert since his time have by no means always been 'devotional' Christians, let alone dutiful children of the Church. Indeed, in recent times this has been spectacularly so.

William Empson is the most surprising instance. He was an atheist and a sworn enemy of Christianity, particularly of the 'torture-worship' entailed in its devotion to Christ's cross. Yet in Herbert's long crucifixion poem 'The Sacrifice' Empson found that the 'presentment of the sacrificial idea is so powerfully and beautifully imagined that all its impulses are involved'. As we have seen, it appealed to Empson as a monumental example of extreme ambiguity. Ambiguity was, for him, the stuff of life. Later he repented that his voracious appetite for it had led him into temporary sympathy for Christianity and was 'keen to stumble away from it'.[6]

A more temperate critic, L. C. Knights, began his essay on Herbert,[7] a model of appreciative critical tact, with these words:

> The poetry of George Herbert is so intimately bound up with his beliefs as a Christian and his practice as a priest of the Church of England that those who enjoy the poetry without sharing the beliefs may well feel some presumption in attempting to define the human, as distinguished from the specifically Christian, value of his work.

Knights noticed that Herbert's best editor, F. E. Hutchinson,[8] had allowed that 'if today there is a less general sympathy with Herbert's religion, the beauty and sincerity of its expression are appreciated by those who do not share it.' 'But', Knights rejoined, 'there is much more than the "expression" that we appreciate, as I shall try to show.' He succeeded, demonstrating that Herbert achieved, and described with frank accuracy, the process of acceptance of life's disappointments, fluctuations and limitations which makes for human maturity. 'The Flower' is a prime example.

Knights concluded his essay by asserting that Herbert's poems handled the changing stages of his life with such honesty and insight that they are 'important human documents' which address 'the questions that, in one form or another, we all have to deal with if we wish to come to terms with life'. Knights described such reconciliation by resorting to a psychology profound enough to get to the heart of the matter without the aid of Christian doctrine:

the recognition, not only of one's limited sphere but (the paradox is only apparent) of one's own value. It is this that gives such wide significance to the poem 'Love bade me welcome: yet my soul drew back', placed deliberately at the end of the poems in 'The Church':

> You must sit down, says Love, and taste my meat:
>> So I did sit and eat.

The achieved attitude – 'accepted and accepting' – marks the final release from anxiety.

Helen Vendler, most subtly sympathetic of Herbert's readers nowadays, takes the view that Love in 'Love (III)' 'is the God Herbert created in his own best self-image – light, graceful, witty, not above a turn of phrase, and yet considerate, careful for the comfort of his guests, affectionate, firm, and above all generous'.[9] A Christian reader might well, and more correctly from the historical point of view, put Vendler's perception the other way round: Herbert created, or rather constructed, himself in life-long response to the Other who was there already, the God who according to his Bible 'is love'.[10] On this crucial question, the question of *whom* Herbert was addressing all the time, Simone Weil's 'presence more personal, more certain, more real than that of a human being',[11] is closer to the poet than Helen Vendler. But Vendler is very close indeed to Herbert's heart, as she shows in the words about the end of 'Love (III)' which close her book: 'a welcome, a smile, a colloquy, a taking by the hand, and a seat at the table stand for all the heart can wish.'

There is an extraordinary clarity in Herbert. It does not exclude difficulty, mystery and the need for patient and close attention, but several of his poems are simple enough to be used as popular hymns sung in churches. A verse of one of these, 'The Elixir', can stand for his poetry as a whole:

> A man that looks on glass,
>> On it may stay his eye;
> Or if he pleaseth, through it pass,
>> And then the heav'n espy

and not 'the heav'n' only or chiefly but the things of ordinary life – its sights and smells, pains and pleasures: all given their true and immediately recognizable shapes. Emerson, Coleridge's American contemporary, accounted for it very precisely: 'Every reader is struck in George Herbert with the inimitable felicity of the diction. The thought has so much heat as actually to fuse the words, so that language is wholly flexible in his hands, and his rhyme never stops the progress of the sense.'[12]

Herbert's clarity of imagination delighted the young John Ruskin. In 1845 he was in Italy, away from his possessive mother for seven months to study Italian painting *in situ*. Fearing for his Protestantism, she had slipped a copy of Bunyan's *Grace Abounding to the Chief of Sinners* into his luggage. He hated it and told her that 'much of Bunyan's feeling amounts to pure insanity', adding that 'the imagination of George Herbert is just as vigorous' but the product of 'a well bridled and disciplined mind'.

> There is as much difference between the writings and feelings of the two men as between the high bred, keen, severe, thoughtful countenance of the one – and the fat, vacant, vulgar, boy's *face* of the other. Both are equally Christians, equally taught by God, but taught through different channels, Herbert through his brains, Bunyan through his liver.[13]

The publisher Pickering had produced a good edition of Herbert in 1835, reprinted in 1838 and 1845: the beginning of the Victorian Herbert boom. Ruskin probably had one of these. Arrived in Florence among the paintings he had long yearned to see, he reverted to Herbert to reassure his mother that 'the fact is, I really *am* getting more pious than I was, owing primarily to George Herbert, who is the only religious person I ever could understand or agree with, and secondarily to Fra Angelico and Benozzo Gozzoli, who make one believe everything they paint, be it ever so out of the way.'[14]

In more recent times plaudits have accumulated. F. R. Leavis noticed his 'free and poised *social* bearing'.[15] The testimony of his fellow-poets is most eloquent of all. When I told James Fenton that I was occupied with Herbert he exclaimed '*The* poet!' and explained, 'Both in intention and execution.' Seamus Heaney has discerned 'in the clear element of Herbert's poetry a true paradigm of the shape of things'.[16] Rowan Williams has expressed his admiration of Herbert as succinctly as Fenton: 'Herbert's the man.'[17]

Elizabeth Bishop's take on Herbert's 'Coloss. 3.3 Our Life is hid with Christ in God' is particularly interesting for its individuality. Among the papers left by this American poet (who, incidentally, believed that 'the only real way to understand poetry is to know the life and beliefs of the poet')[18] are some notes for a talk about the writing of poetry.[19] 'Writing poetry is an unnatural act,' she begins. 'It takes great skill to make it seem natural. Most of the poet's energies are really directed towards this goal.' She quotes Coleridge's praise of 'our elder poets' for 'conveying the most fantastic thoughts in the most correct and natural language'. Then, prompted by Coleridge's admiration of Herbert but disregarding his Christian exclusiveness, she goes on to quote from no fewer than five of Herbert's poems.

In the middle of this selection Bishop interposes a declaration of 'the three qualities I admire in the poetry I like best: *Accuracy, Spontaneity, Mystery*.' Herbert has them all. After looking at other poets similarly qualified – Hopkins, Auden, Frost, Dylan Thomas and her friends Marianne Moore and Robert Lowell – she ends up with a quirkily personal paragraph on Herbert's poem 'Coloss. 3.3 Our life is hid with Christ in God'. First, the poem itself. ('Coloss.' is an abbreviation of 'Colossians' meaning St Paul's Epistle to the Christians in Colossae.)

Coloss. 3.3.
Our life is hid with Christ in God.

My words and thoughts do both express this notion,
That *Life* hath with the sun a double motion.
The first *Is* straight, and our diurnall friend,
The other *Hid* and doth obliquely bend.
Our life is wrapt *In* flesh, and tends to earth:
The other winds towards *Him*, whose happy birth
Taught me to live here so, *That* still one eye
Should aim and shoot at that which *Is* on high:
     Quitting with daily labour all *My* pleasure,
       To gain at harvest an eternal *Treasure*.

Ostentatious hiding makes up the poem. The words of the text (Herbert changes 'with Christ in God' into the more ardent '*in him that is my treasure*') run diagonally through it, their presence advertised by italics and capital letters. While its lines go straight down with no indentation, thanks to a simple couplet rhyme scheme, the biblical text goes obliquely across and through them. So it imitates what was then believed to be the sun's 'double motion': straightforward through the single day, curving around the earth and through the zodiac during the year. 'Winds' in the sixth line means 'bends'. It all ends with harvest, the crown of the year.

'Coloss. 3.3 Our life is hid with Christ in God', for all its cunning crafting, is in fact an image of Herbert's life and being and not just a clever contrivance. The verse from the Epistle to the Colossians, the poem's title and spine, mattered deeply to him. According to John Aubrey on Bemerton Church: 'In the Chancel are many apt sentences of the Scripture. At his Wife's Seat, *My life is hid with Christ in God* (he hath verses on this Text in his Poems). Above, in a little window – blinded, with a Veil (ill-painted) *Thou art my hiding place*.'[20] The poem is nothing less than a picture of what it was to be George Herbert. His life had 'a double motion'. He lived an ordinary life, a public life going 'straight' through time and with it. Simultaneously, he lived an inner or hidden life, obliquely set on his 'Master', Christ who was 'on high' and also a perpetual presence in his heart. Put in less specifically religious terms, this is about everybody's preoccupation with getting through the day as best one can, while at the same time having an 'eye' to the overall parabola of one's destiny, of what one would ideally hope to be. Herbert's religion was such a perpetual dialogue. It stretched between the immanently actual and the transcendently possible – both of them Christ's and so both of them his. The worst thing in life was to feel excluded from its exchanges, the best to enjoy them in harmonious mutual response. In that sense 'Coloss. 3.3 Our life is hid with Christ in God' is a key to his poetry.

Elizabeth Bishop's very personal response to it shows an appropriately Herbertian wit in its happy doubling of the trivial with the poetically significant. She was fascinated by the squinting entailed by the 'double motion' of Herbert's life in which 'One eye/Should aim and shoot at that which is on high.' It reminded her of a feature of her childhood.

My maternal grandmother had a glass eye. It fascinated me as a child, and the idea of it has fascinated me all my life. She was religious, in the Puritanical, Protestant sense and didn't believe in looking into mirrors very much. Quite often the glass eye looked heavenward, or off at an angle, while the real eye looked at you.

> 'Him whose happy birth
> Taught me to live here so, that still one eye
> Should aim and shoot at that which is on high.'

Off and on I have written out a poem called 'Grandmother's Glass Eye' which should be about the problem of writing poetry. The situation of my grandmother strikes me as rather like the situation of the poet: the difficulty of combining the real with the decidedly un-real; the natural with the unnatural, the curious effect a poem produces of being as normal as *sight* and yet as synthetic, as artificial, as a *glass eye*.

'As normal as *sight* and yet as synthetic, as artificial, as a *glass* eye' fixes the poem as precisely as only another poet could do.

In 1967 Bishop's lover, Lota de Macedo Soares, came to see her in New York and straight away took a big overdose. While Lota was lying between life and death in hospital, Bishop wrote to Joseph Summers, thanking him for sending her his book on Herbert.[21] 'Before L came I did read [the] introduction and thought it a beautiful job – I've been reading some of the poems too – some even help a bit, I think.'[22] Once again, as with Cowper, Herbert's hope that his poems might 'turn to the advantage of any dejected poor soul' was fulfilled, if only 'a bit', in his fellow-poet.

Finally, the novelist, biographer and poet Vikram Seth.[23] Having long, though 'neither Christian nor particularly religious', admired Herbert for 'his clarity, his depth of feeling, his spiritual struggles . . . His delight in the pleasures of nature and music, his wit, his strange juxtapositions, his decorous colloquiality', he found one day that Bemerton Rectory was for sale – and bought it. Herbert's spirit, he felt sure, 'might influence me but would not wish to wrest me from myself'. And indeed he proved 'a tactful host', his presence and poetry 'kindly influences'. Seth wrote six poems for his partner the violinist

Philippe Honoré to play, set to music by Alec Roth. Their occasion was grievous: Philippe had left him. Their poetic achievement is singularly interesting. In form and metre they imitate Herbert, with a marked preference for the figure poems which Hobbes and Dryden despised – two dangerous options. In content they are quite different and are filled with his sorrow at Philippe's departure. Herbert's 'Paradise' and Seth's 'Lost' (a Miltonic contrast) are as close as twins, yet utterly different: a poem of hope and a poem of hopelessness.

Paradise

I bless thee, Lord, because I GROW
Among thy trees, which in a ROW
To thee both fruit and order OW.

What open force, or hidden CHARM
Can blast my fruit, or bring me HARM,
While the inclosure is thine ARM?

Inclose me still for fear I START.
Be to me rather sharp and TART
Than let me want thy hand and ART.

When thou dost greater judgements SPARE,
And with thy knife but prune and PARE,
Ev'n fruitful trees more fruitful ARE.

Such sharpness shows thy sweetest FREND:
Such cuttings rather heal than REND:
And such beginnings touch their END.

Seth's poem uses the same device of snipping off one letter after another from the words at the end of each line, but with him the diminishment is bleakly just that, not the work of the benevolent gardener-God in his walled paradise-garden. The word 'tune' occurs three times, recalling the sound of Philippe's violin, always coupled with 'word', Seth's business.

Lost

Lost in a world of dust and spray,
We turn, we learn, we twist, we pray
For word or tune or touch or ray:

Some tune of hope, some word of grace,
Some ray of joy to guide our race.
Some touch of love to deuce our ace.

In vain the ace seeks out its twin.
The race is long, too short to win.
The tune is out, the word not in.

Our limbs, our hearts turn all to stone.
Our spring, our step lose aim and tone.
We are no more – and less than one.

There is no soul in which to blend,
No life to leave, no light to lend,
No shape, no chance, no drift, no end.

Not only has Seth risen to the formidable challenge of imitating one of Herbert's most formidable forms – perhaps *the* most formidable. He has also imitated – if that is the word – Herbert's most fundamental virtues: in his own words 'his clarity, his depth of feeling, his spiritual struggles'. They both tell it, though 'it' is so different for each of them, as it is. This is what separates Seth from those poor early imitators of Herbert in Chapter 10, Harvey, Goodman and Knevet, and puts him with Crashaw and Vaughan, who had learned from Herbert to be themselves. But Seth imitates Herbert's very tricky form as well and so, as poet, deuces his ace.

12

The Bread of Faithful Speech

Among the poems that have not figured in this book so far are several which demand attention by their sheer beauty – a beauty which is bound up with their truthfulness, marked by accuracy and candour. The purpose of this chapter is to read some of them in the interests of getting some understanding of how this was achieved.

'THE CENTRAL MAN'

The truth-to-experience of Herbert's poems is a product of their extraordinary transparency, a quality which he celebrated in those lines from 'The Elixir':

> A man that looks on glass,
>   On it may stay his eye;
> Or if he pleaseth, through it pass,
>   And then the heav'n espy.[1]

The American poet Wallace Stevens, whose phrase provides the title of this chapter, was insistent on it, writing of the poet that:

> He is the transparence of the place in which
> He is and in his poems we find peace.[2]

Peace because the clarity of the poem, its truth, enhances our perception and apprehension of the world, making it more our own. For Stevens, the poet is:

The man who has had the time to think enough,
The central man, the human globe, responsive
As a mirror with a voice, the man of glass,
Who in a million diamonds sums us up.[3]

Herbert is such a man, a poet par excellence who takes something out there in the world or in there in the mind, fashions it into an appropriate form and gives it to the reader, now humanized and clarified by his skill (Herbert's word was 'art'). His candour has made it clearer and kinder – in the sense of more akin.

The subject of 'The Glance' is eye-contact, as important as it is unspoken in the everyday communications of person with person. As usual with Herbert, one of the persons is God, but the atheist reader is not thereby barred from its truth to the universal experience, from cradle to grave, of reading and exchanging looks or glances.

The Glance

1
When first thy sweet and gracious eye
Vouchsaf'd ev'n in the midst of youth and night
To look upon me, who before did lie
    Welt'ring in sin;
    I felt a sugar'd strange delight,
Passing all cordials made by any art,
Bedew, embalm and overrun my heart,
    And take it in.

2
Since that time many a bitter storm
My soul hath felt, ev'n able to destroy,
Had the malicious and ill-meaning harm
    His swing and sway:
    But still thy sweet original joy,
Sprung from thine eye, did work within my soul,
And surging griefs, when they grew bold, control,
    And got the day.

3
If thy first glance so powerful be,
A mirth but open'd and seal'd up again;
What wonders shall we feel, when we shall see

Thy full-ey'd love!
When thou shalt look us out of pain,
And one aspect of thine spend in delight
More than a thousand suns disburse in light,
In heav'n above.

The first verse shows Herbert's ability to recapture past feeling, the overpowering delight of adolescent religious emotion, in all its original reality. It is followed in the second verse by recollection of sadder times when its power was reduced to that of memory. In the third verse the singular 'I' is superseded by the plural 'we' as the poet becomes maturely social and projects his theme into future, ultimate and steady bliss. Only at the end is the full content and possibility of the theme, the kindly eye, realized. In the first verse it is love's 'sweet and gracious eye' imparting 'sugar'd strange delight'. In the second verse that 'sweet [again!] original joy,/Sprung from thine eye' is a memory and pledge to set against present troubles and exert some control over them. In the last verse something even better supersedes it. The raptures of the first verse were 'a mirth but open'd and seal'd up again', momentary and fugitive. But now, looking ahead,

What wonders shall we feel, when we shall see
Thy full ey'd love!

'Full ey'd love' is a transcendentally captivating image, out-topping even the 'quick-ey'd love' of 'Love (III)'. And it is followed by the equally captivating 'when thou shalt look us out of pain' with its homely suggestion of a comforting mother cheering up her hurt child with sympathetically coaxing smiles. These wonderful images make the comparison with 'a thousand suns' in the last lines read like a slightly forced anticlimax, for all their recall of the glories of the final vision in the biblical book of Revelation where 'God shall wipe away all tears from their eyes' in the heavenly city, where 'they shall need no candle, neither light of the sun; for the Lord God giveth them light.'[4] To be honest, we are more moved by and more attached to the wonderfully accurate lines about eye-contact which went before, giving us the joy of recognition of something real and deeply significant: as in that phrase 'look us out of pain'.

For Herbert happiness was always just such a reciprocal and not a solitary matter. It was his when he was on good terms with the life which he derived from his creator. When the exchanges between them were kind and lively, all was well. But it was not so when 'things sort not to my will'[5] and when God was unresponsive – and that is the situation in 'Denial'. Accurate about contact, he could be just as truthful about no contact.

Denial

1
   When my devotions could not pierce
      Thy silent ears;
  Then was my heart broken, as was my verse:
     My breast was full of fears
       And disorder:

2
   My bent thoughts, like a brittle bow,
      Did fly asunder.
  Each took his way: some would to pleasures go,
     Some to the wars and thunder
       Of alarms.

3
   As good go anywhere, they say,
      As to benumb
  Both knees and heart, in crying night and day,
     Come, come, my God, O come,
       But no hearing.

4
   O that thou shouldst give dust a tongue
      To cry to thee,
  And then not hear it crying! all day long
     My heart was in my knee,
       But no hearing.

5
   Therefore my soul lay out of sight,
      Untun'd, unstrung:
  My feeble spirit, unable to look right,
     Like a nipt blossom, hung,
       Discontented.

O cheer and tune my heartless breast,   6
Defer no time;
That so thy favours granting my request,
They and my mind may chime,
And mend my rhyme.

Herbert found physical images and, above all, a form and metre to express psychological disjunction. Iambs (short–longs) jostle discordantly with trochees (long–shorts). The lines of each verse are, apart from the two minimally two-feet lines, unequal in length (four, two, five, three, two feet). There is near-chaos. Most effectively of all, the endings of the last lines of each verse fail to rhyme, discomfiting the reader. The most frustrated last line of all, 'But no hearing', comes up – emphatically – twice in the centre of the poem. On the other hand, the very last line of all, 'And mend my rhyme', is emphatic in a positive way. It rhymes with 'Defer no time' three lines before and also with 'my mind may chime' in the previous line. The long-deferred satisfaction is well fastened. Yet it is still a matter of hope, of maybe and not of present experience. Herbert is clear about that.

'Confession', a later poem, depends entirely on metaphors for the precise description of pain in its first three verses. Being chosen from the everyday world of household furniture, craftsmanship and gardening (the mole), gives them the requisite air of plain reality. In the first verse, grief's ability to invade and penetrate is set against a household metaphor: the closet. Closets provided the best in seventeenth-century privacy and security. They were either little rooms or, more fashionably, elaborate cabinets with multifarious locked drawers and secret compartments for the storage of intimate letters and documents. Herbert refers to both kinds. In the closets of his heart he has chests (of drawers): cabinets containing boxes and 'in each box, a till' or little treasure box – all with Chinese ingenuity – 'yet grief knows all, and enters when he will.' The second verse uses still more commonplace metaphors: the carpenter's screws and 'piercers' (awls), God-sent tortures such as rheumatism. In the third verse burrowing moles catching worms and the ingenuity of locksmiths defeated by lockpicks reinforce pain's relentless invasion of the self.

Confession

1
        O what a cunning guest
Is this same grief! Within my heart I made
    Closets; and in them many a chest;
     And, like a master in my trade,
In those chests, boxes; in each box, a till:
Yet grief knows all, and enters when he will.

2
        No screw, no piercer can
Into a piece of timber work and wind,
    As God's afflictions into man,
     When he a torture hath design'd.
They are too subtle for the subtlest hearts;
And fall, like rheums, upon the tend'rest parts.

3
        We are the earth; and they,
Like moles within us, heave, and cast about:
    And till they foot and clutch their prey,
     They never cool, much less give out.
No smith can make such locks but they have keys:
Closets are halls to them; and hearts, highways.

The metaphors and similes in these first three verses make pain palpable: all the more effectively by being so quotidian and material. They are also fascinating and, as such, paradoxically pleasurable to the reader who can admire their wit. That, and Herbert's poetic craft, tying up each excruciating verse with a rhyming couplet, win a kind of diagnostic control over grief by describing it so accurately and with such 'transparence', to use Stevens's word. Diagnosis opens the possibility of cure. Abandoning the elaborate security of ingeniously private closets and cabinets, in the fourth verse Herbert proposes the opposite: the openness of confession as cure and prophylactic. As against all those screws, gimlets, moles and lockpicks:

4
        Only an open breast
Doth shut them out, so that they cannot enter;
    Or, if they enter, cannot rest,
     But quickly seek some new adventure.

> Smooth open hearts no fast'ning have; but fiction
> Doth give a hold and handle to affliction.
>
>   Wherefore my faults and sins,   5
>   Lord, I acknowledge; take thy plagues away:
>   For since confession pardon wins,
>   I challenge here the brightest day,
>   The clearest diamond: let them do their best,
>   They shall be thick and cloudy [compared] to my breast.

When Herbert writes, at the end of the fourth verse, that 'fiction/Doth give a hold and handle to affliction' he is using the word 'fiction' in the negative sense of dissimulation and lying – things which make any situation worse.[6] He wants to get at the truth. So what about the bravado of the last verse? Does such a triumphant end match up to such an excruciating beginning? It has been prepared for by the previous verse with its clever conceit that openness by definition denies intrusion (no contest) and the engaging image of personified griefs finding nothing to do and so sauntering off 'to find some new adventure'. Adroit as this is, metaphor seems to be getting ahead of reality. Closer attention shows that this last verse does not really cover what has gone before. Herbert clears his breast by open confession of his sins, ensuring God's pardon of them. He is happy and confident in having done his part. God, on the other hand, has yet to do his: 'take thy plagues away' is the poet's challenge to him, not a fait accompli. It has yet to happen. This needs to be noticed because it is immediately overtaken by the dazzling rhetoric of Herbert's delight in confession's power to clear and cleanse, challenging 'the brightest day/ The clearest diamond'. But this triumphant flourish hangs in the air, waiting for the divine response which is not forthcoming.

The kind of almost-happy ending of 'Denial' and 'Confession' is absent from 'Grief'. It is among Herbert's later poems. The first twelve lines are wearisomely rhetorical, calling on clouds, rain and rivers to give him tears adequate to his sorrow in monotonous iambic pentameters. He is on unusually poor form. But at the thirteenth line it suddenly comes alive. The inadequacy of art in the face of reality can be painfully evident to the true artist, who wants not merely to produce art but to cope with intractable reality.

Verses, ye are too fine a thing, too wise
For my rough sorrows; cease, be dumb and mute,
Give up your feet and running to mine eyes,
And keep your measures for some lover's lute,
Whose grief allows him music and a rhyme:
For mine excludes both measure, tune, and time.
　　　　　Alas, my God!

Grief is a mortal threat to Herbert's whole understanding of his situation in the world and his very ability to write poetry. He renounces his great project of redeeming poetry from its erotic preoccupations, and sends it back, with all its technical apparatus of feet and measures, to sex. It is just not adequate to his grief – so immeasurably deeper and sharper than that of all those conventionally complaining lovers with their lutes in pastoral fiction. There is nothing like one's own, real pain. It wrings from him that last line, its brevity bringing the poem to a shuddering halt. The lack of longed-for reciprocity is complete. The truth is out and there are only those three words for it, 'Alas, my God'. Not only does his God not answer him in his trouble. The redress of his poetry, so truly admired by Seamus Heaney,[7] does not answer either – 'answer' in the sense of being fit for purpose.

'Heaven' is a climactic fulfilment of Herbert's longing for the reciprocity denied in 'Denial'. In the early Williams Manuscript it was already the next poem to the final one, 'Love (III)': a distinguished place, which shows Herbert's high estimation of it. It draws on the two foundations of his education, classical myth and the Christian Bible. In Book III of his *Metamorphoses* Ovid told the story of Echo, a mountain nymph who was punished by the goddess Juno. Her chatter had diverted Juno from noticing one of her husband Jupiter's affairs. The punishment was that Echo could no longer speak for herself but only repeat, echo, the last word of what anyone had said to her. The rest of her died. Only her derivative voice remained. This was an aetiological myth, delightful to children, explaining why your last word comes back to you when you halloo some words in a hollow place. Echo was 'born among the trees and leaves'. So when she repeats 'leaves', the Christian poet can steal her trick and reiterate 'leaves' as the leaves of a book: the book of books, his Bible, whose

leaves never fade and fall but 'abide'. A further Christian, and a further pagan, ingredient are both worth noticing. The Church's Morning
and Evening Prayers were largely responsive, a sentence by the minister answered by another from the congregation. In *The Country
Parson* Herbert insisted that 'the people's part to answer' should be
done properly and thoughtfully. He also valued the Socratic to-and-fro
of catechizing because 'when one is asked a question, he must discover who he is.'[8]

Heaven

O who will show me those delights on high?
     Echo.   I.
Thou *Echo*, thou art mortal, all men know.
     Echo.   No.
Wert thou not born among the trees and leaves?   5
     Echo.   Leaves.
And are there any leaves, that still abide?
     Echo.   Bide.
What leaves are they? impart the matter wholly.
     Echo.   Holy.   10
Are holy leaves the Echo then of bliss?
     Echo.   Yes.
Then tell me, what is that supreme delight?
     Echo.   Light.
Light to the mind: what shall the will enjoy?   15
     Echo.   Joy.
But are there cares and business with the pleasure?
     Echo.   Leisure.
Light, joy, and leisure; but shall they persever?
     Echo.   Ever.   20

Reading 'Heaven' one senses that his many disappointments in life
have made the poet doubtful about the assurance of 'those delights on
high' promised by his Bible, particularly the eternal city-cum-orchard
of the last chapters of Revelation. 'Are [the Bible's] holy leaves the
Echo then of bliss?' The answer is 'Yes'. Echo, then, is not just the
pagan nymph but also the Holy Scriptures. All the same, experience

has made the poet wary. It is hard for him to believe his luck. He is even a touch tetchy and hectoring with his challenges: 'show me', 'impart the matter wholly', 'tell me' and 'But are there . . . ?' But Echo responds with serene wit. Her answers are puns, as well as aural repetitions, which turn his querulous questions into calm and lambent answers, becoming steadily more so as he goes on in a crescendo through 'light', 'joy' and 'leisure' to 'ever'.

There had been echo poems before: Sidney wrote one and Herbert's brother Edward wrote a couple. But none of them is a patch on Herbert's. In her treatment of it, Helen Vendler has this to say:[9]

> The form in this case is not unique to Herbert: echo poems pre-existed *The Temple*, both in the classical and modern languages and in English. The form, however, is sufficiently difficult so that even poets of undoubted mastery faltered under the test. Sidney's echo poem in the *Arcadia* is shocking, by comparison, in its woodenness, its lack of invention, and its slavish repetition of identical words:
>
> > Echo, what do I get yielding my sprite to my grieves?
> > > Grieves.
> > What medicine may I find for a pain that draws me to death?
> > > Death.
> > O poisonous medicine! What worse to me can be than it?
> > > It.

And so on for a hundred lines. Not only is Herbert, wisely, shorter. He also takes artifice to a depth of understanding where the theology of reciprocity is at one with human speech – and human speech becomes musical. Vendler again:

> Listen to ourselves and we will find God, the poem says. The verses are, in this way, a radical endorsement of the human: in our yearning we speak God's language. When we find words of the right sort to ask about the divine – words like 'delight', 'enjoy', 'pleasure' and 'persever' – God can do nothing better than answer us in our own vocabulary.

SENSUAL SENSIBILITY

'Words of the right sort to ask about the divine': Herbert liked them to have the truth of sensual immediacy, rather than the remote abstraction of theology's vocabulary. In 'Confession' he made mental anguish so physically palpable that it hurts. The screws and piercers of God's tortures make the reader wince. The rope wound about the heart and cutting it in 'The Cross' have the same effect. Pleasure is given the same actuality – not least the pleasures of language. 'I like our language,' he wrote in 'The Son', and in 'The Forerunners' he calls it:

> Lovely enchanting language, sugar-cane,
> Honey of roses

stimulating the reader's taste buds. To describe the spirituality of prayer, in his dazzling sonnet with that title,[10] he appeals to the senses: to the palate with 'the Church's banquet'; to the eye with 'sinner's tower' and 'the bird of paradise'; to the ear with 'thunder', 'church bells' and 'a kind of tune'; to the touch with 'softness'; to the nose with 'the land of spices'; eventually to the mind in the conclusive 'something understood'. The luscious sensuality of 'The Odour', where Herbert squeezes the words '*My Master*', his customary appellation of Christ, to extract their scent and taste from their sound, has already been noticed.[11] So has:

> I once more smell the dew and rain,
> And relish versing

in 'The Flower'.

Making spirit sensuous is something very close to making the word flesh, the key divine act of incarnation in Christian belief. It brings actuality to the ethereal. The same thing could be achieved by presenting biblical antiquity in modern – meaning seventeenth-century – dress. The pages of the Bible were not meant to be read as mere historical record but as present reality, as in that tour de force of bringing bygone events into the present which is 'The Bunch of Grapes'.[12] It happens again in 'Decay'. Here the pastness of the past is affirmed in a mood of nostalgia, but with a homely realism which makes those good old days, with Aaron transformed into a country parson, a vivid contrast with the sorry state of things now. Then God was commonly around the place and only temporally elusive. Now he is confined to 'some one corner of a feeble heart', eventually to return to the external world with the fires of judgement. There are many biblical references. God in the form of a man wrestled with Jacob at Genesis 32:24–30. God's angel sat with Gideon under an oak at Judges 6:22. God and Abraham discussed ('advised') the fate of Sodom at Genesis 18:23–32. At Exodus 32:9–10 God, exasperated by the obstinacy of the Israelites, says, 'Now therefore let me alone, that my wrath may wax hot against them.' God appeared to Moses in a bush at Exodus 3:2–6. His word came to Elijah in a cave at I Kings 19:9. He provided Hagar with a well at Genesis 21:16–19. He came down to Mount Sinai at Exodus 19:20. Aaron had bells on his chasuble at Exodus 28:33.

Decay

Sweet were the days, when thou didst lodge with Lot,
Struggle with Jacob, sit with Gideon,
Advise with Abraham, when thy power could not
Encounter Moses' strong complaints and moan:
     Thy words were then, Let me alone.

One might have sought and found thee presently
At some fair oak, or bush, or cave, or well:
Is my God this way? No, they would reply:
He is to Sinai gone, as we heard tell:
     List, ye may hear great Aaron's bell.

But now thou dost thyself immure and close
In some one corner of a feeble heart:
Where yet both Sin and Satan, thy old foes,
Do pinch and straiten thee, and use much art
     To gain thy thirds and little part.

I see the world grows old, when as the heat
Of thy great love, once spread, as in an urn
Doth closet up itself, and still retreat,

Cold Sin still forcing it, till it return,
    And calling Justice, all things burn.

'Is God around?' The inquiry here is very like that in 'Redemption' when the tenant farmer went to his landlord's manor house to find him and:

They told me there, that he was lately gone
    About some land, which he had dearly bought
Long since on earth, to take possession.

In both instances, divine absence comes between previous and later presence, and this grand biblical pattern of history is handled with light, quotidian wit.

CANDOUR AND WIT

Wit, intellect at play to find truth, is one of Herbert's most endearing qualities. It hardly needs saying that he was a very clever man. His contemporaries knew it, and so did he. But there is a kind of suffering which is particularly painful to the witty: dullness bordering on depression. He gets a grip on it by writing wittily about it in his poem 'Dullness'. He is annoyed by the love poets, so sprightly with their conventions (we would call 'window songs' serenades) while he is downcast, although he has a better subject. 'Pure red and white' echoes Shakespeare's *Venus and Adonis* (line 10) and the affected lover Armado in *Love's Labours Lost*, 'My love is most immaculate white and red.'[13] For Herbert these, reversed, are the colours of Christ's body and blood, the sum of all perfections.

Dullness

Why do I languish thus, drooping and dull,
    As if I were all earth?
O give me quickness, that I may with mirth
    Praise thee brim-full!

The wanton lover in a curious strain   5
    Can praise his fairest fair;

And with quaint metaphors her curled hair
    Curl o'er again.

Thou art my loveliness, my life, my light,
10   Beauty alone to me:
Thy bloody death and undeserv'd, makes thee
    Pure red and white.

When all perfections as but one appear,
    That those thy form doth show,
15   The very dust, where thou dost tread and go,
    Makes beauties here.

Where are my lines then? my approaches? views?
    Where are my window-songs?
Lovers are still pretending, & ev'n wrongs
20   Sharpen their Muse.

But I am lost in flesh, whose sug'red lies,
    Still mock me, and grow bold:
Sure thou didst put a mind there, if I could
    Find where it lies.

25   Lord, clear thy gift, that with a constant wit
    I may but *look* towards thee:
Look only; for to *love* thee, who can be,
    What angel fit?

The image of the mind, hidden somewhere in the flesh if only he could find it, is a gem of self-irony, suggesting a cluttered writing-table. Clarity is what he needs: a clear sight of ultimate 'thee'. Given that modest requirement, the precondition of reciprocity, its final fulfilment as love can be postponed for the present. Transparency and 'a constant wit' will do for now.

Herbert takes up with the world of 'sug'red lies' again, repeating the phrase in 'The Rose' – but this time with a more courtly elegance and sophistication. The gift of a single rose has long been a love-token: from Herbert's contemporaries Edmund Waller ('Go, lovely Rose,/ Tell her that wastes her time and me ...') and Robert Herrick ('Go happy rose and .../... bind my love'), through Richard Strauss's

Rosenkavalier to the flower-sellers who go round the tables in res-
taurants. The poet is in dialogue with a worldly tempter, some
insidiously plausible Satan. The first part treats him dismissively:
somewhat vehemently so, with its damning criticism of his case. With
the gift of the rose at line 15 the tone changes to the winning – in both
senses. The reference to the rose's use as a laxative in lines 17–20,
effective as an enemy to the constipated bowels, brings things down
to earth.

The Rose

Press me not to take more pleasure
    In this world of sug'red lies,
And to use a larger measure
    Than my strict, yet welcome size.

First, there is no pleasure here: 5
    Colour'd griefs indeed there are,
Blushing woes, that look as clear
    As if they could beauty spare.

Or if such deceits there be,
Such delights I meant to say;   10
There are no such things to me,
    Who have pass'd my right away.

But I will not much oppose
    Unto what you now advise:
Only take this gentle rose,   15
    And therein thy answer lies.

What is fairer than a rose?
    What is sweeter? Yet it purgeth.
Purgings enmities disclose,
    Enmity forbearance urgeth.   20

If then all that worldlings prize
    Be contracted to a rose;
Sweetly there indeed it lies,
    But it biteth in the close.

25   So this flower doth judge and sentence
          Worldly joys to be a scourge:
      For they all produce repentance,
          And repentance is a purge.

      But I health, not physic choose:
30   Only though I you oppose;
      Say that fairly I refuse,
          For my answer is a rose.

'My strict, yet welcome size': the phrase defines both Herbert's self-fashioning and his fashioning of verse. What Helen Vendler shrewdly calls 'his more-than-delicate conscience'[14] makes him wary of the pangs of remorse attendant upon excess. He valued economy, and practises it here very effectively. After line 17 'rose', and rhymes with it, come at the end of every other line up to line 24. The penultimate verse uses other rhymes, but the last verse reverts to 'oppose' rhymed with 'rose' – the last word. The lines are short and sweet. The concentration on the emblematic rose allows a confident and balanced stance which does not need to raise its voice. 'A courtly bow and a rose', writes Helen Vendler, 'is what the advocate of worldliness receives when he comes to call.'[15] The poised ambiguity of Herbert's feelings about sensual pleasure – to which, as we have seen, he was no stranger – give a piquancy to the poem.

      What is fairer than a rose?
          What is sweeter? Yet it purgeth.
      Purgings enmities disclose,
          Enmity forbearance urgeth.

      If then all that worldlings prize
          Be contracted to a rose;
      Sweetly there indeed it lies,
          But it biteth in the close.

It hurts you: when you close your hand on it, or in the end ('close' could mean either).

MINIATURES

'Antiphon (1)' is a late poem, in current use as a hymn. Its marginal directions, 'Cho.' and 'Vers.' stand for the antiphonal voices of a church congregation (as chorus) and its priest (as the solo singer of versicles). Here the versicles are a couple of trimeter couplets, four short lines, set between the choruses. A country congregation is imagined, bellowing its psalms in Sternhold and Hopkins's clunky version and audible in the fields beyond its door. Clear as a bell, with its musical form fashioned to match and reflect its content, the poem's two little stanzas encompass the whole world announced in the first line: heaven and earth, community and individual – the cosmos in a nutshell. The last of all, the patiently enduring heart, brings all this exuberant praise home to a slightly rueful conclusion.

Antiphon (1)

Cho.   Let all the world in ev'ry corner sing,
          My God and King.

Vers.   The heav'ns are not too high,
       His praise may thither fly:
       The earth is not too low,
       His praises there may grow.

Cho.   Let all the world in ev'ry corner sing,
          My God and King.

Vers.   The church with psalms must shout,
       No door can keep them out:
       But above all the heart
       Must bear the longest part.

Cho.   Let all the world in ev'ry corner sing,
          My God and King.

The sheer smallness of some works of art gives them a particular and immediate appeal: to the child in us, it would seem. There is something inherently precious about them. Toys are usually miniatures of some kind. Miniature portraits were prized in Herbert's day: the works of Nicholas Hilliard and Isaac Olivet, painting in watercolour with miraculous fineness on exiguous pieces of parchment or ivory. Poems in miniature, of a dozen lines or less, are a feature of Herbert's later verse. Their 'strict, yet welcome size' appealed to him: perhaps as a man who believed childhood to be the best of human life, and certainly as a poet who responded keenly to their demands on his skill. Here is an example. It is based on St Paul's poetic wish for his gospel of Jesus to be written, not just in ink, 'but in fleshy tablets of the heart'.[16] There was also a long tradition in poetry, from Petrarch onwards, of names carved in hearts. The reader needs only to know that 'parcels' means little pieces, and that the letter 'J' was often written as the letter 'I' at the time. In the King James Bible of 1611, it was always 'I', and so it is in the Bodleian Manuscript, made at Little Gidding, of this poem. I will use it here because the sense of the penultimate line depends on it.

Iesu

Iesu is in my heart, his sacred name
Is deeply carved there: but th' other week
A great affliction broke the little frame,
Ev'n all to pieces: which I went to seek:
And first I found the corner, where was *I*,
After, where *ES*, and next where *U* was graved.
When I had got these parcels, instantly
I sat me down to spell them, and perceived
That to my broken heart he was *I ease you*,
       And to my whole is *Iesu*.

'A great affliction', a sorrow which breaks the poet's heart, and the name of Jesus engraved on it, into three pieces, is treated like a domestic accident – and resolved by finding the fragments and putting them together again. Herbert's great Christian theme of man's disintegration and redemption is securely held in his domestic parable of breaking and mending. His story is wonderful as he sets and settles his small-scale imagery into the grand narrative of salvation: the breaking and restoring of Christ's body parallels the breaking and restoring

of the poet's heart. It is all done with a few quiet words and, smaller
still, by the single four-letter word, Iesu, broken up and put together
again at the very end.

Clearly, Herbert liked his miniatures and liked them to come out in
the form of puzzles, miniature toys for the mind. In 'Hope' he sets one
to the reader. Just as 'Iesu' contained in small compass the mystery of
salvation, so 'Hope', in a mere eight lines, encapsulates (the word is
unusually apt here) Herbert's theme of hope denied or deferred. In
'Denial' he brought out its full anguish. Here, on the other hand, he
puts it in little jokes or emblematic riddles. The pleasant social custom
of exchanging gifts is its setting, so the poem is pleasant too.

Hope

> I gave to Hope a *watch* of mine: but he
> An *anchor* gave to me.
> Then an *old prayer-book* I did present:
> And he to me an *optic* sent.
> With that I gave a vial full of *tears*:
> But he *a few green ears*.
> Ah Loiterer! I'll no more, no more I'll bring:
> I did expect a ring.

Hetbert's editor F. E. Hutchinson proposes the following solution:

> The *watch* given to Hope suggests the giver's notion that the time for
> the fulfilment of hopes is nearly due, but the *anchor*, given in return,
> shows that the soul will have to wait for some time yet; the *old
> prayer-book* tells of prayers long used, but the optic, or telescope,
> shows that the fulfilment can only be descried from afar off; tears
> receive in turn only *a few green ears*, which will need time to ripen for
> harvest; and then the donor's patience gives out.[17]

That just about covers it. But 'I did expect a ring' deserves a little
more attention. It is not necessarily a wedding ring, although any ring
signifies eternity by being unending, and commitment by its bonding.
Rings were often given to a friend as tokens of love and fidelity. Donne
gave Herbert one engraved with 'the figure of *Christ crucified* on an
Anchor, which is the emblem of Hope' accompanied by a Latin poem,

to which Herbert responded with a Latin poem of his own.[18] The traditional emblem made Christ the object of hope, leading some critics to believe that personified Hope in this poem is really Christ crucified, lending a dark and deep touch to it. Apart from that, 'I did expect a ring' is one of those last lines of Herbert which discloses a poem's subtext: what it has really been about all the time. Like the end of 'Grief', it is a final (if more muted) expression of disappointment with God. Herbert does not hesitate to call his divine partner-in-exchange by the opprobrious term 'loiterer'. It is a sting in the tail. All the playfulness was in deadly earnest after all. Herbert's art is up to treating profound, existential problems with wit.

In another eight-line miniature a riddle is set and solved – with a twist.

Love-Joy

As on a window late I cast mine eye.
I saw a vine drop grapes with *J* and *C*
Anneal'd on every bunch. One standing by
Ask'd what it meant. I, who am never loth
To spend my judgement, said, It seem'd to me
To be the body and the letters both
Of *Joy* and *Charity*. Sir, you have not miss'd,
The man replied; It figures *JESUS CHRIST*.

Such an aptly transparent poem needs little comment. It shows Herbert's faith in dialogue, question-and-answer, as the way to truth. He had learned that at Westminster and Cambridge. 'I, who am never loth/To spend [expend] my judgement' is an endearingly ironic piece of self-criticism, agreeing with his acquaintances in 'The Answer' that he was 'eager, hot, and undertaking'. It gives the poem a personal reality. The 'body' in 'the body and the letters both' is, in the first instance, the vine with its grapes in the stained-glass window. Secondly, though, it points to the solution of the riddle: Christ the true vine of John 15 and the embodiment of the virtues. The italics do their work: from single capital letters on to whole words in capitals and lower case, finally the two consummate words in capitals. The final twist is that the poet got it right – or just about: the nicely anonymous 'One standing by', who had asked the question, congratulates him but provides the full answer. Concord and harmony prevail, in contrast to the cross words which end 'Hope'.

As a last example of Herbert's ingenuity in a small compass – an ingenuity expressing true feeling and not merely artificial – 'The Call' is another modest masterpiece. Herbert has plundered the secular love poets to write a serenade or 'window-song' to his Master, Jesus. So, in the first instance, it is a good idea to read it for its easy music or listen to Vaughan Williams's gently flowing setting of it in his *Five Mystical Songs*.

The Call

> Come my Way, my Truth, my Life:
> Such a way, as gives us breath:
> Such a Truth as ends all strife:
> Such a Life as killeth death.
>
> Come my Light, my Feast, my Strength:
> Such a Light as shows a feast:
> Such a Feast, as mends in length:
> Such a Strength, as makes his guest.
>
> Come, my Joy, my Love, my Heart:
> Such a Joy, as none can move:
> Such a Love, as none can part:
> Such a Heart as joys in love.

But as one sings along with the lines (all metrically paced by long–short trochees, but with the final short lacking – thus escaping monotony)[19] two structural features of the poem impinge.

One is that each of the three nouns, summoned or invited in the first lines of each verse, is then given a line to itself in which a verb moves it into work and action. This formula – and decidedly formulaic it is – shapes everything until the very last line, where it is not abandoned but enhanced: by transforming the noun 'Joy' into the verb 'joys' Herbert fashions this last line out of the nouns of the verse's first line: 'Joy', 'Love' and 'Heart'. This is economy pitched to ecstasy, craft expressing emotion. It is worth noticing that by making 'joy' into a central verb, Herbert can reshuffle the order of the first line and put 'Heart' first and, triumphantly, 'love' as the last word.

The second feature which impinges on the reader-just-for-sound is that some kind of progression, some movement on, down and up pervades the poem. In spite of its formulaic pattern, and a formula being such a static and resolved thing, there is a lively flow, lightened by all the words except 'killeth' being monosyllables, towards a happy end. The listening ear catches it as the words in the first lines go from the closed and forward-in-the-mouth sound of 'Way', 'Truth' and 'Life' to the softer and more open sounds of 'Joy', 'Love' and 'Heart'. The eye on the page confirms it. The trio of nouns in the first verse is biblical: Jesus said 'I am the way, the truth and the life' at John 14:6. So poet and reader are together on familiar ground and it is clear that Jesus is being addressed. The trio in the second verse is neither biblical nor so abstract. They belong in the earthly setting of a dining room, lit for a feast – and indeed the 'Strength' which 'makes his guest' recall the same setting in 'Love (III)': 'A guest, I answer'd, worthy to be here:/ Love said, You shall be he.' We are in the world of domestic courtesy rather than the theology of the first verse. In the last verse this inherent dialogue between poet and Jesus melts into identity as the happiest feelings of the human heart are also the qualities of its indwelling divinity, Jesus. The reader has reached the heart of things – of everything – for Herbert, and the progression of the poem is revealed as a homecoming. The whole thing is, in small and modest compass – 'strict, yet welcome size' again – a triumph of craft: complex weaving of simple truths into happiness.

Working with minute care on a very small surface does not in the least constrict Herbert's mind. He may look like a minor poet, in contrast, say, to his friend Donne's magnificent theatricality, but the content of his refined craft shows that he is not. Not only could he take on the grand themes of myth, as in the tormented eloquence of 'The Sacrifice',[20] he could invent a myth of his own. 'Redemption', discussed in the Interlude, presents the myth of salvation in a sonnet. 'The Pulley' is Herbert's myth of creation in four five-line verses. It is extremely daring and independent of him to make such a new tale when his authoritative Bible had one already, also answering the riddle of the unsatisfactoriness of existence. But this does not hold him back, stunt his inventive creativity or cause him to hesitate in picturing the Creator working at his bench, having second thoughts in the middle of the job and revising his plan. The title is an image not used in the poem, but if the reader pauses on it long enough to picture a pulley, he or she is given a clue: if you sling a rope over a fixed wheel, by pulling it down at one end you lift up a weight at the other. Downwards becomes upwards or, psychologically, depression becomes uplift. So it 'generates', in Seamus Heaney's words, 'that compensatory pressure which all realized works exert against the surrounding inconsequentiality. In its unforced way, it does contain within itself the co-ordinates and contradictions of experience, and would be as comprehensible within the cosmology of Yin and Yang as it is amenable to the dialectic of thesis, antithesis and synthesis.'[21]

The Pulley

When God at first made man,
Having a glass of blessings standing by;
Let us (said he) pour on him what we can:
Let the world's riches, which dispersed lie,
Contract into a span.

So strength first made a way;
Then beauty flow'd, then wisdom, honour, pleasure:
When almost all was out, God made a stay,
Perceiving that alone in all his treasure
Rest in the bottom lay.

For if I should (said he)
Bestow this jewel also on my creature,
He would adore my gifts instead of me,
And rest in Nature, not the God of Nature:
So both would losers be.

Yet let him keep the rest,
But keep them with repining restlessness:
Let him be rich and weary, that at least,
If goodness lead him not, yet weariness
May toss him to my breast.

A resonant saying of Herbert's beloved Augustine is visibly at work: 'Thou hast made us for thyself, and our hearts ate restless until they rest in thee.'[22] Herbert plays with it, punning on the two senses of 'rest', rest as repose and rest as remainder, then tying them together in 'restlessness'. This contributes to the engaging wit of the whole invention. But it is deep too, and in its depth he is with Augustine. John Burnaby, Augustine's modern interpreter,[23] asserts that 'there can be no question of what is dominant in his conception of Christian love. It is *desiderium* – the unsatisfied longing of the homesick heart.' Burnaby goes on to quote from Augustine's commentary on the First Epistle of John, a biblical book preoccupied with love.

> The whole life of the good Christian is a holy longing. What you long for, as yet you do not see ... by withholding of the vision God extends the longing, through longing he extends the soul, by extending it he makes room in it ... So let us long, because we are to be filled ... That is our life, to be exercised by longing.

Augustine's search ended with the passionate cry 'At long last I have loved Thee, O Beauty of all beauties oldest and newest!'[24] *Desiderium* led Herbert, the priggish teenage poet who had advertised to his mother his refusal of *eros*, to the same reward.

13

Music at the Close[1]

Izaak Walton writes of music in Herbert's last days:

The Sunday before his death, he rose suddenly from his bed or couch, called for one of his instruments, took it into his hand, and said,

> My God, my God!
> My music shall find thee.
> And ev'ry string
> Shall have his attribute to sing.

And having tuned it, he played and sang:

> The Sundays of man's life,
> Threaded together on time's string,
> Make bracelets to adorn the wife
> Of the eternal glorious King.
> On Sundays heaven's door stands ope;
> Blessings are plentiful and rife,
> More plentiful than hope.

Thus he sang on earth such hymns and anthems as the angels, and he, and Mr. Ferrar, now sing in heaven.[2]

That last sentence of Walton's is cloyingly sanctimonious. Nevertheless, it rehearses the widespread notion, ardently held by Herbert, that music is an art which goes beyond the material and is heavenly in origin and destination. It is therefore a particularly comforting accompaniment to the soul in transit from earth to heaven, waiting at the threshold of death. Herbert's friend John Donne, when he had thought he was dying of plague in 1623, wrote his 'Hymn to God my God, in my Sickness', which begins with the verse:

> Since I am coming to that holy room,
>> Where, with thy choir of saints for evermore,
> I shall be made thy music; as I come
>> I tune my instrument at the door,
>> And what I must do then, think now before.

There are reasons for supposing that Walton's account of Herbert singing and playing on his deathbed is authentic. He got it from Arthur Woodnoth, who was there. And the quotation from Herbert's 'The Thanksgiving' is not copied from *The Temple* where it lacks the first line, 'My God, my God!' and prints Walton's further three lines as two. Aural memory is at work: which is far from being a proof of authenticity but is a modest suggestion of its possibility.

Herbert 'called for one of his instruments', which implies that he had a collection of them in the rectory. Aubrey knew a man who had known him when he was living at Dauntsey and recalled 'that he had a very good hand on the Lute, and that he set his own lyrics or sacred poems'.[3] Like Thomas Campion, he was a composer-poet. None of his compositions survive, but the presence and effect of music in his poetry is pervasive. It mattered to him as much more than a pastime. Words had qualities of sound which music could deliver and enhance. It was transformative, joining people together in 'consort' and mediating between them and God: a virtual sacrament and a heightening of prayer (which Herbert in his poem 'Prayer (1)' called 'a kind of tune, which all things hear and fear'). Walton was emphatic about it.

His chiefest recreation was music, in which heavenly art he was a most excellent master, and did himself compose many divine hymns and anthems, which he set or sung to his lute or viol; and, though he was a lover of retiredness, yet his love to music was such, that he went usually twice every week on certain appointed days, to the cathedral church in Salisbury; and at his return would say, that his time spent in prayer, and cathedral music, elevated his soul and was his heaven upon earth. But before his return thence to Bemerton, he would usually sing and play his part, in an appointed private music-meeting; and, to justify this practice, he would often say, Religion does not banish mirth, but only moderates, and sets rules to it.[4]

Not only did music liberate feeling, it gave it form, 'measure, tune and time':[5] the great achievement of art.

Herbert wrote 'Church Music' before he went to Bemerton, probably when he was at Trinity College, Cambridge, where the Master, his friend Thomas Nevile, had done much to improve the standard of music in the chapel. As a schoolboy, he had heard the music in Westminster Abbey, met William Byrd and John Bull at his mother's dinner parties and gone to his parish church of St Martin-in-the-Fields where the rector was a music-lover.

Church Music

Sweetest of sweets, I thank you: when displeasure
  Did through my body wound my mind,
You took me thence, and in your house of pleasure
  A dainty lodging me assign'd.

Now I in you without a body move,
  Rising and falling with your wings:
We both together sweetly live and love,
  Yet say sometimes, *God help poor Kings.*

Comfort, I'll die; for if you post from me,
  Sure I shall do so, and much more:
But if I travel in your company,
  You know the way to heaven's door.

In an earlier version there was an extra verse between the second and the third.

O what a state is this, which never knew
  Sickness, or shame, or sorrow:
Where all my debts are paid, none can accrue
  Which knoweth not, what means Tomorrow.

Music as present rapture, way out of ordinary time and misery: it testifies to Herbert's delight, but he cut the verse out – no doubt because he felt it went too far and was, in any case, wrong in asserting that music was a stranger to sorrow.

Herbert had read Richard Hooker's *Of the Laws of Ecclesiastical Polity*, the foundational defence of the Church of England as an organic, natural and humane institution. In Book V Chapter 38 of this treatise, published in 1597, Hooker discussed church music with warm and perceptive appreciation. There are distinct echoes of it in Herbert's poem (I have put three of them italics). That, and its own merits, make it worth quoting extensively.

> Touching musical harmony whether by instrument or by voice, it being but of high and low in sounds a due proportionable disposition, such notwithstanding is the force thereof, and so pleasing effects it hath in that very part of man which is most divine, that some have been thereby induced to think that the soul itself by nature is or hath in it harmony. A thing which delighteth all ages and beseemeth all states; a thing as seasonable in grief as in joy; as decent being added unto actions of greatest weight and solemnity, as being used when men most sequester themselves from action. The reason hereof is an admirable facility which music hath to express and represent to the mind, more inwardly than any other sensible mean, the very standing, *rising, and falling*, the very steps and inflections every way, the turns and varieties of all passions whereunto the mind is subject; yea, so to imitate them, that whether it resemble unto us the same state wherein our minds already are, or a clean contrary, we are not more contentedly by the one confirmed, than changed and led away by the other. In harmony the very image and character even of virtue and vice is perceived, the mind delighted with their resemblances, and brought by having them often iterated into a love of the things themselves ... And that there is such a difference of one kind from another we need no proof but our own experience, inasmuch as we are at the hearing of some more inclined unto sorrow and heaviness; of some, more mollified and softened in mind; one kind apter to stay and settle us, another to move and stir our affections; there is that draweth to a marvellous grave and sober mediocrity, there is also that carrieth as it were into ecstasies, filling the mind with an *heavenly joy* and for the time in a manner *severing it from the body*.[6]

Inevitably, Hooker invokes David, believed to be the author of the Psalms, as having 'singular knowledge not in poetry alone but in music also . . . and was farther the author of adding unto poetry melody in public prayer, melody both vocal and instrumental, for the raising up of men's hearts, and the sweetening of their affections towards God'.

Hooker took the stance of an appreciative listener to music. Herbert could add to that his experience as an expert maker of it. The tuning of stringed instruments was the crucial preliminary. There were no tuning forks, so it was a matter of negotiated agreement. For the individual or solitary player this meant tightening or slackening each string until they were all in harmony. For the group or 'consort' it involved all its participants coming together. It took some time and trouble to get everything in tune, into the kind of balance which was called 'temper': a word used for a good state of mind or body as well as for well-tuned strings. It is the title of two poems by Herbert, both complaining of his oscillation between emotional extremes, heaven and hell. In the sixth verse of 'The Temper (I)' he resigns himself to the problem by saying to God:

> Yet take thy way; for sure thy way is best:
>> Stretch or contract me, thy poor debtor:
>> This is but tuning of my breast,
>>> To make the music better.

The financial metaphor of stretching or contracting a debt, extending or abbreviating the time for its repayment, brings to Herbert's mind the tightening and loosening of strings needed to get his lute or viol tempered and 'make the music better'.

It was a struggle, as he says in 'Easter'. The second verse of that poem is a startling musical metaphor. It brings the struggle into a focus which contains its extremities of meaning and feeling. Christ's body stretched on the cross is a lute with its gut strings stretched over its resounding hollow wooden frame. So Herbert and his saviour are united in music. Within all this, there is an emotional unity of extremes appropriate to the Easter season: sorrow and pain (Good Friday) with joy (Easter Day). Agony becomes lyrical.

Awake, my lute, and struggle for thy part
     With all thy art.
The cross taught all wood to resound his name,
     Who bore the same.
His stretched sinews taught all strings, what key
Is best to celebrate this most high day.

Hooker praised music for its ability both to represent feeling 'more inwardly than any other sensible means' and to change feeling into something 'clean contrary'. 'We are not more contentedly by the one confirmed, than changed and led away by the other.' Herbert was fascinated by this state of affairs. The title of his sonnet 'Joseph's Coat' comes from the 'coat of many colours' which Jacob had made for his darling son Joseph.[7] It brings to Herbert's mind the multi-coloured spectrum of human life, its forever-changing grief and happiness and their strange combination. In the middle of the poem, life is a race to the grave. But this is framed by the thought contained in the title: while it goes on, life is changing all the time and – more than that – art, God's art and man's, can make joy painful and sorrow pleasant. The art concerned is music. The 'both' in line 8 are grief and his heart, the 'both' in line 9 his heart and body – and 'due' means owed.

Joseph's Coat

Wounded I sing, tormented I indite,
  Thrown down I fall into a bed, and rest:
Sorrow hath chang'd its note: such is his will,
Who changeth all things, as him pleaseth best.
    For well he knows, if but one grief and smart
Among my many had his full career,
Sure it would carry with it ev'n my heart,
And both would run until they found a bier
  To fetch the body; both being due to grief.
But he hath spoil'd the race; and giv'n to anguish
One of Joy's coats, 'ticing it with relief
To linger in me, and together languish.
    I live to show his power, who once did bring
My *joys* to *weep*, and now my *griefs* to *sing*.

The mutability of music helps him to bear the mutability of life. Shelley noticed it too:

> Our sincerest laughter
> > With some pain is fraught;
> Our sweetest songs are those that tell of saddest thought.[8]

'Saddest thought' was all too familiar to Herbert. His daily recitation of the Psalms, so abundant in complaint as well as cheerfulness ('why art thou so full of heaviness, O my soul: and why art thou so disquieted within me?'),[9] encouraged him to express it. So did the contemporary cult of melancholy which had its full treatment in Robert Burton's widely read *Anatomy of Melancholy*, published in 1621 and going through no fewer than five editions before 1640; and its greatest musical expression in the songs of John Dowland. Dowland often wrote the words as well as their lute accompaniment, as Herbert pictures himself doing in 'Ephesians 4.30, *Grieve not the Holy Spirit, &c.*'. There is a pun: bowels were considered the seat of feeling and, taken from animals such as cats, provided strings for lutes and viols.

> Oh take thy lute, and tune it to a strain,
> > Which may with thee
> > All day complain.
> There can no discord but in ceasing be.
> > Marbles can weep; and surely strings
> > More bowels have, than such hard things.

Herbert shared with St Paul an interest in groaning. 'Even we ourselves groan within ourselves, waiting for the adoption, to wit, the redemption of the body.' 'We groan, earnestly desiring to be clothed upon with our house which is from heaven ... we that are in this tabernacle do groan, being burdened.'[10] For St Paul, groaning was unfulfilment longing for fulfilment, the negative on the verge of the positive: *desiderium* again. Herbert transposed the apostle's eschatology into musical metaphor. In 'Sion' he considered the ornate glories of Solomon's temple, particularly its colossal bronze urn, described at length in I Kings 7. But all this did not impress God, 'did not affect thee much, was not thy aim'. God's concern was with the interior depths of the human heart – the source of groans.

All Solomon's sea of brass and world of stone
Is not so dear to thee as one good groan.

And truly brass and stones are heavy things,
Tombs for the dead, not temples fit for thee:

But groans are quick, and full of wings,
And all their motions upward be;
And ever as they mount, like larks they sing;
The note is sad, yet music for a King.

Groans defy the gravity to which architecture is subject and, in their upward flight, are changed into the music – the sad music – which gave delight in the court of the heavenly king, as in that of Elizabeth and James I. Music transforms cacophonous groaning into sweet melody. Noise becomes harmony. In 'Gratefulness' God puts up with the importunate 'perpetual knockings at thy door' of urgent prayer by hearing it as music, albeit the 'country airs' of a village band or choir (the poem is late, perhaps written at Dauntsey or Bemerton where he would have heard such rough and groaning music-making, accompanying the rough verse of Sternhold and Hopkins's metrical psalms).

This notwithstanding, thou went'st on,
And didst allow us all our noise:
Nay, thou hast made a sigh and groan
Thy joys.

Not that thou hadst not still above
Much better tunes than groans can make;
But that these country airs thy love
Did take.

He ends the poem by asking for 'such a heart, whose pulse [musical "beat"] may be/Thy praise'. Like Donne, Herbert wanted to *be* music with all his being.

William Byrd, a Catholic but a loyal admirer and beneficiary of James I, was a friend of the Herbert family, dining with them three times in 1601 when George was eight. There is an interesting passage in the 'Dedication' of his *Gradualia*, printed in 1605, about the close and mysterious relation of words to music.

In the very sentences (as I have learned by experience) there is such a hidden and concealed power that to a man thinking about divine things and turning them over attentively and earnestly in his mind, the most appropriate measures come, I know not how, as if by their own free will, and freely offer themselves to his mind if it is neither idle nor inert.[11]

Byrd's religious music, such as the *Gradualia* for the seasons of the catholic year and his *Cantiones Sacrae*, was vocal chamber music to be performed in the same domestic context as his secular songs. His fellow catholics liked to worship in their 'fair large chambers', where music 'mingled indistinguishably with the cycle of hospitality and the musicians who served for the Mass would also serve for entertainment'.[12] The singers were of both sexes. And being printed, his music was available to the households of his Anglican friends. It was a time when 'music for a King' escaped for good from the court into the houses of the amateurs.

William Byrd's world of music, inspired by the hidden power of words, both combined in a domestic piety, was Herbert's too. It nourished his longing for reciprocity, for an answering voice to the complaints and praises which the changing circumstances of his inward and outward life induced. Unlike many of his best readers nowadays, he had a personal God to address them to. But that God was as mutable in his dealings with him as the life which the divinity had made and then – inscrutably – governed. What never changed was love. The lines from T. S. Eliot's 'Little Gidding', which were quoted at the beginning of this book, reassert themselves at the end.

> Who then devised the torment? Love.
> Love is the unfamiliar Name
> Behind the hands that wove
> The intolerable shirt of flame
> Which human power cannot remove.
> We only live, only suspire,
> Consumed by either fire or fire.

Eliot ended his pamphlet on Herbert by quoting that masterpiece, 'Love (III)', Simone Weil's 'most beautiful poem in the world', as an indication of 'the serenity finally attained by this proud and humble man'.[13] But this book should end with a poem of Herbert's own. 'Bitter-sweet' is one of his consummately crafted miniatures. The tone is less grandiloquent than Eliot's. Its lower key matches the maturity of its acceptance: its 'yes' to life. Herbert settles for life's ambivalence more quietly than Eliot's 'fire or fire' (the fires of Pentecostal spirit or of hell) and 'shirt of flame'. But the two poets agree about the word which is, in the last analysis, the last word: for Eliot 'the unfamiliar name' but for Herbert the entirely familiar one which closes 'Bitter-sweet'. So long as reciprocity – so perfectly achieved by that poem – matters, Herbert will matter too.

Bitter-sweet

Ah my dear angry Lord,
Since thou dost love, yet strike;
Cast down, yet help afford;
Sure, I will do the like.

I will complain, yet praise;
I will bewail, approve:
And all my sour-sweet days
I will lament, and love.

Notes

ABBREVIATIONS

Autobiography   Edward Herbert, *Autobiography*, Walter Scott, 1888.

Brief Lives   *Aubrey's Brief Lives*, ed. Oliver Lawson Dick,
Secker & Warburg, 1949.

Charles   Amy Charles, *A Life of George Herbert*, Cornell
University Press, 1977.

Ferrar Papers   *The Ferrar Papers*, ed. B. Blackstone, Cambridge
University Press, 1938.

Life   Izaak Walton, *The Life of Mr. George Herbert*, London,
1670, reprinted in *George Herbert: The Complete
English Works*, ed. and introduced by Ann
Pasternak Slater, Everyman, 1995, pp. 338–85.

Vendler   Helen Vendler, *The Poetry of George Herbert*, Harvard
University Press, 1975.

Works   *The Works of George Herbert*, ed. with a Commentary
by F. E. Hutchinson, Oxford University Press, 1945.

PREFACE AND ACKNOWLEDGEMENTS

1. *The Country Parson* is currently best consulted in *George Herbert: The Complete English Works*, ed. and introduced by Ann Pasternak Slater, Everyman, 1995.
2. Also in ibid., Appendix 3, referred to hereafter as *Life*.
3. David Novarr, *The Making of Walton's Lives*, Cornell University Press, 1958.
4. Amy Charles, *A Life of George Herbert*, Cornell University Press, 1977 (hereafter Charles).
5. Joseph Summers, *George Herbert: His Religion and Art*, Chatto & Windus, 1954.

6. Helen Vendler, *The Poetry of George Herbert*, Harvard University Press, 1975 (hereafter Vendler).
7. Chana Bloch, *Spelling the Word: George Herbert and the Bible*, University of California Press, 1985.
8. Helen Wilcox, *The English Poems of George Herbert*, Cambridge University Press, 2007.
9. *A Concordance to the Complete Writings of George Herbert*, ed. Mario di Cesare and Rigo Mignani, Cornell University Press, 1977.
10. *The Works of George Herbert*, ed. with a Commentary by F. E. Hutchinson, Oxford University Press, 1945 (hereafter *Works*).
11. Izaak Walton, *The Life of Mr. George Herbert*, London, 1670, reprinted in *George Herbert: The Complete English Works*, ed. Pasternak Slater (hereafter *Life*), p. 380.
12. George Herbert Palmer, *The English Works of George Herbert Newly Arranged and Annotated and Considered in Relation to his* Life, Houghton Mifflin, 1895.
13. The Williams Manuscript, of which more later.
14. T. S. Eliot, *George Herbert*, Longmans Green, 1962, pp. 13 and 25.

INTRODUCTION: HERBERT'S WORLD

1. Michael C. Schoenfeldt, *Prayer and Power: George Herbert and Renaissance Courtship*, University of Chicago Press, 1991.
2. I John 4:16.
3. Genesis 3:19.
4. Isaiah 25:6.
5. *Country Parson*, Chapter XXII.
6. Simone Petrement, *Simone Weil: A Life*, Mowbrays, 1976, p. 330.
7. *Works*, pp. 321–55.
8. *Country Parson*, Chapter XXXV.
9. David Harris Willson, *King James VI and I*, Jonathan Cape, 1959, p. 123.
10. John Hacket, *Scrinia Reserata*, Samuel Lowndes, 1692, vol. I, p. 175.
11. William Barlow, quoted in Patrick Collinson, *The Religion of Protestants: The Church in English Society 1559–1625*, Oxford University Press, 1982, p. 28.
12. 'Justice (I)'.
13. Thomas Plume quoted in Collinson, *The Religion of Protestants*, p. 95.
14. Ibid., p. 96.
15. *Two Sermons Preached at the Funerals of Mrs. E. Montfort . . . and Dr T. Montfort*, J. Norton, 1632.

16. Daniel W. Doerksen, *Conforming to the Word: Herbert, Donne, and the English Church before Laud*, Bucknell University Press, 1997, pp. 52–8.

17. Collinson, *The Religion of Protestants*, pp. 101–2.

18. *Country Parson*, Chapter XXXII.

19. Collinson, *The Religion of Protestants*, p. 177.

20. *Country Parson*, Chapter VIII.

21. Ibid., Chapter XXIII.

22. Collinson, *The Religion of Protestants*, p. 202.

23. *Country Parson*, Chapter VIII.

24. See Ian Green, *Print and Protestantism in Early Modern England*, Oxford University Press, 2000, especially Part 2.

25. *The Sermons of John Donne*, ed. George R. Potter and Evelyn M. Simpson, University of California Press, 1962, vol. I, p. 375, referring to vol. III, p. 177.

26. *Country Parson*, Chapter IIII.

27. Ibid., Chapter XXXIV.

28. Ibid., Chapter XXXV.

29. Mark Johnston, *Saving God: Religion after Idolatry*, Princeton University Press, 2009, quoted in Galen Strawson's review in the *London Review of Books*, 2 June 2011.

30. Lancelot Andrewes, *Preces Privatae*, trans. and ed. F. E. Brightman, Methuen, 1903, reprinted by Living Age Books, 1961.

31. *Life*, p. 380.

32. *Scripture Women: Rose Thurgood, 'A Lecture of Repentance' and Cicely Johnson, 'Fanatical Reveries'*, ed. with an introduction and notes by Naomi Baker, Trent Editions, 2005.

33. Ibid., pp. 12–14.

34. Ibid., p. 22.

35. *Tottel's Miscellany: Songs and Sonnets of Henry Howard, Earl of Surrey, Sir Thomas Wyatt and Others*, ed. Amanda Holton and Tom MacFaul, Penguin, 2011, p. 3.

36. *The Art of English Poesy by George Puttenham: A Critical Edition*, ed. Frank Whigham and Wayne A. Rebhorn, Cornell University Press, 2007, p. 95.

37. Sir Philip Sidney, *An Apology for Poetry or The Defence of Poesy*, ed. Geoffrey Shepherd, Nelson, 1965, p. 141.

38. 'The Son'.

39. John Donne, *Upon the Translation of the Psalms by Sir Philip Sidney and the Countess of Pembroke his Sister*, in John Donne, *The Major Works*, ed. John Carey, Oxford University Press, 1990, p. 303.

40. Sidney, *Apology*, p. 102.
41. *Life*, p. 380.
42. Sidney, *Apology*, p. 137.
43. 'A Wreath': a highly wrought poem, wreathing key words together by sustained repetitions, 'simplicity' being the key instance and, with masterly paradox, the poem's effect.

CHAPTER 1: CHILDHOOD

1. *Autobiography*, p. 5
2. Ibid.
3. At Powys Castle.
4. Edward Herbert, *Autobiography*, Walter Scott, 1888 (hereafter *Autobiography*), p. 4.
5. Geraint Dyfnallt Owen, *Elizabethan Wales*, University of Wales Press, 1962, p. 178 (no source given for this incident).
6. *Autobiography*, p. 5.
7. Ibid., p. 11.
8. Ibid., p. 3.
9. Now at Weston Park, Shropshire. See p. 35.
10. Quoted in Nikolaus Pevsner, *The Buildings of England: Shropshire*, Penguin, 1958, p. 30n, but not in the new edition of 2006.
11. Mark Girouard, *Elizabethan Architecture: Its Rise and Fall*, Yale University Press, 2009, pp. 35 and 464 n. 103.
12. Isaac Watts, *The Psalms of David*, J. Clark, 1719.
13. Genesis 3:19.
14. John Donne, *A Sermon of Commemoration of the Lady Danvers, Late Wife of Sr. John Danvers*, Scholars' Facsimiles and Reprints, 2006, p. 138 (Magdalen had married John Danvers, her second husband, in 1609).
15. Ibid., p. 140.
16. Ibid., p. 131.
17. See p. 20.
18. Donne, *A Sermon of Commemoration of the Lady Danvers*, p. 138.
19. At Powys Castle, description and facsimile in Amy Charles, 'Mrs. Herbert's *Kitchin Book*', *English Literary Renaissance*, IV (Winter 1974), pp. 164–73. There is a résumé of its contents in Charles, pp. 38–47.
20. *Life*, p. 52.
21. Jeffrey Powers-Beck, *Writing the Flesh: The Herbert Family Dialogue*, Duquesne University Press, 1998, pp. 45 and 46.

22. See Schoenfeldt, *Prayer and Power: George Herbert and Renaissance Courtship*, Chapter 5, 'Standing on Ceremony: The Comedy of Manners in "Love (III)"', from which the following extracts are taken.

23. Adam Nicolson, *Power and Glory: Jacobean England and the Making of the King James Bible*, HarperCollins, 2003, p. 16.

24. *Autobiography*, p. 12.

25. I Samuel 3.

26. L. C. Knights, 'George Herbert', in *Explorations: Essays in Criticism Mainly on the Literature of the Seventeenth Century*, Chatto & Windus, 1946, p. 127.

27. Summers, *George Herbert: His Religion and Art*, p. 92.

28. 'The Retreat'.

29. Richard Hooker, *Of the Laws of Ecclesiastical Polity*, 1597, Book V, Chapter lxiv.2, in *The Works of Richard Hooker*, ed. John Keble, Oxford University Press, 1836, vol. II, pp. 394–8.

CHAPTER 2: WESTMINSTER

1. *Life*, p. 22.

2. 'The Church Porch' 17, in *Works*, p. 10.

3. *Memoriae Matris Sacrum* 2, lines 37, 63 and 64, in *Works*, pp. 422 ff.

4. See p. 124.

5. 'Epigram XIV', in Ben Jonson, *The Complete Poems*, ed. George Parfitt, Penguin, 1996, p. 39.

6. For life at Westminster School see J. Sargeaunt, *Annals of Westminster School*, Methuen, 1898, pp. 36–50, and L. Tanner, *Westminster School*, Country Life, 1934.

7. *Autobiography*, p. 12.

8. 'The Son'.

9. Genesis 11:1–9.

10. Thomas Fuller, *Church History*, 1655, Book XI, p. 126.

11. Milton, 'Elegia Tertia', and Crashaw, 'Upon Bishop Andrewes his Picture before His Sermons'.

12. Hacket, *Scrinia Reserata*, vol. I, pp. 44–5.

13. It can be read in Lancelot Andrewes, *Sermons*, ed. G. M. Story, Oxford University Press, 1967, pp. 143–67.

14. T. S. Eliot, *Essays Ancient and Modern*, Faber & Faber, 1936, p. 21.

15. Andrewes, *Sermons*, p. 163.

16. Ibid., p. 109.

17. T. S. Eliot, *Collected Poems 1909–1962*, Faber & Faber, 1974, p. 99.

18. Lancelot Andrewes, *Selected Sermons and Lectures*, ed. Peter McCullough, Oxford University Press, 2005, p. xxxiii.
19. Ibid., p. 108.
20. William Empson, *Seven Types of Ambiguity*, Chatto & Windus, 1930.
21. Ibid., p. 295.
22. Ibid., p. 286.
23. In 1963 Empson took it all back: 'I put "The Sacrifice" last of the examples in my book, to stand for the most extreme kind of ambiguity, because it presents Jesus as at the same time forgiving his torturers and condemning them to eternal torture. It strikes me now that my attitude was what I have come to call "neo-Christian"; happy to find such an extravagant specimen, I slapped the author on the back and egged him on to be even nastier ... Clearer now what the light illuminates, I am keen to stumble away from it.' 'Herbert's Quaintness' (1963) in William Empson, *Argufying: Essays on Literature and Culture*, Chatto & Windus, 1987, p. 257.
24. Galatians 3:13.
25. Hebrews 2:14.
26. *Aubrey's Brief Lives*, ed. Oliver Lawson Dick, Secker & Warburg, 1949 (hereafter *Brief Lives*), p. 173
27. Ibid., pp. 173–4.
28. Aubrey MS Bodleian Library, folios 53–7, transcribed in Charles, pp. 62–4.
29. George Herbert, 'Unkindness', line 11.
30. *Brief Lives*, p. 173.
31. Three, flattering but of no particular interest, are printed in George Saintsbury's edition of Walton's *Lives*, Oxford University Press, 1927, in an appendix of letters by Herbert and Donne published in 1675. The fourth, discussed here, is in the main text of *Life*.
32. R. C. Bald, *John Donne: A Life*, Oxford University Press, 1970, p. 182.
33. Pliny, *Naturalis Historia*, viii.33.
34. Isaiah 59:4–5.
35. *Life*, p. 349.

CHAPTER 3: A YOUNG MAN AT CAMBRIDGE

1. G. M. Trevelyan, *Trinity College: An Historical Sketch*, Cambridge University Press, 1943, p. 21 for this quotation and for Nevile's building projects.

2. Nikolaus Pevsner, *The Buildings of England: Cambridgeshire*, Penguin, 1970, p. 171.
3. Ibid., p. 172.
4. Thomas Plume, ed., *A Century of Sermons . . . Preached by John Hacket*, Robert Scott, 1675, pp. v–vi.
5. *Life*, pp. 345–6.
6. *Country Parson*, Chapter III.
7. *Life*, pp. 344–5; *Works*, p. 207.
8. See p. 75.
9. See Peter Mack, *Elizabethan Rhetoric: Theory and Practice*, Cambridge University Press, 2002, p. 61 n. 79.
10. *Spectator*, 16 Sept. 1712.
11. Mack, *Elizabethan Rhetoric*, p. 73, quoting Robert Sanderson, 1615.
12. Letter to Lady Beaumont, 18 March 1826, in *Memorials of Coleorton*, ed. William Knight, D. Douglas, 1887, vol. II, pp. 248–9.
13. Matthew 26:15.
14. Quoted in Charles Taylor, *Sources of the Self: The Making of the Modern Identity*, Cambridge University Press, 1989, p. 242. Taylor is so struck by this succinctly brilliant sentence as to make it the title of one of his chapters.
15. Philippians 2:6–8.
16. 'The Circus Animals' Desertion', *Collected Poems*, Macmillan, 1950, p. 391.
17. *Works*, pp. 432–4.
18. Catharine MacLeod, *The Lost Prince: The Life and Death of Henry Stuart*, National Portrait Gallery, 2012.
19. *Works*, pp. 432–4.

CHAPTER 4: 1618

1. 'Affliction (I)', in *Works*, p. 47, line 45.
2. *Works*, p. 363.
3. Ibid., pp. 364 f.
4. Ibid., pp. 369–70.
5. Ibid., pp. 365 ff.
6. *Life*, p. 346.
7. Quintilian, *The Orator's Education*, ed. Donald Russell, Loeb Classical Library, Harvard University Press, 2001.
8. Mack, *Elizabethan Rhetoric*, pp. 49 and 50.
9. *The Autobiography and Correspondence of Sir Simonds D'Ewes*, ed. J. O. Halliwell, Richard Bentley, 1845, vol. I, p. 121.

10. Hacket, *Scrinia Reserata*, vol. I, p. 175.
11. *Works*, pp. 367–9.
12. Ibid., p. 368.
13. *Autobiography*, pp. 107–8.
14. British Library, Add. MS 70001 (Harley).
15. British Library, Add. MS 7081.
16. British Library, Add. MS 7082.
17. Edward, Lord Herbert of Cherbury, *de Veritate*, trans. and ed. Meyrick H. Carre, J. W. Arrowsmith, 1937, p. 310.
18. *Autobiography*, pp. 176–7.
19. Exodus 20.
20. Herbert, *de Veritate*, p. 120.
21. Ibid., p. 136.
22. *Autobiography*, p. 176.

CHAPTER 5: DEPUTY TO ORATOR

1. *Works*, pp. 369–70.
2. Ibid., p. 370.
3. Ibid., pp. 184–5.
4. 'A True Hymn'.
5. *Works*, p. 371.
6. *Life*, p. 350.
7. Ibid., pp. 348 and 349.
8. 'The Temper (I)', in *Works*, p. 55.
9. *Works*, pp. 440–44.
10. This and the previous quotation are from Baker's Cambridge Collections quoted in ibid., p. 600.
11. This and subsequent translations of this oration are by Jasper Griffin, sometime University Orator of Oxford, kindly and expertly made for the author.
12. See Sam Smiles, 'John White and British Antiquity: Savage Origins in the Context of Tudor Historiography', in Kim Sloan, ed., *European Visions; American Voices*, British Museum Research Publication 172, 2009 for a full treatment.
13. *Works*, p. 196.
14. 'Affliction (1)', line 45.

CHAPTER 6: FRANCIS BACON

1. *Works*, p. 460.
2. Ibid., pp. 435 and 436.
3. Ibid., p. 467.
4. Sir Francis Bacon, *The Advancement of Learning*, ed. G. W. Kitchin, Everyman, 1973, p. 25.
5. Ibid., p. 72.
6. Ibid., p. 7.
7. Ibid., p. 215.
8. Ibid., p. 213.
9. Ibid., pp. 79 and 106.
10. Ibid., p. 66.
11. Ibid., p. 82.
12. Ibid., p. 177.
13. Ibid., p. 34.
14. *Works*, p. 438.

INTERLUDE: THE WILLIAMS MANUSCRIPT

1. Dr Williams's Library, MS Jones B 62. *The Williams Manuscript of George Herbert's Poems: A Facsimile Reproduction with an Introduction by Amy M. Charles*, Scholars' Facsimiles and Reprints, 1977.
2. Matthew 21:8 etc.
3. See Allan G. Debus, *The English Paracelsians*, Watts, 1966.
4. *Autobiography*, p.106
5. *OED* 'Tincture'.
6. *Works*, pp. 200–204.
7. Ibid., p. lvi.
8. 'A Wreath'.
9. 'Holy Baptism (II)'.
10. 'Prayer (I)'.

CHAPTER 7: LOST IN A HUMBLE WAY

1. Romans 12:9.
2. Søren Kierkegaard, *The Last Years: Journals 1853–1855*, ed. and trans. Ronald Gregor Smith, Collins, 1965, p. 368.
3. The country parson 'admires and imitates the wonderful providence and thrift of the great householder of the world'. *Works*, p. 241.

4. 'The Answer'.

5. See 'The Size', line 32.

6. 'Employment (II)', in *Works*, p. 79.

7. 'Edward Lear', in W. H. Auden, *Collected Poems*, ed. Edward Mendelson, Faber & Faber, 1991, pp. 182–3.

8. S. R. Gardiner, *History of England 1603–1642*, vol. V: 1623–1625, Longmans Green, 1883, pp. 225–34.

9. *Journals of the House of Commons*, vol. I, London, 1802, pp. 707–96.

10. *Works*, p. 277.

11. Ibid., p. xxx.

12. B. Dew Roberts, *Mitre and Musket: John Williams, Lord Keeper, Archbishop of York, 1582–1650*, Oxford University Press, 1938, p. 8.

13. Ibid., p. 18.

14. Ibid., p. 78.

15. Ibid., p. 33.

16. Hacket, *Scrinia Reserata*, vol. I, p. 62.

17. Dew Roberts, *Mitre and Musket*, p. 121.

18. Ibid., p. 17.

19. *Works*, p. 137.

20. Ibid., p. 283.

21. Ibid., p. 353.

22. Dew Roberts, *Mitre and Musket*, p. 52.

23. Ibid..

24. *Life*, p. 352.

25. The reasons for supposing so are given in Charles, pp. 123–4, quoting a letter from the deputy archivist of the Lincolnshire Archives Office dated 1973. There was no service of induction in the Book of Common Prayer. But according to Walton (*Life*, p. 361), when Herbert was later inducted to Bemerton the law required him to be alone in church while everyone else waited outside and to toll the bell 'to make his induction known to his parishioners'.

26. Quoted by Dew Roberts, *Mitre and Musket*, p. 123.

27. *Life*, p. 357.

28. *Works*, pp. 291–303 and notes.

29. *Life*, p. 353.

30. Matthew 26:42.

31. *Life*, p. 353.

32. Nikolaus Pevsner, *The Buildings of England: Bedfordshire and the County of Huntingdon and Peterborough*, Penguin, 1968, pp. 282 and 283.

33. *Life*, p. 353.

34. *The Ferrar Papers*, ed. Bernard Blackstone, Cambridge University Press, 1938 (hereafter *Ferrar Papers*), p. 59.
35. *Works*, pp. 378 and 379.
36. Ibid., pp. 135–6.
37. *Life*, p. 358.
38. *Brief Lives*, p. 172.
39. John Ferrar, *A Life of Nicholas Ferrar*, in *Ferrar Papers*, p. 58.
40. John 20:23.
41. *The Book of Common Prayer*, Holy Communion, ed. Cummings, p. 138.
42. See Collinson, *The Religion of Protestants*, p. 93 for this and generally.
43. Ibid., p. 92.
44. Ibid., quoting Joseph Hall and p. 95 quoting Hacket.
45. *Country Parson*, Chapter XIX.
46. Donne, *The Major Works*, pp. 286–8.
47. 'The Answer'.
48. II Samuel 6.
49. Jeremiah 18.
50. *Life*, pp. 358–9.
51. *Brief Lives*, p. 218.
52. Ibid., p. 190.
53. *The Poems of Richard Lovelace*, ed. C. H. Wilkinson, Oxford University Press, 1930, p. 96. In an endnote on p. 293 Wilkinson asserts that *bona roba* was 'a common expression for a harlot', which fits Shakespeare's usage better than Aubrey's or Lovelace's.
54. 'The Thanksgiving'.
55. *Country Parson*, Chapter IX.
56. Nikolaus Pevsner, *The Buildings of England: Wiltshire*, Penguin, 1975, pp. 234–9.
57. *Much Ado about Nothing*, II.i.
58. 'Lent', line 19.

CHAPTER 8: BEMERTON:
BEING A COUNTRY PARSON

1. 'The Jews', lines 3 and 4.
2. See Michael Cowan, *Floated Water Meadows in the Salisbury Area*, South Wiltshire Industrial Archaeology Society, Historical Monograph 9, 1982, reprinted in 1998 by the Friends of Harnham Water Meadows Trust; and Hadrian Cook, Michael Cowan and Tim Tatton-Brown, *The Harnham Water Meadows*, Sarum Studies 3, Hobnob Press, 2008.

3. *Life*, p. 359 is probably mistaken in thinking that it was his brother Philip, who had not yet succeeded him. See Charles, p. 145.
4. *Life*, p. 359.
5. Ibid., p. 360.
6. *Brief Lives*, p. 225.
7. Joseph Mede to his cousin Sir Martin Stutevile, in Thomas Birch, ed., *The Court and Times of Charles the First*, Henry Colburn, 1849, vol. II, p. 74.
8. *Life*, p. 361.
9. Matthew 13:45 and 46.
10. *Life*, p. 362.
11. *OED*.
12. *Life*, p. 363.
13. Ibid., p. 364.
14. In the library of Magdalene College, Cambridge, published in *Ferrar Papers*, pp. 266–9.
15. *Ferrar Papers*, p. 267.
16. Luke 9:62.
17. *Brief Lives*, pp. 225–6.
18. *The Diaries of Anne Clifford*, ed. D. J. H. Clifford, Alan Sutton, 1990, p. 94.
19. Quoted by R. T. Spence in *The Oxford Dictionary of National Biography*, 'Anne Clifford'.
20. *Life*, p. 363.
21. 'The Flower', line 29.
22. Numbers 13:23.
23. Genesis 9:20.
24. *Life*, p. 380.
25. In the library of Magdalene College, Cambridge, published in *Ferrar Papers*, pp. 269–70 with a facsimile.
26. Philippians 4:8.
27. An echo of 'The Pilgrimage', verse 3.
28. *Brief Lives*, p. 218.
29. Crown Green Bowls, rather than the nowadays more common Lawn Bowls, is in mind. Crown Green Bowls is played on an extensive green, which is not dead flat but undulating and hilly so that the 'bias' is an integral part of the green itself. Thus in this poem 'the wide world runs bias from his [the bowler's] will.' The bowling green which was the centrepiece of Sir John Danvers's famous garden at Chelsea was circular, and therefore laid out for Crown Green Bowls.

30. *Works*, pp. 375–6.
31. *Country Parson*, Chapter XXIII.
32. Ibid., Chapter IIII.
33. Ibid., Chapter XXIII.
34. Ibid., Chapter XXII.
35. Ibid., Chapter XXI.
36. *Life*, p. 382; *Brief Lives*, p. 218; 'Easter', 'Christmas', 'Joseph's Coat', 'Praise (II)', 'Church-Music'.
37. *Life*, pp. 372–3.
38. Ibid., p. 371.
39. William Barlowe, *The Summe and Substance of the Conference at Hampton Court*, quoted in Kenneth Fincham, ed., *The Early Stuart Church 1603–1642*, Routledge, 1993, pp. 198–9.
40. Ibid., pp. 168 and 215.
41. *Oliver Heywood's Life of John Angier of Denton*, ed. E. Axon, Chetham Society, 1973, p. 50, cited in Collinson, *The Religion of Protestants*, p. 244.
42. *Life*, p. 368.
43. Ibid., p. 353.
44. Genesis 2:7.
45. Exodus 16.
46. *Ferrar Papers*, p. 58.
47. Letter of John Ferrar to Nicholas Ferrar (away visiting his niece Susannah Mapletoft in Essex) of 30 July 1632 in ibid., p. 276.
48. *Ferrar Papers*, p. 59.
49. Hebrews 11:13 and I Peter 2:11.
50. *Life*, p. 376.
51. *Autobiography*, p. 12.
52. The second collect at Morning Prayer in *The Book of Common Prayer*, ed. Cummings, p. 111.
53. The refrain of his poem 'The Posy'.
54. Shakespeare, Sonnet 146.
55. Dylan Thomas, *Collected Poems*, Dent, 1971.

CHAPTER 9: HERBERT'S DAYS AND YEARS

1. Psalm 39:4.
2. Matthew 6:34.
3. Andrewes, *Preces Privatae*.

4. Psalm 130:3.
5. John 3:16.
6. Luke 23:45.
7. See Job 1:6–12.
8. Saint Augustine, *Confessions*, trans. Henry Chadwick, Oxford University Press, 1992, VIII.18.
9. Jonson, *The Complete Poems*, p. 256, 'In Authorem' (Breton).
10. *Country Parson*, Chapter VIII.
11. *Works*, p. 375.
12. Luke 2:7.
13. And reference to Isaiah 1:3: 'The ox knoweth his owner and the ass its master's crib: but Israel doth not know, my people doth not consider.'
14. Luke 2:8.
15. Luke 2:20.
16. See pp. 271–2.
17. Luke 22:44.
18. John 19:34.
19. 'The Church Porch', line 25.
20. Exodus 24:12.
21. Louis MacNeice, *Variety of Parable*, Cambridge University Press, 1965, pp. 8 and 50.
22. See the text and discussion of this poem on pp. 271–2.
23. Wilcox, *The English Poems of George Herbert*, p. 142.
24. I Corinthians 13:13.

CHAPTER 10: HEIRS AND IMITATORS

1. W. H. Auden, 'In Memory of W. B. Yeats', *Collected Poems*, ed. Edward Mendelson, Faber & Faber, 1991, p. 247.
2. H. W. Garrod, 'The Latin Poem addressed by Donne to Dr Andrews', *Review of English Studies*, 21 (1945), pp. 38–42. Dr Andrews was not Lancelot but a physician called Richard Andrews.
3. Quoted in H. R. Woudhuysen, *Sir Philip Sidney and the Circulation of Manuscripts 1558–1640*, Oxford University Press, 1996, p. 14. The Introduction to this authoritative book is the best treatment of the whole complex question.
4. Ibid.
5. John Donne in *Letters to Several Persons of Honour*, 1651, pp. 21–2; see R. C. Bald, *John Donne: A Life*, Clarendon Press, 1970, p. 342.
6. *A Life of Nicholas Ferrar*, in *Ferrar Papers*, p. 59.

7.   Zadok the priest, whom, shunning power and place,
       His lowly mind advanced to David's grace. (lines 864–5)

(See *Dryden: Selected Poems,* ed. Paul Hammond and David Hopkins, Longman, 2007, p. 218.) For David read Charles II and for Zadok, Sancroft. Zadok was the priest who followed King David about during his civil wars carrying the Ark of the Covenant and obeyed his command to take it back to Jerusalem (II Samuel 15:24–9 and a tacit reference to the rebuilding of St Paul's).

8. G. Burnet, *History of his Own Times,* T. Davies, 1766, vol. I, p. 553: 'He had put on him a monastic strictness, and lived abstracted from company.' Burnet nursed a grudge against Sancroft for resisting his (Burnet's) consecration as bishop of Salisbury on account of his relaxed theological views.

9. A 'diplomatic edition' of it is available: *George Herbert: The Temple: A Diplomatic Edition of the Bodleian Manuscript (Tanner 307),* with Introduction and Notes by Mario A. di Cesare, Medieval and Renaissance Texts and Studies, 1995.

10. David McKitterick, *A History of Cambridge University Press,* vol. I, Cambridge University Press, 1992, pp. 169–75.

11. I am grateful to Ian Maclean for information about Cambridge printing and publishing practice.

12. 'Jordan (II)'.

13. 'The Son'.

14. 'The Author to the Critical Peruser' in Thomas Traherne, *Poems, Centuries and Three Thanksgivings,* ed. Anne Ridler, Oxford University Press, 1966, p. 3.

15. Cardell Goodman, *Beawty in Raggs,* ed. R. J. Roberts, School of Art, University of Reading, 1958, p. xiv.

16. Ralph Knevet, *The Shorter Poems of Ralph Knevet: A Critical Edition,* ed. Amy Charles, Ohio State University Press, 1966, pp. 275 ff.

17. Richard Crashaw, *The Verses in English of Richard Crashaw,* Grove Press, 1949, pp. 202 and 210.

18. Empson, *Seven Types of Ambiguity,* p. 280.

19. Many of these are picked up by Alan Rudrum in the notes of his edition of Henry Vaughan, *The Complete Poems,* Penguin, 1995.

20. Bees were a model of poetic productivity for Herbert in 'Employment (I)':

> All things are busy; only I
> Neither bring honey with the bees,
> Nor flowers to make that, nor the husbandry
> To water these.

21. Philip West, *Henry Vaughan's Silex Scintillans: Scripture Uses*, Oxford Univerity Press, 2001, is a through, sensitive critique of Vaughan's debts to the Bible and Herbert.
22. 'H. Baptism (II)'.
23. Mark 1:10.
24. It is beautifully set in Britten's *Spring Symphony* for solo tenor with a background of shimmering strings.
25. According to Sir Thomas Herbert (a very distant relation, but at Trinity College from 1621, when George Herbert was there) in his *Memoirs of the Two Last Years of the Reign of Charles I*, Robert Clavell, 1702.
26. *Oxford Dictionary of National Biography*, 'Ralph Cudworth', by David Pailin.
27. *Country Parson*, Chapter XXXV.
28. 'The Windows'.
29. Jackson was an opponent of Calvinist predestination: 'Grant me, *saith he*, but these two things, that God has a true freedom in doing good, and man a true freedom in doing evil; there needs be no other controversy betwixt the opposites in point of Providence and Predestination.'
30. Donne's famous Meditation XVII ('never send to know for whom the bell tolls; it tolls for thee') in *Devotions upon Emergent Occasions*, in Donne, *The Major Works*, p. 344.
31. *Life*, p. 384.
32. *Country Parson*, Chapter XXXV.
33. *Oxford Dictionary of National Biography*, 'Thomas Laurence', by A. J. Hegarty; and Charles, pp. 229–31.
34. Detected by Caroline Elam.
35. Genesis 28:17.
36. *Brief Lives*, p. 217.
37. See p. 192.
38. *Brief Lives*, p. 173.
39. Gardiner, *History of England 1603-1642*, vol. VI: *1625–1629*, p. 340.

CHAPTER 11: HERBERT'S READERS

1. *Life*, p. 380.
2. His thoughts on Herbert are collected in C. A. Patrides, ed., *George Herbert: The Critical Heritage* Routledge, 1983, pp. 166–73 along with extracts from many other commentators.
3. Psalm 90:3, 5 and 6.
4. Eliot, *George Herbert*, p. 25.

5. Ibid., p. 19.
6. John Haffenden, *William Empson: Among the Mandarins*, Oxford University Press, 2005, p. 6.
7. Knights, 'George Herbert', in *Explorations*.
8. *Works*, p. l.
9. Vendler, p. 275.
10. I John 4:16.
11. Jacques Cabaud, *Simone Weil: A Fellowship in Love*, Harvill Press, 1964, p. 237.
12. R. W. Emerson, 'English Literature: Ben Jonson, Herrick, Herbert, Wotton', in *The Early Lectures of Ralph Waldo Emerson*, vol. I: *1833–1836*, ed. S. E. Whicher and R. E. Spiller, Harvard University Press, 1959, pp. 337–55.
13. *Ruskin in Italy: Letters to his Parents 1845*, ed. Harold Shapiro, Oxford University Press, 1972, pp. 17–18
14. Ibid., p. 108, letter of 9 June 1845.
15. F. R. Leavis, *The Common Pursuit*, Penguin, 1962, p. 52.
16. Seamus Heaney, *The Redress of Poetry*, Faber & Faber, 1995, p. 10.
17. Rowan Williams, *Guardian Weekend*, 9 July 2011, p. 29.
18. Elizabeth Bishop, *Poems, Prose, and Letters*, The Library of America, 2008, p. 639.
19. Ibid., pp. 702–6.
20. *Brief Lives*, p. 218.
21. Summers, *George Herbert: His Religion and Art*.
22. Bishop, *Poems, Prose, and Letters*, p. 876.
23. Vikram Seth, 'Shared Ground', in *The Rivered Earth*, Hamish Hamilton/Penguin, 2011, pp. 51–9.

CHAPTER 12: THE BREAD OF FAITHFUL SPEECH

1. 'The Elixir'.
2. Wallace Stevens, 'Asides on the Oboe' II, in Wallace Stevens, *Collected Poetry and Prose*, The Library of America, 1997, p. 227.
3. Ibid.
4. Revelation 21:4 and 22:5.
5. 'The Cross', verse 3.
6. His only other use of the word 'fiction' is in 'Jordan (I)' where he puts 'fictions' with wigs ('false hair') as properties of untruthful poetry.
7. In Heaney, *The Redress of Poetry*, pp. 9–16.
8. *Country Parson*, Chapters VI and XXI.

9. Vendler, pp. 223 ff.
10. Discussed on pp. 243–4.
11. See pp. 213–15.
12. See pp. 222–4.
13. *Love's Labours Lost*, I.ii.90.
14. Vendler, p. 86.
15. Ibid., p. 87.
16. II Corinthians 3:3.
17. *Works*, p. 520.
18. Ibid., p. 599; and see p. 80.
19. For a discussion of this metre see James Fenton, *An Introduction to English Poetry*, Viking/Penguin, 2002, Chapter 9.
20. See pp. 67–70.
21. Heaney, *The Redress of Poetry*, pp. 12–13.
22. Augustine, *Confessions*, I.1.
23. John Burnaby, *Amor Dei: A Study of the Religion of St Augustine*, The Hulsean Lectures for 1938, Hodder & Stoughton, 1938, pp. 96–7.
24. Augustine, *Confessions*, X.38.

CHAPTER 13: MUSIC AT THE CLOSE

1. Shakespeare, *Richard II*, II.i.11.
2. *Life*, p. 382.
3. *Brief Lives*, p. 218.
4. *Life*, pp. 371–2.
5. 'Grief'.
6. Hooker, *Works*, vol. II, pp. 203–4.
7. Genesis 37:3.
8. 'To a Skylark', *Percy Bysshe Shelley: The Major Works*, ed. Zachary Leader and Michael O'Neill, Oxford University Press, 2003, p. 466.
9. Psalm 42:6 – among many examples.
10. Romans 8:23 and II Corinthians 5:2 and 4.
11. William Byrd, *Gradualia I* (vol. I), 1605–10, ed. Philip Brett, Stainer & Bell, 1989, p. xvii. I am indebted to the Right Reverend Mark Santer for this reference.
12. William Byrd, *Gradualia II* (vol. I), 1607–10, ed. Philip Brett, Stainer & Bell, 1997, p. xviii.
13. Eliot, *George Herbert*, p. 34.

Select Bibliography

Andrewes, L., *Preces Privatae*, trans. and ed. F. E. Brightman, Methuen 1903, reprinted by Living Age Books, 1961.

——, *Sermons*, ed. G. M. Story, Oxford University Press, 1967.

——, *Selected Sermons and Lectures*, ed. Peter McCullough, Oxford University Press, 2005.

The Art of English Poesy by George Puttenham, ed. Frank Wigham and Wayne A. Rebhorn, Cornell University Press, 2007.

Augustine, Saint, *Confessions*, trans. Henry Chadwick, Oxford University Press, 1992.

Bacon, Sir F., *The Advancement of Learning*, ed. G. W. Kitchin, Everyman, 1973.

Bald, R. C., *John Donne: A Life*, Oxford University Press, 1970.

Bishop, E., *Poems, Prose, and Letters*, The Library of America, 2008.

Bloch, C., *Spelling the Word: George Herbert and the Bible*, University of California Press, 1985.

The Book of Common Prayer: The Texts of 1549, 1559, and 1662, ed. Brian Cummings, Oxford University Press, 2011.

Bottrall, M., *George Herbert*, John Murray, 1954.

Brown, D., *Selected Poems of George Herbert with a Few Representative Poems by his Contemporaries*, Hutchinson, 1960.

Burnaby, J., *Amor Dei: A Study of the Religion of St Augustine*, The Hulsean Lectures for 1938, Hodder & Stoughton, 1938.

Carey, J., *John Donne: Life, Mind and Art*, Faber & Faber, 1990.

Clarke, E., *Theory and Theology in George Herbert's Poetry*, Oxford University Press, 1997.

Collinson, P., *The Religion of Protestants: The Church in English Society 1559–1625*, Oxford University Press, 1982.

Cook, H., Cowan, M., and Tatton-Brown, T., *The Harnham Water Meadows*, Sarum Studies 3, Hobnob Press, 2008.

Cowan, M., *Floated Water Meadows in the Salisbury Area*, South Wiltshire Industrial Archaeology Society, Historical Monograph 9, 1982, reprinted in 1998 by the Friends of Harnham Water Meadows Trust.

Crashaw, R., *The Verse in English of Richard Crashaw*, Grove Press, 1949.

Debus, A. G., *The English Paracelsians*, Watts, 1966.

Dew Roberts, B., *Mitre and Musket: John Williams, Lord Keeper, Archbishop of York, 1582–1650*, Oxford University Press, 1938.

Doerksen, D. W., *Conforming to the Word: Herbert, Donne, and the English Church before Laud*, Bucknell University Press, 2007.

Donaldson, I., *Ben Jonson: A Life*, Oxford University Press, 2011.

Donne, J., *The Major Works*, ed. John Carey, Oxford University Press, 1990.

——, *A Sermon of Commemoration of the Lady Danvers, Late Wife of Sr. John Danvers*, Scholars' Facsimiles and Reprints, 2006.

Eliot, T. S., *Essays Ancient and Modern*, Faber & Faber, 1936.

——, *George Herbert*, Longmans Green, 1962.

——, *Collected Poems 1909–1962*, Faber & Faber, 1974.

Empson, W., *Seven Types of Ambiguity*, Chatto & Windus, 1930.

Fenton, J., *An Introduction to English Poetry*, Viking/Penguin, 2002.

Fincham, K., ed., *The Early Stuart Church 1603–1642*, Routledge, 1993.

Fish, S., *Self-Consuming Artefacts: The Experience of Seventeenth-Century Literature*, University of California Press, 1972.

——, *The Living Temple: George Herbert and Catechizing*, University of California Press, 1978.

Free, C., *Music for a King: George Herbert's Style and the Metrical Psalms*, Johns Hopkins University Press, 1972.

Gardiner, S. R., *History of England 1603–1642*, Longmans Green, 1883.

Girouard, M., *Elizabethan Architecture: Its Rise and Fall*, Yale University Press, 2009.

Goodman, C., *Beawty in Raggs*, ed. R. J. Roberts, School of Art, University of Reading, 1958.

Green, I., *Print and Protestantism in Early Modern England*, Oxford University Press, 2000.

Hacket, J., *Scrinia Reserata*, Samuel Lowndes, 1693.

Haffenden, J., *William Empson: Among the Mandarins*, Oxford University Press, 2005.

Heaney, S., *The Redress of Poetry*, Faber & Faber, 1995.

Herbert, E., *The Poems of Lord Herbert of Cherbury*, ed. G. Moore Smith, Oxford University Press, 1923.

——, *de Veritate*, trans. and ed. Meyrick H. Carre, J. W. Arrowsmith, 1937.

Hooker, R., *Works*, ed. John Keble, Oxford University Press, 1836.

Hyde, A. G., *George Herbert and his Times*, Methuen, 1906.

Johnston, M., *Saving God: Religion after Idolatry*, Princeton University Press, 2009.

Jonson, Ben, *The Complete Poems*, ed. George Parfitt, Penguin, 1996.

Kierkegaard, S., *The Last Years: Journals 1853–1855*, ed. and trans. Ronald Gregor Smith, Collins, 1965.

King, Bishop H., *The Poems*, ed. John Sparrow, Nonesuch, 1925.

Knevet, R., *The Shorter Poems of Ralph Knevet: A Critical Edition*, ed. Amy Charles, Ohio State University Press, 1966.

Knights, L. C., *Explorations: Essays in Criticism Mainly on the Literature of the Seventeenth Century*, Chatto & Windus, 1946.

Lull, J., *The Poem in Time: Reading George Herbert's Revisions of 'The Church'*, University of Delaware Press, 1990.

McCloskey, M. and Murphy, P., *The Latin Poems of George Herbert: A Bilingual Edition*, Ohio University Press, 1965.

Mack, P., *Elizabethan Rhetoric: Theory and Practice*, Cambridge University Press, 2002.

McKitterick, D., *A History of Cambridge University Press*, vol. I, Cambridge University Press, 1992.

MacNeice, L., *Variety of Parable*, Cambridge University Press, 1965.

Martin, J., *Walton's Lives: Conformist Commemorations and the Rise of Biography*, Oxford University Press, 2001.

Martz, L., *The Poetry of Meditation*, Yale University Press, 1962.

Maycock, A., *Nicholas Ferrar*, Society for Promoting Christian Knowledge, 1938.

Nicolson, A., *Power and Glory: Jacobean England and the Making of the King James Bible*, HarperCollins, 2003.

Novarr, D., *The Making of Walton's Lives*, Cornell University Press, 1958.

O'Day, R., *Education and Society 1500–1800: The Social Foundations of Education in Early Modern Britain*, Longman, 1982.

Palmer, G. H., *The English Works of George Herbert Newly Arranged and Annotated and Considered in Relation to his Life*, Houghton Mifflin, 1895.

Patrides, C. A., ed., *George Herbert: The Critical Heritage*, Routledge, 1983.

Pevsner, N., *The Buildings of England*, Penguin/Yale, various dates.

Powers-Beck, J., *Writing the Flesh: The Herbert Family Dialogue*, Duquesne University Press, 1998.

Sargeaunt, J., *Annals of Westminster School*, Methuen, 1898.

Schoenfeldt, M. C., *Prayer and Power: George Herbert and Renaissance Courtship*, University of Chicago Press, 1991.

Scripture Women: Rose Thurgood, 'A Lecture of Repentance' and Cicely Johnson, 'Fanatical Reveries', ed. with an introduction and notes by Naomi Baker, Trent Editions, 2005.

Sidney, Sir P., *An Apology for Poetry or The Defence of Poesy*, ed. Geoffrey Shepherd, Nelson, 1965.

——, *The Old Arcadia*, ed. Katherine Duncan-Jones, Oxford University Press, 1999.

Singleton, M. W., *God's Courtier: Configuring a Different Grace in George Herbert's 'Temple'*, Cambridge University Press, 1987.

Smiles, S., 'John White and British Antiquity: Savage Origins in the Context of Tudor Historiography', in Kim Sloan, ed., *European Visions; American Voices*, British Museum Research Publication 172, 2009.

Stevens, W., *Collected Poetry and Prose*, ed. Frank Kermode and Joan Richardson, The Library of America, 1997.

Stubbs, J., *Donne: The Reformed Soul*, Viking, 2006.

Summers, J., *George Herbert: His Religion and Art*, Chatto & Windus, 1954.

Tanner, L., *Westminster School*, Country Life, 1934.

Tottel's Miscellany: Songs and Sonnets of Henry Howard, Earl of Surrey, Sir Thomas Wyatt and Others, ed. Amanda Holton and Tom Macfaul, Penguin, 2011.

Trevelyan, G. M., *Trinity College: An Historical Sketch*, Cambridge University Press, 1943.

Tuve, R., *A Reading of George Herbert*, Faber & Faber, 1952.

Vaughan, H., *The Complete Poems*, ed. Alan Rudrum, Penguin, 1995.

Vendler, H., *Invisible Listeners: Lyric Intimacy in Herbert, Whitman and Ashbery*, Princeton University Press, 2005.

West, P., *Henry Vaughan's Silex Scintillans: Scripture Uses*, Oxford University Press, 2001.

White, J. B., *'This Book of Starres': Learning to Read George Herbert*, University of Michigan Press, 1994.

Willson, D. H., *King James VI and I*, Jonathan Cape, 1959.

Woudhuysen, H. R., *Sir Philip Sidney and the Circulation of Manuscripts 1558–1640*, Oxford University Press, 1996.

Index of Works

General Index

Abbot, George, Archbishop of
  Canterbury 165
Adam and Christ, typology of 68–9
Addison, Joseph 314
Advent 262–3, 276
Aeneas 124
Aesop, Fables 56
alchemy 146–8
Alfred, King 127
ambiguity 69–70, 319
America, discovery of 125
Andrewes and Dury, map of Wiltshire
  190, 204
Andrewes, Lancelot, bishop of Winchester
  36, 60–68, 61, 81, 115–17, 132,
  135, 164, 166, 194, 241
  Christmas Sermon 64–5
  Good Friday Sermon 62–7, 267
  Preces Privatae 15, 257
Angelico, Fra 321
Anyan, Thomas 164
Apocrypha, 'The Song of the Three Holy
  Children' 107
  see also 'Benedicte Omnia Opera'
Aristotle, Rhetoric 101
Armagh, James Usher,
  Archbishop of 311
Ascham, Roger, The Schoolmaster 55
Aubrey, John 71, 79, 133, 189, 200–201,
  216, 217, 227, 239, 248, 254–5,
  309, 311, 323, 352
  Brief Lives xvi

Auden, W. H. 162, 322
Augustine, St 107, 252, 261, 350
  Confessions 17, 252
  Works 51

Bach, Johann Sebastian, St John
  Passion 272
Bacon, Sir Francis 12, 57, 130–38, 131,
  144, 166, 212, 236, 279
  created Viscount St Alban 132
  The Advancement of Learning
    (de Dignitate et Augmentis
    Scientiarum) 130, 132–4
  Instauratio Magna 130, 132
  Translation of Certain Psalms into
    English Verse 133, 135
Bald, R. C. 75
Bancroft, Richard, Bishop of
  London 242
Barker, John 43
Bath, Somerset 107
Baynton Manor, Wiltshire 197–8,
  198–9, 207, 215, 309
  St Mary's, St Katherine and All Saints
    (Edington Church) 202
Bemerton, Wiltshire 203–48, 204–5,
  295, 308, 309–10, 352, 358
  church 323
  Rectory xvi, 7, 18, 45, 164, 203,
    215–16, 257, 324, 352
'Benedicite Omnia Opera' 107
Bernini, Gian Lorenzo 244, 293

385